T0281850

Under the Iron Heel

The publisher and the University of California Press
Foundation gratefully acknowledge the generous support of
the Peter Booth Wiley Endowment Fund in History.

Under the Iron Heel

*The Wobblies and the Capitalist War
on Radical Workers*

Ahmed White

UNIVERSITY OF CALIFORNIA PRESS

University of California Press
Oakland, California

© 2022 by Ahmed White

Library of Congress Cataloging-in-Publication Data

Names: White, Ahmed, 1970– author.
Title: Under the iron heel : the Wobblies and the
    capitalist war on radical workers / Ahmed White.
Description: Oakland, California : University of
    California Press, [2022] | Includes bibliographical
    references and index.
Identifiers: LCCN 2021062859 (print) | LCCN
    2021062860 (ebook) | ISBN 9780520382404
    (hardback) | ISBN 9780520382411 (ebook)
Subjects: LCSH: Industrial Workers of the World—
    History. | Labor unions—United States—History—
    20th century.
Classification: LCC HD8055.I5 W48 2022 (print) |
    LCC HD8055.I5 (ebook) | DDC 331.880973—dc23/
    eng/20220325
LC record available at https://lccn.loc.gov/2021062859
LC ebook record available at https://lccn.loc.gov
    /2021062860

Manufactured in the United States of America

31 30 29 28 27 26 25 24 23 22
10 9 8 7 6 5 4 3 2 1

*To the memory of Troy Allen,
and to the Wobblies*

We will grind you revolutionists down under our heel, and we shall walk upon your faces. The world is ours, we are its lords, and ours it shall remain.

—Jack London, *The Iron Heel*

Contents

Introduction

Face to Face with Tragedy

In the late afternoon of May 18, 1922, a man named Joseph Neil stepped up to a "portly built gentleman" on a street in Hutchinson, Kansas, and asked if he might spare twenty-five cents.[1] Thirty-two years old and with a wistful and slightly melancholy look about him, Neil had sailed many seas and traveled all over North America and Europe. He had worked a great number of jobs, roaming around like this. And he had come to Hutchinson for the wheat harvest, one of many thousands of workers making their way through the region that summer, hiring out on one farm after another as they followed the ripening grain northward. The wheat around Hutchinson was not ready to be cut, though, and Neil, who had arrived that morning, was "dead broke," without "a red copper," and needed something to tide him over. But rather than reaching into his change pocket, the portly built gentlemen alerted the police.[2]

This encounter put Neil behind bars for six years, although not for soliciting the bestowment. As Neil told an organization trying to secure his release, "Every job I ever had, I worked too hard."[3] This life of wandering about and working too hard had led him to join the Industrial Workers of the World (IWW). He enrolled to "better my own conditions" and to see that "other working men might know the principles of better working conditions."[4] But if Neil's membership in the IWW, which police discovered after they arrested him for vagrancy, had bettered his conditions, it also got him imprisoned for violating Kansas's "criminal syndicalism" law, which forbade advocacy of "political or industrial change" by means of "sabotage," "terrorism," or other criminal acts and barred membership in organizations that promoted change by these means.

Over a three-year period that began just before America's entry into the First World War, twenty states, two territories, and a number of cities enacted criminal syndicalism laws. The aim was to destroy the IWW and punish its members, and the laws were put to these purposes. Between 1917 and 1925, police arrested and jailed roughly 2,000 "Wobblies," as everyone called the IWW's members, on some type of criminal syndicalism charge, and state prosecutors and judges imprisoned over three hundred for the crime.[5] Federal authorities also joined in this drive. In the late summer and fall of 1917, federal agents and military personnel began raiding IWW offices and gatherings throughout the country, arresting hundreds of Wobblies and detaining hundreds more. Along with private detectives and state agents, they infiltrated the IWW, seized its mail, and confiscated tons of union records. The following year, federal prosecutors conducted the first of several large show trials of Wobblies. These prosecutions, which resulted in the imprisonment of almost all of the IWW's leadership on conspiracy charges, rested mainly on provisions of the Espionage Act that had been devised with the destruction of the IWW in mind. The statute proscribed interference with the war effort. But as with the criminal syndicalism laws, the ultimate basis of guilt when Wobblies were prosecuted was their membership in the union.

In the course of this campaign, many thousands of Wobblies were also arrested and prosecuted on relatively minor charges, particularly vagrancy. The inherent vagueness of this crime and the slender procedures required to enforce it made vagrancy ideal for harassing these men—running them out of town; disrupting their meetings, organizing efforts, and picket lines; forcing them to work; or, as Neil's case reveals, holding them until more serious charges could be lodged. Vagrancy was also well suited for preemptively punishing them, as it provided grounds for locking them up for days, weeks, even months, in municipal and county jails that were, as a rule, degrading and dangerous. Nevertheless, in their eagerness to criminalize Wobblies, some jurisdictions went even further by rewriting their vagrancy laws to expressly criminalize the IWW, while others made it an act of criminal contempt merely to belong to the organization.

There was considerable lawlessness in this campaign of legal repression. Not only were all these laws conceived and enforced in haphazard and corrupt ways, but also the union's lawyers were harassed and threatened, its defense efforts disrupted, and its witnesses prosecuted. In some cases, too, Wobblies were simply framed on murder charges. And the legal repression the union experienced also converged with outright vigilantism. Everywhere the IWW was active in the late 1910s and early 1920s, its members were victims of what one scholar calls "bourgeois vigilantism," rooted not so much in popular sovereignty as in the prerogatives of class.[6] With shocking regularity, Wobblies were beaten, run through gauntlets, tarred and feathered, chased out of town or across state lines, or simply murdered by businessmen and professionals, self-described patriots, local toughs, college students, soldiers, and police.

. . .

Such treatment of Wobblies was consistently justified by charges that the IWW was a criminal organization, composed of men bent on sedition, wanton disorder, and, especially, sabotage. Contrary to what some of the union's defenders have argued, these accusations were not entirely untrue, at least with respect to sabotage. For years, Wobblies reveled in the concept of sabotage. For them, sabotage usually meant working slowly or inefficiently or otherwise "striking on the job." But not always: more than a few saw in the practice of damaging employers' property not only another way of striking on the job but also a means of vindicating the union's philosophy of class consciousness and turning back upon capital the kind of violence and destruction that capital inflicted upon them.

This is not to say that such destruction was especially common or, as a rule, particularly serious, or that it justifies or truly explains what was done to the union and its members. Wobblies were more inclined to talk about sabotage than to engage in it. They were not nearly as destructive as they were reputed to be. And they were generally much less violent than those who tormented them. But these facts did little to change the way that sabotage was used, together with broader charges of union criminality, to justify the Wobblies' persecution and to conceal the fact that the main reason these men faced such extraordinary depredations was that they hoped to better their immediate conditions and, in the process, to change the world.

The Wobblies believed capitalism irredeemable and illegitimate and thought that it was the destiny of workers themselves to rule. They aimed to educate and organize the entire working class into "one big union," to relentlessly pressure the capitalists, and finally to topple capitalism with a

FIGURE 1. Striking IWW lumber workers near Elma, Washington, 1917. Ralph Chaplin Collection, Washington State Historical Society, Tacoma.

massive general strike and build in its place a workers' commonwealth. For a decade after it was born in the first years of the new century, the IWW struggled to build itself into a functional organization and to move any distance toward realizing this revolutionary vision. But during the war its fortunes changed. On the strength of favorable economic conditions and the union's remarkable success in organizing, especially among migratory workers and in industries like agriculture, lumber, and mining, membership surged. Enrollment is difficult to calculate, but by 1917 it may have reached 150,000 or more, and the union's influence extended over several times this number of workers. Among radical leftist organizations in American history, it attained a prominence rivaled only by the Socialist and, later, Communist parties, and built upon its leadership of hundreds of strikes.

The organizing gains that underlay the union's growth were concentrated in the western two-thirds of the country, on the rapidly industrializing frontiers of American capitalism, where relentless exploitation had sown the seeds of bitter class conflict. Although the IWW never came close to achieving its revolution, the union's surge positioned it to threaten the interests and social visions of powerful capitalists and politicians in that region. More than anything, this surge is what inspired the enactment of criminal syndicalism laws and the Espionage Act, propelled enforcement of these laws as well as vagrancy statutes, and underlay the increase in lawless repression that members endured during this period. In this way, it is also, ironically, a principal reason why, by the time Joe Neil was released in 1928, the union had been effectively destroyed.

As historians of the IWW have long understood, many factors contributed to its demise. Among these were rapid changes in technology, social structure, and the nature of work that eroded the ranks of the migratory, largely unskilled workers from which the IWW came to draw most of its members and reduced the effectiveness of its organizing methods. The IWW also had to contend with far-reaching and well-cultivated opposition to its radical ideas, which were probably more appealing than generally thought and yet never overwhelmingly popular. It had to deal, too, with the rise of communism, which emerged as a competing ideology and confounding political movement at a crucial time in the union's history. And it was likewise ravaged by deep and long-festering conflicts between rival factions within the organization, which by 1924 had left the union thoroughly divided against itself.

As nearly everyone who has studied the IWW also recognizes, repression was a crucial factor in the union's demise, one that saddled it with crippling expenses, disrupted its organizing efforts, incapacitated its leadership, and widened the fractures within its ranks. But repression's role in destroying the IWW has yet to be fully documented or adequately appreciated. For all their attention to the issue, historians have looked at repression too narrowly, focusing on local or regional events, on the Espionage Act cases, on sensational episodes of vigilantism, or on the fate of the union's more prominent leaders without ever reckoning with repression's cumulative effects or giving sufficient attention to the experience of everyday Wobblies like Neil. And compounding this is a tendency not to adequately consider the more intimate means by which repression accomplished its purposes.

Famous for his obsessions with historical memory, political subjugation, and matters of human endurance and suffering, the writer Eduardo Galeano once observed that "hunger looks like the man hunger is killing."[7] So it is with the repression that the Wobblies endured: its consequences are impossible to comprehend without considering what it did to the men on whom it was inflicted. And yet it is exactly this aspect of the story that has been least well examined in studies of repression and the IWW, aside from some scattered reflections here and there and a handful of biographies of prominent Wobblies, where the complicated truth of the matter is often obscured by an understandable but one-sided emphasis on the remarkable resolve these men showed.

To understand what repression did to the IWW one must not forget what it did to men like Joe Neil, whose only prominence came from his imprisonment. While in prison in Kansas, he received a visit from a fairly famous woman named Marcet Haldeman-Julius, a stage artist, writer, banker, and leftist who was also Jane Addams's niece. Meeting Neil "in the insane ward," where he spent four years, Haldeman-Julius discovered a man of "quiet nobility" and great resolve, with "a restless, eager mind that has sought somewhat blunderingly, but no less passionately" than the likes of Bertrand Russell and Oscar Wilde, "after the truth." The IWW was a "religion" to Neil, she marveled; the "conditions of his class are his chief concern."[8]

Such devotion and resolve were common and often explicitly based in the principles of solidarity and class struggle that defined the IWW, as the experience of Neil's fellow Wobbly, Howard Welton, underscores. In late 1921, Welton wrote from California's San Quentin State Prison to the trial judge in his case, declining the judge's offer to help secure either a pardon or parole. Arrested earlier that year for chairing a meeting that featured a leftist preacher—and a government spy—Welton had been convicted of criminal syndicalism. Now, in a lengthy letter to the judge, he rejected the offer of assistance. For Welton, "accepting a pardon implies, to my mind, that one has committed some crime. I have not." In his view, "Our 'crime,'" consisted only of "advocating a social change by peaceful, orderly, efficient methods." Moreover, Welton said, he found himself incarcerated with other Wobblies who were "no more guilty of any crime than I am. If I should be released, they should be released."[9]

Hundreds of Wobblies followed Welton's course, disdaining the clemency of governors, prosecutors, judges, and even U.S. Presidents, sometimes celebrating their convictions and often demanding they be prosecuted and punished in lieu of or alongside their fellow Wobblies. From witness stands and jail and prison cells, they met degradation with a surpassing courage and an astonishing dignity that should long ago have made legends of them all. Among themselves, they fashioned persecution as its own victory over a system that was in their minds utterly unacceptable. This was Joe Neil's perspective. In a letter written just after his release, he told fellow Wobblies that "one who goes to prison for the I.W.W. should be proud of his sacrifice for the principle of industrial unionism, and I am justly proud of mine."[10] But this is not all that Neil said. In this same letter he spoke frankly of the "extreme brutality" he endured. And when Haldeman-Julius met him there in the prison, she recognized all the ways that Neil had been battered by his time in custody and found herself, "face to face," she said, with both courage and tragedy.[11]

Countless thousands of Wobblies languished in foul, dangerous, and overcrowded jails for weeks or months, convicted of vagrancy or awaiting trial on more serious charges. Thousands were injured, sometimes severely, and occasionally killed, by police, jailers, or vigilantes. For the hundreds who were sent to prison, the crushing loneliness, the draining fears, and the stupefying controls of life behind bars were compounded by frequent beatings, arduous labor, and the likelihood that they would be held, sometimes for weeks or even months, in solitary confinement or, worse, in hellish places variously known as the "dark hole," the "dungeon," or the "slaughter house." And unlike Neil, whose "lunacy," according to the prison doctor, was expressed in the fact that he "speaks of being persecuted," more than a few were driven insane by what was done to them.[12] Several committed suicide and perhaps a dozen died of natural causes while incarcerated, coming, by these dark roads, to the same end as those whose association with the union got them murdered. Untold others, either members or potential members, witnessed this suffering and drew from it undeniable conclusions about what affiliation with the union held in store for them, as well.

To understand what became of the IWW requires that one confront repression on these terms, appreciate its vast scale and comprehensive reach, and see how in wrecking lives it also wrecked the union. The IWW had offices and finances, publications and reputation, and leaders; what happened to these is part of the story too. But the union's strength and vitality depended on both the well-being of the people who comprised it, including the thousands whose only notoriety, like Neil's, came with this persecution, and the willingness of everyone who might associate with the organization to risk persecution as a condition of membership. For all their resolution, these men—and the victims of the kind of repression this book is concerned with were virtually all men[13]— were not invulnerable. If the arrests, prison terms, and assaults could break or come close to breaking them, and if knowledge of such practices could create enough general apprehension and uncertainty, then the persecution could accomplish its intended role of destroying the IWW. And that is exactly what occurred.

. . .

While his clients suffered, the union's leading lawyer, George Vanderveer, tried to get a fellow lawyer to appreciate what was being done to

FIGURE 2. Striking IWW miners being deported from Bisbee, Arizona, July 12, 1917. Walter P. Reuther Library, Archives of Labor and Urban Affairs, Wayne State University.

them. No decent person, he told the man, would stand to see racial minorities treated the way these IWWs were. Yet "decent" people not only tolerated the mistreatment of the Wobblies, they were responsible for it.[14] Yet again, these decent people often knew what the IWW was and what the union's members endured, even if they approved of the persecution. Nowadays, when histories of the civil rights and women's suffrage movements flourish, the story of the IWW is all but forgotten. Outside of leftist and labor circles, most people know little about the union. And they know even less about the people who formed its ranks, about America's own heroes of unwritten story, in whose struggles and sufferings can be found no better record of what this country was and what it is likely to remain.

Almost as regrettable as rank ignorance about the Wobblies is that when their history has been written, it has often been to serve a narrative about the advancement of civil liberties in this country. This is common among liberals, whose faith in the legal system usually overrides their interests in radical industrial unionism. It is also, to be sure, somewhat understandable, given that the persecution of the Wobblies did indeed present the country's political and legal elite with essential questions about the rights of free speech and association and the state's prerogative to repress radicals. But what happened to the Wobblies shows how little footing civil liberties have when honoring them requires impingement on the interests and values of the truly powerful. So it was that complicity in the campaign to destroy the union was widespread not only among ignorant and overexcited locals, greedy businessmen, and intolerant reactionaries but also among Progressives of the highest standing. Among these were President Woodrow Wilson, who oversaw the federal assault on the IWW, as well as U.S. Supreme Court Justices Oliver Wendell Holmes and Louis Brandeis, who, in fashioning the "clear and present danger test," devised a way of reconciling the persecution of Wobblies and other radicals with a veneration of the First Amendment to the U.S. Constitution.

Indeed, precisely because they wish to preserve the notion that the values of freedom of speech and association endured even as the Wobblies and their ideals foundered, many liberal historians, if they reckon with the IWW at all, dismiss what was done to the union as aberrant products of the First World War and the "Red Scare" that followed. As they tell it, these were times when irrational impulses briefly triumphed over law and reason. And there are some grounds to believe this reading of the history. The IWW was the most prominent among several radical groups targeted with repression during these periods. Moreover, the Espionage Act was enacted in wartime and the majority of criminal syndicalism laws were adopted either during the war or the Red Scare. It was also during these periods, which were indeed marked by surging militarism and xenophobia and elements of hysteria, that arrests, prosecutions, and vigilantism were at their worst.

Much about the union's experience contradicts this narrative, however. The repression that the IWW endured began to escalate well before America entered the war and persisted until the union was broken, which in many places meant long after the Red Scare had ended. Moreover, repression of the IWW was at least as much a function of the union's strength and the threats it posed to powerful people as of any broader shifts in the country's politics or mood. And what happened to the union was, in the end, much more a matter of class conflict than most liberals have been inclined to believe—or, for that matter, can reconcile with their ultimate faith in the social order that these Wobblies so vehemently rejected.

In fact, an honest telling of what happened to the IWW not only casts great doubt on traditional liberal narratives. It also is destined to disappoint those leftists and unionists who have found in the Wobblies' experience a hopeful augury of a revival of today's labor movement and the working class's eventual triumph, expressed in the audacity and fortitude that these men showed in the face of overwhelming opposition. Instead, what this story really does is confirm the Wobblies' own, darker anticipations as to the nature of capitalist rule, which align with the dismal fate of the labor movement and the radical left since the IWW's decline, as well as the prophecies of the Wobblies' most famous champion, the writer Jack London.

London is a recurrent figure in this book because, more than any other writer or intellectual, he at once enthralled the Wobblies and helped them to understand their world. He studied them, learned from them, and then offered through some of the very works that so captivated them important insights about who they were, about the world they inhabited, and about how they understood that world. London knew, as did the Wobblies themselves, that reformism presented its own perils, some ultimately greater than those of revolutionary activism, and he understood, as they did, the essential truth that the capitalists and their allies would inevitably reckon ruthlessly with those who really dared to defy their reign.

London related this most effectively in his 1908 novel *The Iron Heel*. An immensely popular text among Wobblies, the book unfolds his political philosophy by recounting, from a vantage seven hundred years in the future, a failed fictional revolution in the early twentieth century, crushed by powerful capitalists allied with reformist forces. The novel thus anticipates the Wobblies' own fate. "Power will be the arbiter," portends London, "as it always has been the arbiter." Armed with such power, "the Oligarchy," or the "Iron Heel," vows to rule, to grind down the revolutionists and walk upon their faces.[15] So did the real-world oligarchs, crushing the IWW while teaching a lesson about the kind of power that their class really wields and about the ways that law lends legitimacy to that power and to the violence of which it must ultimately consist.

To their everlasting credit, the Wobblies, more than London, adhered doggedly and fatalistically to their revolutionary hopes, notwithstanding this dim judgment about the world. But their experiences give reason to believe that the judgment was by no means wrong. Like the Christian martyrs to whom they have been likened, the Wobblies were left to find confirmation and redemption mainly in their own destruction. The chapters that follow are a record of this defeat, a history written "in drops of blood," as a union pamphlet put it. Heroic at times and often tragic, the history told in these chapters is largely unmoderated by talk of triumph, unless by this one means the way these dreamers and rebels suffered and what they, in their suffering, revealed about how power arbitrates and how capital, in a capitalist world, is bound to rule.

CHAPTER 1

Socialism with Its Working Clothes On

Industrial Capitalism, Radical Unionism, and the Roots of Repression

Just after ten o'clock on the cool and dreary morning of June 27, 1905, two hundred three delegates assembled in Chicago's Brand's Hall, an inexpensive venue on the southeast corner of Clark and Erie. They were there to convene what one of their number, a thirty-six-year-old miner named William Dudley Haywood called the "Continental Congress of the Working Class." Its mission, he said, was to be "the emancipation of the working class from the slave bondage of capitalism."[1] Haywood was secretary-treasurer of the Western Federation of Miners (WFM), a union whose resolution a year earlier had led to this convention. A big and rugged man, born on the frontier in 1869, he called the convention to order by banging a two-by-four on the podium.[2]

Many of those gathered in the smoky hall with "Big Bill" Haywood were revolutionaries, including Socialist Party leader Eugene Debs and Lucy Parsons, widow of executed anarchist Albert Parsons. And they had assembled at a propitious time. The realms of art, literature, and science were alight with astonishing advances in form and meaning. In world politics, titanic changes were also afoot. A month before the Chicago convention, the Imperial Russian fleet was destroyed in the Battle of Tsushima, guaranteeing Russia's defeat in the Russo-Japanese War and giving impetus to a cycle of conflict that featured, shortly before Haywood banged his two-by-four, a mutiny on a battleship named *Potemkin*. Indeed, unrest was close at hand: the delegates convened amid the prolonged collapse of a chaotic and violent teamsters' strike in Chicago that had raged since April, claimed the lives of about twenty people, and led to the prosecution of union leaders on conspiracy charges.[3]

Unlike the teamsters' strike, the bid to form a new "labor trust," as the *Chicago Daily Tribune* put it, barely made the major newspapers.[4] Nevertheless, the delegates moved efficiently toward the realization of their purpose. When they adjourned sine die on the afternoon of July 8, they had established the Industrial Workers of the World (IWW) and made clear what this new union was about. The preamble to its constitution opened with the pronouncement that "the working class and the employing class have nothing in common" and boldly declared a state of class war.[5] Repudiating the craft unionism that had predominated among American labor organizations and that had built unions around groups of skilled workers of narrowly shared interests, the IWW's founders proposed to organize the entire working class regardless of industry or skill. Unlike most unions and the great majority of civic organizations in the country, they opened the union's membership to everyone, without regard for sex, age, race, or nativity. All workers would be welcomed into an organization dedicated to overthrowing capitalism and abolishing wage labor. Through the union, the workers would rise in irresistible number and build a commonwealth, governed by workers themselves in the interests of all humanity. They would, in Haywood's words, make good a vision of "socialism with its working clothes on."[6]

. . .

When Haywood called the convention to order at Brand's Hall, industrial capitalism had already worked a revolution in American life. Amid massive growth in employment in manufacturing and industries like mining, forestry, and construction, the nation's population exploded, especially in urban areas and disproportionately in the West, where great cities and states sprang up far beyond the earlier frontiers of industrial society.[7] The economy surged in size as well, becoming, by the early twentieth century, the largest in the world, amid tremendous changes in technology, production, and daily life. But nothing about industrial capitalism implied a revolution in fairness or humanity in the world of work, as this new order was captive to the logic of unending accumulation of capital, the principles of ruthless competition, and the dictates of efficiency, maximum return on investment, and profit. These commitments reformed the relationship between workers and employers, which had been governed to some extent by principles of mutuality and community, into a nakedly economic association between alien and profoundly unequal parties. In the decades that followed the Civil War, they remade "free labor," which was the promising but ambiguous legacy of that great struggle, into a license for employers' indifference to workers' interests, backed in law by the pretenses of free contract and "employment at will."

As the IWW put it, industrial capitalism created a class of "ownerless slaves," consigned to lives of deprivation and insecurity.[8] Indeed, in contrast to chattel slavery, this system of "wage slavery" relieved employers of any direct interest in the physical well-being of the men, women, and children they employed. It set these people to work among unprecedentedly powerful machinery and an extraordinary array of toxic substances, often with little training and every expectation that complaints would result in discharge. For these reasons, industrial capitalism also yielded a great harvest in death and injury. Each year in the early twentieth century around 25,000 people died as a direct result of accidents at work and as many as 1.5 million suffered disabling injuries as a consequence of what one historian aptly calls a system of "industrial violence."[9]

This kind of violence was essential to the experience of industrial workers, as Big Bill Haywood well knew. A strong orator who would lead the IWW through its headiest years, Haywood had a habit of saying "I've never read Marx's *Capital,* but I have the marks of capital all over me."[10] "Indentured" at age nine, Haywood began working the mines at fifteen, where later his hand was crushed so badly by falling rock that he could not work, leaving his family to survive on the generosity of fellow workers. As revealed in the many descriptions of scars, broken bones, and missing fingers in their prison records, Haywood's fellow Wobblies often shared this kind of experience.[11] Take Patrick Murphy, for instance, who was locked up on criminal syndicalism charges in 1921. An "I.W.W. at heart," according to his records, Murphy had been badly hurt a decade earlier when a twenty-five-foot pole fell on him while he was working as a lineman for the Washington Water Power Company.[12] "The injury seemed to weigh on his mind," said a lawyer, writing the pardon board. He doubted that Murphy, who was seriously injured again while working for a magnesite company in Idaho, had "entirely recovered," before finding his way into the Idaho State Penitentiary.[13]

Work was crushing in other ways, too, as workers toiled in conditions that were frequently sweltering or frigid; dusty, dank, or noisy; monotonous and frenetic; tedious and back-breaking. In some industries, a more literal kind of violence also prevailed, as workers had to jostle, cajole, bribe, and sometimes fight their way into a job, only to be hectored and harried, sometimes assaulted, and frequently threatened by the foremen, supervisors, and other sorts of bosses who ruled the workplace. Lucky if they got any meaningful breaks, many labored ten and twelve hours a day, sometimes longer, for six and seven days a week, with no time off for vacations and no guarantee that an absence because of injury or sickness, exhaustion, or family emergency would not result in discharge.[14] To quote the historian E. P. Thompson, such was life in a world in which the "work-clock" had "engrossed the universe," where the worker's time had become "money, the employer's money," and was no longer "passed but spent."[15]

Life outside of work offered few compensations for those who endured these conditions. Poverty consigned millions of workers to lives in squalid urban slums, shanty towns, and rural camps and hovels, where they were plagued by violent crime and delinquency, alcoholism and drug abuse, and the frequent disintegration of family under the strains of daily existence. Hunger, malnutrition, and premature death from illness, injury, and malaise were commonplace.[16] Leisure was an extravagance, no less than learning, in a world that made prodigal luxuries of proper schooling and the serious pursuit of art, music, and literature.

This was all endured in view of rapidly increasing social wealth and the promise that humankind was poised to build a society free of poverty and compliant with enlightened, humane sensibilities. The world found itself, as Theodore Dreiser reflected in his novel of that age, *Sister Carrie,* "still in a middle stage, scarcely beast in that it is no longer wholly guided by instinct; scarcely human, in that it is not yet wholly guided by reason."[17] Reason remained captive to the contrary dictates of industrial capitalism, which removed vast wealth from the hands of industrial workers into the books of corporations and businesses, and from there into the accounts of capitalist owners. Some capitalists never accumulated more than a modest store of wealth, and some failed. But many were oligarchs in every sense of the word: when the IWW was formed, two hundred families or individuals in America were worth at least $20 million each, and this when a working class family might try to live on $500 a year.[18] And virtually all capitalists claimed what labor historian Selig Perlman famously called the "effective will to power" that inhered in their ownership of the means of production.[19]

For Haywood, as for many industrial workers, to appreciate the logic of capitalist exploitation did not require a deep reading of Marx's

FIGURE 3. William "Big Bill" Haywood delivering a speech, location and date unknown. Walter P. Reuther Library, Archives of Labor and Urban Affairs, Wayne State University.

Capital so much as a simple recognition that "if one man has a dollar he didn't work for, some other man worked for a dollar he didn't get."[20] But just as important to this story and the grievances that many workers harbored is the inequality that reigned within the working class. Although the hardships of life and work in industrial America befell all workers to some extent, they affected some more than others. Overall wages increased from the Civil War into the twentieth century, but these gains accrued disproportionately to skilled workers.[21] Less favored were the growing legions of unskilled and semiskilled workers, a great number of them blacks, recent immigrants, those born poor or thrown out of their trades or off the land by capitalism's progress, or those who, for one reason or another, defied the "work clock." These "vendors of muscle," as one-time Wobbly Charles Ashleigh put it, whose value as workers reduced to their physical strength, dexterity, and endurance, were the most aggrieved victims of this new order.[22]

It was quite often the inexorable progression of automation and mechanization that brought workers face to face with their true worth in this order and reduced many of them to vendors of muscle. Haywood himself explained how the introduction of power drills devastated the lives of hard-rock miners and drove them into the ranks of the WFM. Not only did the machines render many workers redundant, but in contradiction of the common fable that progress on this front makes work easier, they were also too difficult for some skilled miners to handle. "No consideration was shown to them," as these men had to accept unemployment or settle for lower-paying jobs. "Fifteen dollars a month less for all miners, thirty dollars a month less for miners who could not handle the big drills. It could be summed up in less food, less clothes, less house-room, less schooling for their children, less amusements, less everything that made life worth living." As Haywood recalled, there seemed "no means of escape from the gigantic force that was crushing all of them beneath its cruel heel."[23]

Decades after his imprisonment for criminal syndicalism, an old Wobbly related something similar to the union's resident historian. A former lumberjack, he criticized a scholar's publication on the subject of IWW activism in the lumber industry. The scholar's work was inexcusable, he said, for its failure to appreciate how the adoption of newer, more powerful "donkey engines" made the work so much more exhausting and dangerous. A person had to know the "sickening fatigue" of a ten-hour day under these conditions to appreciate what drove the men to unionize and led them to strike, he avowed.[24]

. . .

Established for the purpose of redressing the depredations of industrial capitalism, the IWW was shaped by the failures and shortcomings of the organizations that had come before, including their indifference or unavailability to workers like this old Wobbly. As the union's preamble makes clear, its founders believed the "trade unions," with their tendency to divide workers against one another, were "unable to cope" with the power of industrial capitalism and were bound instead to "mislead" the working class. During the drafting of the preamble, the delegate most responsible for its composition, a Marxist Roman Catholic priest, Thomas Hagerty, proposed that the document should conclude with words that announced their organization's very different orientation: "an injury to one is an injury to all." Hagerty had gotten this language, which quickly emerged as an enduring battle cry, from an organization that all of the delegates knew well: the Noble and Holy Order of the Knights of Labor, whose slogan was "an injury to one is a concern of all."

Established in 1869 as a secret society, the Knights of Labor shed its secrecy and briefly rose to great prominence in the mid-1880s. And then it disintegrated, partly because of its defeat in the "Great Southwest Railroad Strike of 1886," lost in part because of repression and lack of support from other unions and in part because of clumsy administration and the incoherence of the Knights' governing ideology. Committed to robust reforms, like the eight-hour day, the organization was nonetheless conflicted about the kind of radicalism and militancy necessary to achieve those aims.[25] The Knights were also not clear in regard to a defining question in American labor history, which was whether the unions that comprised it would organize on an industrial basis or on the basis of skill or craft. And as it came apart, a group of unionists committed to this latter form of unionism and angered by the Knights' intrusions into their jurisdictions formed what was to become the country's largest and most venerable labor federation: the American Federation of Labor (AFL). Nearly two decades later, when the IWW was born, the AFL consisted of about 118 affiliated unions entailing three-quarters of the country's two million unionized workers.[26]

True to the AFL's origins, most of these unions were craft-based organizations. As some historians have lately been keen to point out, they could be "progressive" and even "radical" in their aspirations and quick to engage in militant and sometimes violent protests. But when the IWW's founders condemned the trade union movement as dysfunctional and reactionary in the union's preamble, it was the AFL and its affiliated unions that they had in mind, and with good reason. Many of the unskilled and semiskilled workers the IWW would organize were ineligible for membership in AFL unions. And in line with the philosophy of long-time AFL president Samuel Gompers, these unions tended mostly toward a businesslike respectability in pursuit of pragmatic, "bread and butter" demands that served the interests of their own, usually narrowly composed, memberships. They often held an indifferent and even hostile view of unskilled and semiskilled workers, including many blacks, immigrants, and women, who loomed as threats to or distractions from their defining purposes. And they struggled mightily to protect their own members from the ravages of industrial capitalism and ultimately showed little interest in making real inroads against this system.[27]

In the years that preceded the IWW's founding, there had been only a small number of industrial unions in the United States, many outside of the AFL's fold. One of these was the WFM, founded in 1893 by the amalgamation of smaller unions of hard-rock miners in the Mountain West.[28] Another was the American Railway Union (ARU), founded in 1893 by dissident railroad unionists who chafed at the dominance of craft-oriented "brotherhoods." Headed by Eugene Debs, the ARU was independent of the AFL and quickly grew to claim a membership of 150,000. In the summer of 1894, it assumed leadership of the Pullman Palace Car Company Strike, which began among that company's manufacturing workers but evolved into a sensational, nationwide railroad strike. By the end of July, the strike had collapsed, crushed by the intervention of thousands of federal troops and an even greater number of local police and private guards, and by a lack of support from Gompers and the AFL. It was during this strike that a young Ralph Chaplin, whose father was a striker and who would later rise to prominence in the IWW and wear chains in payment, saw a worker "shot in cold blood."[29]

Debs's prominence and his first appointments behind bars came much sooner than Chaplin's. Jailed briefly during the Pullman strike, he served six months the following year in a cell at the McHenry County Courthouse in Woodstock, Illinois, alongside several other ARU leaders, for contempt of a federal judge's injunction ordering the strikers to cease interfering with the railroads. The strike lifted the one-time locomotive fireman out of obscurity and helped to convert him into a Marxist and a socialist. But its failure, which was the culmination of a long series of defeats for workers in other strikes, divested Debs of much of his faith in strikes and other kinds of "direct action" and steered his socialism into a "parliamentary" direction. In 1897, Debs transformed the ARU into a socialist party called the Social Democracy of America, which then became the Social Democratic Party. In 1901, it was reformed again, with dissident elements of the Socialist Labor Party, into the Socialist Party of America, or simply the Socialist Party.

The Socialist Party was very soon the dominant leftist party in the United States and at the forefront of socialism's emergence as a coherent political movement in America. By 1912, the party had about 100,000 members, and Socialist politicians held over 1,000 offices in 340 jurisdictions across the country. That year, Debs, in the fourth of his five candidacies for president of the United States, garnered nearly 6 percent of the popular vote.[30] But while their party remained a leading force in left-wing politics well into the twentieth century, the Socialists were unable to build on these gains or achieve significant reforms, and their momentum stalled, the victim of an America whose political system was no less dominated by powerful capitalists than were its factories and mills and its fields of labor struggle.

. . .

Like Debs, Charles Ashleigh would later be prosecuted under the Espionage Act. But Ashleigh, who started out a Socialist, rendezvoused with this destiny by a different course, one that he described in his semiautobiographical novel, *The Rambling Kid.* The book documents the wanderings of a young Wobbly named Joe Crane who is captive from an early age to the "romance which lives amidst the suffering."[31] Brief and furtive though it may be, this description of the "rambling kid" expresses something essential about the Wobblies, about how they came to be, about how they sought to escape what industrial capitalism had in store, and about how all of this shaped the union that claimed their allegiance.

Faced with the grim realities of life under industrial capitalism, some workers turned away from the mines and mills and toward schemes like running a small ranch or farm or ensconcing themselves in some kind of little business. One-time Wobbly and future Communist Party leader William Z. Foster briefly homesteaded. So did Big Bill Haywood. And so would have Nicholaas Steelink, after he emigrated from Holland, had things worked out as planned. Instead, Steelink, the son of a grocer, "pounded the sidewalks for nine weeks" before managing a "ten dollar a week job doing clerical work and delivering haberdashery" in Seattle, where he fell in with the IWW.[32]

There was often a nostalgia in this desire to work the land, one that idealized a past which seemed more secure and less alienating, even if it was also impoverished and likewise physically taxing. Recalling his youth in Chicago, Ralph Chaplin little wondered why, with the family's life awash in turmoil and hardships, "Dad spent his time longing for Kansas," where he had raised livestock. Nor was Chaplin surprised when his father moved the family to Iowa, where "there were no railroad yards or smoky warehouses, no strikes, no Pinkertons, no policemen, and, for a change, no wolf at the door," then back to Kansas, and then suburban Chicago, before each time returning in defeat to the city where, as his son put it, there was injustice on every side.[33]

Other workers embraced the uncertainties of the age, turning to lives of adventure framed by insecurity. When asked by prison officials why they left home, a remarkable number of Wobblies offered the simple response "to see the world," often followed by amazing accounts of all the places they had lived and worked. Some had followed in the wake of their idol, Jack London, who personified the physical courage and indifference to risk that life demanded of men like themselves. In his youth, London had turned away from industrial labor to become for a time an oyster pirate—a "capitalist," as he put it, who stole not with the services of a senator or supreme court justice but rather at the point of a gun.[34] Many industrial workers, including some who would end up in the IWW, made a similar turn, resorting to various rackets and schemes, hustling and stealing to get by. Others traced London's footsteps to the world's remotest regions, sailing, hunting, fishing, or prospecting for gold and silver. In this last category was A. S. "Sam" Embree. Before he emerged as a key figure in the IWW, Embree headed twice to the Klondike, where conversations about socialism were apparently much easier to find than gold and where the spirit of socialism governed what happened to much of the gold that was found. Like London, who developed acute scurvy in the subarctic, Embree fell ill and almost died on his first trip north.[35]

The Mexican Revolution also called to these men. For years, Jack London supported the revolution. So did Wobbly Leo Stark, a Mexican national whose prosecution for conspiracy in federal court in Kansas in 1919 highlighted his revolutionary commitments.[36] It is not clear whether Stark ever bore arms in the cause, but other Wobblies certainly did. In November 1915, Joe Hill, the union's gifted songwriter, was famously executed by Utah authorities for a murder he likely did not commit, mainly because, in a remarkable display of the fateful determination that could be found among the union's members, he preferred martyrdom to a messy betrayal of a romantic entanglement. Hill had served under the command of John "Jack" Mosby, a deserter from the U.S. Marines and one of two Wobblies to lead military elements of the uprising that unfolded in Baja California, Mexico, in 1911 under the ideological leadership of the anarchist and IWW supporter Ricardo Flores Magón and his brothers Enrique and Jesús. Captured when the rebellion was defeated that June, "General" Mosby said he would testify against Ricardo and Enrique at their trial in San Diego the next summer on charges of violating the federal Neutrality Act. But once on the witness stand, Mosby defended the revolution. When asked who was behind the unrest, he pointed at the federal prosecutor and shouted, "That is the man!" Later convicted of desertion and sentenced to six years in prison, Mosby was shot and killed while being taken to the federal penitentiary at McNeil Island, Washington, supposedly while he was trying to escape.[37]

Another who found his way to Mexico in this tumultuous time was the enigmatic B. Traven. He built one of his acclaimed novels, the semi-autobiographical *The Cotton-Pickers*—first titled *Der Wobbly*—around the Mexican adventures of a wayward American IWW named Gerald Gales who is bound in hardship and exploitation to a racially diverse miscellany of workers, all of them pushed to the edges of humanity by industrial capitalism. Much about Traven, including his real name, remains clouded by the deceptions of an exile who probably fled to Mexico to escape execution for his part in founding the Bavarian Socialist Republic. It is not clear whether Traven was a Wobbly—although always much stronger in the United States than anywhere, the IWW established a presence in much of the world—but certainly he was a Marxist and a radical. Through the laconic, hard-bitten Gales he suggests how he came to these politics. "I was forced," says Gales, "to become a rebel and a revolutionary, a revolutionary out of love of justice, out of a desire to help the wretched and the ragged." So it was that a "strike always broke out where I was working or where I had been working."[38]

Gales's—or Traven's—fellow workers, ambling through life, trying as he says to "save our fancies from starvation," are drawn into a game they cannot win. The idea of "attempting to save a little money and start a small business, or scrape together the fare for a try somewhere else," is a dead end that pits workers one against another and sets them up for greater exploitation. "Everybody is his own best friend. If the grass gets scarce while I'm grazing I'll pull up the roots as well," muses Gales about a world in which the pursuit of one's fancies leads inevitably to defeat.[39]

For most workers there was little chance of escaping capitalism's global reach, and little to gain by chasing visions of a bygone world. "Do you not know the West is dead? / Now dismal cities rise instead / And freedom is not there nor here—/ What path is left for you to tread?" wrote Ralph Chaplin, also a gifted composer of song and verse, after an adventure out West.[40] Indeed, wandering was usually less about adventure than scraping together a living. According to researcher Nels Anderson, a transient himself in his youth, in the decade following the IWW's founding, each year there were perhaps 10,000 migratory workers in Chicago alone, and more than 300,000 moved through the city or spent the winter there. Writing in the early 1920s, Anderson called these workers "hobos," subscribing to a common way of distinguishing them from "bums," "tramps," and other homeless types who either did not wander or seldom worked. These categories were not inaccurate. But they were indefinite in practice, as many moved freely from one to another. Indeed, transience itself was frequently transitory, modulated by the business cycle and the changing demands of industry and fortunes of life. As a result of all these factors, neither Anderson nor anyone else could determine with very much accuracy how many people were sleeping rough or on the road. All that is clear is that, courtesy of industrial capitalism, these conditions were the fate of millions in the early twentieth century, and millions of these were workers.[41]

Just as they were becoming a preoccupation of the IWW, these men also emerged as a concern of the U.S. Commission on Industrial Relations, the most important of a number of official bodies to investigate labor conflict and the conditions of industrial labor in this period.[42] The sympathy for them that ran through the first of the three reports that awkwardly comprise the commission's 1916 "final report" was palpable enough, and its indictment of industrial capitalism sufficiently compelling, that the IWW printed a pocket version of the document for members—one which, when found on their persons, occasionally furnished evidence of sedition when they were prosecuted.[43] But the commission was hardly a revolutionary body. Its other reports were not so critical of industrial capitalism. And like much Progressive research and commentary, including Anderson's work as well as studies by his colleague Don Lescohier, an economist who described workers' transient lives as a process of "degeneration," even the most sympathetic report saw transience as a serious pathology marked by a certain contempt for family, private property, and other preconditions of the social order. In typical Progressive fashion, it proposed to treat this pathology by reformist measures, like subsidized rail travel and the establishment of "hotels" and "colonies and farms" for the "down and out," that did not really threaten that social order.[44]

This attitude toward transience would be an important impetus behind the prosecution of men like these who traded the pursuit of "anachronisms," as Jack London put it, for a more practical radicalism. Joe Neil was one of these men. He had left home when he was only fourteen because, he told prison administrators, he wanted "to see the world" and to escape "home surroundings" that were "unpleasant." But what this meant was that he worked. With "no people nor family," Neil was an immigrant from Austria who had been in Holland and Germany. He had lived in Gulfport, Mississippi; in Halifax, Nova Scotia; in Toronto and Montreal; in Detroit. When arrested in Kansas he had been a fisherman on the Gulf of Mexico; he had been a merchant seaman and had harvested wheat on the Great Plains; he had "roamed all over the world" working like this. In testament to where this life had taken him, he wanted "no one notified in case of accident except I.W.W. headquarters in Chicago."[45]

Likewise, the thirty Wobblies who served time for criminal syndicalism in the Idaho State Penitentiary came from six foreign countries and ten states. Workers all, most had lost one or both parents, even though their average age was about thirty-six; and about one-third did not know whether one or both parents were still alive, or, if they were dead, when they had died. The men had left home, on average, at age sixteen. One had been on his own since age six, another since age nine, and another, John O'Hara, who was born in England, "never had a home." Fourteen, including O'Hara, could not or would not name any living relative. As if to confirm the worries of those who saw menace in their supposed hostility to traditional notions of home, nine offered as the "name and address of living relative" the local or national office of the IWW.[46]

. . .

The world these men inhabited had been rent by labor unrest since before the day that many were born. Each year between 1888 and 1905, American workers engaged in over 1,000 strikes. In 1903 alone, there were almost 3,500, and these were only those known to the government.[47] Some were large and well-organized. Many, like the Pullman strike, were marked by impressive displays of solidarity and militancy. More than a few were successful bids to ensure union recognition or defend wages and working conditions. But many were broken. In fact, in some years, a majority were broken, often decisively and not infrequently by the use of great force.[48]

Many companies maintained their own well-armed militias, or they purchased these services from strikebreaking and "detective" firms, like the Pinkerton National Detective Agency, which helped drive Ralph Chaplin's father back to the farm, the Thiel Detective Service Company, and later, the William Burns Agency.[49] But powerful employers also routinely mobilized police and sheriff deputies, state militias, and federal troops to meet "labor troubles." In conflict after conflict, these forces worked alongside private forces to drive workers off picket lines, force them back to work, arrest them and charge them for strike violence, and otherwise punish them for their insubordination.

These troubles and the corruption of state power in service of explicitly private purposes that they produced were among the reasons that, by the end of the nineteenth century, classical liberalism, with its valorization of free markets and skepticism of state power, had lost much of its capacity to legitimate industrial capitalism or provide a coherent framework for governing society. So were all the social problems that underlay this unrest and seemed to call for more government-sponsored reforms. This old liberalism therefore yielded ground to a new liberalism that openly justified the resort to law and the power of the state as means of managing and defending the social order. Known as Progressivism, this new liberalism was premised on the realistic and pragmatic view that capitalist society was not reliably self-regulating in the ways imagined by classical liberals but instead rife with dysfunctions and in need of many reforms. And yet Progressivism, which was always a fundamentally middle-class movement, was also, from the outset, characterized by its deep faith in the social order it meant to reform. This orientation underlay the dissonant and sometimes contradictory way that its adherents approached both unions and radicals. In line with their commitments to reform, Progressives were often ready to ratify the rights of labor and the principles of tolerance and due process. But they could be just as quick to abrogate these principles when unions or radicals threatened the social order, challenged their values or interests, or impinged on their own sovereignty over the direction and nature of reform.

In line with these tendencies, Progressives often saw in unionism a social problem, not unlike the poverty, transience, and poor working conditions that they intended to redress. But more than most social problems, unions, with their organized activism and, in some cases, calls to class consciousness and conflict, were also threatening to the Progressives' agenda and social vision. With some Progressives, the hostility was fairly comprehensive. More than a few supported the "open shop" movement, an ideological and political program that cunningly packaged an aggressive and sometimes violent resistance to unions as sanctioned by congenial, libertarian values; "open shop" thus became a watchword for treacherous anti-unionism. But whether they could be called champions of the open shop or not, most Progressives were eager to distinguish between legitimate and illegitimate unions. And in drawing this line they distinguished between those that were tolerably moderate and responsible in their methods and aims and those that were intolerably militant or radical. The former might be accommodated, but the latter were to be held in check.[50]

Like most of what the Progressives sought to achieve, managing the "labor problem," as it was called, was ideally done by means of the law—in particular, laws expertly conceived and administered in professionalized ways that complied with neutral, self-justifying principles and standard operating procedures. Vigilantism and other irregular or extralegal practices were sometimes acceptable, to be sure, particularly in exigent circumstances, and these practices could even be construed as lawful in their own right, if not by the self-justifying logic of those who engaged in them, then by practical reflection on how much they really differed from conventionally lawful methods. But as a general rule, Progressives preferred that the violence they called on to deal with labor and class conflicts conformed to more conventional conceptions of law. They took the lead in imposing legal reforms on capitalists and using the force of the law to protect the prerogatives of unions and even, on occasion, the rights of radicals. But they could also get behind the idea of pointing guns at errant workers and irksome revolutionaries, putting them behind bars, and sometimes killing them, and they would fatefully join with various kinds of conservatives and reactionaries in normalizing this kind of violence as well.[51]

. . .

The organization that would do more than any other to bring to the surface Progressivism's capacity for repression got off to a rocky start. During its first two or three years, the IWW was more fully occupied with internal discord than the enlistment of new members. Although influenced by personal rivalries, the core problems concerned ideology and strategy. One faction, composed disproportionately of westerners and transients who had nowhere to vote anyway, and led by Haywood, rejected "parliamentary socialism" and favored instead an approach focused on strikes and similar kinds of activism at "the point of production." Another, composed mainly of eastern socialists, had a more positive view of political activism. This internal struggle gave rise to not one but two rival IWWs in addition to Haywood's faction. One of these splinter organizations lasted only about a year. The other, under the direction of Daniel De Leon, leader of the Socialist Labor Party and a delegate at the IWW's founding convention whose theoretical acumen was overwhelmed by his dogmatism and talent for alienating would-be allies, endured for another two decades but never really found its footing. In the meantime, many other socialists, including Eugene Debs, drifted out of the union; and jurisdictional conflicts between the IWW and the WFM opened a rift between the two organizations that ended, in 1907, with the WFM withdrawing from the organization it helped create and later expelling Haywood from its ranks.[52]

Haywood's faction, also known as the "Chicago" group or the "overalls brigade," emerged from all of this as the true IWW. The factional conflicts cost the organization members, political support, and morale, while exposing, without fully resolving, conflicts that would later cause even more trouble. While these developments did not yet entrench the western orientation and the emphasis on migratory workers that would determine the IWW's destiny, they set the union on these paths.[53] They also left the union with a great clarity of purpose and identity, reflected in a set of revisions to its preamble that consecrated the organization's complete repudiation of political activism in favor of what it would soon call a program of "direct action."

The union harnessed this belief in direct action to a revolutionary agenda, one that saw capitalism as inherently exploitative; envisaged the world as captive to historical laws and defined, above all, by struggle; celebrated the philosophical and historical potency of labor and the working class; distrusted the very concept of the state, along with the kinds of reforms it might administer; and broadly embraced union activism as the proper mode of revolutionary organization. This agenda drew on the arguments and insights of a great variety of thinkers. From Karl Marx and Friedrich Engels, for instance, came notions of historicism and economic exploitation, the sanctity of labor, and universality of class conflict; from Mikhail Bakunin and Georges Sorel came favorable conceptions of anarchism and syndicalism and accompanying methods of protest; and from Charles Darwin, Herbert Spencer, and H. G. Wells, came the sense of the world as bound equally by the laws of evolution and the inviolate logic of struggle. However, in his own way no thinker was more important to the Wobblies or more useful in understanding them than Jack London.

Wobblies regularly highlighted London's relevance to their way of seeing things, and prosecutors affirmed this, presenting London's work in court as an exposition of the Wobblies' philosophy and proof of their seditious ways. In some respects, the link between the writer and the union might seem odd, as London was the most popular author in the world and earned a fortune from his publications, and by the time the IWW came to prominence he lived a very different life than that of men like Big Bill Haywood, let alone Joe Neil. But in other respects, London's appeal among people like these is easy to understand. A true child of the working class, London had worked twelve- and sixteen-hour days while still a young boy. He had suffered poverty and a fractured home life. Before becoming famous, he had been "on the bum," wandering about, and had gone to sea. He knew what it was like to dodge the police, to scape and brawl, and to wonder how he might find his next meal or where he would rest his head when the day was done.[54]

Early in his short life, London had become convinced of an essential truth he shared with many Wobblies and, like them, embraced with religious favor: that the world was a cruel and pitiless place whose essential brutality could nonetheless be transcended and supplanted by reason and morality, although only by the hands of those prepared to see past its many falsities and charades and many legalistic and sentimental simulations and reckon with it on its own, ruthless terms.[55] It was primarily because London propounded this truth, which underlay his faith in "a socialism that deals with what is, not with what ought to be" and yet "desires for goodness" and "right," that the Wobblies gravitated to him.[56] And it is for this reason, above all, that London stands as the leading intellectual light in a union whose members, as Melvyn Dubofsky notes, never produced a prominent scholar from their own ranks but found in the teachings of others what they needed to better comprehend the things "they already knew from life."[57]

James P. Cannon, who organized for the IWW for several years, was typical of many Wobblies in recounting how voraciously he consumed London's writings and how important they were to his political development.[58] And the Wobblies' obsessions with London went beyond his writings. If, like Big Bill Haywood, who had dinner with London, or Ralph Chaplin, who first met him in an Oakland saloon before, like other Wobblies, corresponding with the man, they managed to make London's acquaintance, the event was recounted with both reverence and a sense that in this figure they had encountered one of their own.[59] *The International Socialist Review,* a left-wing publication that allied with the IWW, spoke for many Wobblies when, upon London's death, it eulogized in verse this "friend" and "comrade": "He who arose from us / And voiced our wrongs; / Who sang our hopes, / And bade us stand alone." On that occasion the IWW's *Industrial Worker* memorialized London in similar but plainer terms, using quotes from his writings to illustrate how in London's life of "struggle and revolt" was a reflection of the Wobblies' own. The union's *Solidarity* went further, mourning the loss of an "ardent friend and sympathizer," a "prophet and seer" who had come to embrace the union's ideals so completely that he was, in fact, "an I.W.W. man."[60]

In 1894, London fell in with George Speed, a tough but scholarly figure who had belonged to numerous radical organizations and later was a founding member of the IWW and chaired the union's general executive board. The two were soldiers of privation in Charles Kelley's "industrial army," the western division of Coxey's Army, as it bummed its way across the country, trying to reach Washington, D.C., where the participants intended to demand government jobs to redress widespread unemployment. Neither London nor Speed completed this first March on Washington. Indeed, only a handful made it to the capital, including the movement's founder, Jacob Coxey, who was arrested for trespassing on the Capitol lawn, and the whole enterprise ended in failure. But for London, who found in Speed's impetuous and virile radicalism something he "believed in," the trip was a formative experience.[61]

London embraced the IWW's aim to build a new society, a workers' commonwealth, emancipated from the tyrannies of wage labor, private property, and bourgeois law and government. He seemed especially drawn to the combative and uncompromising way the union planned to achieve this commonwealth, including its most militant tactics. London went so far as to endorse one of the most controversial examples of IWW literature: a 1913 pamphlet called *Sabotage: Its History, Philosophy, and Function* that celebrates the tactic in its most destructive forms. In a note to the author, Walker Smith, which was soon added as a coda to the text, London said, "I do not find a point in it on which I disagree with you. It strikes me a straight-from-the-shoulder, clear, convincing, revolutionary statement of the meaning and significance of sabotage."[62] As London's daughter, Joan, put it, her father considered the IWW's founding a "corroboration of the correctness of his own disagreement with the policies of the Socialist party," whose program of capturing the machinery of the state by electoral means he came to doubt and whose commitment to the class struggle he increasingly found wanting.[63]

London wrote *The Iron Heel* as these realizations were coming to him, in the glare of the 1905 Russian Revolution and in the light cast by the formation of the IWW. Although engaging endorsements of socialism and biting critiques of capitalism run through much of London's early writing, this book best expresses its author's radical worldview. At the novel's center is an unsparing account of how "the Oligarchy," wounded by a revolutionary general strike and a broad uprising, regained its sovereignty via its control of the state and its legal apparatus and the support of a perfidious "labor caste," and then, in the guise of punishing sedition, brutally secured its rule for three hundred years. An anticipation of a strain of political theory that came into its own later in the twentieth century, in leftist critiques of capitalist rule and of liberalism's potential to descend into authoritarianism, the book alienated London's friends in the mainstream of the Socialist Party. They found its brutal view of the world too much, recoiled at its contempt for conventional unionism and its notion that overthrowing capitalism by legislation or

FIGURE 4. Jack London, lower right, at an encampment of Kelley's Army, somewhere in Iowa, April or May 1894. Wisconsin Historical Society, WHI-143480.

reform was doomed to fail, and rejected its suggestions that a proper place to situate a revolution was at the point of production.[64]

Indeed, the IWW's belief in revolution and direct action sanctioned using strikes, slowdowns, and the like to organize, educate, and radicalize the working class, with the aim of eventually calling a vast, general strike by which it would lay siege to the economy and compel the capitalists to surrender ownership and control of the means of production. "If the workers take a notion," as Joe Hill's "Workers of the World, Awaken!" puts it, they could bring the world to a standstill and seize its institutions and machinery for themselves. Violence would inevitably follow, although for the Wobblies, unlike for many anarchists and, later, communists, this would arrive not at their instigation but rather from the capitalists. Big Bill Haywood realized this from the outset. He warned the delegates at the IWW's founding that when the capitalists came to understand the union's agenda, they would subject its members "to every indignity and cruelty that their minds can invent."[65] With the benefit of a few years of the IWW's existence to work with, London foresaw the same. In *The Iron Heel*, the Oligarchy "believed that they alone maintained civilization" and that without them "humanity would drop back-

ward into the primitive night out of which it had so painfully emerged."
Out of this perspective was derived a set of moral standards and political
and juridical principles that aligned entirely with their interests and that,
in turn, gave credence to whatever kind of repression they elected to
impose on those who would deign to challenge their reign.[66]

Not itself a work of scholarship, and also crude and hyperbolic at
times, *The Iron Heel* has nowhere near the empirical foundations, ana-
lytical rigor, and theoretical depth of Marx's *Capital,* Darwin's *On the
Origin of Species,* or even Spencer's *Social Statics.* Nor does the book
compare favorably in these ways to the writings of European anarchists
and syndicalists, whose ideas were especially crucial in shaping the
union in its early years, when its fate was more fully in the hands of well-
educated intellectuals, many of them immigrants in eastern cities.[67] But
as the IWW developed a dominant base among transients in the West,
this "thrilling primer" on philosophy, political economy, and revolution, which managed to condense most all the IWW's other intellectual
influences, became more relevant to the Wobblies than any other book.[68]
Shaped around the enthralling idea that a decisive struggle against the
Oligarchy would be led by figures not unlike themselves, and written by
a man who could easily have fallen into their own ranks had he not
become a wealthy writer, this "small folk bible" of radicalism was
widely read by the union's membership, given as a reward to industrious
members, and commonly recommended to new recruits. It could be
found, well-used, in IWW establishments all over the country.[69]

The union would have plenty of occasions to describe *The Iron Heel*
as "not fiction but fact," to quote the IWW's *Solidarity* when, speaking
of the Oligarchy grinding down the revolutionists and walking on their
faces, it eulogized London.[70] Already when London wrote the book and
described the "high ethical righteousness" that would drive the Oligarchy to crush the kind of radicalism the Wobblies offered, it was becoming more common, in line with increasing worries about the IWW's
program, for real-world capitalists to denounce the IWW as a criminal
organization and to seize upon every episode of violence that could be
used to justify this charge. Prominent among these was the assassination of former Idaho governor Frank Steunenberg, killed on December
30, 1905, by a bomb attached to a gate outside his home in Caldwell.
Six weeks after the bombing, police and operatives of the Pinkerton and
Theil agencies kidnapped Big Bill Haywood and Charles Moyer, president of the WFM, as well as George Pettibone, another labor activist,
from Denver and brought them to Idaho to be tried for the killing. The

men were alleged to have conspired to kill Steunenberg, a Populist Democrat elected with the miners' support, because he had betrayed them during a bout of labor trouble in 1899.

Steunenberg had indeed betrayed the miners, and it is possible the three were behind his death. However, it is also possible that they were innocent. Jack London was one of many leftists who thought so. In his view, the prosecution occurred because Haywood and company stood "between the mine owners and a pot of gold."[71] Offered his own pot of gold by the *San Francisco Examiner* if he would report on the trial, London refused, donated money to the defense, and spent his time instead writing *The Iron Heel,* whose plot he built around the fate of a messiah figure who resembles Big Bill Haywood and is targeted in a frame-up by the Oligarchy.[72]

In fact, in this "greatest battle ever waged between intrenched [*sic*] capital and organized labor," as the union put it, the prosecution's case rested on the word of a deranged man named Albert Edward Horsley, alias Harry Orchard, who planted the bomb but said he had been recruited to this task by the defendants.[73] Whatever the truth of that, Orchard had certainly been employed as an informant by the mine owners. He was also groomed throughout the case by the famous Pinkerton agent James McParland, whose record of provocation and intrigue stretched back to the Molly Maguires affair of the 1870s—a murky episode which resulted in the execution or imprisonment of some twenty Pennsylvania coal miners for various crimes that McParland had confected, fomented, and fabricated. This was too much even for a panel of conservative Idaho jurors. After indulging an epic closing argument by Haywood's lead counsel, Clarence Darrow, the jury acquitted him in July 1907. Moyer and Pettibone were exonerated soon after.

A decade earlier, Darrow had defended Eugene Debs against contempt charges arising out of the Pullman strike. Now Debs expressed his support for the defendants in the Steunenberg case. While the men sat in jail awaiting trial, he penned a widely circulated tract titled *Arouse, Ye Slaves,* in which he predicted that if the "capitalist tyrants" should kill Haywood, Moyer, or Pettibone, "a million revolutionists, at least, will meet them with guns."[74] Debs's pamphlet may have heartened the defendants, but as powerful people began to awaken to the threat the IWW might pose to their interests and values, it also provided grounds for condemning the union as a dangerous, criminal organization. So did Jack London's support, which was entwined with his own public endorsements of revolutionary violence. And then there was

Haywood's trial itself, which, despite his acquittal, produced lurid testimony about IWW intrigues that featured very prominently in the nation's newspapers.

. . .

In the years that followed Haywood's trial, people hostile to the IWW searched widely for ways to present the union as a dangerous organization. They could find some evidence of this in Mexico. Their numbers may have been relatively few but Wobblies like Joe Hill and Jack Mosby did bear arms for the revolution, and their actions, though without official sanction, were touted in one of the union's main newspapers, the *Industrial Worker*. There was also Hill's conviction and execution, which were regarded as proof of the Wobblies' wanton and murderous ways. Still, evidence of IWW criminality was at first lacking, even by the loose standards that defined this quest. But its detractors found some of what they sought in the "free-speech fights" for which the union became famous.

Waged mainly between 1907 and 1917, and mainly in western cities like Spokane, Washington, Minot, North Dakota, and Fresno, California, these struggles unfolded when Wobblies were arrested for speaking on the streets, usually in places where this privilege was freely granted to less radical groups, and other members stepped into their places in great numbers with the idea of overwhelming authorities' ability to jail them all or honor their demands for jury trials. In fact, such fights were often tumultuous affairs that seldom occurred without scores, sometimes many hundreds, of Wobblies arrested and packed into fetid jails or confined in open-air "bullpens." Reinforced by local businessmen, college boys, and random assortments of miscreants and toughs, police beat the Wobblies, turned fire hoses and dogs on them, froze them, starved them, even branded a few with hot irons.[75] The free-speech fights could sometimes become deadly, too. For instance, the union's 1912 free-speech campaign in San Diego, a city under the effective rule of railroad and real-estate baron John Spreckles, was met with exceptional brutality and ended in a rout and the deaths of at least two Wobblies.[76]

It was not uncommon for local authorities to relent and grant the Wobblies at least a limited right to speak, although at the expense of charges, circulated widely in mainstream newspapers, of the union's irresponsibility and penchant to sow mayhem and disorder. The cost of these affairs eventually led to the Wobblies themselves becoming more circumspect about their true value. However, the fights were not without practical purpose. They came into greatest use just as the IWW

FIGURE 5. Wobblies being fire-hosed during the San Diego free-speech fight, probably late spring or summer 1912. The police station and city jail are in the background. University of Washington Libraries, Special Collections, SOC 3829.

began to focus on organizing migratory workers. In nearly all the cities where these affairs occurred, these workers were hired off the streets by farmers, foremen, or labor agents and were not always easy to reach by other means. The soapbox speeches that gave rise to the free-speech fights were well suited to the purpose. And if neither the speeches nor the free-speech fights frequently produced a great number of recruits, the latter, especially, took much courage and helped establish the union's credibility as an organization whose members were prepared to make real sacrifices in the name of industrial unionism.[77]

This penchant for sacrifice, which would show itself in so many ways, rested on the Wobblies' extraordinary faith in the union's program and ideals. Roger Nash Baldwin, principal founder of the American Civil Liberties Union, was, with Helen Keller and Rockwell Kent, among a handful of intellectual and cultural elites who joined the IWW. He saw this conviction and understood its deeper roots. A wealthy heir and a Harvard graduate, Baldwin's brief membership in and longtime affinity for the IWW rested partly upon the impression the organization made on him at a forum in Saint Louis, where he "just marveled at how these working people could talk on such a high level about public issues."[78]

Baldwin's judgment would hardly have surprised the Wobblies themselves. This is clear from the recollections of Wobbly Hagbard Edwards, for instance, who served over three years in California's San Quentin for criminal syndicalism. Edwards remembered how in the late 1910s, the IWW speakers he heard on Seattle's skid row "rekindled an interest in reading which had been dormant since arriving from Norway." He remembered going to the main public library at Fourth and Madison where he consumed the works of Upton Sinclair, Henry George, Robert Ingersoll, and Jack London and where he fell in with an old Wobbly "known by the sobriquet of Pork Chop" who, after sustaining an injury working as a shingle weaver, had been studying there every day for two years.[79]

Wobblies like Edwards and Pork Chop could also do their studying in the IWW's halls, which served many purposes beyond the conducting of conventional union business. Sometimes stocked with musical instruments, they hosted speakers and debates and frequently featured libraries of their own, often with hundreds, even thousands, of volumes on subjects from Western philosophy, to evolutionary biology, to classical poetry and literature.[80] In addition to the halls, the union sponsored workers' schools and colleges, where members could take courses in all manner of topics, not just those of immediate relevance to the union and its purposes.

Nor were these the only ways in which the Wobblies put an erudite and principled edge to their brusque challenge to the reign of capitalism. The speakers who so impressed Edwards or figured in the free-speech fights could also be found in hobo "jungles," job sites, and work camps, explaining the logic of capitalist exploitation and the IWW's program, condemning racism and other impediments to working class solidarity, and urging workers to desist from alcohol and drugs, dime novels, vaudeville shows, the services of prostitutes, and other distractions from their cause. Similar discourses appeared in the great number of pamphlets and newspapers the IWW published, which featured essays, news stories, editorials, letters, poems, and cartoons, many of a high quality.[81] Members were expected to read and promote these texts, which reveled in the union's strength while relentlessly affirming the IWW's founding ideal that it was the Wobblies' mission and purpose to realize humanity's destiny, even if this came at great costs to themselves.

Songs were also central to the way the IWW defined itself and articulated its vision of the world, as Wobblies often sang as they worked, traveled, protested, and roosted in prison or jail. The most important appear in the union's famous *Little Red Songbook,* first published in 1909 and distributed in huge numbers. The booklet is a compendium of Wobbly grievances and aspirations set to lyrics. In it can be found not only selections like Joe Hill's "There Is Power in a Union" and "Workers of the World, Awaken!" and Richard Brazier's "A Dream," with their messianic visions of a spectacular new world born out of workers' sacrifices and struggles, but likewise Laura Payne Anderson's "Industrial Workers of the World," which addresses "ye brave Industrial Workers," the "vanguard of the coming day." There is the IWW's version of "L'Internationale," whose first stanza closes with the arresting line "We have been naught, we shall be all." And then there is a song that some anonymous Wobbly forged from Rudyard Kipling's "Song of the Dead," a song that defied the common slander of the union as a bunch of worthless "I Won't Works" and insisted that even the most transient and impoverished in their ranks were neither tramps, nor bums, nor other hopeless victims, but workers of the most vital sort, endowed with an inviolable claim to remake the world in line with a vision which was uniquely theirs to realize. Its title: "We Have Fed You All for a Thousand Years."[82]

But if these things impressed the likes of Roger Baldwin and Helen Keller, they did nothing for the union's critics who, if they acknowledged the IWW's culture of revolution and solidarity, saw in it the irresponsible indulgence of people who had little to lose, were headed nowhere, and could scarcely comprehend the union's program anyway.[83] These were the judgments not only of the union's crudest detractors but also of Progressive scholars, particularly when, in the 1910s, the union's ranks swelled with migratory workers. This was the underpinning of the patronizing views of Nels Anderson and Don Lescohier, for instance. And it was also the perspective of Robert Hoxie, a University of Chicago economist who served as an investigator for the Commission on Industrial Relations. Hoxie's 1913 article "The Truth about the I.W.W."—with its descriptions of the union as a "pathetic" organization of "desperate elements" who were undernourished, lacking the "broad-headed" and "square-jawed" features essential to proper labor activism, incapable of fully understanding their own program, and destined to fail—set the standard for this kind of work.[84]

One whose writings often met this standard was Carlton Parker. A Berkeley professor and later a dean at the University of Washington who had been a miner in his youth, Parker acknowledged that the Wobblies "read and discuss abstractions to a surprising extent." But he assured readers of his extended, psychoanalytical study of the IWW that the

Wobbly "mind" was "stamped by the lowest, most miserable labor conditions and outlook which American industrialism produces." Anticipating the condescending way courts would occasionally justify overturning Wobblies' convictions, Parker concluded that the IWW was composed of "neglected and lonely" men, "usually malnourished and in need of medical care," whose command of their own philosophy was limited and whose enterprise was a futile exercise in desperation and despair.[85]

These Progressive critics were right on many points. The IWW was shaped by Wobblies' lives on the precarious margins of a capricious and rapidly changing society— it was not a collection of affluent graduate students, earnest Boy Scouts, or pious choir boys. More than a few Wobblies were sick or injured. Some were only casually connected to the union. As the union grew, some paid dues just to get along better with their fellow workers, or for the privilege of sleeping in the union's hall or in the jungles its members controlled, or to more easily ride on freight trains full of Wobblies without being hassled.

These critics were also right to note the Wobblies' lack of formal education. There were some exceptions. Leo Laukki taught at a workers' college in Minnesota and would go to federal prison. Fred Esmond, who would join him there, was educated at Oxford. A. S. Embree, who would also serve time in prison, likewise had some college, as had at least three defendants convicted of conspiracy in Kansas. Nicholaas Steelink had studied English, French, and German, as well as bookkeeping, shorthand, and mathematics, before landing in prison. However, most Wobblies were just "everyday" working men, as Arthur Berg, on trial for criminal syndicalism in Oklahoma in 1923, characterized himself in response to a prosecutor's attempt to cast him as conniving seditionist steeped in atheism and anarchism.[86] And most had only a few years of formal schooling, if that. Some struggled with their reading, and some could not read at all. Like Joe Crane in Ashleigh's *Rambling Kid,* many were "really not interested in anything very much, except the small daily drama of living."[87]

Nevertheless, the habit of dismissing the Wobblies' comprehension of and belief in the union's teachings says more about those promulgating such views than about who these people really were. A great number of the people who joined the union, especially in the late 1910s and early 1920s, were true believers, Wobblies in the most authentic sense, as one of the union's leaders mused a half-century later.[88] And they were not stupid. Joe Neil's prison record describes his "grade of education" as "none," and he was no intellectual. But when Marcet Haldeman-Julius

FIGURE 6. IWW Hall, Everett, Washington, probably 1916. Walter P. Reuther Library, Archives of Labor and Urban Affairs, Wayne State University.

met him behind bars she found a man who had no regrets and was still keenly interested in the union's ideas. He was "content to have found a philosophy that satisfied him, and to discuss it with those whom chance and the fortunes of the road threw in his way."[89] Like Ashleigh's Joe Crane, who later embraces the union's philosophy, Neil was one of countless Wobblies to immerse himself in the IWW's teachings. Like thousands of these men, Neil's commitment to this philosophy passed the sort of acid tests of ideological fealty that people like Hoxie and Parker have never been required to take.

None of this should be surprising. For can a man who is unschooled never gain a deep understanding of the world? Can a rogue not also be a radical? And can poverty and adversity not be more direct and reliable entrées to enlightenment than lives of privilege and ease? How else can we reckon why, as they suffered in prison, hundreds of Wobblies felt that what they most needed to be sent to them were more books?[90] How else might we consider the reflections of an old Wobbly on how the IWW had saved him from a life of criminality and brought him to higher reflections: "Through the IWW I began to consider how man had risen from the beastly stage through the ages. I could see a future that I could be part of creating. I began to see how you contribute to my well-being and I to yours. I saw what love was in the finest sense."[91]

. . .

The Wobblies' commitment to their union's program was further confirmed in a string of large and notable strikes during the IWW's first eight years of operation. Among these was the country's first documented sit-down strike, which occurred in 1906 and involved 3,000 workers at a General Electric plant in Schenectady, New York. That affair was followed by a series of strikes in the mining towns of Goldfield and nearby Tonopah, Nevada, extending from late 1906 through the end of 1907. The union made progress in pursuit of an eight-hour day despite company-sponsored intrigue and conflict with the WFM. But its gains were undone by repression. The IWW's general secretary, Vincent St. John, was shot in the hand by a hostile WFM member and hunted by a lynch mob before union activism was put down by federal troops, deployed on the pretext of reining in IWW-sponsored violence.[92]

In 1909, the union insinuated itself into a chaotic and bloody walkout among 6,000 terribly exploited workers at Pressed Steel Car Company in McKees Rocks, Pennsylvania.[93] That struggle ended with some concessions, and the workers established a union, the Car Builders Industrial Union, affiliated with the IWW. But the concessions were actually little more than a restoration of conditions prevailing before the strike, and the IWW affiliate soon faded away, leaving the workers without effective union representation and the IWW without any real membership gains. Moreover, the company and its supporters in the newspapers and in local government affixed much of the blame for strike violence, which claimed the lives of a dozen people, on the IWW, even though its organizers had used their limited influence to counsel restraint.[94]

These strikes were among several hundred protests, large and small, that the union organized or led between 1906 and 1913. A fair number were out West, and not only in industries like lumber, mining, and construction, where the union would later make significant gains, but also among cannery and electrical workers in California, for instance.[95] However, most were in industrial cities east of the Mississippi River. Among these were prominent struggles involving railroad car builders in Hammond, Indiana; construction workers in Chicago; shoe workers in Brooklyn; meat packers and tobacco workers in Pittsburgh; rubber workers in Akron, Ohio; and one among steel workers in New Castle,

Pennsylvania, that got the whole staff of the union's newspaper, *Solidarity*, thrown in jail.[96] The strikes sometimes produced concessions, but like those that followed the trouble in McKees Rocks, they were usually modest and generated little in the way of lasting support for the union. Such was also the case with the union's two most storied strikes in its early years: the "Bread and Roses Strike," in Lawrence, Massachusetts, in 1912, and the Paterson Silk Strike, in Paterson, New Jersey, in 1913.

In both places, IWW organizers were able to exert considerable influence among hard-pressed, predominantly immigrant textile workers not originally in the union's fold, and to mount impressive protests and propaganda and relief campaigns. In each city, what began as small, spontaneous walkouts that challenged regressive company policies imposed on top of long-standing exploitation grew to entail about 25,000 workers. But in the end, neither strike was successful. The Lawrence strike ended with significant concessions, but the companies soon reverted to prestrike policies, while in Paterson the strike collapsed without any meaningful concessions. And although the union signed up roughly 10,000 new members in each city, these gains proved fleeting, as nearly all of the new recruits drifted away within a year.

Both strikes unfolded in the face of considerable repression. Hundreds of union people were arrested and untold numbers beaten, including in one notorious incident in Lawrence, dozens of children awaiting evacuation from the city during what was partly a humanitarian measure and partly a brilliant propaganda coup organized by the IWW. Five people were also killed in these strikes, three in Lawrence and two in Paterson. One of the dead in Lawrence was a striker named Anna LoPizzo, shot down during a riot. LoPizzo's death led to a drawn-out but unsuccessful murder prosecution of two of the union's lead organizers, Joe Ettor and Arturo Giovanitti, who were miles away when LoPizzo was killed, almost certainly by a policeman. Most other union people arrested during these strikes were released without charge or faced minor charges. But several union leaders and supporters were imprisoned because of their actions in Paterson. Four strike leaders were charged with inciting a riot by holding a meeting, and one of them, Patrick Quinlan, was convicted and served two years in prison. A Socialist newspaper editor, Alexander Scott, was convicted of criminal libel and sentenced to one to fifteen years. And Socialist journalist and IWW supporter Frederick Sumner Boyd was convicted of sedition for inciting sabotage of mill property and sentenced to one to seven years.[97]

The repression that featured in these strikes did not evolve into a sustained campaign to destroy the IWW, however, mainly because the union that stood behind all this turmoil remained so ephemeral. Nor, as bad as these things were, did they differ very much in intensity or from what many other unions faced in this period. Nevertheless, the strikes themselves did much to define the union's fate. Their failure reflected the limits of the IWW's opportunistic organizing methods as well as the apparent extent of its appeal among the more sedentary, often foreign-born industrial workers of the East, at least given the methods being used. They marked the pinnacle of the IWW's attempts to establish itself among such workers and anticipated its retreat from this front of activism and its turn toward the West, where a more sustained and telling encounter with repression awaited.

. . .

Despite their earlier rupture, the Socialist Party had remained entwined with the IWW and supported it in some of these strikes. But that situation was not stable. In 1911, the party was divided between a left and right wing. Representatives of the right wing were presenting recent gains in membership and election victories as validation of the moderate program they favored, while condemning the IWW and its members and supporters within the party as reckless adventurers whose impetuous practices and radical vision could undo these accomplishments. The solution was to end the party's association with the IWW and expel its members. So these rightists adopted the methods of the capitalists and cast the union's commitment to direct action as a plan for violence and destruction.

At the head of this campaign was Morris Hillquit, a lawyer from New York whom Leon Trotsky famously dismissed as the "ideal Socialist Leader for successful dentists."[98] Hillquit detested the IWW and especially Haywood. He therefore led a group that tried unsuccessfully to block Haywood's appointment to the party's national executive board. Several days after being elected to the board in December 1911, Haywood gave a speech at New York's Cooper Union in which he summarized his views on the relative merits of political activism and direct action. Published two months later in the *International Socialist Review,* Haywood's brief for radical industrial unionism was compatible with a program of peaceful direct action but was also unsparingly critical of the legal system. "Do you blame me when I say I despise the law?" asked Haywood, venturing that "no Socialist can be a law-abiding citizen."[99]

Hillquit's group included powerful figures like Congressman Victor Berger, and it resumed its attacks on the IWW at the party's convention in the summer of 1912. Although Haywood and the IWW enjoyed significant support, Hillquit's faction pushed through an amendment to the party's constitution that mandated expulsion of "any member of the party who opposes political action or advocates crime, sabotage or other means of violence as a weapon of the working class."[100] Approved in a referendum in which only a fraction of members voted, the amendment led to a vote that removed Haywood from the board and effectively ejected him from the party. Although some union members quit the IWW in support of Hillquit's position, the party lost 20,000 members within four months of Haywood's expulsion, on top of over 30,000 who left after it adopted the amendment.[101]

. . .

It was not at all surprising that these attacks on the IWW focused on sabotage. Within five or six years of the union's founding, the IWW's publications began to frequently celebrate the concept, often with clever cartoons featuring pictures of a wooden shoe, images of a pensive black cat, conceived by Ralph Chaplin, or exhortations like "wear your shoes." Sabotage featured in many IWW songs, including Joe Hill's version of "Ta-Ra-Ra-Boom De-Ay," his "Casey Jones—the Union Scab," and a number called "Liberty Forever," which concluded with the lines, "To organize and teach, no doubt, / Is very good—that's true, / But still we can't succeed without / The Good Old Wooden Shoe." Soapbox speakers endorsed the practice, in part because their audiences found it so thrilling. And at the union's ninth annual convention in 1914, the main governing body, the general executive board, resolved without objection that speakers urge "the necessity of curtailing production by means of 'slowing down' and sabotage."[102]

Rooted in French slang, the word *sabotage* originally signified working awkwardly, incompetently, or in overly deliberate or otherwise inefficient ways. In this country, it remained foreign to the vocabulary of labor protests until about 1910, which is when the term began to appear with increasing frequency, alongside "direct action," in the IWW's rapidly expanding array of publications. The word still had its original connotation of work done slowly or badly. But by that time, it also had a rival meaning, consistent with both the rhetoric and practice of revolutionary syndicalism in France. This rival meaning invoked kicking or throwing wooden shoes, or sabots, into machinery and suggested violent destruction as a legitimate form of protest.[103]

This kind of destructive sabotage never constituted IWW policy, at least not in any formal or organized way.[104] Many instances of sabotage of this sort that did occur were the doings of workers who, whether IWWs or not, were acting on everyday grudges, something writer Louis Adamic, for instance, noted when he recounted what he witnessed during his time as an industrial worker.[105] In some cases, destructive sabotage was the work of provocateurs. Much of what was taken to be sabotage was also nothing of the kind, but instead the result of accidents or acts of god in a context where union people often indulged the rhetoric of destruction.[106] In plenty other cases, reports of sabotage were simply the lies of hostile newspaper reporters, capitalists and their managers, or private detectives and government officials.

For these reasons, many of the union's supporters, along with some historians, have denied that Wobblies engaged in much sabotage at all, contending that no Wobbly was ever caught committing serious acts of destructive sabotage or, if the testimony of turncoats and snitches is set aside, proven in court to have engaged in this kind of thing. As one Wobbly put it, referring to the rhetoric of sabotage, "Joe Hill was a poet. We understood that."[107] But poets often relate the truth in ambiguous and nuanced ways; and it is clear that while sabotage, as actually practiced by the IWW, was usually another name for "striking on the job," it was not only that.

In 1910, the "one big union" that, in the Wobblies' imagination, would bring the capitalists to their knees was a long way off. In this context, sabotage loomed as an effective form of protest in a world that otherwise afforded even the most militant workers few means of effectively challenging the terms of their exploitation. It offered to workers a way of meeting the violence of industrial capitalism on comparable terms, becoming in this manner central to the IWW's assertion of workers' class consciousness and their sovereignty over capital and the production process. As Walker Smith wrote in his pamphlet, "Is the machine more than its makers? Sabotage says 'No!' Is the product greater than producers? Sabotage more says 'No!' Sabotage places human life—and especially the life of the only useful class—higher than all else in the universe."[108] This kind of judgment about capital and work could be effectuated in passive ways or contemplated, as Wobblies often did, in rousing fantasies about destruction. But for many Wobblies, actual destruction was sometimes called for, something made evident in the wake of events in 1913, at a hops "ranch" near Wheatland, north of Sacramento.

. . .

That summer the Durst family, which owned the ranch, had used promises of high wages and good working conditions to recruit nearly twice as many piece-rate workers to harvest their crop as the undertaking required. Nearly 3,000 men, women, and children, of a great range of ethnicities, descended on the place, only to find exceptionally low wages and inhumane living conditions. But against the Dursts' expectations, the workers began to organize. The harvest had hardly begun when, on August 2, a couple dozen workers went down to manager Ralph Durst's office and demanded improved pay and accommodations, under threat of a strike. Some of these people were Wobblies, and others, representing what had already become an important element of IWW affiliation, were not members but were nonetheless associated with the union. Durst wanted nothing to do with any of them and brushed them off. In fact, by most accounts he either slapped or slugged their leader, a Wobbly whose membership had lapsed named Richard "Blackie" Ford, and tried unsuccessfully to get Ford arrested by a local constable. The organizers responded by calling for a mass meeting the next day.

As hundreds of workers gathered peacefully on the ranch that Sunday afternoon, singing IWW songs, Ralph Durst decided he was losing control of the place and summoned Yuba County sheriff George Voss. When Voss arrived, accompanied by local district attorney Edward Manwell and a dozen deputies, his group headed to the speakers' stage, intent on ordering everyone to disperse and arresting Blackie Ford. The facts have never been entirely clear, but as these men pushed their way through the throng of anxious workers, one of the deputies fired his shotgun into the air. Perhaps this was an accident; more likely, it was intended to intimidate the crowd. In any event, it threw the tense scene immediately into disorder and violence. In the "brief but furious battle" that ensued, fists and clubs flew through the air and twenty more shots were fired, some by the authorities, others by the workers. Two boys were killed, an Englishman and a black Puerto Rican. So were Manwell and a deputy, both, it would appear, beaten and then shot by the Puerto Rican after he had disarmed another deputy but before being struck down himself.[109]

Rushed to the scene on orders of Governor Hiram Johnson, National Guardsmen found the place deserted early the next morning. As soon as the shooting stopped, nearly all the pickers had fled in haste, carrying what they could and hoping to avoid being arrested. Some of the state's newspapers wrote, provocatively and falsely, of hordes of Wobbly fighters heading into the area, as in the free-speech fights. Jack London, who had watched the fires that followed the 1906 San Francisco earthquake with Joe Ettor, witnessed hordes of frightened workers heading away from the ranch and thought they resembled the shattered refugees from that calamity. About a hundred who remained at the ranch or were tracked down fell into the hands of the Burns Detective Agency, various vigilante groups, and Yuba County deputies. Some of these men were subjected to beatings, death threats, and starvation. One, a worker named Nels Nelson, who had lost an arm because of a gunshot sustained in the riot, hung himself. Another attempted suicide, and yet another had a mental breakdown and had to be committed. This "investigation" ended with four defendants charged with Manwell's murder: Blackie Ford, Walter Bagan, William Beck, and Herman Suhr, an active member of the IWW who was secretary of the impromptu local the union had established at the ranch.[110]

The state's case was premised on the notion, backed by a coroner's judgment, that the union had incited Manwell's killing and that since these defendants were leaders in the union, they were responsible. Aided by sympathetic Socialists, the IWW organized a well-funded defense headed by a lawyer named Austin Lewis. But the case was heard before a judge who had been friends with Manwell and in a town barely ten miles from Durst Ranch. On January 31, 1914, after two and a half weeks of trial, the jury acquitted Bagan and Beck, whose leadership in the strike was not as significant, but convicted Ford and Suhr, who were sentenced to life in prison.[111]

The Wheatland affair confirmed for many people in California and the West that the IWW was a dangerous organization that needed to be contained. They believed this, in part, because of the work of the California Commission of Immigration and Housing (CCIH). Created a year before the events at Durst Ranch, the CCIH flourished in their aftermath and quickly emerged as a model for Progressive redress of this kind of labor unrest. Charged with unearthing and addressing the causes of the trouble on Durst Ranch, the CCIH dedicated itself to improving working and living conditions for migratory workers in the state. But it also developed an obsession with undermining the IWW and coordinating the efforts of businessmen and politicians who shared this goal.[112]

The CCIH's hostility to the IWW was framed not only by the riot, its aftermath, and the trial, but also by attempts by the union to secure the release of Ford and Suhr. After legal appeals failed, the union organized a campaign of direct action aimed at inducing the hop growers to use the power they had wielded to put these men in prison for the purpose of getting them out. When the Wobblies' deadline of August 1, 1915, came and went without results, the union began its protests. Wobblies set up picket lines at a significant number of hop ranches, which diminished the availability of workers and cost some of the hop growers, including the Dursts, considerable money.[113]

This was not all, though. There were also fires, broken machines, and dead orchard trees all over California's Central Valley, particularly, it seems, after the results of striking and picketing fell short of union expectations. Some of this was attributable to nature and accidents and some was likely the work of detectives. But in this case direct action was not limited to a withholding of labor or inefficient work. Articles in the IWW's newspapers brazenly endorsed destructive sabotage as a necessary means for winning the release of Ford and Suhr. The union's leadership, including Big Bill Haywood himself, seemed at least to appreciate the value of threatening this kind of action. And while it seems doubtful that there was ever any coordinated campaign of sabotage, let alone one actually directed by the union itself, it seems certain that some of the destruction was indeed the work of Wobblies.[114]

In the scheme of things, the destruction that summer and fall did not amount to very much, and the whole thing might well be seen as a reckless but understandable reaction to what had happened to workers on Durst Ranch, to what workers endured throughout the region, and to what had been visited on union people arrested and prosecuted after the riot. But as people like Haywood should have known, the union's radicalism and its impingement on the economic interests of powerful people largely denied it the benefits of this kind of forbearance. Their headlines ablaze with sensational stories of IWW plots and schemes, the state's newspapers were certainly not so inclined.[115] Neither were its politicians, especially not after Pinkerton detectives, employed by the CCIH, helped produce a confessed IWW arsonist in the person of a sick and mentally ill man named James McGill, who said he was part of a gang that had set numerous fires at the direction of the IWW. Although McGill's statements were incoherent and implausible, this mattered little, and he was convicted of arson and sentenced to fifteen years in prison.[116]

Some staff at CCIH doubted that Wobblies were actually responsible for much destruction, and after interviewing McGill, Governor Johnson also developed doubts about his veracity. But these concerns did not stop CCIH from using the confession to justify intensified efforts to undermine the IWW. Nor did they inspire restraint on the governor's part. Indeed, for Johnson, IWW sabotage provided a rationale for denying Ford and Suhr clemency and also underlay his decision to enlist the federal government in a campaign to destroy the union.[117] Johnson recruited to this cause Oregon governor James Withycombe, Washington governor Ernest Lister, and Utah governor William Spry. In the fall of 1915, the governors dispatched Lister's friend, the U.S. Secretary of the Interior, to meet with Woodrow Wilson and secure his support. With Johnson's endorsement, the CCIH also sent its own emissaries to Washington to lobby Wilson.[118]

Federal authorities had honored the request from Nevada officials and businessmen to suppress the IWW at Goldfield and Tonopah in 1906 and 1907, never mind that charges of union-sponsored violence used to justify it were largely untrue. In the early 1910s, federal authorities also deported a few foreign-born Wobblies on ideological grounds and engaged in sporadic surveillance of the union. But the government had demurred in 1912 when five hundred influential Californians, annoyed by IWW activism in their state and led by John Spreckels and *Los Angeles Times* publisher Harrison Otis, demanded a federal campaign against the union. And it demurred again on this occasion. One reason for this is that the federal government was then very short on policing resources. In the mid-1910s, the U.S. Justice Department's Bureau of Investigation had only a hundred forty-one employees. Another reason is that the department's agents decided that the IWW was not creating nearly as much trouble as the governors and the CCIH contended.[119] Indeed, despite this business in California, the union was not capable of making very much trouble.

. . .

The lost strikes, the split with the Socialist Party, and its organizational difficulties had left the IWW not only isolated but, in Melvyn Dubofsky's words, on "the verge of disintegration."[120] Enrollment is an uncertain way to measure the strength of any union and a particularly dubious way to establish where the IWW stood, given how completely poor record-keeping and a footloose membership have frustrated even the most dogged attempts by researchers of this question. Nevertheless, what can be uncovered makes clear that, without ever having achieved much in the first place, the union was indeed in decline. Enrollment may have peaked at 60,000 shortly after its formation, much of it composed of WFM members; but by 1910 there might have been only a few thousand dues-paying members in the entire IWW. After rebounding in 1911 and 1912 to perhaps 20,000, membership collapsed again following the Paterson Silk Strike. In the recession years of 1913 and 1914, the entire organization counted maybe 5,000 members and possibly only half that number.[121]

The union was also bereft of funds and by 1914 was engaging in little organizing or activism. In fact, by this time, the death of "socialism with its working clothes on" seemed imminent. But events would soon save the IWW from this fate, even as, shaped by the union's reputation for sabotage and other forms of militancy, they also answered the appeal of a character in another of London's writings, *The Dream of Debs*. Published in 1909 in the *International Socialist Review* and illustrated by Ralph Chaplin, the short story chronicles a successful general strike by the "I.L.W." The strike is "the biggest and solidest organization of labor" in the country's history. "The tyranny of organized labor is getting beyond endurance," says the narrator, a wealthy victim of the uprising. "Something must be done."[122]

CHAPTER 2

Protecting the Business People

Class, Law, and the Criminalization of
Radical Industrial Unionism

In May 1916, the International Shingle Weavers of America, affiliated with the American Federation of Labor (AFL), called hundreds of shingle workers in Everett, Washington, out on strike in a bid to overturn wage cuts imposed eighteen months earlier, near the end of the nationwide recession. By late summer, the strike was weakening but had attracted the attention of the IWW, whose organizers decided they might revitalize the struggle and strengthen the union's presence among these terribly exploited workers. But when Wobblies began to enter the city in significant numbers to support this effort, they confronted Sheriff Donald McRae, who was ready for them with "San Diego-style measures."[1]

A Progressive and himself a former member of the shingle weavers union, McRae had the support of the Commercial Club, composed mainly of mill owners, as well as something called the Open Shop League, comprised of professionals and lower-level managers from the city's firms. He also had in his command an army of deputies, made up of scores of similar figures and a great number of local toughs and bullies, that repeatedly closed the union's hall, arrested its members, often on grounds of speaking without a license, sometimes beat them, and ran hundreds out of town. Nearly two dozen were seized on a single day in August, held overnight, and put on a boat to Seattle the next morning. In this group was a "black-haired volatile Irishman," as one historian describes him, named James Rowan, who had been arrested days earlier and deported but had returned and resumed organizing. While being marched to jail with his fellow captives that day in August, Rowan slipped away and delivered another speech, only to be arrested yet again.[2]

It was not the IWW's way to yield easily to repression, and the struggle quickly came to resemble a free-speech fight. On September 9, a small boatload of Wobblies attempted to sneak into Everett. McRae's men captured the infiltrators, beat them, and held them for a time without arraignment or trial. On October 30, a boatload of forty Wobblies arrived at the public dock from Seattle, thirty miles south on Puget Sound. Summoned by the lumber-mill whistles, McRae and two hundred men were waiting. They beat the Wobblies, loaded them into automobiles, and brought them to a place called Beverly Park. There, in a driving rain, they "warned" their captives against coming back to Everett by running them through a gauntlet, again beating them severely, and then ordering the men, some badly hurt, to walk back to Seattle.[3]

It says much about where the IWW found itself in the fall of 1916 that the nation's newspapers could indulge their growing obsession with the union not with accounts of these ominous events in Everett but with breathless stories, instead, of William Brown, a Wobbly who had been murdered under suspicious circumstances on October 29 in San Mateo, California, and of Joseph Schmidt, a Wobbly who, facing very questionable murder charges in Minnesota, had been granted bail and was racing to Scranton, Pennsylvania, to bury his infant son and visit his wife on her deathbed. These events and the coverage they received reflected an upwelling in repression, one that, in turn, showed how much progress the union was making toward finally finding its footing. The events in Everett were part of this trend, and the city would very soon earn its place in the national headlines.

On the morning of November 5, 1916, several hundred IWWs marched four abreast from the union hall in Seattle down to the Colman Dock. With pooled money the men secured passage to Everett on the *Verona* and the *Calista*, small steamers that provided service between the cities. The *Verona* set out first, loaded to the legal limit with two hundred fifty passengers, mainly Wobblies but also some sympathetic students and adventurers. When the boat pulled into the dock in Everett at about two o'clock that afternoon, the Wobblies were belting out "Hold the Fort," an old gospel hymn, remade by the Knights of Labor and the British Transport Workers Union before finding its way, remade again, into the IWW's songbook: "We meet today in Freedom's cause, / And raise our voices high; / We'll join our hands in union strong, / To battle or to die."

Battle and death awaited that Sunday, as there on the waterfront were McRae and his two hundred deputies, well-armed, in many cases drunk, and fed up with the Wobblies' perseverance. While the *Verona* was tying up, the sheriff challenged them. "Who is your leader?" he demanded. "We're all leaders," someone replied. "You can't land here," said McRae. "The hell we can't," was the reply. That moment, a gunshot rang out, probably fired by one of McRae's men, who immediately enfiladed the boat. The *Verona* nearly capsized when passengers rushed to the seaward side, seeking cover from a hail of gunfire. Some leapt and others fell overboard, only to be shot at in the water. A few fired back. Held fast by lines that none aboard could safely reach, the ferry drew fire from the dock and from a tugboat where McRae's men had also taken position. For maybe ten minutes, bullets tore through the *Verona's* deckhouse and through her passengers, too. Finally a union man cleared the engineer's mind of indecision by sticking a gun in his face and got the vessel underway, snapping the mooring lines in the process.[4]

When at last the *Verona* pulled out of range, two deputies lay dead on the dockside and about twenty, including McRae, shot through the leg, were wounded. The *Verona* bore four dead, all Wobblies; another union man was mortally wounded; and about thirty others were hurt, most of them Wobblies and most of them with gunshot wounds. As many as six or seven Wobblies may have ended up dead in the water, but that was never clear. Another man, J. A. Kelly, died several years later, possibly from the lingering effects of having been shot that day. In any event, further loss of life was probably averted when the *Verona* hailed the *Calista* out in the sound and desperately warned her crew to head back. Waiting there in Seattle for both vessels were the police, who took the seriously injured to the hospital and marched the other Wobblies to jail.[5]

. . .

In the aftermath of the shooting, hundreds of deputies patrolled the streets of Everett, securing their victory over the Wobblies. From one vantage, little of what was done in Everett that summer and fall to these "soldiers of discontent," as Charles Ashleigh called his fellow Wobblies, had any basis in the law.[6] So said the mayor of Seattle, Hiram Gill, in fact. But for Sheriff McRae, said by Wobblies to have been granted lifetime employment at the state capitol as a reward for his service, for his men, and indeed for nearly everyone else who persecuted the union's members, the law was a contradictory and ambiguous thing. Although in some ways it set limits on what they might do to the Wobblies, it was also a broad license, only modestly constraining, to deal harshly and expeditiously with people they declared genuine threats to the values of their community and its interests.

Indeed, one can appreciate that in some very meaningful ways McRae and his men, like many others who wore badges and guns and were never prosecuted for this kind of behavior, *were* the law. Yet one might nonetheless wonder why they did not often rest their authority on the pedestal of vagrancy law. Although some Wobblies were arrested on this charge prior to the *Verona* incident, apparently none was ever prosecuted.[7] Had officials in Everett relied more on this charge, they might have been defeated by the Wobblies, as their counterparts in cities that confronted free-speech fights this way sometimes were. But they also might have accomplished their purposes, and done so with the kind of legitimacy that McRae's fellow Progressives were inclined to prefer. And maybe they would not have had to shoot so many people.

In 1916, the State of Washington had a vagrancy law. So did Everett, an ordinance whose use against unionists and working people had garnered complaints from Socialists and labor people for years. And so did nearly all American jurisdictions in the early twentieth century. A fixture in American jurisprudence since Colonial times, particularly at the county and city level, many of these laws had been reformed in the late nineteenth century. The revisions, which often made vagrancy laws easier to enforce and sometimes authorized harsher punishments, left intact the essential function for which they had first been conceived in fourteenth-century England, the same that underlay the complaints of Everett's Socialists: they make criminals of poor, able-bodied, unemployed people, especially if they are found where people like Donald McRae decide they do not belong.[8]

Vagrancy laws helped codify the vision of "free" labor that came to prominence in post–Civil War America. They enforced the belief that workers' freedom consisted of an obligation to care for themselves and a duty to accept employment at prevailing conditions and wages, and they did so with a level of legal efficiency and straightforwardness that befit not only the social realities of industrial capitalism but also the preference among the architects of this age to rely on law in the formal, conventional sense as a means of regulating the economy and stemming the tides of disorder. So it was that the new vagrancy laws enacted in the late nineteenth and early twentieth centuries were championed by forward-thinking, philanthropic, and progressive-minded people.[9]

What suited vagrancy laws so well for these purposes is that they were written such that almost anyone could be arrested and prosecuted. The ordinance in Fargo, North Dakota, which would get much use against Wobblies, was typical. It made a potential vagrant of anyone who "shall be found loitering or strolling about the streets, alleys, avenues or lanes, or public or private places in the city," and it criminalized everything and everyone from "juggling" to "pilferers, confidence men, common drunkards, [or] common nightwalkers." In confirmation of E. P. Thompson's judgment about work and capitalism, it even criminalized "misspending" one's time.[10] The ordinance was likewise typical of most vagrancy laws in that neither defendants' "intent" nor the question of whether they had committed any particular act were necessarily material to proving guilt, as well as in that defendants could be arrested without a warrant and convicted and sentenced in trials without jury or much other legal process.

Jack London famously came to see all of this in the summer of 1894, after the threat of destitution and the dawning futility of the venture forced him to take leave of Kelley's Army and strike out on his own. He had slept in a field in Niagara Falls, New York, in hopes of seeing the falls but was arrested for vagrancy early the next morning and brought to trial that same day. The judge "was in a hurry," and it was "fifteen seconds and thirty days to each hobo." When London's name was called he planned to assert a "liberty those ancestors of mine had fought and died for" by saying something in defense of himself. But before he could say his piece, he had gotten thirty days too. "His Honor paused long enough to say to me, 'Shut up!'"[11]

London observed that the operative notion of guilt in the courtroom transcended the question of who had a job, could give a good account of himself, or even was dissolute or a drunkard. The terms of the law, in these formal respects, meant nothing. Rather, the trials were exercises in disciplining the defendants because they were presumed to have rejected what the social order had to offer them. This is why one of London's codefendants who insisted that he had not quit his job but that "his job had quit him" was promptly sentenced to twice as long in jail. It is also why London's later demand for a lawyer elicited laughter.[12] He and his codefendants were chained up and marched to the Erie County Penitentiary, where brutality and indignity were the orders of the day. Like most defendants, they served their time without appeal, as doing so usually required that they raise hundreds of dollars to bond an action that would likely take much longer to litigate than their sentences would run and was destined to fail anyway.[13]

It was London's misfortune not simply to be run out of town, either by the police or by the judge as a condition of his sentence, as this was the fate of many vagrants. But in other respects, London's punishment was typical. Well into the twentieth century, county jails all over the country were generally deplorable and altogether unsafe places where, as reform-minded sociologist Stuart Alfred Queen noted in 1920, "The great majority of convicted men are simply locked up in cages like wild animals." In his study of jails, Queen likewise found it all too easy to muster evidence of the extraordinarily casual and arbitrary ways in which most vagrants, along with other petty offenders, ended up in these facilities in the first place.[14]

To be sure, vagrancy laws served other purposes besides dealing with defiant or wayward working men. They were often used to make preemptive or investigatory arrests of common, sometimes genuinely dangerous, criminals and likewise to regulate prostitution, the drug or alcohol trade, and other everyday threats to bourgeois norms and public order. These functions, too, were framed by competing class interests and values. But in the early twentieth century, it was in the contexts of strikes and organizing efforts that vagrancy laws' congenital character as means of class control showed itself most clearly. This was quite evident in their use against the IWW, not only in many free-speech fights but in a more pervasive way in the cities and towns of the Great Plains, from whence a great number of "the boys" who descended on Everett to support the IWW struggle had come.[15]

. . .

By the early twentieth century, the Great Plains were fully within the orbit of industrial capitalism. A vast prairie five hundred miles wide running through the center of the continent, from central Canada down into Texas, it had been converted into tens of thousands of privately owned farms producing grain for a global market. Corn, oats, rye, barley, and other grains were grown, alongside beets and potatoes. And there were livestock farms too. But wheat was the dominant crop. Each year in the late 1910s and early 1920s, the "wheat belt," as it was known, produced nearly half a billion bushels on roughly five million acres of land.[16]

Improvements in machinery and cultivation techniques allowed a farmer and his family to grow perhaps four or five hundred acres of grain without requiring much, if any, hired help. Although some operations were much larger, that was about the average size of the region's

FIGURE 7. Threshing Crew, Reno County, Kansas, probably 1915. The farmer, John P. Linscheid, stands at the far right; his two sons are to his right. John P. Linscheid Collection, Mennonite Library and Archives, Bethel College.

wheat farms. But in these days before the widespread use of the motorized combine, when farmers relied on binders and headers to cut the grain and threshers to extract the seeds, it took much more labor to harvest the wheat than to grow it. Drawn by horses and mules, or, in the case of some binders, early tractors, these implements typically required several men and could cut only about fifteen acres a day. The threshing rig usually consisted of a large steam engine and a grain separator, along with water wagons, power belts, and other cumbersome equipment, and it could require a dozen or more men to operate.[17]

The labor needed at harvest was therefore considerably greater than the region's communities could provide, and workers had to be brought in in large numbers. The numbers could never be determined with great certainty, but by the late 1910s and early 1920s, across the wheat belt more than 250,000 hired hands, including perhaps 100,000 transient workers "from other states," were needed each summer to bring in the crop. Mostly single, white men, these migratory workers included students, thrill-seekers, and bored or down-and-out tradesmen or businessmen. But the core of the workforce, particularly the part that worked the whole season, consisted of transients who moved between the harvest and jobs in industries like lumber, mining, and oil and urban industrial workers driven to the fields by unemployment.[18]

Some hands made a decent "stake" in the harvest. But it was a struggle, at typical rates of three to five dollars a day. Work on each farm, whether bringing in the grain or threshing it, usually lasted a couple of weeks. After each job, the hands would head to another farm, often following the ripening grain from south to north over the course of the summer and early fall, "catching up" with it in what were usually hundred-mile jumps, before moving on to other types of work.[19] Along the way, they went long stretches without pay, reliable shelter, or basic amenities, navigating a perilous landscape and encountering conditions that taught a very young Ralph Chaplin, when he worked the harvest, "how the underdog was forced to live."[20]

Railroads had built the region and were the only practical way for the hands to travel any significant distance, given the state of the roads and the unavailability of automobiles. Most could not afford to make their way by Pullman or coach, and so they traveled out to and through the wheat belt by the dangerous means of hoboing on freight trains.[21] This often meant riding atop the cars, under them, or nestled inside, and it also meant hustling between cars and climbing on and off of the rolling stock. A great number of harvest hands—scores, at least—were among the several thousand "trespassers" who died on the railroads each year, crushed by shifting loads or between the cars, killed in falls, run over, caught under the wheels, or killed in the collisions and derailments that were extraordinarily common.[22]

Traveling by freight was also a good way to fall into the hands of common criminals, if not on the trains, then in the rail yards and jungle encampments where hoboes gathered and where gangs of "yeggmen," "jack-rollers," and "hi-jacks" plied their trade. Robbery and assault were common, and murder was a real possibility. And because riding the freights was illegal, as was trespassing in the yards or on the railroads' right of way, police and trainmen had ample prerogative to create all kinds of trouble for these men—which they did, for reasons that ranged from a simple sense of job and duty to a hatred of hoboes that verged on the pathological. Often they cleared the trains of hoboes and arrested or drove away those who were "undesirables" or whose labor was not needed in the area. It was not uncommon for them to beat the illegal riders or even throw them off the trains while they were rolling. Nor was it uncommon for police and trainmen to "harvest the harvesters," as the IWW put it, demanding money that went straight into their own pockets.[23]

Sometimes harvest hands fought back. Twelve years before he was charged with criminal syndicalism in Kansas, Joe Neil and several other

Wobblies were hoboing in Wisconsin when a brakeman threw them off a train "in none too kindly fashion." The Wobblies responded by bombarding the brakeman with rocks, which got Neil convicted of assault and sentenced to a year in prison.[24] Although trouble like this rarely resulted in felony prosecution, harvest hands were occasionally charged with very serious crimes, including the murder or attempted murder of trainmen.[25] In 1915, for instance, Wobbly James Schmidt was prosecuted in Aberdeen, South Dakota, for murdering a brakeman who, according to Schmidt, tried to shake him down and shoot him. Schmidt benefited from a mistrial when the jury, which largely favored his self-defense claim, could not reach a verdict.[26]

Trainmen and police were workers themselves and, out of feelings of solidarity or basic humanity, were not always intolerant of illegal riding and trespassing. Because they were destined to carry most of the grain these men harvested, sometimes the railroads welcomed the hands on board.[27] Likewise, the commercial and professional people who ran the region's towns had interest in getting the crops in, and so could also see their way clear to accommodate the "indispensable outcasts," as historian Tobias Higbie describes them, particularly if there was not too much disagreement about going wages and not too many hands looking to earn them.[28]

Len De Caux, who left Oxford University to "join the working class," discovered this in the early 1920s, long before he rose to prominence in the labor movement. De Caux found himself among a great bunch of hoboes who alighted from a train in a small town west of Minneapolis only to be confronted by a "burly and stout" sheriff at the head of "a small posse." But rather than hassling the men, as they expected, the sheriff welcomed them, smiling and friendly, and told his deputies to see to their needs. De Caux recalled how two Americans at Oxford had assured him that in this country "the laboring man is highly respected—when labor is in high demand."[29]

Sometimes there was also an element of genuine decency in the way the townspeople treated the hands, even when they were organized to raise wages. In the summer of 1924, 117 IWWs convening for union business in the small town of Kenmare, North Dakota, were greeted warmly by the mayor, who expressed the town's appreciation for their labor and presented the Wobblies with a donation of fifty dollars raised by town businessmen, which the Wobblies used to pay for meals.[30] Such consideration was hardly universal, however, and the hands were often right to expect trouble. The unpredictable and disorganized nature of the harvest and the unreliable means by which the men traveled meant that scores or even hundreds often descended on a place at one time, many of them young and bawdy, hanging about on the streets and in the rail yards or in nearby jungles for days, singing and drinking, sometimes brawling and gambling. This was reason enough for townspeople, police, and trainmen to make life difficult for them, even if the men were needed, and even when they were not threatening revolution, organizing strikes, or sabotaging farm equipment. And it is the reason that in places like Fargo the coming of the harvest brought a dramatic increase in police activity and daily arrests on charges like vagrancy.[31]

More likely to sympathize with these workers were the farmers themselves, and not only because their need for labor was most immediate. Although large compared to their eastern counterparts, a majority of the region's farms were owned by people who were far from wealthy. Most farmers hired their own harvest labor directly. However, most could not afford to own a threshing rig and engaged the services of a thresherman who, in turn, usually hired his own labor. Working alongside the hands, many farmers felt a certain kinship with them, paid what they honestly believed was fair and provided decent food and accommodations. When the union made inroads, some farmers, especially the smaller ones of modest means who shared the Wobblies' grievances, would go so far as to actively support the IWW and seek out union hands. In some places, farmers like these influenced the state or local officials to lighten up on the hands, including those who were Wobblies. But such attitudes were not the norm. "John Farmer," as the IWW called him, was essentially a capitalist, after all, and even more so were the threshermen, whose ties to the hands were more attenuated and who frequently complained that the workers sabotaged their equipment. Driven by desperation, greed, or good business sense, and justified by the workers' supposed fecklessness or criminality, many who engaged them served their hands bad food and alkali water, directed them to sleep in rough sheds or on bare ground, haggled over wages, or even ran them off without pay once the job was done.[32]

Making it to the harvest was no guarantee of steady work in any event, as the men, sometimes induced by misleading advertisements or dishonest labor agencies, faced the constant risk of traveling great distances only to find they were not needed. As Joe Neil discovered in Hutchinson, Kansas, this was a good way to get arrested for vagrancy. When they did get work, it was often a grueling marathon, under the direction of farmers constantly worried about weather and falling prices. This was the reality behind IWW organizer E. F. Doree's declaration that for harvest hands, the eight-hour day meant "eight in the morning and eight in the afternoon."[33] And it gave truth to the lyrics of Joe Hill's version of the song "Ta-Ra-Ra-Boom-De-Ay," with its celebrations of sabotage: "I had a job once threshing wheat, / Worked sixteen hours with hands and feet. / And when the moon was shining bright, / They kept me working all the night." With pay organized by the day, farmers and threshermen often did demand service from "can to can," and even beyond. Ten- to eleven-hour days were typical, which was plenty when the time was filled with arduous and sometimes dangerous labor.

Doree claimed that in one county in Kansas on a single day in 1914, twenty-five men died of heat stroke.[34] This is surely not true. But Wobbly Jack Miller probably remembered right when he recalled working on a farm near Lincoln Center, Kansas, for ten days straight in temperatures well over one hundred degrees Fahrenheit and watching five men "go down with heat exhaustion."[35] Indeed, as regular reports in the region's newspapers made clear, death by heat stroke was a possibility, as was being killed or seriously injured by lightning and draught animals, and sometimes by the machinery—including, in the most spectacular way, explosions of the boilers that fired the thresher engines or of the great clouds of dust generated by this process.[36]

These conditions in the fields and on the road produced a natural solidarity among the harvest hands, rooted in common struggle and reflected in the surprisingly cooperative culture in the jungles and on the trains and in the close, though usually temporary, bonds that developed among small groups as they traveled and worked the harvest. As Ralph Chaplin witnessed, these men "would stand together, fight for one another, steal for one another, and share [their] last crust of bread with one another." They could also be organized. Chaplin recalled how, years before the IWW made headway in the industry and before he had himself joined, he and his fellow "rebels" at their jungle campfires "heard rumors about a proposed organization of agricultural workers. We listened greedily."[37]

. . .

The IWW made some attempts to organize harvest workers during its first decade. But headlined by free-speech fights in places like Kansas City, Missouri, and Fargo and Minot, North Dakota, these efforts were haphazard. The union recruited few members and achieved few improvements in compensation or working conditions.[38] However, things began to change in 1914, when, with the endorsement of Big Bill Haywood and a prominent member named Frank Little, the IWW's general executive board established a Bureau of Migratory Workers. The following spring, the union convened in Kansas City, Missouri, and created the Agricultural Workers Organization No. 400 (AWO)—the "400" being a sardonic reference to the "list" of oligarchic families said by themselves and their sycophants to represent the only people who mattered in New York "society."

The formation of the AWO was part of a broader shift in IWW structure. In its first decade, the IWW was characterized by a lack of clear strategy on every front and an altogether casual approach to the management of its affairs. This was reflected in the free-speech fights, which began largely unplanned, and in the union's equally improvised interventions in places like McKees Rocks, Lawrence, and Paterson. Doing things in this way honored the IWW's footloose and adventurous spirit. But it was hard not to believe that the union's precarious situation was attributable to this manner of conducting business. Haywood and Little were among a number of the union's leaders to embrace this conclusion, along with Chaplin, who had joined the IWW in 1913 and soon became an important figure in the organization. At the union's tenth convention in 1916, changes were ratified that centralized authority in the Chicago office and augured a more careful and deliberate approach in general.[39]

Although the immediate effects of these changes were generally positive, they set the stage for future conflict within the organization. They also contrasted with a very different development at the local level. Until the AWO's founding, IWW organizing was built, if not upon the union insinuating itself into existing conflicts or working through isolated, industry-specific locals, then upon a scattering of "mixed locals" whose members included workers from any number of industries. These mixed locals fit with the IWW's faith in industrial organizing and its idea that workers should be free to move between industries without taking out new union memberships. But the model deprived the IWW of both focus and the ability to coordinate its efforts across specific industries. Worse, the union relied primarily on so-called stationary delegates as front-line organizers, charging them with enlisting new members and negotiating with employers on the basis of fairly rigid guidelines already prescribed by the union and usually from immobile union offices. This was all poorly suited to the circumstances the IWW encountered in the field, especially as its attentions shifted westward.

By 1912 a consensus had already begun to emerge within the union that it should restructure its organizing efforts such that organizers spent more time in the field. When the IWW created the AWO, it embraced this philosophy, substantially replacing the stationary delegates with "roving delegates," "camp delegates," and "job delegates," as they were variously called, who worked the jungles, trains, bunkhouses, mills, and camps where workers congregated, while often laboring alongside the men they sought to organize. Constrained by a loose set of priorities, they had considerable discretion to decide how best to enlist new members and bargain over terms.

By putting more organizers in the field and blurring the lines between them and other workers, the new approach made every member a more likely target for arrest, assault, or discharge. And because it had delegates travel around burdened with dues money, membership cards, and dues books, it also rendered this material vulnerable to being lost, stolen, or seized by police or vigilantes. Nevertheless, the virtues of this approach far outweighed its liabilities. Besides expanding the number of organizers, the job delegate system gave organizing a more democratic character. And its inherent flexibility was ideal for dealing with small employers or autonomous foremen in varied and often isolated locations, allowing organizers to broker sensible compromises on wages and working conditions that could produce surprisingly congenial relations, even with cynical police and wary townspeople.[40]

The delegate system was especially well suited to the AWO's situation. Under the leadership of a "no-nonsense Wobbly" named Walter Nef who had done nearly every kind of migratory labor, the AWO focused on achieving better wages and working conditions and barring discrimination against IWW members. Although the AWO adhered to the IWW's policy of rejecting written contracts as fetters on worker militancy, it discouraged members from abrogating the agreements it did reach. It discouraged them from traveling around in overly large, threatening groups, as these vulnerable workers had become used to doing. And with an understanding that some confrontational tactics, like the free-speech fights, were often counterproductive, the AWO likewise moved to rein in unnecessary protests.[41]

The AWO deployed these methods throughout the West, including Washington, Oregon, and California, where it was active in the grain fields and among orchard workers, hop pickers, and table-vegetable workers, many of whom were women and children. It organized, too, among beet workers on the Great Plains and even in the "corn belt" that ran east to west, transecting the wheat belt. It was in the wheat belt, though, with its large, seasonal demand for migratory labor, that the union made its biggest mark. There, in both the southern winter-wheat zone centered in Kansas and in the northern spring-wheat region that ran from eastern Montana into western Minnesota and from the Dakotas into Canada, the union sought to establish what it called an "eight-hundred-mile picket line" with which to force concessions from employers and establish control over working conditions in the industry. But to do this, the Wobblies would have to run an eight-hundred-mile gauntlet of men who were committed to breaking their union.

. . .

The new harvest workers union created a great stir during the 1916 harvest when it organized workers behind a baseline demand of four dollars a day, along with fifty cents an hour overtime and decent food and accommodation. That summer, Kansas newspapers were full of talk of "industrial warfare," Wobbly "invasions," and, in one instance, a "black plague" of 150 "negroes"—IWWs—descending on a small town.[42] The harvest began with numerous clashes between Wobblies and local police and townspeople. One of these occurred in early July, in WaKeeney, when tensions escalated between IWW men and "scissorbills," as the Wobblies called nonunion men willing to work for lower wages, who had gathered by the hundreds in the town. The police responded by raiding the IWW camp and searching everyone. Finding a gun in the possession of a man named Earl, or Clifford, Lake, they arrested Lake and brought him before the police court, where he was convicted the next morning on a weapons charge. That night, the evening of July 8, a large group of Wobblies made good on a threat to storm the jail. They liberated Lake and jailed the sheriff. Before they could escape, a group of 150 "citizens," summoned by fire alarm and telephone before the Wobblies could cut the lines, freed the sheriff, recovered the prisoner, herded every suspected IWW out of town, and, in the process, accidently shot and wounded two union men.[43]

Local officials predicted that the "disgruntled bums" would return to WaKeeney to "sack the town."[44] They never did. But in the week that followed, there was more trouble around Salina, 125 miles to the east, where newspapers reported burned wheat, the arrest of IWW organizers, and a great number of scuffles between Wobblies and police, vigilantes, and nonunion harvest hands. Several people, both IWW and nonunion, were reported shot and others beaten up before the end of the harvest later that summer.[45]

This trouble in Kansas arose directly out of the union's success in organizing men behind its bargaining demands, as the campaign led to a great number of hands loitering in small towns until these terms were met and in bigger cities awaiting word of where good jobs could be found. Conflict with police and townspeople followed the hands as they followed the harvest. The summer was marked by clashes also in small towns in Nebraska and adjoining parts of Iowa, as well as larger towns like Omaha, Sioux City, and Council Bluffs, where police and vigilantes either warded off the Wobblies or arrested them in large numbers.

Some of the worst trouble occurred in Lincoln, where an attempt to cleanse the city of Wobblies produced a rumpus on July 13, during which an IWW struck the sheriff's father in the head with a frying pan. This led to the arrest of a number of Wobblies and, in turn, the influx of some two hundred IWWs determined to secure the release of two of these arrestees. The Wobblies failed to push their way into the jail and failed, too, to compel the police, in the fashion of a free-speech fight, to arrest them en masse. But their threats to bring many hundreds more union men into the town were preempted by an agreement to release the two prisoners. Meanwhile, police in Omaha dealt with their IWW problem by loading nearly all the men into box cars and shipping them north.[46]

The union's success in achieving higher wages and better conditions helped bring more men to the harvest, which meant more trouble. By midsummer, large groups of workers were congregating in and about the region's railroad towns. Divided into "armies" of IWW men and scissorbills—or "independents" or "yellow card men," as they were also called—these groups engaged in several "battles." One of these occurred on the afternoon of July 27 in Council Bluffs, where hundreds of hands were encamped and where an attempt by Wobblies to organize a hold-out for four dollars a day resulted in a general melee. No one was seriously injured. But a similar affray in Redfield, South Dakota, that day among hundreds of hands produced an exchange of gunfire that left three Wobblies injured. The next day, another huge clash between these factions a hundred miles south in Mitchell, South Dakota, resulted in gunplay and left several people injured and several others under arrest.[47]

While all this was occurring, a large number of Wobblies, probably around fifty—although some newspapers claimed several hundred—marched down to the jail in Ortonville, Minnesota, just over the South Dakota border, and compelled the police to release one of their men.

Dozens of townspeople armed with guns and bats responded, driving all the Wobblies out of town. Indeed, that summer large groups of armed citizens frequently mobilized against the union men. The force that intervened to end the riot in Mitchell captured 250 IWWs, held them all night crouched in a circle under the lights of automobiles, and then shipped them north on a freight train. As other trains pulled into town over the next few days, police and townspeople either turned them back, sent them through without permitting anyone to detrain, or stopped them so that union organizers and men carrying weapons could be identified and taken to jail.[48]

By the time the harvest reached North Dakota, the situation was quieter, partly, one suspects, because authorities were ready. The *Fargo Forum and Daily Republican* applauded police practices in that city to ensure that the men went to work the fields without holding out for higher wages, including those meant to "walk" the "pep" out of union organizers. "Keeping the men constantly on the move, picking out the leaders and running them out of the country whenever possible," is how the paper praised the efforts.[49] Harvest hands who held out for wages higher than what the police thought "fair" were liable to be preemptively deemed IWWs and either run out of town or arrested. If arrested, they faced several weeks in jail, maybe breaking rocks or working on the roads during the day, or the option of harvest work at proffered wages.[50] Said the *Ward County Independent,* "The working man finds a welcome in Minot, but the trouble makers will be given a decidedly interesting time."[51]

. . .

The AWO's limited campaign in 1915 had produced a promising yield of 2,000 to 3,000 members. Despite all of the trouble the union encountered in 1916, it surged forward that season, signing up between 16,000 and 20,000 new members.[52] Some sense of how it recruited these men and how it soon extended this surge across other industries can be gotten from what Wobblies arrested in a fall 1917 raid on a union convention in Omaha told federal agents. A great number of these men had been recruited in the harvest. A few said they had signed up because everyone else in their work crew was IWW; some cited a political purpose, like "the emancipation of the working class"; and one said, "I joined the IWW because I got kicked by a sheriff." But by far the most common answer was simply "to better my condition." When asked if their condition had improved, nearly all said yes. Most pointed to higher wages and better food; one, alluding to something that suggested how it was that the bettering of conditions actually served the union's political aims, said that what had made his life better were the friends he had found through the union.[53]

As the AWO's membership grew, the union was better able to organize the hands to hold out, more successful in delivering higher wages and improved working conditions, and in turn more successful recruiting members. It was able to reach better accommodations with police and townspeople, who were often averse to conflict with large, organized groups of men.[54] Its members were likewise able to turn the tables on criminals, beating them or throwing them off the trains and ejecting them from the jungles. As Wobbly William Dimmit put it, "the high jack has not been tolerated." "His rule of freights and jungles" was "overcome by organized force."[55] Similar treatments were inflicted on independents, something Len De Caux discovered some years later when, before joining the IWW, he nearly got himself ejected from a train while working the harvest, and then again when he had to convince his fellow riders that his card for the One Big Union, the Canadian cognate of the IWW, was sufficient for passage.[56] This kind of thing sometimes crossed into the realm of gratuitous, even brutal, acts of violence and sometimes resulted in prosecution. But, justified or not, violence was one means by which Wobblies in the harvest sought to hold their eight-hundred-mile picket line.[57]

Confronted by large numbers of organized men, the trainmen had to back off as well, a fact amusingly reflected in a report from the summer of 1916 about a group of Wobblies who commandeered an entire train in Jamestown, North Dakota, and drove it some distance, apparently "just for the fun of handling things themselves."[58] Of more practical advantage was the success Wobblies had in compelling trainmen not only to think twice before assaulting them, summoning the police, or taking their money but also to accept the union's red card as license to ride without being hassled and even to help hold the picket line by granting this privilege only to union men.

There were other benefits to joining the AWO, some prosaic and some less practical but nonetheless essential. Membership in a growing organization allowed the men to use the union's expanding network of headquarters as banks where they could send their pay against the risk of robbery or expropriation by police or judges. They could avail themselves of the IWW's cultural offerings and sometimes sleep and wash up in union properties. They could rely on fellow members for help if they were short of funds, needed to deliver a message to someone across

FIGURE 8. IWW organizers conducting a vote among harvest hands, somewhere on the Great Plains, probably between 1916 and 1920. Walter P. Reuther Library, Archives of Labor and Urban Affairs, Wayne State University.

country, or desired someone to look after them if they were hurt, fell ill, or died on the road. They could find friendship, as the one worker told federal officials in Omaha.[59] And they could indulge the belief that they had made their way into an organization that not only bettered their conditions but gave historic meaning to their difficult and lonely lives.

. . .

The IWW's gains in the wheat belt and its changing strategies positioned the union to make progress in another important industry where it had organized for years without accomplishing much. Like the harvest, the lumber industry employed a highly transient workforce of the sort that the IWW was destined to do well at organizing. This was the rueful judgment of Cloice Howd, an investigator with the U.S. Department of Labor, who found lumber teeming with "rebels" and refugees from industrial society, some of "great genius," others woefully deficient, and many lacking in any case what he called "the mental ability to make the adjustments necessary for life in our complex social environment."[60] These workers were vulnerable to the IWW's entreaties, as Howd saw things; and at the root of these vulnerabilities were the industry's terrible working and living conditions.[61]

Focusing on western states, Howd found that in many logging camps and sawmills in the late 1910s, seasonal turnover ran as high as 100 percent, and on some jobs four or five men were hired for each position in the course of a week.[62] Among the reasons for this was something even truer here than in the harvest: the great danger of the work. In "the woods," where lumberjacks labored, it was easy to be killed or seriously injured by a falling tree or by falling from a tree, into the upper reaches of which men were sent with saws and axes. It was also easy to be cut by a saw or axe or crushed or mangled by the logs or the machinery used to move them out of the woods.[63]

In the lumber mills, where boards, shingles, posts, and the like were produced, workers labored around saws, rasps, and splitters, amid the crude engines and elaborate belt and pulley systems that powered them, and among piles of wood and stacks of logs that were prone to tumble without warning. Hazardous conditions were aggravated by a pace of work that was often ruled by the speed of the machinery and the owners' demands to extract the greatest value from their investments. "Lumber is not the only product of sawmills. There is also a frequent harvest of cripples," said an IWW publication.[64] And not just cripples, as the story of William "Billy" Gohl attests. A powerful AFL labor leader in Aberdeen, Washington, Gohl's reputation as a prolific serial killer—the "Ghoul of Grays Harbor"—following his 1910 conviction for murder may well have been based, in part, on the great number of deaths of sailors, longshoremen, and lumber workers in the area that were actually caused by workplace accidents.[65]

The Pacific Northwest, including California, Idaho, and Montana, and the Upper Great Lakes region, were the main focal points of IWW activism in lumber. There, much of the timber stood in very remote tracts.[66] This meant that the lumberjacks who harvested these tracts had to reside in camps that were often isolated deep in these forests. Constructed with great frugality, these rude outposts typically comprised a scattering of shoddy bunkhouses that were crudely furnished, lacking in sanitary facilities, poorly lit, eternally damp, inadequately heated and ventilated, and awash in filth and vermin.[67] There, the workers got what rest they could and took meals that "one had to be 'hungry as lumberjacks' to enjoy," as one veteran of this life remembered.[68]

Outside of the South, where as many as half were black, the industry's workers were nearly all English speaking, typically single, and mostly native born whites, with a disproportionate number of Scandinavian heritage. Workers in the lumber camps, especially, were apt to also work the harvest, construction, or other transient jobs.[69] The work was in any case unreliable. Even when the men wanted to stay on the

FIGURE 9. Lumber workers pose with "steam donkeys" in Washington State, probably around 1910. Charles R. Pratsch Photographs, Manuscripts, Archives, and Special Collections, Washington State University Libraries, PC 018.

job, their fortunes were determined by the rate at which tracts of timber were cleared, by seasonal factors like snowfall and water flow in the rivers and streams that were often used to move the wood, and by the caprices of a volatile global market for wood.[70]

The lumber industry was dominated by large, sometimes gigantic producers like Weyerhaeuser and the Northern Pacific and Southern Pacific railroads. In the Pacific Northwest, the Upper Great Lakes, and the piney woods of Louisiana and Texas, where most of the country's timber was found, 22 companies owned over a quarter of the wood and 195 concerns owned nearly half. These big operators got these holdings by something akin to theft: through cut-rate leases, land grants, and discounted sales of government holdings, what had been a public resource came to be owned in this fashion. Indeed, by the time the IWW was founded, private parties controlled 80 percent of the country's standing timber. With the resource in their hands, these interests viewed labor as the key to competition, with the result that wages were pushed down to the "barest sustenance level."[71]

Throughout the industry a ten-hour day was typical, although some workers were expected to put in twelve. Most worked six days a week and some seven. Wages could exceed the going rate for agricultural labor, but were nonetheless low, averaging from twenty cents to fifty cents an hour in the late 1910s. In the absence of union representation, rates were typically, as Howd put it, "entirely a matter of individual bargaining" and subject to arbitrary change "according as [the boss] thought men were scarce or plentiful."[72] Supervision was also oppressive. The foremen treated the men "as so many machines," periodically pushing them to work at an incredible pace in order to compensate for perceived "inefficiency and laziness." And while not every employer would fire a man just for belonging to the IWW, most would promptly discharge any "labor agitator," regardless of his affiliation.[73]

The IWW's initial efforts in the industry were improvised and generally ineffective. There were a few union-led strikes, like one that began among Portland mill workers in the spring of 1907, spread to a dozen mills, and seemed destined to provoke a significant settlement until the Oregon Central Labor Council, which was controlled by the AFL, withdrew its support and the walkout collapsed.[74] Two years later, organizing efforts in western Montana culminated in a confusing series of walkouts around Kalispell and Missoula that local authorities met with beatings and arrests.[75] In October, this conflict evolved into a full-blown free-speech fight on the streets of Missoula under the leadership of a teenager named Elizabeth Gurley Flynn, who was well on her way to becoming the most prominent woman in the IWW. Hundreds of people descended on the small city and, as the *Butte Miner* put it, scores of "laborites," including some women, were thrown in the local "dungeon."[76] That same month, a much bigger free-speech fight on the other side of the Idaho panhandle, in Spokane, reached its apogee. Having begun in the spring of 1909, and framed partly as a protest against exploitative employment agencies, the struggle extended into the spring of 1910. Among the five hundred people jailed was journalist and future Communist Party chairman William Z. Foster, who, while imprisoned for forty days, "frosted" his feet and joined the IWW.[77] There, the IWW got the ordinance that had been used to prevent members from speaking overturned, although the struggle also cost the lives of perhaps three Wobblies.[78]

These free-speech fights, along with another in Aberdeen, Washington, that began in 1911, grew out of speaking campaigns that drew some lumber workers into the union. They gave impetus to a chaotic succession of strikes that began in the spring of 1912. Organized around a new IWW local, the National Industrial Union of Forest and Lumber Workers, these strikes brought out hundreds of workers in western Washington. Scores of strikers were arrested and a handful seriously injured in clashes with police and company men. Amid all this trouble, company men tried to drive several hundred Greek and Finnish mill workers from Raymond and another 150 from Hoquiam, and they would have succeeded had not the sheriff and sympathetic railroad workers come to the workers' aid. This strike was followed soon by another, composed of lumber workers in western Washington, and according to the union, it brought 5,000 men off the job and closed forty-six camps.[79]

As had become common with IWW strikes, the protests led to some improvements in wages and accommodations but left the union with few lasting gains in membership. In line with its nationwide decline, by 1913 the IWW was nearly defunct in the region's camps and mills. Membership in the National Industrial Union of Forest and Lumber Workers had fallen to fewer than seven hundred, and the Seattle local, which had been a cornerstone, had maybe fifty members. That year, with the entire union struggling to survive, the IWW's Spokane-based *Industrial Worker,* which was one of its two main newspapers and one heavily oriented toward efforts in lumber, suspended publication. And that year and throughout the following, IWW activism in the region mainly consisted of organizing marches of people thrown out of work by the recession, inciting small strikes here and there, and protecting its members and property from occasional attack.[80]

These developments followed on the heels of the union's failure to establish itself two thousand miles away, in southwest Louisiana and southeast Texas. There, the Brotherhood of Timber Workers (BTW)—founded in Louisiana in the last weeks of 1910 by two lumberjacks with socialist leanings, Arthur Lee Emerson and Jay Smith, and an enterprising IWW intellectual named Covington Hall—had made impressive organizing gains among both black and white workers. But it also provoked a "war" with lumber companies that extended through 1911 and into 1912 and left the union battered by blacklistings, layoffs, yellow-dog contracts, and extended lockouts. Anxious for support, the BTW proposed to affiliate with the IWW. Haywood himself attended the BTW's second annual convention in May 1912 at the opera house in Alexandria, Louisiana, in order to consummate this relationship. When he found the proceedings segregated, Big Bill insisted that the workers defy Jim Crow law and custom. "You cannot possibly do business this way," he told them, and if meeting as equals was against the law, "the law should be broken." So it was, as the workers convened together and elected an integrated slate of delegates.[81]

Following the convention, the BTW presented the lumber companies with a list of demands. "Aghast," the companies imposed another series of lockouts and began importing strikebreakers. The union responded by organizing mass rallies. It was in the course of such an event that, on the evening of July 7, 1912, one hundred strikers and their families assembled near a crossroads called Grabow, Louisiana, not far from the union's stronghold of DeRidder. Arthur Lee Emerson was delivering a speech from the back of a wagon when company guards sprang an ambush. Ten minutes of gunfire killed two union men, a bystander, and a company guard, and forty people, among them women and children, were injured.[82]

Hundreds of angry farmers and lumber workers gathered that evening bent on revenge but were convinced by Emerson and other union men to "let the law take its course." And it soon did: sixty-five union men, including Emerson and a conspicuous number of black workers, were charged with murder, and nine were brought to trial that fall in Lake Charles before a jury purged of pro-union men. But despite this, the ardent efforts of a trust-busting, Progressive congressman named Arsène Pujo, who served as a lawyer for a lumber company and organized the prosecution, and the investigations of a hundred Burns Agency detectives, the defendants were acquitted. After hearing from the prosecution's star witness that the company gunmen had been liquored up for a planned attack, the jury needed only "a few minutes." No company men were ever prosecuted, never mind the local coroner's conclusion that hirelings of the Galloway Lumber Company were to blame. But the long stay in the Calcasieu Parish jail left the Wobbly defendants demoralized, and in the case of Emerson, too sick and tired to resume effective leadership. According to the union newspaper, *Solidarity*, these events demonstrated the "Iron Heel on Dixie."[83]

Continued repression helped prevent the BTW making any further inroads. A lockout at a large mill in Merryville, Louisiana, in November 1912 led to a strike of about 1,300 workers that was suppressed by mass arrests and violence. By February company guards and vigilantes had imposed a "reign of terror" in the town, one that led to an exodus of several hundred union people from the region.[84] There were a few other strikes, all small and unsuccessful. But the struggle ended the following

summer in defeat for the union, which faded away. According to
E. F. Doree and Jack London's old acquaintance, George Speed, the
"iron heel" had accomplished its purpose.[85]

The union's fortunes in lumber were poised to change, though, if not
in the South then in the Northwest and the Great Lakes region, partly
because of the advent of the job delegate system. The system was actually pioneered in lumber camps around Marshfield, Oregon, in 1911.
But only after it was successfully deployed in agriculture did it have a
significant effect in lumber. In 1915, the IWW's national income was less
than $10,000, and the cash balance at the Chicago headquarters fell to
only $22.44; a year later, with fifteen cents of every AWO member's
fifty-cent monthly dues going straight to the IWW's central treasury, the
union's income was about $50,000 and its cash balance nearly $19,000.[86]

So great was the AWO's success, and so overwhelming its support,
that IWW officials, including Haywood, worried that the AWO might
eclipse the national union or even secede from it.[87] Soon after it was created, the agricultural union began to enlist workers from outside of agriculture, especially lumberjacks. By the fall of 1916, several thousand
lumber workers had joined the AWO and were recruiting more workers
and making demands in lumber camps across the Northwest and northern Minnesota. But rather than expanding its jurisdiction or forsaking its
parent union, the AWO became the basis for the IWW's expansion. It
first financed the revival of *Industrial Worker* and then, at its annual
meeting in Minneapolis in the fall of 1916, urged the lumber workers in
its ranks to form their own affiliate. The IWW itself endorsed this initia-
tive at its convention a few weeks later. This led to a convention in
Spokane in the first week of March 1917. A majority of the seventeen
delegates were from the AWO. When they concluded their business, they
had formed the Lumber Workers Industrial Union No. 500 (LWIU).[88]

. . .

The LWIU was one of dozens of new unions chartered by the IWW in
1916 and early 1917 and one of several with a nationwide jurisdiction.
At its founding, the LWIU already had as many as 6,000 members, was
rapidly growing, and would soon take its place next to the agricultural
union as the most important local in the IWW. As with the AWO, growth
built upon itself, as organizers delivered better pay and working conditions in the camps and mills and, in more than a few cases, backed by
larger numbers, were able to coerce reluctant workers to enlist. One
Wobbly recalled that, in dealing with young and eager organizers, espe-

cially, "at times it would not do to persist in refusing to take out a card."[89] But the LWIU's surging membership just as quickly inspired efforts to check the organization, not least in Idaho, where "the better class of citizens of the northern part of this state" decided that "some kind of legislation" was required with which to "protect the business people of the State from the malicious and destructive activities of the I.W.W.s."[90]

These men appointed one of their number, lumberman and former sheriff Charles Leaf from Benewah County in the heavily forested panhandle, to convey to the legislature a bill they had composed. The draft gained a hearing but was met with skepticism by the state's senate judiciary committee, whose staff considered it overly broad and ambiguous and yet also "inadequate to accomplish the avowed purpose." So Leaf and his colleagues turned for help to Boise lawyer Benjamin Walker Oppenheim.[91]

Oppenheim's clients and the people behind them were typical of those who would spearhead legislative efforts to destroy the union. For them, the Wobblies were criminals in both their methods and their aims. What was needed, above all, was a statute that could be used to "shut up" these "agitators" and keep them "off the job."[92] This was not such a simple task, however. A bill that directly punished Wobblies for destructive and violent behavior would be both superfluous, as such things were already crimes, and ineffectual, as few Wobblies actually engaged in such conduct. Even a law that directly criminalized sabotage would fall short, as this was never a widespread or everyday practice and would be difficult to prove in any case. Nor would it do to criminalize common union activities like striking, because doing so would generate unwanted resistance from conventional unions and their supporters, if not also the courts. It would also not suffice to blatantly declare the IWW a criminal organization or criminalize belonging to the union, as judges and legislators might well consider this unconstitutional.

Oppenheim's solution was clever, if not ingenious. The statute he wrote made it a crime, criminal syndicalism, to promote, in the fashion that jurors and others could be relied on to presume the IWW to do, social change by means violence, terrorism, and, notably, sabotage.[93] More specifically, his bill made it a felony, punishable by up to ten years in prison and a fine of up to $5,000, to advocate or organize for, become a member of, or assemble with any organization that advocated criminal syndicalism.[94] The bill also made it a misdemeanor for an "owner, agent, superintendent, janitor, caretaker, or occupant of any place, building or room" to knowingly allow the premises to be used for the purposes of promoting criminal syndicalism, if the defendant had notice that the place were being "so used."[95]

The bill was introduced by a Republican senator from northern Idaho, a Scotsman named W. S. Walker. Seventy-one years old, Walker had been a cavalryman during the Civil War, a minister, the factor of a post office, and a merchandiser, and he had founded a military school for boys. Now retired, still possessed of his Scottish accent, and prone to wearing some sort of elaborate military uniform on the floor of the legislature, Walker was usually more spectacle than statesman. But his moment had arrived. He knew Charles Leaf and shared his views about the IWW, made good use of his ministerial background and militaristic pose to parry criticisms, and was able to move the bill through the legislature quite effectively.[96]

The bill passed in the state house by a vote of 60–0 and in the senate, where Walker promoted it with a "vehement anti-I.W.W. speech," by a vote of 32–3. "Debate" consisted of a great number of vituperative anti-IWW speeches accompanied by the distribution of printed copies of IWW literature. Those historian Eldridge Dowell wryly calls the "friends of labor" in the legislature offered but "slight resistance" to the manner in which the legislation was rushed through. Having earlier killed a slate of anti-IWW bills that threatened their constituents by targeting things like picketing and quitting work, these pro-labor legislators had also worked successfully to pass several statutes on mine safety. But they voted for the criminal syndicalism bill.[97] On March 14, 1917, almost a month after it had been introduced and about a week after the formation of the LWIU, the statute was signed into law by Governor John Haines.[98]

. . .

Another new affiliate created by the IWW during this period was the Metal Mine Workers Industrial Union No. 490, founded in February 1916 and assigned the job of organizing miners in the Midwest and Montana. Its creation positioned the IWW to assume leadership of an important strike by iron-ore miners in the Mesabi Range of northern Minnesota. Production there was dominated by Oliver Mining Company, a subsidiary of the world's largest corporation, U.S. Steel. The strike began at the instigation of an Oliver worker named Joe Greeni, angry about inadequate pay under a piece-rate system that was capriciously and corruptly administered. On June 3, Greeni brought forty men out on strike at a mine in Aurora. By the end of the month, the majority of the range's workforce of 16,000 had joined the walkout, along with thousands of others in the surrounding ranges. Production of iron ore was crippled.[99]

Mining was marked everywhere by inadequate pay as well as perpetually dangerous working conditions, poor accommodations, and, if not piece-rate and subcontracting schemes, then an entrenched culture of bullying by foremen and superintendents. But the Mesabi's mines, situated in this isolated, nearly subarctic region and operated for the benefit of steel companies that were as aggressive about controlling costs as they were about promoting the open shop, stood out in this regard. The mines were the scene of low-level conflict going back to the 1880s but not much effective union representation. In 1907, the Western Federation of Miners had managed to lead a strike involving as many as 15,000 of the region's miners. After two months it was broken, done in by hundreds of arrests and the importation of thousands of strikebreakers. Attempts in 1913 by organizers like Frank Little and E. F. Doree to establish the IWW in the region produced few new members, although they did give the union something of a toehold in the region.[100]

When the 1916 strike began, Wobbly organizers and stalwarts among the miners quickly asserted effective leadership of the strike and enlisted perhaps 4,000 members. But the strike was soon awash in violence that claimed the lives of three people and was, inevitably, blamed on the IWW. One of the dead was miner John Alar. Shot down June 22 in front of his home when mine guards fired on a miners' parade in the town of Virginia, Alar was buried at a funeral at which organizer Carlo Tresca asked mourners to swear that "if any Oliver gunmen shoot or wound any miner, we will take a tooth for a tooth, an eye for an eye or a life for a life." The two other dead were a delivery driver and a deputized mine guard, James Myron, who were killed when a group of guards forced their way into the home of striker Philip Masonovitch in Biwabik in the early hours of July 3, on the pretext of arresting him for bootlegging. It is not clear exactly how the men died, although they were likely felled by shots fired by company men during the melee.[101]

These incidents were partly the fault of Governor Joseph Burnquist, who had licensed the deputizing of hundreds of mine guards. Oliver and other mining companies also instigated the violence by deploying hundreds of well-armed guards and deputies and cooperating with police and local officials to ban union gatherings and arrest scores of strikers, including much of the strike's leadership. Most of those arrested faced minor charges. But several organizers, including Tresca, were indicted for criminal libel, because a large sign at Alar's funeral read, "Murdered

FIGURE 10. Funeral procession for slain IWW striker John Alar in Virginia, Minnesota, June 26, 1916. Walter P. Reuther Library, Archives of Labor and Urban Affairs, Wayne State University.

by Oliver Gunmen." And eight people were indicted on the governor's orders for supposedly murdering Myron. In this latter group were all the miners present at Masonovitch's house, as well as several union leaders, including again Tresca, who were nowhere near that place but were alleged to have incited the killing.[102]

As soon as these men had been arrested, the local newspapers were reporting that strikers were going back to work, and by mid-September, the strike had definitely been broken, a casualty of repression, company intransigence, and the departure of many workers for the harvest fields and lumber camps.[103] As Socialist journalist Leslie Marcy put it, the strike showed that London's *Iron Heel* was a "cold blooded fact."[104] The murder case was resolved in December by a deal that had three local strike leaders, all miners, plead guilty to manslaughter while the other, better connected defendants were freed. In the latter group, with Tresca, was Joseph Schmidt, the man we saw earlier who had been granted bail so that he might bury his son and visit his dying wife. The arrangement followed unsuccessful efforts to enlist as defense attorney Frank Walsh, the left-leaning Progressive who chaired the Commission on Industrial Relations. And it may well have been supported by the IWW's top leadership. However, Haywood soon condemned the deal and blamed it on the poor judgment of Joe Ettor and Elizabeth Gurley Flynn, who had been sent to manage the strike and had helped arrange the deal. Later, claiming a specialty in labor defense work, Flynn regretted the agreement and wondered if her romantic relationship with Tresca, with whom she had faced riot charges after the Paterson strike, had compromised her judgment. But she also blamed Haywood, contending that the whole thing was rooted in inadequate funds from the Chicago office.[105]

This episode led Tresca and Ettor to quit the IWW, and by the summer of 1917, Flynn was also gone, for all intents and purposes. Whoever was to blame, the mess hardly inured to the union's credit. But local leaders in Minnesota channeled the frustrations of the rank and file into another strike in the state's lumber camps and mills. Just after Christmas, they led a walkout of a thousand workers at a mill in Virginia, said to be the largest in the world, where low wages and eighty-four-hour workweeks were typical. Support for the strike was sporadic, as it extended into 1917, but it soon entailed another large mill in International Falls, as well as perhaps two thousand men in the lumber camps. Like the miners' strike, this walkout was checked by well-organized repression: thousands of deputies and vigilantes arrested several hundred Wobblies on vagrancy and other charges, banished all strikers from Virginia, and drove many others out of the state.[106]

The IWW called off the lumber strike on February 1, pointing to improvements in working conditions and higher wages as vindication. But if the lumbermen were willing to make modest concessions, they were not inclined to accede to this surge in IWW-led protest. Before the lumber strike ended, a delegation met with Governor Burnquist and pleaded for more help in suppressing the union. They also enlisted the support of state legislators and mining interests, as well as the state labor federation, which, despite occasional gestures of solidarity with the IWW, apparently saw an opportunity to advance its own position at the Wobblies' expense. This coalition demanded that, along with the militia, more police and deputies be dispatched to areas of unrest. It also promoted a legislative response to "permanently settle" the IWW problem.[107]

These efforts began to bear fruit in January 1917, when the state legislature convened hearings in which testimony was taken from a great number of police and lumber and mining capitalists and their various operatives, who attested to the supposedly excellent working conditions in the camps and mills and told lurid, and no doubt exaggerated, tales of IWW-sponsored mayhem and sabotage. AFL officials likewise condemned the IWW and presented the situation as proof of why the state's lumbermen and mine owners should work with their unions. But legislators also heard from a lawyer and some farmers who were sympathetic to the IWW and even from some Wobblies.

Among the IWW "agitators" and "propagandists" to appear was Joe Ettor, in his last days of service to the union. Smiling Joe, as he was known in the union, demanded that he be allowed to examine witnesses, which was granted on the condition that company lawyers could also do so. The proceedings that followed descended into outbursts of shouting and disorder, which were inevitably cast as further proof of the IWW's unfitness to operate in the state. Nevertheless, the main thing the hearings demonstrated was what Eldridge Dowell calls "a singular absence of violence on the part of the I.W.W" during the trouble of the preceding months. They also went a long way toward confirming the horrible working conditions that actually prevailed in the mines, mills, and camps and fueled the unrest, as well as the extent to which the lumbermen and their allies had resorted to violence and corrupted public authority.[108]

The legislature's report on the hearings condemned many of these conditions without calling for any stern action against the union. But in the spirit of Progressivism, it broadly endorsed the expansion of public authority over labor disputes and in this way gave credence to the idea that some kind of anti-IWW legislation should yet be enacted. Sure enough, in March, Leonard Nord, a senator and real-estate man from International Falls, introduced a criminal syndicalism bill that was very similar to the bill enacted in Idaho. Nord's colleagues of both major parties embraced its "exceedingly drastic" provisions as exactly what was needed, and the bill passed with only a single negative vote in each chamber, both cast by Socialists, and was signed into law by Burnquist on April 16.[109]

. . .

The push to criminalize the IWW extended into Washington State, where it drew impetus from the union's progress in lumber as well as fallout from the events at Everett. On February 16, 1917, a bill almost identical to the one enacted in Idaho was introduced in the state legislature. Debate on the senate floor included a frank description of the legislation as a way to put the IWW "out of business" and a means of sending "cattle" to the penitentiary and stopping IWWs from getting away with short jail terms for vagrancy. The proceedings in the senate also featured a listing of the IWW's many alleged crimes and a reading, as well, of the IWW song "Christians at War." A standard of the *Little Red Songbook,* the song was a biting parody of the hymn "Onward Christian Soldiers," and its opening verses, "Onward Christian soldiers! Duty's way is plain / Slay your Christian brothers, or by them be slain," sent the senators "into a frenzy." In the house, a legislator held aloft a bottle of phosphorous, said to have been taken from an IWW saboteur, while others shouted down a colleague who tried to explain that "Christians at War" was actually an attack on militarism and not a call to murder Christians.[110]

The bill passed in the senate by a vote of 32–5 and then cleared the house, 83–12.[111] Besides being a near copy of the Idaho bill, the statute was positioned to become the first criminal syndicalism law enacted anywhere, as the final vote occurred on March 6, over a week before Idaho's law was enacted. This happened to be the day after Wobbly Thomas Tracy went to trial in Seattle on murder charges for killing deputy sheriff Jefferson Beard during the clash in Everett. Tracy was to be the first of seventy-four defendants to be tried, the theory of the case being not only that he and his fellow defendants were party to an elaborate IWW conspiracy featuring arson, sabotage, and other acts of wanton destruction, and that the fracas at the waterfront was the inevitable product of this, but also that he was among a number of Wobblies who maliciously fired at the deputies.[112]

Prosecutors mustered a great number of witnesses to support these claims, but they lost the case. Heading Tracy's defense was George Vanderveer, who had served two terms as prosecuting attorney for King County, Washington. Vanderveer successfully petitioned to have Tracy's case moved to Seattle, where there was less animosity toward the IWW. During cross examination, he and his colleagues discredited many of the prosecution's witnesses. To contradict the state's case, they also put on the stand a number of townspeople, including some women who had been roughed-up while trying to stop the shooting, as well as men who were aboard the *Verona,* among them a few who had been shot. By these means the defense made clear who the real victims were that day. On May 5, 1917, the jury acquitted Tracy and prosecutors dropped charges against the other defendants.[113]

Two weeks into Tracy's trial, Governor Ernest Lister vetoed the criminal syndicalism bill. This was the first and last time this kind of legislation was effectively vetoed. According to the Socialist publication

Northwest Worker, it occurred because of the "rebuke" Lister, a banker and owner of a wood manufacturing business, received from "the people" for his support of an antipicketing bill the previous year.[114] He was loathe to offend them again, the newspaper concluded. In fact, Lister was no friend of the IWW. He believed the union's doctrine to be "false," would soon propose the formation of a statewide system of vigilantes called the "Patriotic League" to take on the IWW, and would generally support the wartime repression of Wobblies in the state.[115] Nevertheless, Lister, a strong Progressive, also thought the legislation represented the wrong way of dealing with the union.

. . .

Early in the Great War, Lister's fellow Progressive, former professor Woodrow Wilson, professed a commitment to neutrality. This helped him gain the support of left-leaning Progressives and unionists, many of them pacifists, and was important to his reelection victory in the fall of 1916. But already by then his stance had begun to shift, and by early 1917, amid an escalation of German attacks on American shipping and fallout from the disclosure of German entreaties to Mexico, which was still wracked by revolutionary turmoil, the president was promoting America's entry into the war as a way to secure the peace and realize Progressive ideals. War would mean the advancement of democracy, at least as he imagined it, and more government regulation of economic production and labor relations of the sort central to his agenda.[116]

In line with this position on the war, the president's Justice Department began in late 1916 to move toward criminalizing espionage and sabotage as well as speech or political associations that undermined the government's security interests. The main fruit of this effort was a bill drafted in early 1917, primarily by legal scholar Charles Warren. A moderate Progressive and Harvard man, Warren was an assistant to Attorney General Thomas Gregory. The bill he produced dealt with everything from the issuance of passports to export controls and the proper conduct of diplomacy. But it made deep inroads on freedom of speech and association, even after a Republican-led majority in the House stripped away a provision that allowed the president to criminalize the publication of such information as he might declare useful to the enemy.

The bill criminalized espionage and interference with military and defense operations that already could have been prosecuted as treason or various sorts of conspiracy or other inchoate crimes. But it also authorized postmasters to bar objectionable materials from the mail. And it empowered the government to criminalize nearly any kind of political activism or dissent, provided that such action was deemed inimical to the war effort. The key provisions in this regard were sections three and four of Title I: section three made it a felony for anyone to "willfully make or convey false reports" with intent to interfere with the military; to "willfully cause or attempt to cause insubordination, disloyalty, mutiny, [or] refusal of duty" in the military; or to "willfully obstruct the recruiting or enlistment service of the United States"; while section four made it a felony to conspire to violate section three.[117]

The legislative history of these provisions is not especially well marked by the manipulations of business interests. But such interests did not have to be blatant, not when, from the outset, there was little doubt in Congress that Title I was rightly aimed at radicals, particularly the IWW and elements of the Socialist Party. Some in Congress viewed these provisions as affronts to the country's founding principles of tolerance or federalism and therefore opposed the bill. But Title I generated relatively little debate beyond partisan concerns about how much or little the legislation would augment the president's power. Overtaken by America's formal entry into the war, the legislation moved inexorably toward enactment. The House passed its bill by a vote of 259–107, and the Senate approved its version 77–6. The bills were reconciled via a conference report, and the Espionage Act was signed into law by Wilson on June 15, 1917.[118]

While the statute was moving through Congress, Wilson created the Committee on Public Information for the purpose of propagandizing the war. At the head of this infamous entity was George Washington Creel, a man who embodied the contradictions of Progressivism as strikingly as anyone. As both a journalist and sometime government administrator, Creel had spent nearly two decades supporting a wide range of social reforms, from women's suffrage, to police reform, to public ownership of utilities, to changes in labor law. But the war and the rise of the IWW brought out another side of his Progressivism. The very day Wilson signed the Espionage Act, Creel's committee issued a statement which anticipated that there would be "numerous prosecutions" under this "most important" new law. Creel himself endorsed the idea that the law be used, albeit in a suitably measured way, to punish the Wobblies for what he and many others in the federal government had come to regard as an intolerable combination of seditiousness and radicalism.[119] Wilson himself felt for a time that the states should continue to take the lead in criminal prosecutions involving the IWW. But it did not take long for the man who believed that world war was the surest path to world peace to fully embrace wartime repression as an appropriate means of securing a vision of freedom that also happened to protect the business people.[120]

CHAPTER 3

In the War of Capital against Labor Someone Must Suffer

The War and the IWW

On July 18, 1917, Frank Little hobbled into Butte, Montana, on crutches because of an injury sustained in a recent automobile accident and in terrible pain from a hernia brought on by a beating he had sustained a few months earlier in Texas. He had gone to Butte, described by writer Dashiell Hammett as "an ugly city of forty thousand people, in an ugly notch between two ugly mountains that had been all dirtied up by mining," to organize copper miners who were striking the Anaconda Copper Mining Company, which controlled twenty mines around the city.[1] The strike was a protest against the open shop and a hiring system called the "rustling card" that was employed to blacklist union men. But it was also a struggle against unsafe working conditions.[2]

On June 8, bad luck and company negligence and greed had produced a horrific underground conflagration known as the Granite-Speculator Mine Disaster, which claimed the lives of 167 men. The disaster underscored the dangers of this kind of work. From 1910 to 1913, 162 men were killed in Butte's mines, caught in explosions or cave-ins, crushed by machinery, or burned in fires. During this same period nearly 6,000 lost time because of injuries. As many as 150 Butte miners also died annually of silicosis and other respiratory disorders attributable to the dust and fumes in the mines.[3]

There were plenty hazards above ground in Butte as well. For several years before the mine disaster, labor relations had been defined by great confusion and intrigue, punctuated by factional conflict and violence.

The worst trouble had occurred in the summer of 1914, when dissension within Butte Miners Union No. 1, the first chartered local of the Western Federation of Miners (WFM), exploded in a series of riots, shootouts, and bombings that demolished the union hall and left at least one person dead. WFM president Charles Moyer—Big Bill Haywood's codefendant in the Frank Steunenberg murder case but now, with their unions at odds, his bitter enemy—had to flee the city ahead of an armed mob of angry miners. After more bombings and disorder, the National Guard was called in to put down the unrest.[4]

The dissidents formed an independent organization called the Butte Mine Workers Union and enrolled over 5,000 members. The union enlisted a few hundred Wobblies, at most, but never affiliated with the IWW. Nevertheless, in the eyes of WFM loyalists as well as officials with Anaconda, the trouble in 1914 was the product of Wobbly machinations. This was not true, and in any case the Butte Mine Workers Union faded. But conflict persisted and by the summer of 1917, another rebellion was afoot. On June 13, five days after the mine disaster and two days after workers walked out in protest, militant miners formed a new union, the Butte Metal Mine Workers Union. Although also nominally independent, it was much influenced by IWW members, and it bitterly opposed the International Union of Mine, Mill and Smelter Workers, which is what the WFM began calling itself in 1916.[5]

The day after his arrival in town, Little delivered a speech to workers gathered at a ballpark in which he wrapped his condemnation of the company and the WFM in an angry tirade against the war. Little recounted what he said he had told Arizona governor Thomas Campbell a few weeks earlier: "I don't give a damn what country your country is fighting, I'm fighting for the solidarity of labor."[6] This was an exceedingly bold thing to utter in a city that teemed with company spies and hardened gunmen who were primed to rationalize their trade as a patriotic calling. But Little personified the cult of "physical daring" that had come to define what it meant to be an IWW and was undeterred.[7] According to Ralph Chaplin, when Little left for Butte he brushed off Chaplin's concerns for his safety. "Don't worry, fellow worker, all we are going to need from now on is guts."[8]

Probably thirty-nine years old, slight of build, and, like Big Bill Haywood, blind in one eye from a childhood accident, Franklin Henry Little had been a miner and WFM member and joined the IWW just after it was founded. On the rebellious wing of a militant union, Little was a persistent advocate of sabotage. He had been on the general executive board for several years, had organized nearly everywhere the union was active, and had been jailed and assaulted many times. Four years earlier in Duluth, Minnesota, Little had even been kidnapped at gunpoint and in broad daylight, and he had to be rescued from a secluded location some thirty-five miles away by armed workers. Now, in Butte, he was abducted again, this time with ghastly results. At three o'clock on the morning of August 1, seven masked men drove up to Nora Byrne's boardinghouse in a black Cadillac and pulled Little from his bed. They beat Little, dragged him behind the car, and hanged him, dead, from a railroad trestle.[9]

Dashiell Hammett worked for the Pinkerton Agency and was sent to Butte, he said, and offered $5,000 to kill Little on Anaconda's behalf. This is how Hammett came to know the place, crafting from the nasty truths he observed a setting that makes his book *Red Harvest* an apt contribution to the list of great American novels. But Hammett refused to wet his hands with Little's blood, abandoned the Pinkertons, and steered a leftward course that would lead to his imprisonment decades later for failing to cooperate in the federal persecution of Communists. This makes Hammett's tale all the more poignant, though of scant help in determining who actually committed the murder. In fact, evidence points to Little's death at the hands not of the Pinkertons but rather of certain operatives of Anaconda who were never seriously investigated.[10] According to Henry Myers, one of Montana's U.S. senators, it was Little who should have faced prosecution. "Had he been arrested and put in jail for his seditious and incendiary talks, he would not have been lynched," said the senator.[11]

. . .

The men who killed Little left a coded message on his body that was thought by some to foretell their next six victims. One of the marked men was William Dunne, a local activist on friendly terms with the IWW who believed that when Little was killed half the IWWs in Butte were company agents and that these men had lured Little to Butte in the first place. Dunne's estimate of informants and plants was no doubt an exaggeration, but by this time, everywhere the IWW was active it was infiltrated by government agents, company operatives, and private detectives. Even Little was thought by some, almost certainly without foundation, to have been corrupted. While the number of spies operating in Butte, or anywhere else, is impossible to calculate, U.S. Department of Justice records make clear that the practice was widespread. What is also clear is that Little's assassination paid dividends beyond eliminating an important IWW leader, as it gave impetus to the occupation of Butte by federal troops and National Guardsmen, who, in the name of maintaining copper production for the war, used heavy-handed tactics to curtail union activities and gradually buried the strike. Little was buried on August 5—in town, on his "battle ground," as Big Bill Haywood decreed. His funeral procession was said to be the largest in the city's history and his burial was watched over by more than five hundred police and guardsmen.[12]

Little's death clearly affected Haywood. But he could not have been overly surprised by the event. Long before America declared war on Germany on April 6, 1917, the IWW denounced the conflict as a senseless sacrifice of workers' lives in pursuit of imperialist interests and pledged to oppose a draft, should there be one. At its tenth annual convention in November 1916, the IWW resolved that members should agitate against the war during peacetime and launch a general strike if the United States entered the conflict. However, once the country was at war, Haywood led a faction of the leadership, backed by top figures in the Agricultural Workers Industrial Union No. 110 (AWIU)—the new name of the Agricultural Workers Organization (AWO) as of March 1917—that moved to rein in the IWW's condemnation of the war and moderate its stance on the draft. Opposing this faction was a group headed by Little and Chaplin and supported by many within the Lumber Workers Industrial Union (LWIU). Despite a great deal of debate, the two sides were unable to reach any clear resolution and left members to decide for themselves whether to dodge the draft or openly oppose the war.[13]

Many Wobblies censored their positions on the war, and it is likely that over 90 percent of eligible union members registered for the draft. Among them was Chaplin himself, who soon struck a more equivocal position, proposing that members register for conscription but also claim, as he did, exemption as conscientious objectors. However, more than a few Wobblies, including a great number of the union's Irish and Finnish members, continued to defy the draft and denounce the war.[14] Among them was Little, of course, whose partial blindness, like Haywood's, guaranteed he would never be conscripted anyway, and who, like Haywood, would also have been too old for conscription until eligibility was extended in September 1918.

It was not only opposition to the draft or the war that marked the union for increasing repression. So did sabotage. As they became alert to the danger that inhered in the IWW's association with sabotage, leaders like Haywood and Chaplin had come to reject the celebration of the practice and even suspended Walker Smith, author of the incendiary pamphlet that Jack London endorsed, from his job as editor of the union's newspaper, *Industrial Worker*. When the political situation surrounding America's entry into war made its evocation especially risky, the general executive board completely repudiated the concept of sabotage, effectively banned its mention in the union's documents, and ordered all copies of Smith's pamphlet destroyed.[15] By this time, most of the rank and file had also become just as careful with the word and concept. When federal agents interrogated fifty-nine Wobblies arrested in November 1917 and asked them to explain the meaning of sabotage, nearly all defined it in terms of slowing down on the job. "As I understand it, bum work for bum food or bum pay," is how one put it.[16]

These precautions and disclaimers did not necessarily diminish the prevalence of destructive sabotage, infrequent though it already was, let alone prevent overblown accusations of sabotage from justifying the IWW's persecution.[17] Nor did the union's distancing of itself from the term have much effect politically, as sabotage came to underlay a broader campaign to denounce the union as seditious and altogether dangerous. Pleading the need to maintain industrial production in wartime and casting their interests and values as indivisible from those of state and society, powerful capitalists and their allies among western politicians deluged the federal government with demands to rein in the union. Their efforts hinged on claims that the IWW was an agent of Imperial Germany, its surge in membership and influence financed by "German gold" in exchange for the union's help in undermining America's military readiness by means of sabotage, strikes, and other intrigues. The newspapers had been trading in rumors of IWW ties to Germany since 1915. But this particular charge was propagated in the summer of 1917 by the U.S. attorney for Oregon, Clarence Reames, and by western congressmen and business interests. It was subscribed to for a time by U.S. Attorney General Thomas Gregory and faithfully and uncritically recounted by newspapermen all over the country.[18]

The charge concerning German gold drew credence from Germany's contrivances to aid Vladimir Lenin's return to Russia so that he might hasten that country's move toward revolution and out of the war. It was consistent with concerns, already widespread and soon manifested in Germany itself, about the ability of radicals to organize or inspire crippling mutinies and sabotage among soldiers, sailors, and industrial workers. It also cohered with the fact that by 1917 German agents, by means of industrial sabotage, terrorism, and biological warfare, had been attempting to undermine American military preparation for two years or more.[19] And of course there was the IWW's strong association with sabotage and criminality, exaggerated though it may have been. In this light, the idea that Germany had conspired with the IWW was not completely implausible. But neither was it true.

At Haywood's invitation, federal agents inspected the IWW's files, and they found no connections to Germany. Still, the charge would not go away. Part of its appeal was that it seemed to explain why such a radical union, composed of men widely dismissed as pathetic and weak, could nonetheless be surging as strongly as the IWW was in 1917. This is apparently why Gregory first credited the story, for instance. But what those who believed this business about German gold refused to see was that the union's increasing activism was not a product of outside financing. Rather it was this increased activism that constituted the true reason for the improvement in the union's finances and overall standing, and in turn the justification for its destruction.

By the time the United States declared war on Germany, better organizing and increased demand for grain, lumber, ore, oil, construction, and shipping, along with a tightening labor market and skyrocketing costs of living, had pushed enrollment in the IWW to perhaps 150,000, and maybe more.[20] Not all the recruits were equally committed to the union's program, as the IWW was always built around a core of members who handled most of the union's business and endured an inordinate share of the repression.[21] But owing in part to its focus on transient workers, there were also, in effect, many more Wobblies than there were people paid up in their dues. By 1917, the IWW had issued several hundred thousand cards to workers whose memberships might have lapsed but who likely remained loyal, and by some estimates only about one-third of those who considered themselves active Wobblies tended to be current on dues at any given time.[22] Moreover, the IWW had the support and allegiance of many who had not yet joined but were poised to do so. Although certainly not universally popular even among industrial workers, the union had already proved this in places like Lawrence, Paterson, and the Mesabi.

By every measure, by the late spring of 1917 the IWW was finally becoming something like the organization its founders had envisaged. And this is what made the union such a worrying specter for powerful people. A broad coalition of Progressives and conservatives in business, government, and the newspapers had already shown considerable ability to mobilize effective opposition to the organization and to bend the truth to that purpose. Now they found themselves at a point in history at which the lines between reckless misapprehension and intentional misrepresentation of the IWW, along with those between lawful and unlawful forms of repression, were never more easily washed away.

. . .

What this meant for the IWW was clearly revealed by events in southern Arizona, which was Little's battleground before his fateful trip to Montana. The scene was Bisbee, a company town under the control of the Phelps Dodge Corporation and a handful of other copper concerns, where a miners' strike had been on since June 27. Part of a larger strike that grew out of the trouble in Butte, the walkout was led by the IWW and may have involved as many as 24,000 workers in Arizona and 40,000 across the West. In Arizona, the IWW's Metal Mine Workers Industrial Union No. 800, which held its first convention in Bisbee on June 15, led the strike. Effectively taking control of the moribund local of the International Union of Mine, Mill and Smelter Workers, it pressed for higher pay and safer working conditions. In Bisbee, as many as 3,000 workers joined the strike, which was enough to shut the mines, curtail production, and prompt state and local officials to demand that federal troops be dispatched.

The military sent only one man, though, a lieutenant colonel who was suspicious of IWW motives but concluded that there was no disorder and therefore no need for army intervention.[23] This left matters in the hands of Cochise County sheriff Harry Wheeler, who had ridden with Theodore Roosevelt's Rough Riders and, after a little prodding from the copper companies, stood ready to rough up the IWW and its supporters. On the evening of July 11, Wheeler convened with copper company officials and an anti-union faction called the Workman's Loyalty League. With assurances from Phelps Dodge and the other mining companies that they would cover the costs, he and his deputies formed a posse of about 2,000 loyal employees, mine company managers, businessmen and professionals, and assorted other locals. Early the next morning, the posse coursed through the town, rounding up an equal number of miners at gunpoint on vague charges of vagrancy, treason, and disturbing the peace. The real crime was being on strike, and any one who did not disclaim this was taken to the town plaza and held under the guard of riflemen and machine gunners. During these proceedings, communications by telephone or telegraph were cut, and

Wheeler was chauffeured around town by a local Roman Catholic priest, a machine gun mounted on the cleric's car. A number of captives were beaten and had their homes ransacked. The "only trouble," according to the *Bisbee Daily Review,* occurred when a contingent of possemen reached the home of Wobbly James Brew. When their leader, a shift boss, ignored Brew's warning and entered his yard, Brew shot him dead. When Brew attempted to surrender, the vigilantes shot and killed him.[24]

As the plaza filled with men, the posse began marching its captives two miles to a ballpark near the train station. When their final demand that the men return to work elicited "hoots and jeers," the posse picked out about 1,200, a majority of Eastern European or Mexican heritage, packed them into cattle cars and boxcars of the El Paso and Southwestern Railroad, which Phelps Dodge owned, and, with a crowd of women and children cheering the spectacle, sent the train two hundred miles east, out onto the desert.[25] Sixteen hours later, the men were dumped in the early morning darkness at the tiny desert hamlet of Hermanas in Luna County, New Mexico. They had minimal supplies and no baggage or money, and many were sick from dehydration and the heat. The main reason none perished is that New Mexico authorities and army units guarding the border against Mexican incursions moved quickly to provide water, food, and shelter. A good number of deportees remained camped in the area for two months or more, in the "protective custody" of the army, which did nothing to facilitate their return to Bisbee. In fact, besides some key men whom the companies needed in the mines and discreetly lured back, most never returned to Bisbee, where a "Citizens' Protective League" required for reentry a document certifying that the holder had not been on strike. The deportees' threat to return to Bisbee en masse went unfulfilled. And those who did go back without permission were arrested for vagrancy, brought before a secret court set up by Wheeler, and run out of town under threat. Needless to say, these measures broke the strike in Bisbee.

When the Bisbee deportation occurred, an extraordinary wave of vigilantism was sweeping the country, engulfing many besides the Wobblies. Hundreds of socialists, pacifists, religious objectors, people of German heritage, and random contrarians were run off their property, beaten, tarred and feathered, threatened with death, shot at, and occasionally killed after being denounced as "slackers" or traitors.[26] Wobblies, of course, had endured this kind of thing for years. But America's official entry into the war came with a surge in attacks on union people

FIGURE 11. IWW deportees being moved through a cordon of possemen and loaded onto railcars, Bisbee, Arizona, July 12, 1917. University of Arizona Libraries, Special Collections.

and property. There were destructive raids on union halls in Kansas City, Duluth, Seattle, and Chicago, and shortly before the Bisbee affair, a hundred suspected IWWs were rounded up in Jerome, Arizona, and two-thirds of them deported by train to California. In fact, so threatening was anti-IWW vigilantism in the summer of 1917 that it inspired desperate and futile pleas from Haywood for federal protection.[27]

These actions drew more approval than criticism from powerful people. A great number of government officials and newspapermen endorsed what happened in Bisbee, too. Some took a position similar to Henry Myers's view of Little's killing, arguing that, even if illegal, the deportation only occurred because better laws were not on hand for dealing harshly with radicals like these.[28] Others believed the workers had gotten what they deserved and that the deportation was lawful in a practical sense. However, such was the sheer impudence of the episode in Bisbee that not everyone who mattered approved of the proceedings, and the Wilson administration was compelled to place the affair before the President's Mediation Commission.[29]

The administration established the commission in September 1917 at the behest of Samuel Gompers and Secretary of Labor William Wilson. Its main purposes were to check labor unrest in order to benefit the war effort, protect American Federation of Labor (AFL) unionists from the spillover effects of wartime persecution, and undermine the IWW. These were encoded in guidelines written by its counsel and secretary, future U.S. Supreme Court Justice Felix Frankfurter. Although it investigated conditions in the lumber industry as well as matters in Butte, the commission first examined the Bisbee affair. After meeting with AFL officials in Phoenix, it convened in Bisbee in November, interviewed Wheeler, some of the deportees, and a slate of local officials, among other witnesses, and took statements from company officials and their lawyers. It then produced a report that concluded that the deportation "was wholly illegal and without authority in law" and closed with five recommendations, among them the pursuit of claims under state law.[30]

State law did nothing to bring about the return of these men to their homes. And although over two hundred members of the deportation mob were charged with kidnapping under state law, the prosecution was a farce, possibly devised to clear Phelps Dodge of civil suits filed by the deportees. When the case went to trial three years later most of the evidence allowed seemed to show the IWW's criminality, and the one defendant chosen for prosecution was acquitted. Meanwhile the civil suits, which named the plaintiffs, served conveniently as blacklists for other companies.[31]

The Mediation Commission did not believe that the deportation violated federal criminal law. Nevertheless, the U.S. Justice Department indicted two dozen people, including Wheeler and the president of Phelps Dodge, Walter Douglas, whom everyone knew to be responsible, charging them with conspiring to deprive the deportees of their right under the U.S. Constitution and federal law to live and travel where they pleased. But in December 1918 the indictment was quashed by the trial court. In 1920 the U.S. Supreme Court affirmed this ruling, deciding that although the U.S. Constitution and federal law did indeed protect the right of the deportees to live and travel where they pleased, the federal government could only enforce that right against states, and because the deportation was somehow, in the court's view, a private affair, the defendants therefore could not be prosecuted.[32]

. . .

The Bisbee affair was no less than "the Iron Heel at work," according to the IWW's newspaper *Solidarity*.[33] In its immediate aftermath, hundreds of IWWs followed Frank Little from Arizona to Montana, where the union's fortunes were shaped not only by America's entry into the war and all the trouble that surrounded Little's murder but also by an intense and chaotic struggle in lumber that evolved into what one scholar declared "the most spectacular and widespread lumber strike ever to occur in the United States." The "Great Lumber Strike" was planned when the LWIU was formed in March 1917. The strike had several ostensible starting dates, including one as late as July 1. But it began more or less spontaneously in April with scattered walkouts at camps in northern Idaho and adjacent parts of Montana and Washington. It gathered strength as it moved into the coastal forests of Washington and into Oregon, drawing out mill workers, miners, and others and converging with a handful of smaller, AFL-led strikes.[34]

The strike was led throughout by delegates with the LWIU, and it demanded better pay, more reasonable working hours, more humane management, and, in the camps, better food, proper beds and bath facilities, and smaller, less crowded, bunkhouses. Like every IWW strike, it was also aimed at building the union's membership and radicalizing the workers. Probably 50,000 lumber workers were idled by the strike, out of a workforce of roughly 75,000. This led to widespread shorthandedness and, according to one historian, brought wood production in the region to a "dead halt."[35]

As with the big IWW-led strikes a few years earlier in the East and the year before in Minnesota, the size of the walkout reflected the union's ability to exert influence well beyond its dues-paying membership. But unlike in those earlier strikes, the union accomplished this with a basis of support that extended from a core of several thousand deeply committed members to many thousands of others who were quite familiar with the organization, eager to answer its call, and liable to stay with it. Moreover, in important testament to what it really meant to be a Wobbly and how the union's membership should be reckoned, while most who struck were not paid-up members when the strike was called, many, perhaps a majority, had been affiliated with the IWW at some point, and many more broadly sympathized with the union.[36]

The lumber companies had no intention of negotiating with the IWW and solicited help in suppressing the strike in the name of military preparedness. In Montana, where the strike coincided with ongoing unrest among miners, their appeals were answered with a wave of vagrancy arrests. IWWs were arrested all over the western half of the state that fall, some individually or in small groups and some in raids on union gatherings and headquarters.[37] The strikers were also met with vigilantism, as by that fall there was "practically no limit to the number of patriotic organizations a person could join," as Clemens Work puts it, and many of these "committees," "leagues," and "societies," if they even bothered with a name, were little more than fronts for anti-union violence.[38]

In Red Lodge a local "Liberty Committee," composed of mining-company agents, commanded by a former sheriff, and said to have hundreds of supporters, abducted and tortured several Finnish IWWs accused of criticizing the war. In November, the committee convened a tribunal in the basement of the courthouse at which two Wobblies were hanged and whipped until blood pooled at their feet and they confessed the names of others.[39] This committee did not kill anyone, but it did get someone killed by one of its victims, a Finnish Wobbly named Emil Koski who was taken before the tribunal that fall on charges of being "disrespectful" to the government and flogged with a rope. A week later, after the sheriff declined to charge Koski, a group of committeemen paid him a nighttime visit for a "second inquiry into his seditious utterances." Koski answered them with a rifle and a shotgun. Unfortunately, the fusillade he unleased struck a neighbor, Kaisa Jackson, who died two hours later.[40]

Amid these dangerous goings on, wealthy Butte mine owner, newspaperman, and former U.S. Senator W. A. Clark declared that "the minute the military here stop detaining men for seditious acts we have got to take it into our own hands and have a mob, and we don't want to start that. I can get a mob up here in twenty-four hours and hang half a dozen men."[41] In fact, the military was on hand in large part because figures like Clark and western governors and other politicians had demanded that federal intervention against the IWW entail the use of the military. In July 1917, the National Guard was federalized for service in the war. So the Wilson administration responded by deploying the army, sending units first to Washington State and Montana, where they augmented National Guard units that had posted there since spring and remained, in some cases, until 1921.[42]

This undertaking represented an extraordinary departure from constitutional norms and federal laws enacted in the nineteenth century, which hold that federal military forces may only be used to enforce civil law and order in cases in which the legislatures of the affected states, or if the legislatures cannot be convened, their governors, certify the need for such measures; and also require that the president issue a proclamation affording the insurgents an opportunity to disperse before using force. Just before America entered the war, Secretary of War Newton Baker unilaterally, with no legal authority and with an eye toward containing the IWW, suspended these requirements. At President Wilson's behest, commanders in the field were ordered to concern themselves only with acts of sedition or serious disloyalty and with the security of installations essential to the military. In fact, army troops and guardsmen were deployed across the West, where they seized control of railroads, ports, smelters and mines, other facilities, and, on occasion, whole counties or towns; assumed broad powers of arrest; barred picketing, even by AFL unions; and, aided by the Office of Naval Intelligence, spied on civilians and threatened them with court martial.[43]

This misuse of the military was entirely in line with the hopes of those who most ardently promoted their deployment as a means of breaking the IWW. To this end soldiers in Whitefish, Montana, for instance, conducted a series of search-and-destroy operations against IWWs as well as railroad workers and common laborers. They seized union property and arrested Wobblies, including one they held without charge for nearly two months.[44] So frequent and aggressive were these practices that in August 1917, Flathead County attorney T. H. McDonald wrote to Attorney General Gregory to remind him that such heavy-handed tactics were counterproductive and to insist that local officials, armed with vagrancy laws, had a handle on whatever trouble the union was causing.[45] Around Butte, especially, the army's habit of arresting large numbers of union men garnered frequent complaints by U.S. Attorney Burton Wheeler and even the attorney general, who felt that the practice at least verged on being unlawful.[46]

These complaints seem to have had only a modest effect in reining in the federal troops. Some officers were hesitant to use their men as labor police, but many obviously had their own view of the law, backed not only by weapons and trained soldiers but also by a perspective they shared with most of the region's businessmen and politicians that the union's strikes were disloyal affairs intended to undermine the war effort. These elements also believed Wobblies to be guilty of much destructive sabotage, an accusation that the newspapers supported by blaming every conceivable calamity on the IWW. The union was said to be at the center of "an international conspiracy of mongrel aliens" who were, among other things, "hiring Mexicans to start forest fires in the mountains of Arizona; Hindus and Chinese to set fire to grain fields; Finns, Austrians, and Italians to start strikes in the Gogebic iron range in Michigan." A week after Little's death, one Montana paper even charged the union with inciting Apaches in Arizona to return to the "warpath."[47]

These stories were ridiculous. But the union was haunted by its frequent endorsements of sabotage in earlier years, by the events that followed the Wheatland affair, and by an element of genuine concern about actual acts of destruction. As in the campaign to gain the release of Blackie Ford and Herman Suhr, sabotage loomed as a way to repay the violence that these workers faced on the job and in the course of their attempts to organize and protest by more conventional means. Not only were the union's attempts to distance itself from the concept ineffective, but there undoubtedly was something of a surge in sabotage during the lumber strike.[48] Nevertheless, it seems that the practice increased far more quickly and threateningly in the imagination of the IWW's enemies than it did at the hands of dangerous Wobblies.

This was something Wade Parks, the county attorney of Sanders County in western Montana, discovered when he answered a request from Wheeler and the governor to determine what was going on in his jurisdiction. In a series of dispatches in August 1917, Parks reported that there were few disturbances either in lumber or in the area's wheat fields; that forest fires in the region were the work of ranchers recklessly burning slash piles; that union people on strike were protesting in an orderly and disciplined way; that the workers had legitimate complaints; that the Wobblies he spoke to were not much concerned with the war anyway; and that such trouble as there had been in the region was often the work of phony IWWs employed by private detective agencies.[49]

Park's findings aligned with reports from U.S. Forest Service supervisors in Montana and Idaho, which attested to the excellent assistance that IWW crews were providing in "protecting Uncle Sam's timber" from the fires that raged through the region. Firefighting was a major source of employment for Wobblies in the 1910s and 1920s, when fires consumed vast swaths of forest and men were needed on a temporary basis to deal with the problem. The work was every bit as tough and dangerous as logging, mining, or the harvest. But even at the height of the lumber strike, during which two Wobblies were killed on the job, the union specifically directed members to continue fighting the fires.[50]

. . .

Arson was the first thing on the minds of many people in Bemidji, Minnesota, on the morning of July 22, 1917, when they awakened to news that the Crookston Lumber Mill, the town's largest employer and, it was said, the second largest mill in the country, had burned down. The fire was no doubt on the mind of Chief of Police Frank Ripple when, later that day, he walked up to Jesse J. "Jess" Dunning, who was dining in a restaurant in town, and detained him on a charge of "suspicion."

With the Beltrami County attorney and a fellow officer in tow, Ripple took Dunning down the street to IWW headquarters so that he could search the place. Ripple's department had strained its budget jailing Wobblies over the preceding twelve months.[51] Now the chief, a young policeman of the new, aggressive, and professional type, had in his custody the secretary of the local branch of the LWIU.

While at the headquarters, Ripple's attention was drawn to a slender volume called *Sabotage* by the French anarcho-communist Émile Pouget. Published in 1898, Pouget's book had been translated by Arturo Giovannitti while he awaited trial in Lawrence, Massachusetts, in 1912, and it was fairly popular among Wobblies. Ripple also noticed a pamphlet titled *Sabotage: The Conscious Withdrawal of the Workers' Industrial Efficiency* by Elizabeth Gurley Flynn. Based on a speech she had given in defense of Frederick Sumner Boyd, the man convicted of inciting sabotage during the Paterson strike, Flynn's pamphlet had been an IWW staple since its publication in 1915—although by the time Dunning was arrested, Flynn, who had witnessed how effectively prosecutors had used the book at Thomas Tracy's murder trial, supported the union's effort to withdraw it from circulation.[52]

Flynn's pamphlet is a relatively moderate text whose main theme is indeed withdrawal of workers' efficiency, while Pouget's, though it defends injuries to employers' property, is more a call to ruin products than a brief for wantonly burning down sawmills.[53] But even though support for the Great Lumber Strike was not particularly strong in Minnesota, where logging operations declined in the summer, the unrest of the previous winter had not faded, and there was plenty of appetite to crush the union. A few days after Dunning was seized, "a posse of citizens" about 150 strong "cleaned house." Armed with clubs and with the mayor in the lead, they rounded up and deported two dozen Wobblies and then threatened the owners of businesses where IWWs had been welcome.[54] In this environment, close readings of radical texts counted for as little as honest reflections on the actual methods and purposes of the IWW, and Dunning was charged with criminal syndicalism.[55]

One of six Wobblies Ripple arrested on "suspicion," Dunning was the only one held for trial. The others were warned to abandon the union and leave town and then released. During his trial, Dunning denied having read either Flynn's or Pouget's pamphlet. He also denied any connection to the fire at the mill, which, as a prominent citizen from Bemidji later admitted, was almost certainly an accident. Nevertheless, on October 3, 1917, Dunning was found guilty of advocating criminal syndicalism and selling literature that advocated criminal syndicalism and sentenced to two years in prison.[56]

Dunning was not the first person convicted of violating a criminal syndicalism-like law. On June 29, three months before Dunning's conviction and eleven days after a hundred National Guardsmen sacked the union hall in Duluth, Arthur Thorne, who was the IWW's secretary in that town, was convicted of violating an ordinance that redefined vagrancy to include advocating "the duty, necessity or propriety of crime or violence as means of accomplishing industrial or political ends." The city council had recently enacted the law on the advice of Minnesota's Public Safety Commission, which had urged the state's municipalities to adopt ordinances that merged vagrancy and criminal syndicalism. In finding Thorne guilty of violating the ordinance, municipal judge W. H. Smallwood explicitly declared membership in the IWW a misdemeanor and opened the door to several more prosecutions that summer and fall. Some Wobbly defendants landed in jail for sixty days, and one was shot in Virginia in the course of a broader campaign in that part of the state to arrest IWW "slackers."[57]

. . .

Dunning was, in any case, the first person anywhere convicted of felony criminal syndicalism.[58] But he only barely attained that distinction. On October 24, Boise's *Evening Capital News* announced that "for the first time in the history of the state the state penitentiary will contain within its grim walls a man convicted on the charge of criminal syndicalism." The man in question was thirty-six-year-old J. J. McMurphy, recently convicted in Wallace. McMurphy sat silent during trial, waiting until he was being sentenced to a year at hard labor plus a $500 fine to unleash what the *Capital News* called "fevered battle cries" of the IWW. Less fevered was McMurphy's judgment about his fate: "In the war of capital against labor someone must suffer and I am one of the men picked out."[59]

McMurphy was an LWIU organizer, arrested on July 17, at the height of the Great Lumber Strike, while giving a speech in the mining town of Burke. His conviction rested partly on his possession of Flynn's pamphlet on sabotage. Meanwhile, the second man convicted of criminal syndicalism in Idaho, John Otis Ellis, was charged with advocating sabotage himself. Arrested in Clearwater County in late July 1917 after a witness claimed that the forty-year-old IWW supporter had urged workers to "cut logs short" if they did not get five dollars a day, Ellis was convicted and sentenced to one to ten years in prison by a judge who later told the state prison board that Ellis was industrious and a man of honesty and integrity.[60] But caught "agitating" and associating with "agitators for industrial reform," Ellis rightly joined McMurphy in prison just before Thanksgiving, according to the judge.[61]

These convictions were the fruits of a statewide campaign against the union that relied on a great number of government-sponsored "home guards" and vigilante organizations. Sponsored by lumber and mining interests, these groups worked in hand with the State Council of Defense, which Idaho, like every other state, had established at the urging of the National Council of Defense. The main purpose of these organizations was ostensibly to bolster wartime production and morale, and they did work toward these ends. But they also joined in the repression of IWWs and other radicals. On July 6, 1917, the Idaho Council of Defense released a report, based mainly on the testimony of people representing lumber interests, which concluded that "shrewd and cunning" IWWs in the lumber camps were distributing literature "of a decidedly treasonable, revolutionary and lawless character" in derogation of the war effort and in violation of the criminal syndicalism law.[62]

The report recommended that Governor Moses Alexander declare martial law and request that federal troops be deployed to the Coeur d'Alene area. Alexander demurred, despite a deluge of letters and telegrams from businessmen and local politicians urging the same action and despite his own strong dislike for the IWW.[63] A Progressive and a Democrat, he was worried about costs and convinced that this was neither the state government's nor the army's proper mission, and he preferred that the matter be dealt with by local authorities. Local police and prosecutors did just that, rallying home guards, local adjuncts of the Council of Defense, and various citizens' groups in a more or less coordinated operation against the IWW.[64]

On July 13, 1917, the day after J. J. McMurphy was arrested, the sheriff of Boundary County, on the Canadian border, had his men round up five hundred suspected Wobblies and "banish" them from the area. That same day, the sheriff of Benewah County, further south in the panhandle, raided the IWW hall, closed it down, confiscated all the union literature, and arrested the union secretary on criminal syndicalism charges.[65] The next day, Moscow, seat of Latah County, at the base of the panhandle, was host to a "citizens' meeting" on the IWW that occurred against a backdrop of complaints from lumber company officials and representatives of the local chamber of commerce about strike-related wood shortages.

FIGURE 12. Striking IWW lumber worker in Idaho, probably summer of 1917. Walter P. Reuther Library, Archives of Labor and Urban Affairs, Wayne State University.

There was another meeting that day in Moscow on how to deal with the union, this one involving Governor Alexander and the region's sheriffs. The solution was obvious, and it involved emulating the measures taken in Boundary and Benewah counties. According to the *Kendrick Gazette*, the sheriffs pledged "to protect every man in north Idaho who wants to work, to arrest every I.W.W. agitator or organizer, to stop every freight train entering the state or a county" and remove every person riding without authorization. The sheriffs also vowed to coordinate with their counterparts in adjacent counties of Washington,

Oregon, and Montana as well as the Idaho Council of Defense and the region's citizens' groups.[66]

Within a few days of the meeting, the sheriffs of Clearwater and Latah counties, armed with a warrant that identified one individual and "500 others whose names are unknown" and working with the Council of Defense and citizen volunteers, seized at least seventy Wobblies and "idlers," gathered them in a "bullpen" at the Latah County fairgrounds in Moscow, and held them on criminal syndicalism charges.[67] Prosecutors were not sure how to proceed, however, and did not immediately file formal charges. But they did complain to Governor Alexander about the expense of keeping these men and the lack of evidence to convict many of them of any crime, even criminal syndicalism, and then contacted the federal government about initiating deportation proceedings against the handful who were foreigners.[68] Meanwhile, IWWs continued to be arrested in batches throughout the northern part of the state.[69] In order to hold them, several more "stockades" or "bullpens" were established in Idaho and Benewah counties. Each of these soon held about fifty captives, some on criminal syndicalism charges and others for vagrancy.

. . .

Everywhere the IWW was active during the first months after America entered the war it faced considerable persecution. One of these places was Oregon, where on July 16, 1917, just after conferring with military and business leaders, Governor James Withycombe urged that all IWWs in his state be rounded up, convicted of vagrancy, and put to work on the rock pile. And he endorsed the idea of raising a battalion of war veterans to accomplish this mission.[70] The battalion never materialized. But even before the governor's announcement, which came just one day after a flour mill burned to the ground in Klamath Falls, plenty of Wobblies were being arrested. And when the governor made his announcement, police began picking up just about every Wobbly they could apprehend. Within a few days, the jail held thirty-five or forty Wobblies on vagrancy charges.[71] On July 31, twenty-one were sentenced to terms that ranged from thirty days and costs to six months and one hundred dollars.[72]

There were plenty of arrests elsewhere in Oregon. Come the end of August 1917, the jail in Portland, for instance, was also full of Wobblies "held on any old charge."[73] And a similar situation prevailed in Washington, where the strike had forced the closure of some lumber mills and created labor shortages in the wheat fields, fruit orchards, and mines. In July, Wobblies were arrested by the dozens in raids in Yakima and North Yakima and around Ellensburg by police and sheriff deputies, federal agents, Washington Council of Defense personnel, federal troops, and citizens groups, typically for vagrancy or on suspicion of interfering with agricultural production.[74] Then, on July 17, a force comprised of contingents of all these groups raided a congregation of IWWs awaiting the start of the region's wheat harvest in the railyard in Pasco, arrested thirty for vagrancy, seized their literature, and replaced the union flag, which had been raised over the yard, with a giant American one.[75] That month, over sixty union men were locked up in a rude "detention camp" on the courthouse lawn in Kittitas County; another sixty were being held incommunicado at a stockade in Chelan County; and seventy-five were in jail in Yakima County. Many of these men would not be released until fall, by which time some looked "more like skeletons than human beings," according to the IWW.[76]

As the union reeled under the weight of all these arrests and detentions and the lumber strike, despite its early promise, threatened to collapse, James Rowan decided to act. Considered by some in the federal government to be "the most dangerous man in the entire I.W.W. movement," this was the same Rowan who had defied Sheriff McRae a year earlier in Everett.[77] Now secretary of the LWIU, on August 13 Rowan telegrammed the region's governors and demanded that the great number of IWW prisoners who were in custody be released within one week. Otherwise, the union would call a general strike. The ultimatum produced immediate results, if not the ones intended. Governor Alexander in Idaho responded by revising his views on the use of federal troops and asking that they become more active in suppressing union activism in his state. With the approval of Washington governor Ernest Lister, he had the Second Idaho Infantry sent across the border to Spokane. Under the command of Major Clement Wilkins, the force descended on IWW headquarters, arrested Rowan and two dozen others, and held most of these men as military prisoners under threat of court martial.[78]

This amounted to an illegal imposition of martial law and prompted IWW lawyers to challenge the men's confinement with a writ of habeas corpus. Turning the central question before him into its own answer, a state judge promptly denied the writ by declaring he had no authority over military affairs.[79] While the union reckoned with this, the general strike foundered. Moreover, as support for the main strike in lumber diminished in the face of repression and the companies' increasing success in restarting production, the LWIU's leadership decided in September to move the strike "to the job."[80] This strategy involved slowdowns, quickie strikes, and probably some acts of sabotage. It allowed the union to maintain pressure on the lumber companies well into the following year and even beyond and helped increase wages and improve working conditions. But it also ensured that members continued into the fall to face arrest and prosecution, vigilantism, and intermittent conflict with military units.[81]

. . .

James Rowan and his fellow captives in Spokane were never court martialed. But Rowan was on a list of forty-four Wobblies wanted that summer for investigation by the U.S. Justice Department. Some, like Emil Pouget, described as an IWW leader, and Walter Raleigh, said to be a construction worker, if not a long-dead Elizabethan gentleman, were, unsurprisingly, destined never to be apprehended.[82] Others, like Butte miner Dan Sullivan, got away. Arrested in Klamath Falls, convicted of vagrancy in July, and ordered to serve six months, on November 15 Sullivan slipped away from a work detail outside the jail and vanished.[83] Rowan, though, was among dozens of Wobblies on the list whose dealings with the Justice Department would last much longer.

On the afternoon of September 5, a small army forced its way into the IWW's national headquarters at West Madison on Chicago's Near West Side. Led by Justice Department officials, its ranks included a miscellany of Secret Service men, deputy U.S. marshals, local police, private detectives, and representatives of the recently formed American Protective League, a 250,000-strong vigilante group that enjoyed the federal government's sanction. The raiders seized control of the place, searched it, and trucked away five tons of materials, including membership and meeting records, letters, books, office equipment, desks and chairs, paper clips and rubber bands, even envelopes containing Joe Hill's ashes. Agents also entered, without warrant, the Chicago homes of prominent Wobblies, ransacked them, and removed all manner of personal property, which was, like most of the material taken from the headquarters, never returned.[84]

The Chicago raids had been preceded by intense surveillance of the union's offices and leaders, and it headlined a nationwide blitz. On September 5 and 6, federal agents raided union offices in nearly fifty other cities, including all of the union's strongholds in the West. There was little resistance, although in Seattle nine hundred protesters gathered in the street as the raid unfolded and sang "Hold the Fort." There were some arrests, too, and at more than a few locations agents tore up union property and occupied or padlocked the buildings for weeks. And the raids continued into the fall, giving credence to Wobbly Chris Luber's observation that the "story of Jack London, entitled . . . *Iron Heel* is taking its rapid, steady progress."[85]

The raids were in many ways the product of the campaign begun by western businessmen and politicians after the deadly riot in Wheatland to put the federal government behind an effort to destroy the IWW. Having launched perhaps a hundred strikes since America entered the war, the union had indeed become the threat that it was not in those earlier years.[86] Working with the California Commission of Immigration and Housing, the governors of eight western states petitioned President Wilson several times in the late summer of 1917 to deal harshly with the union's members, including, by one proposal, by confining them in concentration camps without due process. Although, as we have seen, the military would do just that, apparently with Wilson's approval, the president otherwise preferred that the government deal with the IWW by more conventionally lawful means.[87]

To this end, the administration embraced a strategy promoted by John Lind. A Progressive Democrat and former governor of Minnesota who had served a term in Congress, Lind headed Minnesota's Public Safety Commission, which had been working to undermine the IWW since its creation in March 1917.[88] A confidant of the president as well, Lind met with Justice Department officials and floated his proposal that federal prosecutions be used to break the union. Simon Lubin had the same idea. A particularly good exemplar of Progressivism's contradictory tendencies, Lubin was heir to a Sacramento department store and a former social worker; he would later be denounced as an IWW sympathizer and, after that, as a Communist sympathizer. But he was the primary figure in encouraging the founding of the California Commission of Immigration and Housing. As president of that organization Lubin had advocated prosecuting the IWW during the trouble that followed the convictions of Ford and Suhr, and he resumed that argument in the summer of 1917.[89]

The September 5 raids in Chicago occurred one day after a federal grand jury in that city had begun to hear evidence against the IWW. Just over three weeks later, the jury indicted 166 union members. There would be more federal indictments. But this was by far the most extensive. Among the defendants were most of the union's leadership, including some already familiar names: Haywood and Chaplin, as well as

FIGURE 13. Minnesota Commission of Public Safety, probably 1918. Governor Joseph Burnquist, the chair, is fourth from the left. Minnesota Historical Society, Minnesota Commission of Public Safety Collection.

Flynn, Rowan, George Speed, and Vincent St. John. Every defendant was charged with five criminal counts, all of conspiracy. Each count alleged that the defendants had conspired to undermine the war effort. And the most prominent counts concerned the Espionage Act.[90] Most of those indicted were arrested in late September and locked up in the Cook County jail, where they endured filthy, overcrowded, and dangerous conditions but also, in the spirit of their union, organized themselves, exercising together, performing skits, and publishing a newsletter called the *Can-Opener.*[91]

. . .

Virtually all of the country's big newspapers endorsed the federal government's move against the union, often in the most intemperate terms. "The snake should be scotched," said the *Washington Post.* "Let its existence end in Chicago where its crushing may teach a salutary lesson in military patriotism," the paper concluded.[92] Even the liberal *Saint*

Louis Post-Dispatch averred that the IWW had "gone a step too far" and faced a proper reckoning.[93] There was no meaningful opinion polling in those days, and it is impossible to say for certain, but it seems very likely that most Americans, plied with propaganda from the government and newspapers alike, and possessed of their own views on the merits of radical unionism in wartime, also supported the government's campaign. Without a doubt, this was the dominant view among the country's middle and upper classes.

In the summer of 1917, this kind of hostility to the IWW was quite evident in the southern half of the wheat belt, where it served capitalist interests and values and underlay a surge in anti-IWW persecution. Parts of Kansas and Oklahoma were turned into occupation zones, teeming with police, vigilantes, and company guards, and arrests of Wobblies were commonplace. R. T. McCluggage, the county attorney of Butler County, Kansas, near Wichita, boasted that his office prosecuted around 1,500 people for vagrancy that season, almost all of them IWWs of some sort. As McCluggage explained, testifying later in a federal criminal trial, "I used the vagrancy law to cover cases where men refused to work at what we considered good wages."[94]

Kansas typically edged out North Dakota as the country's largest producer of wheat, while Oklahoma also harvested a very substantial crop. The two states together accounted for some 12 million acres, or 19,000 square miles, of wheat on farms that required an inordinately large amount of transient labor at harvest time.[95] And wheat production, like lumber and mining, was an essential industry during wartime. It is therefore not at all surprising that many of the arrests of Wobblies in Kansas and Oklahoma were related to IWW activism among harvest hands. But a lot of the trouble in the region was also connected to oil, as both states were home to several subfields of the Mid-Continent Oilfield. These fields were the country's most productive, filling a demand for petroleum products that had been rapidly increasing even before the war.[96]

The IWW was never as successful organizing in oil as it was in wheat, lumber, and mining. But oil suited the union's efforts in some of the same ways as those industries. Hiring practices were casual and abusive and subject to capricious boom and bust conditions, while drilling wells and laying pipelines was dirty and dangerous and required that the men reside in grimy, crime-infested, and vice-ridden camps and boomtowns. The workforce was starkly divided between a small contingent of well-paid skilled workers and a great number of hard-pressed, poorly paid, unskilled and semiskilled workers. And a great many of these less skilled workers also worked the harvest or the woods and sometimes in mining and construction. Indeed, more than a few were already IWWs when they arrived in the oil fields.[97]

The IWW first established a dedicated local of oil workers in the region in 1907. But for nearly a decade it achieved little, as recruitment suffered from recessionary conditions and the usual problems of haphazard organizing methods and sporadic repression. However, improved economic conditions, better organizing tactics, and healthier union finances underlay a rise in membership. Initially enrolled in the AWO, these new recruits were soon organized in the Oil Workers Industrial Union No. 450 (OWIU), chartered on January 1, 1917. With the support of the AWIU, the OWIU launched an organizing campaign that spring and thus increased the Wobblies' exposure to persecution.[98]

The union's fate in Oklahoma and Kansas was joined with that of something called the Working Class Union (WCU), which had been founded in Louisiana in 1913 from the remnants of the Brotherhood of Timber Workers. Notwithstanding this connection, the WCU had little of the hesitation about the use of violence that, despite its dalliances with sabotage and its commitment to self-defense, always characterized the IWW. Indeed, as it established itself in Oklahoma, the WCU conformed to the outlaw culture for which the region, the "Old Southwest," was well known. The organization was soon implicated in burning barns and dynamiting livestock-dipping tanks in protest of burdensome measures imposed by the state government to control Texas cattle fever. Its members had a record, too, of night-riding attacks, intimidating and sometimes whipping exploitative landlords and uncooperative farmers. And they occasionally robbed banks and stole horses and other property. They also strongly opposed the war and resented conscription—so much so that, in the late summer of 1917, as many as a thousand adherents launched an armed revolt across three counties south and east of Oklahoma City.

The Green Corn Rebellion—so called because the rebels supposedly intended to spread their cause by marching across the country foraging on corn and livestock—was characterized by widespread skirmishing. The revolt was quickly put down, but it resulted in three deaths and the arrest of 450 WCU people, of whom 150 were convicted on various charges. Despite the fact that there were certainly Wobblies and IWW sympathizers among the rebels, and that the organizations shared a contempt for the war and a deep resentment of the region's capitalists, actual ties between the WCU and the IWW were minimal, and the IWW certainly did not organize the uprising. But federal agents, police, newspapers, and the region's elites readily assumed that the groups were closely entwined and drew on this assumption in justifying the intensifying campaign against the IWW in the region.[99]

. . .

That summer, Wobblies were also presumed to be behind a campaign of destruction in South Dakota. These charges were primed in the late spring by a fire that burned down a giant International Harvester warehouse in Sioux Falls.[100] Then in early July came "reliable information" from army officers that the IWW had positioned men around South Dakota in preparation for a concerted campaign to burn the state's wheat fields.[101] There was evidence to support neither this nor any claim of IWW involvement in the warehouse fire, but the accusations nevertheless inspired attacks on union that summer, including several incidents in Aberdeen. There, on July 23, 1917, police seized fifty Wobblies and turned them over to a "large group of prominent businessmen," who, according the union, beat the men "until the blood oozed from their skin."[102] A week or so later, with the harvest in full swing, "home guards" in that city intercepted all trains leading into the town and purged them of suspected IWWs, while a group of citizens sacked the AWIU hall and savagely beat the men they found inside. The next day, after the police had seized its contents, the town declared the hall a public nuisance and closed it down. The IWW responded with something resembling a statewide strike, which may have pushed up wages in the harvest but was met with a wave of vagrancy arrests and waned after a few weeks.[103]

The situation in North Dakota was somewhat different, and not only because of a dearth of charges of sabotage but also because of the influence of the Nonpartisan League. A leftist farmers' organization with a strong presence in the northern wheat belt, the League was founded in 1915 to counter the exploitative practices of railroads, banks, and flour companies. Its stronghold was North Dakota where, in the fall of 1916, it elected one of its own, Lynn Frazier, governor. Within two years, it would control both houses of the state legislature and elect a supporter to Congress. The League's membership was diverse and its politics sometimes confused, but the organization's main constituents were less prosperous farmers whose socialistic ambitions, soon realized in the establishment of a state-owned bank, flour mill, and grain elevator and a state-administered hail-insurance program, coexisted alongside a consuming skepticism about the compatibility of corporate capitalism with democratic government in America. For reasons related to these beliefs, the League also opposed the war and the draft. As a result, its members were assaulted by mobs, deported from their own hometowns, and occasionally charged with sedition or criminal syndicalism or violating the Espionage Act.[104]

Given all of this, it is not especially surprising that, despite several attempts by supporters of such a statute, North Dakota was alone among wheat belt states in not adopting a criminal syndicalism law, despite several attempts, and that federal troops played no significant role in the state during the war.[105] Nor is it surprising that conflicts involving the IWW were somewhat muted in the state, as well as in adjoining parts of Minnesota and Montana, where the League was also strong. This was true even in 1917, when many farmers were desperate to recover from the previous season, when bad weather and disease had decimated yields.[106] In fact, as the 1917 harvest approached, the League invited the IWW to discuss a harvest labor agreement covering North Dakota. These talks foundered, mainly because as the union's political position deteriorated, elements of the League, especially in prosperous eastern counties, balked, and the League feared a schism over the issue. Nevertheless, the negotiations helped ratify an informal understanding whereby many individual farmers would meet the union's reasonable demands regarding pay and working conditions and the hands would deliver reliable work.[107]

In the wake of the failed talks, Governor Frazier ordered state law enforcement officials not to interfere with men who were holding out for higher wages. But Frazier's influence over county sheriffs and city police was limited. And if farmers and the League often stood in solidarity with the IWW, the commercial and professional interests in the towns, who generally opposed the League, took a very different view of the IWW.[108] They resented the union's radicalism, loathed its habit of organizing hands to congregate in the towns while holding out for higher wages, and often endorsed the practices of simply running these men out of town, making them work, or throwing them in jail.[109] When the United States entered the war, this program came to predominate throughout the state, including in the largest city, Fargo. In the summer of 1917, the police department not only hounded harvest workers but also set itself up as a labor agency. Its boast during the harvest of having summarily sent five hundred men to the fields was corroborated by a piece in the *Fargo Forum*, which announced, "Get Men Here," directing interested farmers to inquire at the jail.[110]

. . .

When the 1917 harvest ended, the situation in the Dakotas fell very quiet. But such was not the case to the south. In the early morning hours of October 29, 1917, a bomb detonated outside of the Tulsa, Oklahoma, home of J. Edgar Pew, vice president and manager of western operations at Standard Oil subsidiary Carter Oil Company. Although the explosion wrecked the front porch of the house, it did little other damage, and no one was hurt. But most of the region's politicians and influential capitalists, along with the state's major newspapers, were quick to blame the bombing on the union, despite the absence of any evidence that Wobblies were involved. They were likewise eager to connect the bombing to the Green Corn Rebellion and to cast it as a portent of more bombings and proof of the need for a strong response to the IWW, including, if necessary, vigilantism. A week after the blast, federal and state authorities raided IWW offices in the city and arrested two dozen.[111]

The city attorney picked out eleven of these men and charged them with vagrancy. Perhaps he supposed that if they could not be prosecuted for the bombing they could at least be brought to trial on this charge. Or perhaps, as events would soon suggest, he was party to a different plan. The trial began on November 8 and ended late the next night with the defendants convicted, essentially, of belonging to the IWW. Judge T. D. Evans, who later became mayor of Tulsa and held that office during the 1921 massacre of blacks in that city, imposed a fine of one hundred dollars on each man and declared that the sentences would be suspended if they left town. Evans then had the police arrest five IWWs who had testified for the defendants, declared them guilty, and imposed the same sentence.[112]

Shortly after Evans pronounced sentence, police hustled all sixteen captives into automobiles, drove them a short distance, and delivered them to representatives of the "Knights of Liberty," a secretive, Ku Klux Klan–like outfit composed of local police and area businessmen. Clothed in black robes and hoods, the Knights took their captives to a secluded spot on the western outskirts of town, where other Knights waited. There, they stripped the union men naked, beat them with ropes, and covered them in tar and feathers. They also burned the Wobblies' clothes and shot at them. Then, with a warning never to return to Tulsa, punctuated by a volley of gunfire over the Wobblies' heads, they left their victims to fend for themselves in the cold and dark.[113]

The day after the "Tulsa Outrage," police in the oil town of Drumright, forty miles to the west, raided the IWW hall. Holding guns on the Wobblies they forced them to wreck their own hall and then took them to jail. This was part of a "general clean-up" of IWWs, as one newspaper called it, which, in the wake of the bombing, spread through Oklahoma and extended into Kansas. In a series of operations concentrated around Wichita, federal agents, police, and vigilantes arrested dozens of "loiterers" and "loafers" and, if they appeared to be IWWs, held them pending further investigation. As many as 350 Wobblies were picked up in this campaign, which was broadly justified as a response to the bombing.[114]

About three dozen of these men were held in Eldorado, Kansas, before being brought to Wichita, where, on December 7, they were charged with vagrancy and "frequenting houses of ill-fame" on the dubious word of a gambler and bootlegger named "Poker Slim." Most were held for over three months without counsel and in lieu of bail that ran from $7,500 to $10,000 for each defendant.[115] This was on the orders of the U.S. attorney for Kansas, Fred Robertson, who regarded the IWW as a collection of "traitors," "jail-birds," and "alley rats."[116] Convinced of German subversion in his state and, later, that he was the subject of several assassination plots by the IWW, Robertson had none of the scruples of his counterpart in Oklahoma, who rebuffed the pressures of oil company executives and refused to prosecute people just because they were Wobblies. On March 6, 1918, a Wichita grand jury convened by Robertson indicted thirty-four of these men on conspiracy charges.[117]

. . .

Oklahoma was not the only place where a mysterious porch bombing led to federal indictments of Wobblies. Just before midnight, December 17, 1917, a bomb exploded next to the back porch of the California governor's mansion in Sacramento. The blast roused Governor William Stephens, his wife, and their servants and shattered windows blocks away. But the bomb was detonated in such a fashion that it was bound to cause no injuries and only minor damage. This gives added credence to the theory, quietly endorsed by the governor's own investigator as well as some federal agents, that behind the blast were operatives of the Pacific Gas and Electric Company and San Francisco district attorney Charles Fickert.

Fickert was looking to defeat a recall initiated by leftists who were incensed by his recent conviction of two men, Tom Mooney and Warren Billings, for the bombing of San Francisco's Preparedness Day Parade on July 22, 1916. That crime, which killed ten people, was likely the work of followers of the shady and morally suspect Italian anarchist Luigi Galleani. But Mooney was well-known in radical and leftist circles in

California and tied to prominent Wobblies like Big Bill Haywood. He had publicly defended the use of violence to secure the release of Ford and Suhr, the Wheatland defendants. He and possibly Billings had briefly been in the IWW. And, when no longer connected to the IWW, both men had been implicated in a sabotage campaign during a 1913 strike against Pacific Gas and Electric. This made them attractive targets for Martin Swanson, a one-time Pinkerton with a vendetta against organized labor who had worked for Pacific Gas and Electric during that strike and was hired, at the expense of open shop interests, to investigate the Preparedness Day bombing. After weeks of machinations and intrigue, Swanson fingered Mooney and Billings, as well as Mooney's wife and two other men. This gave Fickert, a virulent opponent of unions and radicalism, an opportunity to strike a blow against labor and the left and possibly to propel himself into the governor's office.[118]

No one connected to Galleani was ever prosecuted for the Preparedness Day bombing. But while their fellow defendants were either acquitted or never brought to trial, Mooney and Billings, who were almost certainly innocent, were convicted and sentenced to life—in Mooney's case after he initially received a death sentence. Neither Fickert nor anyone with the utility company was ever charged in the bombing of the mansion. Instead, a few days after the incident, police followed up on an informant's tip and arrested two Wobblies, William Hood and George Voetter, when they went to a Sacramento Wells Fargo office to pick up a shipment of dynamite.[119]

A cook at construction sites and lumber camps who told his interrogators that "the I.W.W. is my country and my soul," Hood was supposed to be a member of a "Cats Claw Club" of IWW saboteurs and was under surveillance. Voetter was a miner of "nervous temperament" and "a German type," according to the papers. The two men said they were going prospecting when arrested. Police and federal agents claimed that, having destroyed the porch at the governor's mansion, their plan was to blow up Pacific Gas and Electric's headquarters. It is possible that Hood and Voetter were plotting something, and Hood later confessed to stealing the dynamite. But there is no real evidence connecting either to the porch bombing, and, as far as this event was concerned, they were convicted six months later only of illegally possessing and transporting explosives. It also seems that if they were involved in a bombing campaign, it was without the IWW's official sanction, as it is hard to see how this kind of terrorism could have advanced the union's vision or interests.[120] The same could not be said for Fickert. The porch bombing occurred on the eve of the recall vote and after Fickert had campaigned on a promise to protect the public against the dangers of radicalism.[121]

If by some chance neither Fickert nor Pacific Gas and Electric was responsible for the bombing, it could have been the work of some other amorphous group looking to sully the IWW's reputation.[122] There was no shortage of such outfits in California, which had been transformed over the previous decade into an "open shop empire" where unions were beleaguered and the IWW reviled. Among the powerful figures and entities behind this development were *Los Angeles Times* publisher Harrison Otis and his son-in-law Harry Chandler, who took over the paper when Otis died in July 1917; reactionary railroad man and philanthropist Henry Huntington; the McClatchy family, which published the *Sacramento Bee,* one of the state's most influential newspapers; local and regional chambers of commerce; and dedicated open-shop organizations like the Merchants and Manufacturers Association.[123] All of these were keen to put the politics of military preparation and state security behind their vision of a world in which unions were weak and the IWW simply did not exist.

These aims were shared by a number of impromptu organizations, like a "committee of wealthy individuals" headed by a justice on the California Supreme Court that petitioned the federal government to allow it to investigate the IWW on the government's behalf.[124] That group's offer was declined, however, mainly because this kind of work was already being done by the U.S. Department of Justice as well as California's Council of Defense. Besides broadly fanning the flames of antiradicalism with patriotic propaganda, the latter featured an "intelligence division" for coordinating investigations with the Justice Department and the military. It also oversaw the establishment of "loyalty committees" in every one of the state's counties, which reported on radicalism, sedition, and, especially, "IWWism."[125]

Partly because of the efforts of groups like these, the IWW had already faced plenty of trouble in California in the months preceding the bombing at the governor's mansion, including a steady stream of vagrancy arrests, a great number of police raids, and a spate of vigilantism, punctuated by an episode in August when some six hundred marauding soldiers demolished the union's Oakland headquarters.[126] And some of the federal raids that fall also occurred in California. The bombing made things worse. Following the arrest of Hood and Voetter, authorities launched another round of raids on IWW meetings and headquarters in Sacramento, as well as in San Francisco, Los Angeles, and Fresno. Statewide, around two hundred, maybe more, were arrested on charges ranging from vagrancy, to crimes related to sabotage, to suspicion of being involved in the bombing itself. Some of the vagrancy cases were adjudicated and, years later, some of the particular claims of sabotage would resurface in state criminal syndicalism prosecutions. But for several dozen of these people, a different fate was in store.

Shortly after Hood and Voetter were picked up, the *Sacramento Bee* declared that the city was "disgraced by the spectacle of a jail full of I.W.W.s" that neither it nor the state could properly punish. What the newspaper called for, and what one of the McClatchy brothers demanded when he communicated directly with Hiram Johnson, California's former governor and junior U.S. senator, was federal prosecution.[127] Pressured as well by the Sacramento chamber of commerce and other business interests, federal prosecutors obliged. They secured three separate indictments, each charging groups of IWWs with a variety of criminal acts before, in October 1918, consolidating the indictments into one that charged fifty-three defendants with conspiracies to impede the war effort.[128]

. . .

In Idaho, the conclusion of the conventional phase of the Great Lumber Strike in September brought an end to large-scale roundups, but arrests persisted and, by Christmas, dozens of Wobblies were being held on criminal syndicalism charges throughout the state's northern reaches. Among the "mischief makers" later brought to trial was William Nelson, a twenty-eight-year-old lumberjack and the union's secretary in St. Maries, Benewah County. Arrested there in December 1917, Nelson was prosecuted in Coeur d'Alene on charges of distributing IWW literature and advocating the spiking of logs.[129]

The decision to move Nelson's trial to Coeur d'Alene in neighboring Kootenai County brought a threatening crowd of IWW supporters to the St. Maries courthouse. When some of them pushed around the county sheriff, a group of "armed citizens," joined by state militiamen and federal troops, rushed to the sheriff's aid. This impromptu posse arrested dozens of Wobblies, ran most of them out of town, and then quarantined the area.[130] Nelson was convicted on April 2, despite the testimony of a fellow Wobbly and former Benewah County sheriff who insisted that the IWW man had never advocated sabotage.[131]

Sentenced to two to ten years, Nelson joined J. J. McMurphy and John Otis Ellis in Idaho State Penitentiary.[132] Other Wobblies soon took up residence there, partly to satisfy the demands of powerful business-men like J. T. Moran of Benewah County, who, just before Nelson was convicted, telegrammed Governor Alexander to insist that "forty or fifty" additional criminal syndicalism prosecutions were needed to stanch the IWW in northern Idaho.[133] On May 28, 1918, not a month after Nelson's arrival in prison, a dozen Wobblies were convicted of criminal syndicalism in a mass trial in St. Maries. A week later, they were sentenced to serve one to ten years in the penitentiary, where, to the great satisfaction of the state's newspapers, they arrived on June 7.[134]

The union's continuing difficulties that winter and spring did not end at Idaho's western borders. Just before the first of the year, the "home guard" around Ione, Washington, near the Idaho and Canada borders, performed a "clean up"—seizing about a hundred IWWs and running them out of town, except for two they kept in jail.[135] In the weeks to come, a great number of Wobblies were arrested for vagrancy in Spokane, where authorities sought to refute claims from government and businesspeople in Idaho that the city was serving as a cross-border haven for Wobblies.[136] Come April, just as Spokane officials escalated a tiff with the governor over their demand that he impose some kind of martial law, twenty-seven Wobblies, who had been culled from nearly a hundred taken in a two-pronged raid on the headquarters of the AWIU and the LWIU, were convicted of vagrancy, sentenced to thirty days in jail and ordered to pay one-hundred-dollar fines. Unusually, there were two women in the group. While one of them, Mrs. Blair Cairns, organ-ized a futile defense, the judge sought to reopen the "rock pile" so he might have some place to put the prisoners to work.[137]

In the meantime, incursions on IWW offices continued in the region. On February 23, for instance, federal agents joined with Portland police in a raid on union headquarters that ended with a hundred men lined up on the street, fifty arrested, and more than a truckload of union docu-ments hauled away.[138] On May 2, city police in Seattle conducted what the newspapers called the region's largest single raid on the IWW and the largest raid of any kind in the city's history. At 8:30 that night, fifty heavily armed officers, led by Chief of Police J. F. Warrant and backed, according to the police, by a crowd of 15,000 people on the street, forced their way into the union's hall on Washington Street. When the police entered, a man identified as C. Swelling was delivering a speech, "How American Justice Works," to the four hundred people gathered inside. Perhaps unable to appreciate that the question had just been conclusively answered, Swelling continued with the lecture while officers dragged over two hundred people out of the building.

The police detained their captives on an "open charge," shuttled them to police headquarters before a cheering throng, and then padlocked the hall. The raid had been launched at the direction of the recently elected mayor, Ole Hanson, with the promise that those taken would be charged with criminal anarchy. This did not happen. But within a week, most had been charged with disorderly conduct, a couple dozen were held on immigration or draft-related charges, and federal agents were poring through stolen union legal defense records in hopes of bringing more charges. Within a few days, three of the men taken that night were charged with violating the Espionage Act. Nearly two weeks after the raid, 150 arrestees still languished in the jail, there to welcome five or so union people taken in yet another raid.[139]

In Spokane these raids found a new purpose that spring in providing the authorities with people to prosecute for misdemeanor criminal syndicalism. Such was the outcome of a May 3 raid on what was described as a new and secret IWW headquarters.[140] Enacted in April 1918 and used more than any other law of this kind, Spokane's criminal syndicalism ordinance was one of twenty adopted by cities in Washington. On June 28, the superior court upheld the ordinance against a challenge by lawyers representing Wobbly Hays Jones, who had been convicted earlier that month and sentenced to thirty days in jail. The lawyers had argued that the law was an unconstitutional example of "class legislation," meaning it unjustifiably imposed upon labor organizations, and upon the IWW in particular, burdens not placed on comparable business organizations. In a ruling that was later affirmed by the Washington State Supreme Court, Judge Bruce Blake rejected this argument out of hand.[141] And with Blake's ruling behind them, city authorities intensified enforcement efforts, arresting and convicting Wobblies on charges of both vagrancy and misdemeanor criminal syndicalism through the summer and holding some for possible federal prosecution.[142]

. . .

On April Fools' Day, 1918, the first big federal case involving Wobblies went to trial. Court convened on the sixth floor of the massive beaux arts federal building in the Chicago Loop for the trial of the Wobblies indicted in that city the previous fall. There were 113 defendants in court, a fair number dressed in overalls and working jackets. Their ranks had diminished by over 50 since the indictment, because some had been misidentified or were never found, one had died in an accident, another had fallen mortally ill in jail, and others had had their cases severed and were never tried. In this last category were Joe Ettor and Carlo Tresca, who had left the union before the indictment, and Elizabeth Gurley Flynn, who was on her way out and had urged Ettor and Tresca to petition for severance. Another defendant was excused when he arrived in his military uniform.[143]

The prosecution of this case was preceded by a handful of smaller but similar federal cases, some involving IWWs. One of these, which may have provided a model for Chicago prosecutors even though it did not involve the Espionage Act, was the case against G. T. Bryant and two other members of a radical tenant-farmer organization called the Farmers and Laborers Protective Association, established in Texas in 1915. Although much about the association's history is still unclear, it was connected to both the IWW and the Working Class Union. Probably a Wobbly himself, Bryant was among fifty-five members of the organization indicted in the summer of 1917 for conspiring to "overthrow" the government and hinder conscription. He and two other defendants were convicted in Abilene, Texas, in October 1917 and sentenced to six years in prison.[144] Convicted on only one count, the men were indicted and tried on eight, which alleged a complicated array of plots and schemes said to have flown, inevitably, from their organization's radical purposes in wartime.

The Chicago case was similarly complicated. It alleged that each defendant was guilty of five conspiracies to hinder the war effort by interfering with production and transportation of war material, with the draft and military recruitment, and with the enforcement or administration of a presidential proclamation and the joint resolution by which Congress declared war on Germany. Altogether, the indictment invoked some twenty provisions of federal law. But at its center were sections three and four of Title I of the Espionage Act.[145]

The judge in the case was Kenesaw Mountain Landis. A patriotic Progressive who became infamous as the first commissioner of professional baseball, Landis had already sent a number of draft evaders and war protesters to prison.[146] He nonetheless handled the trial in an outwardly fair and decent way. Concerned about the poor quality of the food at the jail, Landis organized lunch for the defendants and released some on their own recognizance during the trial. When illness threatened defendant Charles Ashleigh's life, Landis even placed him in the care of his own physician. And he insisted that courtroom procedures adhere to the precepts of due process and ensured that conditions in court were comfortable and congenial. During much of the trial, he even dispensed with his robes and sometimes came down from the bench during testimony.[147]

The defendants were represented principally by seven attorneys: Otto Christensen, William Cleary, Caroline Lowe, John Metzen, Harold Mulks, Jesse Quitman, and, in the lead, George Vanderveer. Hired when Clarence Darrow declined, to his regret, because he was otherwise obligated, Vanderveer was arrested in December on the morning of the arraignment when he entered the courthouse with an "automatic pistol" on his person. He failed in his attempts to settle the case before trial, and he is reputed to have drunk heavily during the trial. Nevertheless, Vanderveer was by all appearances a good choice. He had a great deal of experience in both prosecution and defense work, had secured Thomas Tracy's acquittal a year earlier, and was by most accounts capable and dedicated, if not entirely reliable.[148]

The prosecution was led by Frank Nebeker, a Progressive corporate attorney from Utah who had been named special assistant to the attorney general, in charge of prosecuting IWWs, and Claude Porter, a Democratic Party operative and special assistant who would work on several other federal prosecutions of IWWs. Aided by the local U.S. attorney and a handful of Justice Department lawyers, Nebeker and Porter seemed from one vantage to have had before themselves a difficult task. Because the indictment alleged that the defendants had conspired to interfere with the war effort by a program of strikes, sabotage, and seditious propaganda, it could therefore be construed to require that the prosecution prove that the defendants had actually done these things. However, this view misconstrues the doctrine of conspiracy.[149]

The essence of conspiracy is that it makes it a crime for defendants to agree among themselves to pursue a criminal purpose. Beyond demonstrating such agreement, which can be tacit in nature and proved by circumstantial evidence, prosecutors are not required to prove that any particular defendants actually did anything. For while conviction also requires that an "overt act" have been committed in furtherance of the conspiracy's purpose, that act need only have been committed by one of the defendants and, furthermore, need not itself constitute a crime or even something essential to the completion of the conspiracy. Indeed, the overt acts identified in the indictment consisted of correspondence or written documents, like the preamble and various documents on the subject of sabotage that Haywood, Chaplin, and others had "caused to be printed." Consequently, Nebeker, Porter, and their colleagues were in a position to convict the defendants almost entirely by convincing the jury that they shared an intention to interfere with the war effort, and they could accomplish this, like their counterparts in the state criminal syndicalism cases, by putting the IWW itself on trial, trusting that if the union seemed unscrupulous and seditious, the jury would reckon that merely being associated with it demonstrated each defendant's culpability.

When they began to present their case in May, this is exactly how prosecutors proceeded. They introduced some fifteen thousand documents in evidence, most seized in raids the previous fall. Nebeker read to the jury from these texts, including selections from the union's newspapers, personal and union correspondence, Flynn and Pouget's pamphlets on sabotage, and, inevitably, the IWW's preamble. This exercise became so tedious that defendants and spectators alike turned to their own reading materials for distraction. But occasionally the testimony brought out something important. A standout was the reading of a collection of letters by Charles Lambert, a member of the IWW's general executive board who had headed the defense committee working on behalf of Wheatland defendants Blackie Ford and Herman Suhr. Written during the campaign to compel the men's release, Lambert's letters celebrated burning crops, poisoning trees, and other acts of destruction and were tailor-made to advance the prosecution's case.[150]

The prosecution also put on dozens of witnesses who claimed to have overheard Wobblies denouncing the war, who said Wobblies had urged them to dodge the draft, who purported to know that IWW strikes were aimed at undermining the war effort, and who attested to the violence of these strikes and the union's commitment to sabotage.[151] Like much of the government's most incendiary literary evidence, which was produced years earlier, many of these allegations were not only beyond the scope of the indictment but also concerned conversations and events that occurred before the declaration of war and the enactment of the Espionage Act. Landis allowed this evidence on the theory that it demonstrated the defendants' intention to conspire. By a different but equally dubious logic, one that presumed the IWW to be a kind of undying conspiracy, Vincent St. John was a defendant in the case, even though he had largely retired from the IWW in 1915 to work a copper claim in a remote part of New Mexico and, when word of his indictment finally reached him, had to hike many miles through the desert to place himself in federal custody.[152]

In any event, only a few witnesses, mostly IWW turncoats, recounted much beyond talk and writings, whatever the time frame. Prosecutors had promised to produce more telling evidence. But if they had this kind of proof, which is somewhat unlikely, they seem to have lost it in the most ridiculous fashion. Ex-governor of Arizona Thomas Campbell, who was supposed to arrive in Chicago with briefcases full of documents that would prove the worst IWW outrages, made it to court without these papers, which he claimed had been purloined in Washington, D.C., by a "negro" IWW disguised as a railroad porter.[153]

Once the prosecution rested on June 19, Vanderveer and his colleagues began their defense. They would call over one hundred witnesses, among them dozens of public officials, farmers, and other employers, and among these, reputable establishment figures. Such witnesses had little reason to support the IWW, and some were openly hostile to the union. Yet they attested to the Wobblies' reliability and good work and contradicted the image of the union as a criminal organization bent on destruction. In this category were some of the Montana officials who had reported to Justice Department officials how peaceable and orderly union men had been during the Great Lumber Strike.[154]

A majority of the defendants also testified. They explained IWW ideology, noting how neither opposition to the war nor the union's affinity for strikes confirmed the violent, destructive, and seditious designs attributed to the organization and its members. And they asserted that the testimony about sabotage was either misrepresented bluster, indiscriminate accounts of accidents, or the doings of rogues and provocateurs. Landis had barred the defense from putting in evidence the *Final Report of the Commission on Industrial Relations,* which Vanderveer and company had hoped to use to demonstrate the legitimacy of the defendants' purposes. But the defendants themselves accomplished much on this front, describing from the witness stand the terrible working conditions that they and their fellow workers had endured and the difficult and tragic lives that had brought them to this fateful moment. A highlight in this regard was the testimony of Big Bill Haywood himself, which was heard by Eugene Debs and venerable labor activist Mary "Mother" Jones. They were among a list of visitors to the proceedings that included celebrity preacher and rabid IWW opponent Billy Sunday, who was Landis's guest, as well as South Dakota's first U.S. senator, Richard Pettigrew, a Populist whose criticisms of the war as a capitalist racket had gotten him indicted under the Espionage Act and who came to support the defendants.[155]

The trial was front-page news, covered by leftist journalists, Carl Sandburg and John Reed, and all of the big newspapers. And as the end of summer approached, speculation abounded about how it would end. When the jury got the case, the defendants and their lawyers, at least, were reasonably optimistic.[156] They should not have been. Landis correctly instructed the panel that membership in the IWW was not tantamount to guilt, even in a conspiracy trial. But he also emphasized that the goals of a conspiracy did not have to be realized to establish guilt. He confirmed that in determining whether the defendants had formed an agreement among themselves, the jury should not expect prosecutors to have proven that this agreement was explicit. He rightly noted that when deliberating the question of an overt act, the jury should remember that an act by one defendant was attributable to all. And he also refused to instruct the jury that the defendants had a right to peacefully express their opposition to the war. In all these respects, Landis's instructions adhered to the meaning of conspiracy and prevailing interpretations of the U.S. Constitution. Haywood, at least, reckoned they were "fair." In fact, they were all but a directive to send Big Bill and his codefendants straight to prison.[157]

When the verdict came, on August 17, about a dozen of the defendants brought to trial had already had charges against them dismissed for one reason or another. Among these were Peter Kirkenen, who had lost his mind, and Roger Culver, an organizer in the Butte strike that had brought Frank Little on his last, fateful trip there, who turned out to be an operative of the Theil Detective Agency and a government informant. This left ninety-seven defendants, every one of whom the jury found guilty on all of the four counts that remained, 388 counts in all, entailing 10,000 criminal allegations. After three and a half months of testimony, they needed but forty-five minutes to decide.[158]

Reporters claimed that Haywood sank into his chair when the verdict was read. Other defendants were visibly shocked, as were Vanderveer and Lowe, who, by one account, wept at the defense table. Packing the courtroom, along with two hundred police and U.S. marshals, were the defendants' loved ones. They had dressed in anticipation of a homecoming and formed a "lane of tears," according to the *Chicago Tribune,* through which the defendants were led into custody, while in the lobby a band played "Hail, Columbia."[159] Two weeks later, Landis brought the defendants back for sentencing in a courtroom packed again with friends, family, and police. Besides a lecture from Landis about the correctness of the verdict, the proceedings featured three hours of statements from the defendants. Among these was a plea from Anson Soper, who asked that he be allowed to serve whatever prison term Landis might impose on fellow defendant Norval Martlatt, in addition to his own, so that Martlatt might go home to his family.

Landis denied being influenced by Soper but ordered Martlatt held pending further consideration, which meant he would not be sentenced at all. He ordered defendant Pete Daily, who was dying, released on the same terms. When court convened the next day, Landis sentenced two others to ten days in jail.[160] Then he commenced sending men to prison. Landis sentenced twelve defendants, including Soper, to a year and a day; thirty-five others to five years; thirty-three to ten years; and fifteen, including Haywood, Rowan, Chaplin, who turned thirty-one that day, and other top leaders, to the maximum term of twenty years. All of the defendants who got prison terms were also fined in amounts that ran up to $30,000 and totaled $2.3 million, or about $42 million in today's funds. A leader of a relatively small but quite successful waterfront local, the Marine Transport Workers Industrial Union No. 8, and recipient of a ten-year sentence, Ben Fletcher was the foremost black Wobbly in a union in which blacks might at times have comprised 10 percent of members. He was also the only black member on trial in Chicago, although not the only one to go to prison.[161] And it fell to him to inject some humor into these grim proceedings. "Judge Landis is using poor English today. His sentences are too long," Fletcher said. But the lengthy sentences were no laughing matter for the defendants, some of whom had allowed themselves to believe that Landis's initial leniency presaged short sentences for all.[162]

Five days after sentencing, while most of the defendants were in jail and Landis vacationed in northern Michigan, a bomb exploded in the entrance of the federal courthouse, which also housed a post office. The powerful blast killed four people, injured dozens, and convinced many more that the trial must have come to the right conclusion. It convinced many Wobblies that someone was trying to kill Haywood, who was at the building that day trying to arrange bail and claimed to have just passed through the entryway when the bomb detonated. Two men were seen planting the device, but no one was ever charged. Two days later, late in the evening, the defendants were piled, shackled and under heavy guard, on a special train bound for the federal penitentiary at Leavenworth, Kansas. They pulled away from the station under the solemn watch of William Bross Lloyd, a wealthy Socialist who put up considerable money for the defense and would soon be prosecuted under Illinois's sedition law.[163]

. . .

The defendants had been at Leavenworth just over a year when the Montana Supreme Court was compelled to take note of their case while deciding the appeal of J. A. Griffith. An IWW job delegate who was on his way to the harvest in North Dakota, Griffith had been charged with violating that state's sedition law after entering the Blue Front Saloon in Billings in July 1918, "confessing" his IWW membership, and expressing there and in a boardinghouse his disapproval of the Chicago conspiracy prosecution. Convicted that December despite Vanderveer's representation, he was sentenced to eight to sixteen years in prison. But in the supreme court's view, Griffith's conviction simply could not stand, as it rested on "nothing more than the expression of an opinion as to the probable outcome of a trial conducted 1,500 miles away."[164]

Griffith was one of about 130 people arrested for sedition in Montana during the war, and one of 45 imprisoned on this charge.[165] Some of these defendants were just random folk who too freely shared their views about the war; some were Socialists or pacifists. But a fair number were either Wobblies or connected to the IWW, charged with violating a law enacted because state officials believed U.S. Attorney Burton Wheeler and U.S. District Court Judge George Bourquin too reticent to imprison people for violating the Espionage Act.[166]

Neither Wheeler nor Bourquin was a radical. Wheeler had not only seen a certain level of anti-IWW repression as necessary to prevent a worsening of mob violence, he had met with the general counsel of Anaconda Copper about prosecuting Frank Little just before Little's murder. But he broadly sympathized with labor, disliked militarism, and was not one to casually bend the law to serve business interests. And he declined to bring Espionage Act charges against Wobblies in his jurisdiction. Likewise, Bourquin, a former miner and cowboy who was the state's only federal judge, was guided by his own belief that the law should not serve as a tool of class rule and should be administered in conformance with principles of due process and the rule of law. As both men saw things, a defendant could not violate the Espionage Act or commit similar federal crimes by mere speech, without actually causing someone to resist the draft, undermining the war effort in some tangible fashion, or conspiring to do this in some clearly manifest way.[167]

In February 1918, Governor Samuel Stewart, backed by the state's newspapers, threatened that if more radicals and "traitors" were not jailed, there would be more vigilantism, and he called a special session to deal with the situation. It was during this session that the legislature enacted the sedition law, along with a seldom-used criminal syndicalism statute and, revealingly, a statute requiring the registration of all privately owned firearms.[168] The legislature impeached a state district court judge deemed too tolerant of dissent. And, at Governor Stewart's urging, it also conveyed legal standing on the State Council of Defense. Besides condemning Wobblies and other "disloyal" elements and attempting to prosecute them for vagrancy and "loafing" through its own administrative orders, the council, in turn, took the lead in trying to force Wheeler and Bourquin from office. Supported by the legislature, most of the state's political elite, and some army officers it recruited to its cause, the council deluged Attorney General Gregory with charges that both men were derelict in their duties.[169]

Under the U.S. Constitution, Bourquin could only be removed by impeachment, and he occupied the bench for another forty years. But Wheeler's days as a prosecutor were numbered. In September 1918, during an IWW strike in support of the "class war prisoners," soldiers in Butte joined with police and Anaconda officials and raided the IWW hall, the Metal Mine Workers Union hall, and the *Butte Daily Bulletin*, a publication that sympathized with the IWW. The mob seized property, roughed up union people, and held more than three dozen on vague charges including sedition and creating a disturbance. This angered Wheeler, who complained to Gregory, pointing to specific cases where soldiers had brutalized their captives. Gregory then reminded the War Department that the army had no authority to engage in any such activity. For a time, it was unclear what might become of this conflict. But on October 9 Wheeler suddenly resigned, worried that his stance would threaten the reelection of his mentor, U.S. Senator Thomas Walsh, who could not afford to alienate the Anaconda Copper Mining Company.[170]

Wheeler left office just in time to represent another person charged with sedition: William Dunne, the man whom Frank Little's killers had threatened and who did not particularly like Little but had nonetheless walked at the head of his funeral procession. The lead editor of the *Daily Bulletin*, Dunne was arrested in September along with colleagues Leo Daly and R. B. Smith, and the three were charged with publishing in that paper an editorial critical of the State Council of Defense. Dunne had testified for the IWW defendants in the Chicago conspiracy trial, was elected to the Montana House of Representatives while under indictment, and was a central figure in a short-lived attempt to organize a Butte "soviet"—a coalition of veterans, unionists, and radicals of a sort that would be organized in several American cities following the armistice. He was the principal target in the case and brought to trial first. Despite Wheeler's representation, he was convicted in February 1919 and sentenced to pay a $5,000 fine. Daly was never brought to trial, but Smith was convicted that June and fined $4,500. And so he and Dunne confirmed by their own experiences their newspaper's repeated admonition "that the age of the iron heel foreseen by Jack London is here."[171]

CHAPTER 4

I'll Take neither Mercy nor Pity

*Repression and the IWW during
the Red Scare*

Five years of organizing and publicity work for the IWW in the 1910s
had gotten Fred Esmond arrested several times, at least. It was because
of one of these arrests that Esmond's draft registration card listed his
residence as the San Francisco County Jail. He spent most of 1918
residing at a different address, though. One of dozens of Wobblies
picked upon in the wake of the bombing of the governor's mansion, he
was indicted and locked up in Sacramento awaiting prosecution on federal conspiracy charges. The Oxford graduate and newspaperman,
who, like Charles Lambert, had rashly threatened sabotage after the
conviction of Wheatland defendants Blackie Ford and Herman Suhr,
had just turned thirty-nine when he surrendered himself to U.S. Marshals that February. For eight months he was confined in solitary, and
for forty-odd days he "fought his battle," as the union put it, with no
bed or blanket, sleeping on the floor of his cell.[1]

Esmond's codefendants in the federal case also suffered—held in
crowded cells too small for all to lie down at the same time—until they
were moved to a slightly less crowded lockup. They made do on inadequate and revolting fare, as money provided by the IWW's California
defense committee to buy provisions was stolen by jailers and the food
that was delivered allowed to rot before the hungry inmates' eyes. Amid
the raging influenza pandemic, a majority fell ill; four died of the virus,
and another succumbed to tuberculosis.[2] For a time, they faced threats
of vigilantism serious enough that George Vanderveer wrote the White

House with his concerns and federal officials at least acknowledged the danger.[3]

In the defendants' ranks were William Hood and George Voetter, the men accused of bombing the governor's mansion and convicted in June 1918 on explosives charges. Now, with their fellow defendants, they faced a prosecution promoted by a great number of government officials and California elites, including the McClatchy family, whose newspaper, the *Sacramento Bee,* had demanded that Wobblies found engaging in sabotage be executed by firing squad "without counsel or benefit of clergy."[4] The case had been pushed, as well, by San Francisco district attorney Charles Fickert, who probably had had the bomb planted at the governor's mansion. However, there was resistance to the prosecution on the part of some influential people, most notably Simon Lubin and George Bell, who as president and chair, respectively, of the California Commission of Immigration and Housing had helped instigate federal intervention against the union in the first place.

Lubin and Bell were allied with Governor William Stephens. And in 1918 Stephens was challenged by Fickert in the Republican Party primary and also embroiled in a squabble with federal prosecutors over control of anti-IWW efforts in the state. Moreover, Stephens's investigator, whose work suggested that Fickert was actually behind the bombing of the governor's mansion, had operated under Lubin's direction. From this vantage, Lubin and Bell could not but see the whole prosecution as politically fraught, if not also morally unjustified. Unlike Fickert, they were not just Progressives, but the kind of Progressives who, while they saw the virtues of repression, did worry about how far it should go. And then, too, there was the plight of a defendant by the name of Theodora Pollok, which seemed to resonate with these two Harvard graduates.[5]

About thirty years old, Pollok was a onetime settlement worker and suffragist from a prominent Baltimore family. She had found her way into the IWW some years earlier and had helped the union with defense work since the Wheatland affair. On December 29, 1917, Pollok was serving as secretary of the California branch of the union's general defense committee. When, in this capacity, she tried to post bail for a group of fellow Wobblies, she was arrested and subjected to a humiliating physical examination of the kind usually reserved for prostitutes—something the U.S. attorney justified as appropriate for IWW women. And then, in October 1918, Pollok was indicted with the others for conspiring to undermine the war effort.[6]

While prosecutors developed their case, police raided the general defense committee's San Francisco office seven times over a six-month period and seized all the office's documents. Others who worked there besides Pollok were repeatedly arrested, typically for vagrancy, and one man who worked in the office was picked up fifteen times in four months. Those who tried to raise defense funds and publicize the union's cause by distributing handbills on the street were also arrested, and the defendants' mail, including communications with lawyers, was intercepted by government agents, who replied under false pretenses and used this artifice to uncover details about the defendants' legal strategy.[7]

This kind of treatment was not unusual. Just two days after the Chicago conspiracy defendants were arraigned in December 1917, federal agents "swooped down" on the union's headquarters in that city, "drove out 150 members, arrested five, and took charge of the place," and in this way interrupted frenzied efforts to prepare for the impending trial.[8] During the trial, agents also intercepted union mail, preventing lawyers from gathering witnesses and raising funds.[9] These practices gave credence to Pollok's suggestion to her codefendants in Sacramento that they accept the inevitability of conviction, engage counsel only to preserve issues at trial for appeal, and refrain from representing themselves. Pollok herself was soon turned against this approach by friends and family, who probably encouraged Lubin and Bell to attempt to intervene on her behalf. But forty-three of the defendants agreed to decline legal representation for any purposes at all, committing themselves to an entirely "silent defense."[10]

When trial began at the post-office building in Sacramento in December 1918, there were forty-six defendants, because, as in the Chicago conspiracy trial, many of the fifty-three originally indicted were released for various reasons or could not be found, while others had been added to the case. There was more suggestion in this case that some of the defendants had engaged in actual sabotage. But for the most part they faced the same charges as their fellow Wobblies did in Chicago and were prosecuted the same. Prosecutors introduced reams of union literature and correspondence and testimony by police and sheriffs who claimed to be privy to antiwar statements by Wobblies. They implied that the defendants were behind the bombing at the governor's mansion, making this point, to the shock of Judge Frank Rudkin, by having the dynamite that Hood and Voetter were arrested with brought into court. They also produced an assortment of IWW turncoats, including three who were initially among those indicted: Wilfred Dennis, Elbert Coutts, and John

FIGURE 14. The "silent defenders" in the Sacramento conspiracy trial departing the Sacramento County jail, 1918. UW Libraries, Special Collections, SOC 0393.

Dymond. A local union official, Dymond had been the only Wobbly allowed to visit the defendants in jail, and he had urged his fellow defendants to plead guilty. Indeed, most defendants in the case had been offered money and freedom to testify against their fellow workers.[11]

Dennis, Coutts, and Dymond regaled the jury with lurid tales of Wobblies burning crops, killing trees, destroying lumber, wrecking machinery, and manufacturing an array of fiendish incendiary devices. Although the "silent defenders" did nothing to challenge this testimony, counsel for Pollok and the two other defendants represented by lawyers exposed the questionable character and dubious motivations of all three and opened other significant holes in the government's case. Pollok herself took the stand, where she spent considerable time defending the IWW and explaining that a poem she had written, "A Soldier with a Broken Nose," was not proof of sedition.[12] But to no avail. Judge Rudkin would later openly question the defendants' culpability and was careful to instruct the jury to weigh the guilt of each and not to convict on the basis of mere membership in the IWW. But on January 16 the jury convicted every one of the defendants on all counts after deliberating for only about an hour. While being led from the courtroom after hearing the verdict, the silent defenders burst into song.[13]

At the sentencing hearing, several defendants broke their silence again, and it was one of the weakest who spoke the loudest. Although visibly ailing and facing years in prison, Fred Esmond struggled to his feet and spoke his piece. "I am not asking for mercy," he told Rudkin. "I'll take neither mercy nor pity from you or any other representative of this government. . . . I want to go on record for myself and the organization as saying that we, the outcasts, have been framed up on, clubbed, beaten, slugged, martyred and murdered," he said, quite truthfully. "Is it any wonder that I do not consider myself bound by your procedure when this court and its proceedings are a disgrace to the United States? You have done more than any I.W.W. could possibly do to drag your Stars and Stripes though the mire."[14] Rudkin sentenced the silent defenders to prison terms ranging from one to ten years, with more than half of them, including Esmond, getting ten years. Five months later, Pollok, who was frail and tubercular, received a one-hundred-dollar fine, and the two others who had counsel got that plus two months in jail.[15]

A week after the trial ended and just a few blocks away, a "militant Progressive" and "spokesman" for organized labor named William Kehoe introduced a criminal syndicalism bill in the California State Senate. The legislation was backed by Governor Stephens, reelected handily on a platform of crushing these "Huns of industry" and "terrorists."[16] The state legislature had gone some distance toward adopting such a law in the spring of 1917. But the measure was tabled, the victim of a stalemate between open shop forces and supporters of organized labor over the implications of terms like *syndicalism* and *sabotage* and the possibility that a law that incorporated them might be used to harass conventional unionists.[17] This time the statute moved inexorably toward enactment.

In fact, virtually the entire business community in the state supported the legislation. So did the newspapers, which ran lurid tales that season of ongoing IWW sabotage and ominous accounts of a tumultuous IWW-led strike in the San Gabriel Valley, east of Los Angeles.[18] And so did most all the state's legislators. This time the bill featured a definition of sabotage as "malicious destruction, damage, or injury to property." And it easily overcame the desultory complaints of some civil libertarian–minded lawmakers and the residual concerns of some skeptical pro-labor legislators who did not share the view of the California Federation of Labor that destroying the IWW should supersede worries about how else such a law might be used. The bill cleared the legislature with only nine negative votes, all in the lower house and mostly cast by Republicans.[19] Signed by the governor on April 30 and immediately effective, the law was enacted alongside "scores of measures advocated by organized labor."[20]

. . .

These developments in California showed that as much as the war had worsened the IWW's situation, its fortunes were not destined to improve in the wake of the armistice of November 11, 1918. This was certainly the case in Washington, as events in Seattle on January 12, 1919, pres- aged. That day a diversity of labor militants and radicals, including a number of IWWs, gathered in an open-air meeting in Seattle to discuss the formation of a "soviet" of workers and to urge a general strike. On orders from Mayor Ole Hanson, club-wielding police descended on the gathering and hauled more than a dozen to jail. The fracas was not much, but the police declared it a "riot," and so did the newspapers, which deemed this collection of radicals carrying red flags a portent of bolshevism and evidence of the need for repressive measures to hold the threat of postwar radicalism in check.[21]

The very next day, the Washington State Legislature convened and moved immediately to override Governor Ernest Lister's veto of the criminal syndicalism bill two years earlier. The few objections were met with rhetoric even more extreme than in 1917, including claims that Lister's veto had been secretly extorted by an IWW threat to destroy the state's orchards with copper nails and a statement by the bill's cham- pion in the lower house that he "would just as soon shoot [his] own brother if he carried the I.W.W. card." Immediately after it convened, the senate passed the criminal syndicalism bill by a vote of 37–5 and sent it to the lower house, where it passed the following day, January 14, by a vote of 85–6.[22]

The head of the Washington State Federation of Labor, an arm of the American Federation of Labor (AFL), likely bargained away opposition to the criminal syndicalism law in exchange for support for the federa- tion's legislative agenda. He later boasted that the legislative session had helped give the state "the most progressive labor laws in the Union."[23] But Washington's mainstream labor movement was not monolithic, and some factions within it, motivated by both wary self-interest and soli- darity, began to mobilize a referendum to repeal the criminal syndical- ism law as soon as it was enacted. Afraid that this effort might gain traction or that they might lose votes, and looking to change percep- tions of the bill, its supporters in the legislature repealed and replaced the just-enacted law with another, one that, in the guise of equality under the law, also made "resisting" economic, industrial, or social change a crime. Confident that this would make no difference in how the law was used, the legislature passed it with only two negative votes, both in the house, and on March 19, Lewis Hart, the lieutenant governor who had taken over for an ailing Lister, signed the bill into law.[24]

These developments unfolded amid a surge in labor unrest propelled by the chaotic demobilization of hundreds of thousands of servicemen, massive wartime inflation, and global political unrest, which gave apparent credence to the hopes of some and the fears of others that some kind of Bolshevik-style uprising was imminent. Although many events in 1919 fit well with these portents, none was more important than what unfolded in Seattle, where a shipyard strike involving over twenty craft unions and 35,000 workers gave rise to one of the most remarkable episodes of labor protest in American history. The shipyard strikers appealed for support from the Seattle Central Labor Council, which was infused with IWWs and Socialists and, more importantly, well attuned to the militant mood of the city's workers. The council responded by calling a citywide general strike on February 6. Supported by at least 65,000 workers, it brought the city's economy nearly to a standstill. The council and the strikers maintained order and essential services, including hospital and food services, and for several days ran the city, despite a raft of threats and provocations emanating from the mayor.[25]

A Progressive with honorary membership in a boilermaker's local, Mayor Hanson boasted of being a union man. But he was a union man who despised radicalism and, especially, the IWW. With powerful interests in lumber and shipping pressing him, Hanson declared that if the strike had not ended by the morning of February 8 he would impose martial law, and he issued a proclamation that implied that anyone who usurped civil authority would be summarily shot.[26] To back this oath, Hanson filled the streets with police, their numbers bolstered by hundreds of temporary officers, including fraternity boys from the University of Washington and members of a statewide vigilante group called the Minutemen, which already had considerable experience assaulting and harassing IWWs. Although Hanson's ultimatum passed without a declaration of martial law, he took advantage of Governor Lister's illness to enlist state officials in a deployment of thousands of federal troops. This, combined with the repudiation of the strike by the national AFL and failing support from the leaders of participating AFL unions, brought the general strike to an end on February 11.[27]

FIGURE 15. Soldiers and trucks at National Guard armory during Seattle General Strike, February 1919. Seattle Museum of History and Industry, 1983.10.10696.

The new criminal syndicalism statute did not go into effect until June.[28] But roused by the surge in radicalism, Seattle prosecutors charged some two dozen Wobblies with violating a disused criminal anarchy statute enacted after the 1909 Spokane free-speech fight. In May they brought one of these men, James Bruce, to trial. Despite producing an array of government agents and informants and offering breathless depictions of radical literature, prosecutors could not convict. Perhaps swayed by George Vanderveer's argument that the IWW was committed to revolutionary change by economic and not political means, and that this law was exclusively concerned with criminalizing the latter, the jury acquitted Bruce. Prosecutors then dismissed charges against everyone else who had been arrested for criminal anarchy.[29]

Meanwhile, in Spokane authorities arrested scores of Wobblies and prosecuted some on lesser charges. On January 23, 1919, for instance, police raided the IWW's new and well-furnished hall. They trashed the place, arrested six, and charged five with misdemeanor criminal syndicalism. A week later, the defendants were convicted and sentenced to thirty days and a one-hundred-dollar fine.[30] Other arrests and convictions followed; by summer's end, several dozen Wobblies were roosting in the city jail on a miscellany of charges, including vagrancy and felony and misde-meanor criminal syndicalism.[31] There, on September 18, 1919, Wobbly Carl Swanson committed suicide by strangling himself with a necktie.[32]

. . .

The removal of the Great Lumber Strike "to the job" had resulted in ongoing conflict in the region's lumber camps and continued wood shortages. It also produced an extraordinary effort to rein in the IWW by different means. Sent to Oregon in October 1917 by the federal gov-ernment to investigate the situation, a Progressive army colonel named Brice Disque visited mills and camps. In the fashion of other Progres-sives, he determined that supposed IWW outrages in the industry, which he took for granted, were linked to the dangerous and inhuman living and working conditions that he witnessed. Disque was therefore primed to be taken with the suggestion from one of the lumbermen that a "loyal legion" of workers be formed to preempt the IWW. He gained approval in Washington, D.C., to create such an organization, and by the end of November had established the first "local" in Wheeler, Oregon. Over the next several months, Disque worked with a corps of junior officers to establish more locals and, in the guise of representing the workers who joined these locals, shrewdly negotiated shorter hours, more stable wages, and better accommodations. By the summer of 1918, the new organization claimed over 100,000 members.[33]

The Loyal Legion of Loggers and Lumbermen got along reasonably well with Samuel Gompers, who had come to despise the IWW, and the AFL. Its mission abetted by Disque's mobilization of 100,000 troops who worked in the mills and camps, the Loyal Legion did indeed blunt the IWW's influence, especially in western Oregon, where there were major stands of Sitka spruce, crucial in the manufacturing of airplanes. But not only did the Loyal Legion accomplish its purpose, in part, by justifying the withering repression already being directed at Wobblies, it also was an undemocratic organization that was completely controlled by Disque and his subordinates, one whose members were often coerced, sometimes violently, into joining. Moreover its success was incomplete. Many workers who joined retained their membership in the IWW and their contempt for the industry's employers. And despite its efforts, there was still considerable conflict in the mills and camps.

Indeed, according to the president of the State Federation of Labor, by the end of the war, a "spirit of unrest and bitterness" prevailed in

Oregon.[34] Much of this was centered in Portland, where thousands of workers and demobilized soldiers and sailors who were struggling to cope with postwar labor conditions gave their support to a new organization, the Council of Workers, Soldiers and Sailors of Portland and Vicinity. Formally established in January 1919 by a diversity of leftists, including many Wobblies, it had at its head a Socialist named Harry Wicks. This soviet, as it was also called, was the product of months of organizing. Its central aim was to establish revolutionary workers councils and use them to unite the working class in protest. With a revolution built upon such organizations unfolding in Russia and similar organizations giving impetus to upheaval in postwar Europe, this episode was quite enough to move Oregon toward the enactment of a felony criminal syndicalism law.[35]

Calls for such a law came from the Oregon bar association, the mayor of Portland, the governor, a host of business organizations, and most of the state's newspapers. The legislature moved rapidly, adopting the criminal syndicalism law alongside a workers' compensation law and a limit on labor injunctions. Debate was somewhat enlivened when labor-friendly legislators introduced bills to outlaw "criminal commercialism" and "commercial sabotage." But these had no chance of passing. And attempts to block passage of the criminal syndicalism law with reasoned rejoinders about how threats of radicalism were inflated or how the new law would undermine conventional unions went nowhere. The statute was enacted with only four negative votes in the house and one in the senate and went into effect on February 3.[36]

Emboldened by the passage of the new law, Portland police "declared war" on radicals, decreed it unlawful for anyone to distribute radical literature on the streets, and began making arrests.[37] In late February, they joined hands with federal agents and sheriff deputies, raided IWW headquarters in the city, seized all the important records, and marched twenty-two members to jail, where five were held for deportation and the others charged with vagrancy.[38] That month, police also arrested radical physician and honorary IWW Marie Equi—who had already been convicted the previous December of violating the Espionage Act for giving a speech at a Portland IWW meeting—and charged her under the new criminal syndicalism statute.[39] Equi served eighteen months at San Quentin for violating the Espionage Act but was one of several dozen people threatened with criminal syndicalism prosecution yet never brought to trial. Fearing they themselves would be charged with criminal syndicalism, landlords evicted both the IWW and the Portland soviet from their respective headquarters, which helped hasten the soviet's demise.[40]

. . .

What the IWW experienced in the spring and summer of 1919 was folded into a nationwide surge in unrest and repression. By the beginning of summer, the first of over fifty race riots had already occurred—riots that would claim hundreds of lives and make the year the bloodiest period of racial strife since the end of Reconstruction. On May Day, several major cities exploded in class violence. In Boston, at least one person, a policeman, was killed, scores were injured, and dozens faced criminal charges. In Cleveland, battles between protestors organized by Socialists and IWWs and a large mob of police, vigilantes, and soldiers left at least two people dead, as many as 50 injured, and 200 arrested. And in New York, 1,500 police were needed to stop 500 soldiers from smashing into a meeting on behalf of Tom Mooney and Warren Billings at Madison Square Garden.[41]

The May Day riots occurred just as the most extensive terror bombing campaign in the country's history occurred. In two separate waves, the first in late April and early May and the second in early June, bombs were anonymously sent to or planted at the homes and offices of three dozen prominent capitalists and government officials. Although the bombs did not kill or injure any of their intended victims, whose ranks included Ole Hanson, Kenesaw Mountain Landis, Frank Nebeker, Charles Fickert, and other IWW enemies, some bombers and innocent workers lost their lives.[42] Like the Preparedness Day bombing that got Mooney and Billings imprisoned, these were likely the work of anarchist followers of Luigi Galleani and not the IWW. A few union members were also militant anarchists, but the Wobblies, who generally considered the "dynamite philosophy," as Wobbly historian Fred Thompson put it, ineffective and morally unacceptable, had no real connection to the Galleanists and their campaign.[43]

Nevertheless, the bombings and unrest that spring lent both legitimacy and urgency to the enforcement of California's new criminal syndicalism law. The San Francisco Police Department's "Neutrality Squad" had been raiding the IWW's Red Branch Hall on Mission Street and other union retreats nearly every week for a year.[44] On May 22, 1919, the squad entered the People's Institute, a workers' school affili-

ated with the IWW and the Socialist Party and housed in a joint establishment called Jack London Memorial Hall, arrested seven men, and
took them to Southern Police Station. The school's secretary and business manager was Emanuel Levin. A former U.S. Marine, Levin later
became a Communist and a leader of the tragic 1932 "Bonus March,"
the gathering of over 40,000 impoverished veterans and their supporters who reprised the idea behind Coxey's Army and went to Washington, D.C., to demand early payment of bonuses owed by the government. That day in 1919, Levin's business was to get these seven men out
of jail. But when he headed to the station to see about arranging bail, he
ran straight into the leader of the Neutrality Squad, Captain Jack
O'Meara. "Who are you?" O'Meara asked. "I am the secretary of the
People's Institute," replied Levin. "That's a radical organization, and
under the new syndicalism law you are guilty of a felony," said O'Meara.
With that, O'Meara made Levin the first person to be charged with
violating California's felony criminal syndicalism law.[45]

The raid had turned up plenty of radical literature, including volumes by Lenin, Trotsky, and Engels, not to mention Jack London, as
well as a great deal of IWW materials. These texts formed the cornerstone of the case against Levin, which alleged no particular acts or
words by which Levin committed criminal syndicalism.[46] According to
prosecutors, Levin's guilt was based on nothing more than his radical
politics, which the literature proved, and on his association with the
IWW.[47] Levin understood this. "My case is not a personal one," he told
the National Civil Liberties Bureau, precursor of the American Civil
Liberties Union (ACLU).[48] But at his trial, which began on December
26, 1919, he denied being an IWW. The jury apparently believed him,
because he was acquitted.[49]

In the meantime, authorities gradually escalated their enforcement
campaign. On June 29, a raid by federal and state agents on a "secret"
union meeting in Stockton netted nineteen men, among them two of the
union's top leaders in California, who were all held on criminal syndicalism charges.[50] By the end of summer, in northern California alone
fifty-seven union men and one woman had either been formally charged
with criminal syndicalism or were being held pending such charges. Up
to that point, most criminal syndicalism cases were in the northern half
of the state. But this soon changed. In the early fall of 1919, the Los
Angeles County Board of Supervisors produced five thousand copies of
the criminal syndicalism act and distributed them to the public in hopes

of receiving aid in prosecuting more Wobblies.[51] The police there also used membership rolls, secured through espionage at the union's Chicago headquarters, to coordinate a series of raids. That October, forty people were hauled before the grand jury in Los Angeles because their names were on a list of contributors to a union defense fund seized in a raid on the IWW's headquarters in the city. Among those implicated, although never brought to trial, were "parlor Bolsheviki": several college professors and, supposedly, a former U.S. senator who was scheduled to be interviewed discreetly by the district attorney.[52]

. . .

By the summer and fall of 1919, it was typical for the slightest measure of IWW involvement in any violent episodes to furnish proof of the union's seditious character, while confirming just how intolerable these episodes were. Such was the case with the May Day riots, in which Wobblies played a modest role, and several large and bloody strikes that unfolded that fall and stood out in this year of exceptional labor conflict. Wobblies played only the most tangential roles in the Boston Police Strike; in the Great Steel Strike, led by William Z. Foster, by then no longer with the IWW, which was the largest U.S. strike to date; and in a sprawling eastern coal strike, which rivaled the steel strike in size and was destined to evolve into years of armed struggle. But these were nonetheless presumed to confirm the threat posed by IWWism. Indeed so were the race riots, which were blamed not only on blacks themselves but also on the IWW, which was said by the big newspapers and by people like Illinois governor Frank Lowden and South Carolina congressman and future U.S. Supreme Court Justice James Byrnes to have inspired their impertinence.[53]

Indeed, for many elites and much of the public, all of the unrest of that year was the work of a perilous amalgamation of anarchism, bolshevism, socialism, IWWism, black radicalism, and feminism, one that truly threatened the social order. This was a central premise of the "First" or "Great" Red Scare, the surge in antiradicalism whose beginning is usually situated, if not around the May Day riots and the bombing campaign, then on November 7, 1919—the second anniversary of the Bolshevik Revolution—when federal agents, police, and vigilantes began a series of nationwide raids that resulted in the arrests of as many as 1,000 radicals and suspected radicals. These were the first of a series of roundups—soon to be known as the Palmer Raids, after U.S. Attorney General A. Mitchell Palmer, who oversaw them—that extended into the next year and resulted in the detention of about 6,000 people.[54]

Often violent, conducted with scant regard for constitutional rights, and accompanied by a swell of intemperate rhetoric, the raids were concentrated in cities east of the Mississippi River and along the West Coast. They netted many more socialists, anarchists, and representatives of the nascent communist movement than IWWs, of whom perhaps a few hundred were seized. They also left the federal government without a ready way of dealing with these detainees.

In May 1918, Congress amended the Espionage Act to directly criminalize speech and expressions of just about any kind that criticized the war effort and likewise to authorize the postmaster general to more easily bar such communications from the mail.[55] But the Sedition Act, as these provisions were called, was intended for wartime use and would be repealed in December 1920.[56] And while western congressmen pushed their colleagues to enact a federal criminal syndicalism bill, this effort came to naught, along with a few other attempts over the next few years, in part because of doubts about the need for such a law and in part because some in Congress thought the federal government's power to enact this kind of statute, as opposed to that of the states, was limited to wartime.[57] Furthermore, while sections three and four of Title I of the Espionage Act could still be enforced on the theory that the Knox-Porter Resolution, which formally ended America's state of war, was not signed into law until July 1921, most people believed the war was already over, and support for continued use of these provisions had faded.[58] This left the federal government, which still had limited resources for policing and prosecution, without a ready means of prosecuting its captives. And it left deportation as the main way of dealing with them. Perhaps 800 radicals met this fate. But probably only two dozen or so of these were Wobblies, as IWWs were more likely to be citizens than were the anarchists and communists who made up the majority of those kicked out of the country.[59]

The deportations were carried along on the current of xenophobia that ran through the Red Scare. Together with the Palmer Raids, they gave the Red Scare an identity and relevance apart from the repression of the IWW, an organization whose members had, in the course of several years, already endured more serious persecution than all other radicals combined and would continue to face this treatment long after the Red Scare. But insofar as it was distinct from what otherwise happened to the IWW, the Red Scare also gave added impetus to the

FIGURE 16. Cartoon published in the *New York Herald* a week before passage of the Sedition Act, a set of amendments to the Espionage Act, May 1918. Cabinet of American Illustration, Library of Congress.

persecution of Wobblies by vigilantes and state and local authorities, whose services federal officials often regarded as a proxy for their own. For it validated the idea that the threats and dangers represented by the IWW transcended the sectarian bounds of early twentieth century left-ism. In the process the Red Scare helped sustain the notion that even those who provoked the union's members in the cruelest ways and paid a commensurate price for this were victims deserving of unqualified reparation.

. . .

This was made tragically evident by an episode in Centralia, Washington, a lumber and mining town of about seven thousand located sixty-five miles south of Seattle. Wobblies had been active there for years and had long faced harassment and assaults at the hands of police and vigilantes allied with local lumber and mining capitalists. During the war, businessmen pressured landlords not to rent the Wobblies space for a union hall. When the union men did secure a property, they were driven out. During a Red Cross parade on April 5, 1918, an assortment of townspeople smashed up the hall. Amid cries to lynch the men, they instead dragged the Wobblies outside, hoisted them up by their ears into the back of a truck, drove them out into the country, and dumped them, with orders never to return.[60]

The following spring, some Wobblies did return, only to be driven from a hall they had set up in a vacant building. In June, a group of vigilantes assaulted Tom Lassiter, a forty-three-year-old Wobbly who had lost his sight in an industrial accident and supported his family with a newsstand. They smashed Lassiter's stand twice in the course of a week, beat him, and dumped him in a ditch out in the country, with a demand that he leave town. Lassiter defied this order but at greater cost. For not only did local authorities ignore the assaults on him, but early the next year they also prosecuted him for criminal syndicalism and threw him in prison for six months.[61]

By the end of summer 1919, the union had been run out of Centralia on four occasions. But come Labor Day, Wobblies had established a new hall on the ground floor of a downtown hotel owned by a sympathetic couple. Hearing rumors that townspeople would soon sack this place too, they consulted a local lawyer: thirty-one-year-old Elmer Smith, whose brother was a Wobbly. Smith told his clients, quite correctly, that they had a right to defend themselves, with deadly force if necessary; but he urged them to seek police protection. Not surprisingly, the chief was of no help, although he also demurred when the town's businessmen, organized around a "Citizens' Protective League," demanded that he preemptively run the IWWs out of town.

Informed by the city attorney that, indeed, the union could not simply be driven out of town, at least not by his reading of the law, the men of this Protective League colluded with members of a newly formed chapter of the American Legion and devised their own means of accomplishing this, one that took advantage of the town's Armistice Day parade.[62] A relatively large affair, the parade was to feature a march by the legionnaires led by post commander Warren Grimm. A stand-out athlete, the city attorney's brother, and a lawyer himself, Grimm was a local hero and had recently served in the American Expeditionary Force in Siberia. He was to lead the legionnaires past the IWW hall, not once but twice, even though parades usually did not travel that route.

When Armistice Day arrived, chilly and grey, respectable citizens were spotted around town brandishing nooses, and rumors abounded that an attack on the hall was imminent. Sure enough, during the parade, just as the legionnaires' formation, about eighty strong, paused in front of the union hall, the mounted parade marshal blew a whistle and the veterans charged the hall. Wielding pipes and clubs, they smashed the door open, only to meet a hail of gunfire from Wobblies, who fired from inside the hall and from buildings overlooking the scene. Within seconds, legionnaire Arthur McElfresh was killed outright and Grimm and fellow legionnaire Ben Cassagranda were mortally wounded. As bullets and screams filled the air, the legionnaires retreated in panic and then regrouped. Their numbers boosted by other townspeople, and wielding firearms retrieved from their homes or seized from local hardware stores, they resumed their assault, pouring gunfire into the hall and taking it without further losses.[63]

Six Wobblies were captured and jailed but several fled amid the confusion. Among them was twenty-nine-year-old lumberjack and army veteran Wesley Everest, who had spent months in the stockade for refusing to salute the flag. Chased down and cornered at the Skookumchuck River by an armed mob, Everest shot and killed one of his pursuers, Dale Hubbard, and was then captured, beaten, and thrown in jail with his fellow Wobblies. Through the afternoon, armed men patrolled the town, seizing more IWWs, warning off strangers, and completing the destruction of the union hall. Later, several dozen convened behind closed doors at the Elks Lodge and then, near midnight, went down to the jail, removed Everest, whom they had mistaken for the union's secretary, Britt "Brick" Smith, and took him to a bridge over the Chehalis River. There, they hanged Everest dead and shot up his body. Everest's last words: "I got my man and done my duty. String me up now if you want to, damn you!" For several more hours, a mob milled about menacingly at the jail, threatening the Wobblies inside. One of these was

James McInerney, alias James Mack, who been aboard the *Verona* at Everett, was among the seventy-four charged with murder in that case, and, although the records are not clear, may have been among those wounded in that massacre. The crowd that night beat him severely and tightened a rope around his neck before finally dispersing.[64]

Three legionnaires had also been wounded in the attack on the union hall, along with one Wobbly. Several other people were injured in the heated days that followed, as police and deputies scoured the area, arresting anyone suspected of being an IWW and roughing up more than a few people. On November 14, a legionnaire shot an innocent traveler in Chehalis when the man did not respond quickly enough to a challenge. The next day, a deputy sheriff was killed in a most ridiculous fashion when two posses composed of what the newspapers called "expert woodsmen," trying to close in on a nonexistent stronghold of IWW "desperadoes," converged in the woods northwest of Centralia and recklessly opened fire on each other.[65]

More IWWs were jailed, besides those taken in the melee at the hall. Elmer Smith was arrested at his law office after the assault on the union hall by none other than the school principal, aided by a company of Boy Scouts. Within two weeks, thirteen men, including Smith and two others who were never captured, had been arraigned for murdering Grimm. Prosecutors apparently thought his death fit best with their story that the Wobblies had attacked the legionnaires without provocation or justification.

The defendants were brought to trial on January 26, 1920, forty miles away in Montesano. At the head of the prosecution was a legionnaire named Clifford Cunningham, a former railroad and timber company lawyer who had attended the meeting that led to Everest's lynching and may have been at the scene when he was killed. The trial judge, John Wilson, openly detested the IWW. Neither he nor prosecutors or police did anything when investigators hired by the defendants' lawyer, George Vanderveer, were assaulted and intimidated as they tried to work the case. Indeed, during the trial, prosecutors had Vanderveer's mail stolen and, with Wilson's approval, presented some of it in court, along with perjured testimony from one of the original arrestees, Tom Morgan, who turned state's evidence. Prosecutors also had several defense witnesses arrested on perjury charges as they left the stand. They did this in a courtroom full of army soldiers and legionnaires who were paid five dollars per day to attend the trial, from a fund endowed by lumber companies.[66]

FIGURE 17. The seven defendants convicted of murder in the Centralia case at the
Washington State Penitentiary in 1921. *Back row, left to right*: Ray Becker, O.C. Bland,
Britt Smith, Bert Bland; *front row, left to right*: Eugene Barnett, John H. Lamb, James
McInerney. Lewis County Historical Museum.

Perhaps most damaging to the defense was Judge Wilson's decision
barring evidence of all the incitements and assaults that preceded the
events on Armistice Day. Nevertheless, the trial did not end quite as
badly for the defendants as it might have. One, a boy of sixteen at the
time of the incident, was adjudged insane and committed to the asylum,
and another had charges against him dismissed. The jury struggled to
decide the fate of the others, delivering an initial, compromise verdict,
partly premised on the crime of third-degree murder, which Washington
law did not recognize. Wilson rejected the verdict and ordered further
deliberation. Late on the evening of March 13, after several more hours
of deliberation, the jurors delivered a new verdict. They acquitted two
of the remaining defendants: Elmer Smith and Mike Sheehan. But they
found the others guilty of second-degree murder. The seven convicted,
all lumber workers and miners, were Eugene Barnett, Ray Becker,
brothers O.C. and Bert Bland, John H. Lamb, James McInerney, and
Britt Smith. The convictions contradicted considerable evidence show-

ing that the legionnaires had attacked the hall unprovoked and rested on several implausible assertions about how Grimm had been shot. Several jurors later said that they had felt intimidated by all the soldiers in court and on the streets and by rumors of an imminent IWW invasion of the town and, further, that they had only convicted because they thought that Wilson would honor their recommendation for leniency. The judge sentenced the convicted men to terms of twenty to forty-five years in prison.[67]

. . .

The murder case was not the only prosecution to come out of the events at Centralia. U.S. Justice Department officials were deluged with letters and resolutions from Legion posts, chambers of commerce, and businessmen condemning the killing of the "heroes" in Centralia and urging decisive federal action.[68] Attorney General Palmer demurred, as he considered this a matter for state and local government, but not all his underlings were as reticent. When the *Seattle Union Record,* a publication of the Seattle Central Labor Council, suggested that the legionnaires had provoked the Wobblies, federal authorities barred the paper from the mail and seized it under the authority of the Espionage Act. On the grounds that by "pretending to . . . advance the interests of laborers as a class" it had interfered with the war effort, they also indicted the paper under that statute, along with its Socialist publisher, Harry Ault; journalist, doctor of philosophy, and IWW sympathizer Anna Louise Strong; and two other people.[69] The case was a very weak one, though, particularly with the war essentially over, and the indictments were quashed early the next year.

In the meantime, thirty-four civic, patriotic, and business organizations telegrammed Washington governor Lewis Hart and demanded that, in light of the "massacre," he use his office to destroy the IWW.[70] Hart obliged, authorizing a wave of arrests and prosecutions that extended across the state. A week after the clash in Centralia, district attorneys from five counties, encompassing the cities of Seattle, Spokane, and Tacoma, reported to the state attorney general that *five hundred* Wobblies were under arrest for criminal syndicalism in their jurisdictions.[71] A union publication claimed that *over eight hundred* were actually in custody, in line with what it described as a plan to overwhelm the union's lawyers and defense committees.[72] These are reasonable estimates, considering that Washington prosecutors ultimately charged over 150 Wobblies with criminal syndicalism, most of them during this period, and probably convicted at least half that number.[73]

Some convicted after the Centralia affair, like "negro" organizer Perry Murphy and two others in Seattle police court, faced misdemeanor charges. But there were plenty of felony convictions. On February 1, thirty-six Wobblies picked up after the Centralia incident were convicted in Tacoma in the largest mass trial in the history of these prosecutions. The jury deliberated fifty-nine hours and recommended the "utmost clemency" in sentencing, believing that they had condemned the organization more than the men. The defendants, for their part, broke out in song upon hearing the verdict. But whether they received the "utmost clemency" is certainly debatable. Eleven were fined and several were ordered to quit the IWW, but twenty-two received sentences ranging from eighteen months to three years.[74] In late February, eleven Wobblies, also rounded up after the trouble in Centralia, were convicted of criminal syndicalism in Montesano and, in the case of four of them, later sentenced to prison in a trial that featured testimony by George Vanderveer, who took temporary leave of his work on the Centralia murder case for this purpose. One of these defendants, Anti Koi, had been driven insane by a vicious beating he endured at the hands of legionnaires after his arrest and was committed to an asylum.[75]

By the spring of 1920, the IWW's bimonthly "Northwest Defense Bulletin" read like a dirge, listing case after case of defendants who had been arrested, tried, and often convicted of criminal syndicalism.[76] Amid all these arrests and prosecutions, rumors abounded of Wobblies murdered by vigilantes in remote areas.[77] Certainly, many were beaten and put to flight, while a great number also suffered while languishing in jail, as revealed in correspondence between Wobbly inmates at the jail in Yakima and the national office of the ACLU. The IWW men, among them one arrested when he came to deliver tobacco to the others, complained that they were being held nearly incommunicado, served horrible food, and confined in miserable, vermin-infested conditions in a "strong tank," also known as the "ice box."[78] The men were never allowed outside, spending all of their time, sixteen of them, in a six-by-thirty-foot room. By the time they dispatched their first complaints to the ACLU in December 1920, they had been locked up for seven months, and some were ill. They remained another five months like this, and five would spend two years in the jail before the criminal syndicalism charges against them were finally dismissed.[79] Still they declared, "We are not giving up the fight."[80]

. . .

In the wake of the Centralia killings and the first raids of the Red Scare, arrests and prosecutions of Wobblies surged in Oregon, as well. Governor Ben Olcott pronounced the union guilty of "nothing short of treason" and called on all the state's peace officers to cooperate in rooting out "the evil."[81] All over that state, authorities responded by arresting Wobblies and, in dozens of cases, charging or threatening to charge them with criminal syndicalism. Enforcement was concentrated in Portland, where, on November 21, 1919, a grand jury indicted twenty-two of the fifty-eight Wobblies arrested in a raid a week earlier.[82] Within two months, according to the union, twenty-nine members were either facing formal criminal syndicalism charges in that city or had already been convicted of the crime.[83]

The campaign against the union converged with an effort to undermine the newly formed Communist Labor Party (CLP), an organization that stood out among several rival parties in the communist movement's early years for its close connections to the IWW.[84] Among those affiliated with both organizations was Joseph Laundy, an IWW, AFL unionist, leader of the Portland soviet, and founding member of the Portland CLP. Laundy was arrested on Armistice Day when he answered a knock on the door at an IWW meeting. His criminal syndicalism trial in April 1920 featured the testimony of A. E. Allen, a former Wobbly who turned government witness. Allen's lurid accounts of how, as a member, he had engaged in and advocated serious acts of sabotage helped overcome a vigorous defense by George Vanderveer, and Laundy was convicted and sentenced to two years in prison.[85]

In Idaho, where the legislature had created a state constabulary for the purpose of better suppressing the IWW, the Centralia affair also produced more trouble for the union. The superintendent of the constabulary, former sheriff Frank Breshears, decided that Wobblies were "swarming" into the state's panhandle region to escape the pressure in Washington and Oregon and ordered the men in his command to work with county sheriffs and arrest every Wobbly they could apprehend.[86] Aided by Governor D. W. Davis's declaration that the IWW was an "outlaw organization" and assisted by "chosen men" of the American Legion, which was quickly coming into its own as enemy of labor radicalism, they undertook, according to the *Caldwell Tribune*, to stamp out the "foolishness" and "handle 'em rather rough."[87] In November, these forces arrested about a hundred Wobblies, mostly in the panhandle region, and held several dozen on criminal syndicalism charges or for possible deportation. The constabulary boasted that in the face of these efforts, Wobblies were tearing up their membership cards and surrendering to police.[88]

One of the people to be convicted of criminal syndicalism in the wake of this campaign was William Dingman, who was among twenty-three Wobblies charged in Bonner County, three days before Christmas 1919. At the conclusion of their trial early the following March, Dingman, the only defendant alleged to be an organizer, was the only one to be convicted. When it decided Dingman's appeal four years later, the Idaho Supreme Court upheld his conviction, along with the basic concept of criminal syndicalism and the method of prosecuting defendants by proving their membership and then deluging the jury with evidence purporting to demonstrate the union's criminality.[89]

Another Wobbly taken in Idaho in the wake of the Centralia affair was Felix Jovanovich. Facing criminal syndicalism charges in Shoshone County in the spring of 1920, Jovanovich was convinced that he would be hanged if convicted and twice attempted to cut his own throat with a razor, once while in jail awaiting trial and again after the trial began, during an overnight adjournment. Then he tried to throw himself from an upper floor window at the hospital. This was all too much for the man, who died May 29, 1920. Although the union did not disagree with the authorities' claim that Jovanovich was in poor health, attributing his vulnerability to exposure to lead in the mines, it declared his "tragical ending" the immediate result of his prosecution and adjudged him "an insane victim of an insane system."[90]

. . .

In late 1919 and early 1920, Wobblies in California faced a significant increase in harassment and assaults at the hands of citizens groups. On November 14, a "citizens committee" confronted Oakland's public-safety commissioner, Fred Morse, to whom the Legion had just offered "1,000 men" to assist in such work, with the demand that every IWW be put "behind bars."[91] That same day, there was yet another raid on Jack London Memorial Hall and Red Branch Hall. During this operation the San Francisco police joined with the American Legion post in demanding that all Wobblies leave town.[92] That night, a club-wielding mob of uniformed ex-servicemen sacked the IWW's hall in Los Angeles. Twenty or thirty men broke up a meeting of fifty Wobblies, smashing furniture, beating anyone they could get their hands on, and sending three union people to the hospital.[93]

The Legion already had a key man at the forefront of the state's efforts to prosecute Wobblies, at least in Southern California. That man was Buron Fitts, a lawyer who served as the state's lieutenant governor in the late 1920s and then, in impressively corrupt fashion, as district attorney of Los Angeles County through the 1930s. In 1919, Fitts was president of the state American Legion and was sworn in that November as a special deputy district attorney in Los Angeles so that he might wage "war on radicals," according to the *Los Angeles Times*.[94] From this office, Fitts promoted the theory that the IWW was at the center of an elaborate plot to violently overthrow the social order and even to harm Fitts himself.[95] As a result of his agitation, authorities posted armed guards at the homes of "officials who are fighting the I.W.W. menace" and extra guards at the county jail to preempt a supposed plan by the IWW to storm the place with hundreds of men and free their fellow Wobblies.[96]

There was also an increasing number of criminal syndicalism prosecutions, beginning late in the year. On December 3, 1919, James McHugo, the second person arrested for felony criminal syndicalism in California, became the first person convicted of that crime in the state. An electrician by trade and secretary of the IWW's Recruiting Union No. 600 in Oakland, McHugo had been arrested at the union hall the previous May. He readily admitted his membership in the IWW, which allowed prosecutors at his trial to establish guilt merely by showing that the IWW itself advocated industrial or political change by unlawful means. For that purpose, they introduced IWW literature in evidence and elicited the testimony of two special agents of the U.S. Justice Department, as well as that of Elbert Coutts and John Dymond, to implicate the union in bombings, sabotage, and other crimes.[97]

Dymond had been a member of the Western Federation of Miners (WFM) before working with the IWW as a delegate and then as union secretary in Fresno. Since testifying in the Sacramento conspiracy trial, he had become a "professional witness" in the guise of serving as an "investigator" for the Los Angeles County district attorney's office. Fresno lawyer Harry McKee told the ACLU's Roger Baldwin that during the Sacramento trial he had tried to warn "the boys" about Dymond, but "they felt sore" at McKee for "mistrusting a fellow worker who was so active and efficient." Dymond efficiently stole $1,400 in defense funds and was later exposed as an agent of an open shop outfit called the Better America Federation and, in line with the Ku Klux Klan's history as an implacable enemy of labor radicalism, a member of that organization as well. But only when he took the witness stand in Sacramento did his astonished victims believe "he was crooked."[98]

Coutts was just as crooked. Also a former member of the WFM, he had joined the IWW back in 1913, when he was about seventeen years old. By his own courtroom testimony, he not only burned haystacks and engaged in other acts of sabotage during his time in the IWW but also occupied himself with burglary, robbery, and similar crimes, for which served twenty months in San Quentin. Unlike Dymond, who seems to have drawn a salary, Coutts was mostly paid at a flat rate of several hundred dollars per trial. He admitted in the early 1920s that testifying against the IWW had become his only legitimate source of income, one sufficient to purchase a forty-acre farm.[99]

Following the McHugo trial, these "Gold Dust Twins," as the IWW called them, appeared scores of times in criminal syndicalism prosecutions, particularly in California, where they consistently delivered questionable but effective testimony. No doubt coached by prosecutors, they knew what they were doing, too. Almost never did they testify about the criminal acts of anyone on trial. Instead, they levied their charges of violence or sabotage against members who were not present and sometimes did not even exist, and in that way avoided opening themselves up to easy contradiction and impeachment.[100]

During this "life and death struggle for the I.W.W.," as the *Los Angeles Herald* called the trial, McHugo was represented by William Cleary. A lawyer who had worked on behalf of the Bisbee strikers in 1917, and for his troubles had been deported along with the miners, Cleary had performed indifferently as one of George Vanderveer's assistants in the Chicago conspiracy trial.[101] But in the course of this trial, which stretched through November into early December, he seemed to do his job well. Drawing on the testimony of A.S. Embree, secretary of the IWW's Metal Mine Workers Industrial Union No. 88, who was awaiting trial on criminal syndicalism charges in Idaho, Cleary challenged the reliability of the state's evidence and countered the prosecutors' inevitable claims that the union was a violent, criminal organization. Nevertheless, it took the jury only five minutes to convict McHugo, who was sentenced to one to fourteen years at San Quentin.[102]

Initially, California prosecutors dismissed most criminal syndicalism cases that came to them. But within a month of McHugo's conviction, the state tried three other defendants on such charges, all in San Francisco. One trial resulted in a hung jury and another, Emanuel Levin's, ended in an acquittal. But a third, James Malley's, resulted in conviction. Malley had been arrested June 26, 1919, while on bail on another criminal syndicalism charge and was arrested again, on November 26, on a vagrancy charge. He began his criminal syndicalism trial representing himself, with no preparation, because his lawyer was detained and the judge would not grant a continuance. Convicted on December 10, a week later Malley was sentenced to one to fourteen years, which was the only prison sentence prescribed by California's statute for convictions on a single count. Malley told the judge that the case against him was "a crime against free speech," to which the judge replied that Malley had committed "crimes of social insanity."[103] As with most defendants in California, Malley's actual sentence was set by the state's prison board, which gave him five years.[104]

While these prosecutions unfolded, the raids and arrests continued. One of the men taken that fall was Nicholaas Steelink, twenty-nine years old and with a potent reputation as a soapbox agitator. First arrested in early October, Steelink was out on bail when arrested again during the veterans' attack on the Los Angeles union hall in November. His prosecution in that city in March 1920 was in some ways a reprise of the Sacramento conspiracy prosecution of a year earlier and notable for the sensational testimony of Robert Connell, who appeared in that trial alongside Coutts and Dymond and testified with them in this case as well. A convicted felon and one-time Wobbly who was among nineteen men arrested in September 1918 and charged with committing industrial arson in the Sacramento area, "Dublin Bob" was every bit as dubious a character as the Gold Dust Twins. The focus of his testimony in both cases was the supposed existence of an IWW "sabotage factory," installed on a Stockton houseboat—an "explosives ark," as it was also called. His assertions backed by the testimony of Coutts and Dymond, Connell claimed to have developed a proficiency in chemistry while in prison and to have applied this skill to the invention of an amazing array of nefarious devices, including various incendiary and explosive mechanisms and even a caustic foot powder for eroding the feet of unwary scabs. On top of all of this, a deputy U.S. marshal contended in Steelink's trial that fires started by IWWs had caused $50 million in damage in California.[105]

This kind of testimony makes Steelink's trial a study in the vagaries of the criminal syndicalism cases and the whole idea that the IWW needed to be destroyed because it was bent on violence and destruction. Even with the full benefit of hindsight, the facts remain unclear. On the one hand, the volume and intricacy of evidence about sabotage makes it difficult to discount the claims entirely, especially when some Wobblies surely did commit destructive acts. On the other hand, the utter unreliability of "special agents" Coutts, Dymond, and Connell and the incredible flourishes that run through their appearances make it easier to see their testimony as an orchestrated frame-up than as proof of some concerted stratagem, let alone something for which Steelink, or for that matter nearly any other Wobbly, could fairly be held responsible, and particularly considering that everyone who confessed to being a party to these schemes was a government informant.

Nevertheless, with such testimony at its center, Steelink's trial moved unswervingly toward conviction. Ten "typical" IWW songs were read into the record.[106] An array of "secret signs" and "codified slang language," said by prosecutors to foster "violence, sabotage, and unrest"— though they may have been nothing more than artifacts of hobo culture used to distinguish accommodating and hostile places to rest or get a meal—were also put in evidence. After hearing from District Attorney Thomas Lee Woolvine that Steelink's lawyer, J. M. Rycman, should be tarred and feathered for deigning to take the case, the jury took only twelve minutes to convict. The judge sentenced Steelink to one to fourteen years in prison, despite the fact that he was suffering from tuberculosis. He arrived at San Quentin in May 1920, where Malley and McHugo, both imprisoned just before Christmas 1919, awaited.[107]

. . .

California prosecutors quickly became very adept at convicting people of criminal syndicalism. Almost always, they took full advantage of the way the crime was defined and charged defendants with being guilty simply because they belonged to the union, an approach that allowed them to obtain convictions mainly by putting the IWW itself on trial. No one better understood this strategy and its implications than Raymond "R. W." Henderson, a blind lawyer with socialist politics who represented a number of Wobblies. A graduate of the Berkeley School for the Blind and the University of California law school, Henderson published a scholarly study of California's criminal syndicalism law in action, which observed that convicting people based on membership alone constituted a "constructive" form of conspiracy liability. It was in this way even more favorable to prosecutors than conventional conspiracy doctrine, which, as evidenced in the federal prosecutions, required at least a tacit agreement to commit a criminal act, as well as an overt act in furtherance of the conspiracy.[108]

All of the Wobblies' lawyers knew this about criminal syndicalism. Time and again, they tried to convince both trial and appellate courts that juries should be required to find that defendants had themselves endorsed the criminality attributed to the union or that, in line with a basic precept of criminal law, they had knowledge of the union's "unlawful character."[109] But the courts routinely demurred, citing the language of the statutes on the first point and on the second simply stating that jurors could infer such knowledge from the defendant's membership in the union.[110] Some courts permitted prosecutors to use conspiracy doctrine to expand criminal syndicalism culpability even further by allowing them to argue that merely to agree with another to promote membership in the IWW was itself a felony.[111]

Given that most of their clients were not inclined to deny membership in the union and would seldom be believed if they did, defense attorneys had few options besides challenging the premise that the union indeed advocated using violent or criminal means to bring about social change, or, in a similar way, contesting the way such means were legally defined in the first place.[112] In some instances, these strategies bore fruit, resulting in acquittals.[113] In one notable case, defendant William Moudy, a delegate arrested in Seattle in 1920 with a "brown grip" full of IWW propaganda, took the stand in his own defense and boldly admitted his work for the organization and unapologetically defended its aims and social vision.[114] The jury deliberated eleven hours before acquitting him.[115] Sometimes, these arguments led to hung juries. But this outcome did not usually count for much, as defendants were frequently retried, sometimes multiple times.[116] Indeed, most were destined to be found guilty whatever the circumstances, given that charges of sabotage and the like offered to prosecutors, judges, and jurors reason to do with these men what many were eager to do anyway.

. . .

For whatever they were worth in such straitened circumstances, good lawyers were in short supply, as Wobbly John Pico discovered early in 1920. Pico was forced to accept representation from a new, court-appointed lawyer the very morning his criminal syndicalism trial began in Clallam County, Washington, because his chosen lawyers, Vanderveer, Ralph Pierce, and J.F. Emigh, were tied up in other cases. "Incensed" and with a "belligerent attitude that further handicapped his counsel and prejudiced the jury," Pico was convicted and sentenced

FIGURE 18. George Vanderveer, location and date unknown, but probably in Montesano, Washington, during the 1920 trial of the Centralia defendants. Walter P. Reuther Library, Archives of Labor and Urban Affairs, Wayne State University.

to one to ten years in prison.[117] But the lawyers were hardly dithering. Emigh, a legionnaire himself who would soon serve as deputy county attorney in Butte, was handling a case in Ellensburg, Washington, which ended with six of seven defendants convicted of criminal syndicalism. Vanderveer was in Montesano, handling the Centralia murder case, which he began underprepared because of work on other IWW cases.

And Pierce, who was Vanderveer's partner and assisted him in Montesano, had been pulled away by yet another case in Tacoma, the one in which thirty-six Wobblies were convicted of criminal syndicalism. In fact, when the verdict came in that case, Pierce was already on his way back to Montesano.[118]

More lawyers might have been willing to take these cases had doing so not been so costly. Mary Gallagher Douglas was a leftist who was very active in IWW defense work, both nationally and in California, where she served on the general defense committee and courted prosecution herself for testifying on behalf of criminal syndicalism defendants. She recalled that most lawyers she knew who were engaged in the work never expected any payment, and none who were paid received much.[119] Those who arranged for pay sometimes found the fees inadequate or slow to arrive. Vanderveer charged the IWW $10,000 to handle the Chicago conspiracy case but found himself without the necessary funds to avoid foreclosure on his home, partly because the union had trouble paying the fee.[120] There were also the fees that lawyers forfeited because they were occupied with these cases or because everyday clients declined to hire them if they represented Wobblies. Harry McKee, who tried to warn the Sacramento conspiracy defendants about John Dymond, told Roger Baldwin that "even socialists who were my warm personal friends came to me and told me they were afraid to bring me their business lest the prejudice of the judges might result in my losing their cases." For this reason he said he was closing his practice.[121]

And these lawyers faced more than financial strain. Besides being deported from Bisbee and being threatened in that town, William Cleary received death threats and demands that he nevermore represent such defendants while trying a criminal syndicalism case in California in 1920.[122] Elmer Smith defied hostile police and a mob when he represented Wobbly defendants in Eureka, California, in 1922.[123] Just over a year later, Smith was arrested for contempt of court while trying to defend a Wobbly in the Centralia police court and later sentenced to three and a half days in jail. A month after that, while organizing union protests to secure the release of IWW prisoners, he was arrested for public speaking in Centralia, convicted of misdemeanor criminal syndicalism, and sentenced to ten days in jail.[124] Vanderveer was pulled from the dais and arrested in Astoria, Oregon, in 1920 as he tried to read the Declaration of Independence to a group of 2,000 workers gathered for a Fourth of July picnic.[125] And Harold Mulks, a capable and devoted lawyer who often worked with Clarence Darrow and became a mainstay for

IWW defendants in the early 1920s, was the victim of an especially serious assault. On the night of January 13, 1922, Mulks was in Shreveport, Louisiana, to look into the case of two IWW organizers who had been convicted of vagrancy and sentenced to sixty days in jail when two masked men abducted him from the lobby of his hotel and delivered him to a mob. Mulks was flogged and then put on a train headed to Texas, where he was hospitalized.[126]

. . .

For the defendants in the conspiracy case that federal officials put together in Kansas, obtaining legal counsel was less of a problem than making it to trial. In jail since late 1917 and first indicted in March 1918, these men were reindicted in September to take better account of the successful prosecution of the Chicago conspiracy defendants, and then again in June 1919 after an aborted trial that March and the quashing of the second indictment on the grounds of incoherence. The final indictment charged the defendants with violating the Espionage Act by conspiring to impede military recruitment and the draft, with conspiracy to violate the Lever Food and Fuel Control Act of 1917 by interfering with the production and transportation of wheat and oil, and with conspiracy to hinder the execution of the laws of the United States.[127]

The defendants had reason to hope that the long delays in the case might end with their release, as this was the fate of fellow Wobblies who faced a similar prosecution in Omaha. On September 5, 1917, the day they launched nationwide raids against the IWW, federal agents forced their way into headquarters of the IWW's Construction Workers Industrial Union (CWIU) in that city. Although they seized all the union's records, they made no arrests. But on November 12, amid worries that the IWW was preparing to meet the "iron heel" with "Russian methods," Department of Justice men, Secret Service agents, local police, and private detectives launched another raid.[128] This one occurred during a convention of the Agricultural Workers Industrial Union (AWIU), hosted by the CWIU, which had been called to try to stabilize the IWW's affairs amid all the raids and arrests. It ended with the seizure of the conventioneers' "entire outfit" and the arrest of sixty-four members present in the hall.[129]

The defendants were thrown in the Douglas County jail where, according to the sheriff, they "fared mighty well," receiving plenty of aid from the union while engaging in "seditious talk."[130] Part of their fare was to be interrogated by federal agents, who asked each of them twenty or more questions, including whether they had read the *Little*

Red Songbook, whether they believed in sabotage, and, with deportation in mind, where they were born.[131] The men remained locked up for months while U.S. Attorney Thomas Allen, whose marriage to William Jennings Bryan's sister might speak to a measure of populist sympathy, communicated his doubts about the case to Attorney General Gregory. The government had "very little against these defendants," who were mostly rank-and-file harvest hands, construction workers, and teamsters. "They were attempting to hold a convention in an orderly way when arrested," Allen noted, "and the only evidence we have is certain books, pamphlets, and letters that were seized at the time of the raid."[132]

In June 1918, with about fifty of these Omaha defendants not yet indicted but still in jail, Allen proposed that they plead guilty to some kind of charge and be sentenced to time served. The Wobblies refused and remained in jail for a year and a half before being freed on bail.[133] Finally, in April 1919, Allen proposed to his superiors that the men be absolved, adding that such a move might lend more credibility to the government's overall campaign against the IWW. After all, wrote Allen, there were not "any vicious men among them."[134] Attorney General A. Mitchell Palmer, who had just taken office, agreed, and the case was dismissed.

There would be no such relief for the Kansas defendants, though. During the two years that they were in jail, union lawyers pushed repeatedly for a dismissal. Palmer had misgivings about this case as well, but U.S. Attorney Fred Robertson persisted, citing IWW activism during the 1919 harvest season. For months, Robertson kept the defendants locked up in jails in and around Wichita, where they made do with unhealthy food and wet, filthy, rat-infested lodgings that were, by turns, freezing cold and broiling hot. But in September, Judge John Pollock yielded to outrage that the defendants' lawyers and the National Civil Liberties Bureau had generated about these conditions and agreed to move the prisoners and the trial itself to Kansas City, Kansas. They were better treated there. But before trial finally opened on December 1, 1919, one defendant had died, others had been stricken with tuberculosis, scarlet fever, typhoid, and influenza, and two were insane.[135]

Unlike in the Chicago conspiracy case, none of these defendants was very prominent, although there were committed organizers among them. Wencil Francik had joined the IWW in Seattle back in 1909 and from then until his arrest "did nothing" but work for the union. F. J. Gallagher, whom federal officials later adjudged "a particularly bad actor" for his "brazen . . . denunciation of the so-called master class," had been "one of the first I.W.W. organizers to appear in the oil fields" in 1917 and "wrote considerable" for the union's newspapers. Michael Sapper was a job delegate and quite active in the oil fields.[136] The most important defendant was C. W. Anderson, who had briefly served as secretary of the AWIU. But most of the defendants were rank-and-file workers who had joined the union between 1915 and the time of their arrest and were caught up in the flurry of anti-IWW persecution in the fall of 1917.[137]

Robertson built his case around proving that the IWW was itself a seditious and criminal organization, so that he might then contend, like so many other prosecutors, that merely belonging to the union was tantamount to guilt. In order to accomplish this, Robertson and his special assistant, "Colonel" Sam Amidon—a close friend of Woodrow Wilson and vice chairman of the Democratic National Committee—gathered together the usual collection of books, pamphlets, letters, and songs, from which they extracted for the jury passages that underscored the union's opposition to the war and seemed to confirm its affinity for sabotage. They made much of the union's success in plastering the state with hundreds of thousands of "stickerettes" bearing IWW slogans. They also used an assortment of snitches and professional witnesses.[138] The most important of these was Frank Wermke, a National Guard deserter and common criminal who joined the IWW under the alias of Frank Wood and became an organizer. Wermke, who had given similar testimony during the Chicago trial, claimed to have spiked logs, burned haystacks, and broken harvest machinery. From the witness stand, he improbably claimed that while heading a "flying squadron" of IWW toughs he had forced men into the union at gunpoint "hundreds" of times.[139]

The defendants agreed to accept legal representation after considering and rejecting the "silent" defense adopted in Sacramento. The man in whose hands they put their fate, Fred Moore, was a Michigan native who wore a cowboy hat and boots, and, like George Vanderveer, was seldom unarmed. He was also a notorious philanderer and rumored to have a cocaine habit. But by the time Moore took on this case, he had considerable experience. He had represented Wobblies in free-speech fights, successfully defended Joe Ettor and Arturo Giovannitti in Lawrence, and played a part in the Thomas Tracy trial after the Everett massacre and in the Chicago conspiracy trial.

Moore was joined by Caroline Lowe. Like Moore, Lowe struggled to reconcile the demands of the case with her many obligations to other IWW defendants. The two did their best to undermine the government's witnesses but otherwise put up no defense. After closing arguments,

Judge Pollock, who helped Robertson to draft the indictments, instructed jurors that if they found the IWW was a "disloyal" organization that had worked to impede the war effort, and that the defendants were committed to the union and its purposes, they should convict.[140] And so they did. A panel composed of nine farmers and three professional men deliberated for twenty hours, perhaps because they "wanted to be sure," perhaps because they were confused, before convicting all of the twenty-eight defendants on trial.[141] That same day the verdict was delivered, December 18, 1919, Pollock sentenced the defendants to prison, except for one man who was on the run and would receive his sentence upon his capture a month later. Their terms ranged from one to nine years and they were, except for the fugitive, dispatched to Leavenworth the next day, joking and singing IWW songs.[142] "Nine years are not long," said C. W. Anderson, "when the cause is considered."[143]

Caroline Lowe understood the cause and determined that these defendants had been prosecuted at the behest of the region's oil interests, including Carter Oil Company, Sinclair Oil Company, and Gypsy Oil Company.[144] The same interests, as everyone knew, were behind the enactment of a criminal syndicalism law in Kansas. This project was spearheaded by Robertson and Amidon, who worked alongside the American Legion and something called the "One Hundred Percent American Club," an organization whose ranks included Governor Henry Allen, Attorney General Richard Hopkins, and other prominent state officials. A statute very similar to Oregon's was enacted in January 1920, the legislature having rejected several more extreme or ridiculous bills, including one whose definition of "criminal syndicalism" included "free love" among the prohibited means of industrial or political change.[145]

It would be a while yet before anyone was prosecuted under the new law. But there were other cases for Lowe and Moore to attend to, including one that followed the bombing of the J. Edgar Pew home in Tulsa back in October 1917. Police and federal agents had attempted to pin the bombing on two Wobblies, Harry Lyons and Harry Casey. But with no evidence to link either to the crime, they fixed their sights on Charles Krieger, a machinist by trade who had mined copper in Arizona and served as an IWW job delegate and then moved to Oklahoma and worked at a boiler and iron works. Krieger was on a job ninety-four miles away when the bomb went off, and the only thing at all fitting to his being charged was his IWW membership. Nevertheless, the state accused him of conspiring to bomb the Pew house and locked him up for two years while it decided how to proceed.[146]

Unlike her cocounsel Moore, who would soon garner both fame and reproach for his representation of Sacco and Vanzetti, Lowe was of unimpeachable character and never as well-known as she should have been. Lowe was a former schoolteacher, an IWW supporter, and a Socialist who had lectured on behalf of the party. She had studied law at a Socialist college in Kansas and passed the bar in time to assist Moore and Vanderveer in both the Tracy trial and the Chicago conspiracy case. Competent, reliable, and dedicated, Lowe donated untold hours of pro bono representation in IWW cases as well as sizeable sums of money to defense efforts; she raised funds for the union and attended to the needs of Wobbly defendants with great compassion and decency.[147]

Krieger's trial ended on November 10, 1919 in a hung jury. Moore and Lowe did challenge the government's case, but the mistrial was the work of a single juror who bore a grudge against Carter Oil, which had posted a $10,000 reward for Krieger's conviction. Prosecutors determined to retry Krieger. While he waited he got a new lawyer, because Moore had missed the key filing deadline concerning the appeal in the Kansas conspiracy case. Frustrated by this act of malpractice, the union's Chicago office allowed Moore to remain for Krieger's second trial, which began in May 1920, in deference to Krieger's wishes, but they added Harold Mulks to the defense. This time, the defense was more successful in exposing the state's case as a crude frame-up based on the perjured testimony of police, Burns detectives, and an IWW prisoner coerced into testifying with the threat of federal charges. On June 8, jurors repaid their efforts by finally acquitting Krieger.[148]

. . .

Even before Krieger's first case went to trial, powerful political and business interests in Oklahoma were certain that membership in the IWW should be directly criminalized by means of a criminal syndicalism statute. Overseeing this effort was the state's Progressive governor, J. B. A. Robertson. A former prosecutor and a named partner in a law firm closely connected to the oil industry, Robertson had made clear his intention to extend wartime repression into the postwar years and had even testified in the Kansas conspiracy case. At his urging, the legislature enacted a criminal syndicalism statute in March 1919, with only four negative votes. Among these was one cast by a representative from Oklahoma City who refused to dishonor the memory of an ancestor who had signed the Declaration of Independence.[149]

The first person prosecuted under the law was Jack Terrell, one of four AWIU job delegates arrested in Enid in June 1919, three months after the law became effective. The state's case against Terrell drew heavily on the introduction of IWW documents found in his possession and seized without a warrant. Terrell, who had a fifth-grade education, had been elected to the general organizing committee of the AWIU. He amazed courtroom spectators with his intelligent and articulate testimony. But despite this and able representation by Fred Moore, the jury convicted in only thirty minutes. Sentenced to seven years, Terrell was allowed to go free while his appeal was pending. When his case finally came before the Oklahoma Criminal Court of Appeals, he was in prison in California, convicted in the summer of 1923 of criminal syndicalism in that state.[150]

CHAPTER 5

Dealing the Death Blow

Repression and the IWW after the Red Scare

When the Red Scare faded in late spring of 1920, A.S. Embree was among only a handful of prominent Wobblies not yet in prison or out on bail while under a sentence. But prison is where he was headed. Arrested in Burke, Idaho, in late May by the sheriff, who recognized him as a witness at the trial of Felix Jovanovich, the young Wobbly who died after trying to kill himself, Embree soon faced criminal syndicalism charges in that state. An immigrant from Newfoundland and a member of the Western Federation of Miners when the IWW was founded, Embree was not one to be deterred from his work. A leader among the 1,200 deported from Bisbee, Arizona, in July 1917, he had been tried and acquitted there of inciting a riot after defying Sheriff Harry Wheeler by returning some weeks later and then was jailed for several months and threatened with death after he returned once again. When he was charged in Idaho, Embree's family lived in Butte, Montana, where he was busy organizing.[1]

On April 19, 1920, organizers led by Embree called a strike at the mines around Butte. Two days into the strike, with most of the mines closed, company guards confronted several hundred picketers who were blocking the road to Anaconda's Neversweat Mine. While the sheriff and Embree were trying to arrange a compromise that would calm the situation, the guards opened fire, shooting sixteen picketers in the back and mortally wounding Wobbly Thomas Manning. Although the shooting apparently began without provocation and on orders from a company official, and ended with the guards clubbing injured union men, an inquest did not assign fault for the "Anaconda Road Massacre," let alone blame the companies.[2]

Federal troops had remained in Montana long after they were removed from most other parts of the West and were set to work breaking up picket lines after the killing. With the help of William Dunne and other sympathizers, Embree and fellow union leaders responded by organizing general strikes and other protests in cities across the state. But these were met with mass arrests, and the strike in Butte steadily collapsed. It had been launched to revitalize the IWW in Butte, but once it was broken, Anaconda decreed that the company would no longer employ anyone connected to the IWW in its Montana mines and reopened them on a nonunion basis.[3]

These events effectively brought an end to years of significant IWW activism, not only in Butte but throughout Montana, where the union's decline showed the toll that sustained repression had taken. It was largely because of repression that neither had the union ever really gathered much momentum in the oil fields of Kansas and Oklahoma nor, for that matter, after the strikes in 1916 and 1917, accomplished much in the lumber and iron-mining areas of northern Minnesota. It is also a principal reason the union gave ground elsewhere in mining, including in Arizona. Throughout much of the West, though, the IWW remained viable beyond the Red Scare. This was true on the waterfronts and in construction and even more in agriculture and lumber, where the organization was probably again adding members. But precisely because the union remained active, the campaign to destroy it also extended into the new decade. Sometimes this involved naked violence and mass arrests, as in Butte. In other instances, it entailed legal repression of the sort that had, by this time, come fully into its own.

How effective this system of persecution had become is evident in the experience of organizer Jack Gaveel. Convicted of criminal syndicalism May 19, 1921, by a Los Angeles jury that heard a week of testimony but took only twenty minutes to reach its verdict, Gaveel had been a member of the IWW since 1913. He had escaped a criminal syndicalism charge in Leavenworth, Kansas, in the summer of 1920 and, like Embree, had become prominent in a union whose leadership had been decimated by prosecutions. But prison is where Gaveel was heading, too. A few days after his conviction, he was sentenced to the statutory term of one to fourteen years and went on to serve three years at San Quentin before being deported, "while very ill," to his native Holland.[4] During sentencing, Gaveel angrily rebuked Judge Frank Willis: "The jails will be full of

I.W.W.'s before you get through." "Yes, they will," said the judge, as long as Wobblies violated the criminal syndicalism law.[5] And so they were, as long as the union remained a viable organization.

. . .

It is not clear how Gaveel avoided being imprisoned on criminal syndicalism charges in Kansas. But two weeks after he was arrested there, fellow Wobbly Harry Breen was taken into custody, in this case three hundred miles to the west in WaKeeney. Also an organizer or delegate, Breen got himself charged after admitting his IWW membership to an undercover volunteer policeman and being found in possession of the IWW songbook, with its image of "noted murderer" Joe Hill "on the first page." Breen had been with the IWW for four years, had wandered "over nearly the whole of the country," and had recently worked the harvest and in construction before ending up in Kansas State Penitentiary.[6]

The state's evidence against Breen at trial that September featured an extensive collection of organizing material, union propaganda and business documents, and legal correspondence related to other cases. This was quite enough to convict him of criminal syndicalism. Found guilty of violating the statute on three counts, Breen was sentenced to three to thirty years. When asked at intake to identify the "main cause of your downfall," a question that usually elicited something at least implicitly apologetic about an inmate's family life or personal failings, Breen answered with defiance: "I.W.W."[7]

Breen was not the only Wobbly arrested in Trego County, Kansas. The same day he was arrested, so were Robert Dilgar, the well-named Thomas Paine, and William Murphy, all picked up in Collyer. The men were jailed in lieu of bail and their cases were continued until the court's December term. This was too much for Dilgar and Paine. On a warm and moonless night in mid-October, the two nearly escaped by using knives and window weights to pry and knock stones out of the jailhouse wall. When brought to trial, they were acquitted of criminal syndicalism but convicted of "aiding and abetting" each other's attempt at escape and, two days before Christmas, sentenced to one to two years in prison.[8] On appeal, lawyer Harold Mulks tried to justify their gambit on the grounds that each had reason to consider the other's confinement unlawful, but the Kansas Supreme Court rejected this argument, and Dilgar and Paine remained locked up.[9]

Their codefendant Murphy had been arrested for vagrancy in Anaconda, Montana, back in 1914 for supposedly leading a group of Wobblies who had "taken possession" of a boiler room. On that occasion he told a policeman, "We are the kind of boys who would rather do a long term in a real prison for something worth while [sic] than to be picked up because we haven't got a job."[10] Four years later and a thousand miles away, facing trial on a criminal syndicalism charge in WaKeeney and looking at a long term in a real prison, Murphy remained defiant. At a preliminary hearing he "stated he was proud that he was an I.W.W." During his trial, Murphy "stood mute" and even refused the assistance of the lawyers the union provided him.[11]

Convicted and sentenced to one to ten years, Murphy arrived at the state prison on Christmas Eve. He declined to give any information about himself, even after he was transferred to the "insane ward." Over a year after his initial imprisonment, prison authorities noted that Murphy still "refused absolutely to answer any questions and said if there were any consequences, he guessed he could take them."[12] Apparently he could. After his release three years later, Murphy was arrested on vagrancy charges in Jamestown, North Dakota, still an IWW. Sentenced to thirty days in jail and a twenty-five-dollar fine, he was threatened with deportation to his native Ireland.[13]

These men were among a handful of Kansas defendants to actually go to prison for criminal syndicalism. But they were not the only ones to face the prospect. Arrests on this charge continued through the summer and into the fall of 1920, in concert with continued organizing efforts in the harvest. On July 4, teenager Robert Barker was arrested at the stockyards in Wichita when police found he was an IWW; he was then charged with criminal syndicalism. That charge was dropped, days before the city adopted its own criminal syndicalism ordinance.[14] Barker instead faced a vagrancy prosecution, but he was released on a writ of habeas corpus by a judge who observed how "this is pretty good government" that protects the rights even of IWWs.[15] A week later, Barker filed a civil suit seeking damages for the severe beating that representatives of this good government inflicted on him when they first took him into custody.[16]

Officials in Kansas had anticipated an "invasion" of one hundred organizers, who would work their way up from Oklahoma during the 1920 harvest. "We will be prepared," said the governor, while the state fire marshal assured that when "one of these men appears you may bet he will be arrested." [17] So many Wobblies were jailed for vagrancy and so debilitating was this for the union that it advised members to stop pleading guilty, in hopes that if they demanded some kind of trial and held out until Caroline Lowe or Harold Mulks could take their case, maybe Kansas authorities would be compelled to ease up.[18]

Despite all of this, authorities were not content to rely on conventional prosecutions to deal with the IWW. In June 1920, Kansas attorney general Richard Hopkins petitioned to have the IWW, the Agricultural Workers Industrial Union (AWIU), the Oil Workers Industrial Union (OWIU), and their officers and members all enjoined from violating the state's criminal syndicalism statute by their mere presence in the state. Hopkins got a judge in Butler County to agree that the order was necessary to interdict twenty-five AWIU organizers who were deploying to the wheat fields from Kansas City and threatening the "public health and lives" of the people of Kansas. The injunction was statewide in scope, published in almost all the state's newspapers, and posted in every county.

Within a month of the injunction being issued, twenty-five IWW "agents" were indeed arrested. After the harvest, newspapers and public officials celebrated the resulting victory over the union. Hopkins declared that the order "greatly assisted the state in curbing the unlawful activities" of the IWW.[19] "The I.W.W. did not have any success operating in Kansas this year," boasted the *Hutchinson Gazette*.[20] In fact, the union did effectively organize some farms, just not enough to have a significant effect on wages and working conditions. The injunction was one reason for this, and Lowe and Mulks sought to have it quashed. Their efforts came to naught, though: the Kansas Supreme Court upheld the order, against the argument that it made criminals of those who were subject to arrest without affording them the procedural rights which are the usual prerequisites of criminal punishment.[21]

Made permanent soon after it was issued, the injunction was still in effect in 1921 when organizer C. L. Johnson was charged with criminal syndicalism in Hutchinson. Johnson was picked up in July while delivering a lecture to harvest workers at a train depot. He dismissed two lawyers provided him by the union—probably Lowe and Mulks—and represented himself at trial. Indeed, Johnson "proved to be quite a lawyer," according to a local newspaper reporter, who called his performance a "strong counter attraction to the Kansas State Fair."[22] After Johnson's cross examination of the prosecution's witnesses, the judge ruled that there was insufficient evidence to convict and ordered him released. Not every organizer fared as well. Arrested in McPherson in the summer of 1921 and charged with criminal syndicalism, John Downs remained in jail until December, when finally he was allowed to plead guilty, pay $450 in fines and court costs, and leave town.[23]

The following year there was more persecution. In June 1922, amid another statewide, harvest-time flurry of vagrancy arrests, five Wobblies were charged with criminal syndicalism in Anthony, in the south-central part of the state.[24] Over two months later, with the harvest over, charges were dropped and the men were released, apparently because the county did not wish to incur the cost of prosecuting them.[25] Not so lucky was Joe Neil, arrested that May in Hutchinson. Brought to trial on October 7, Neil was convicted the same day, not for membership, but for advocating criminal syndicalism "by word of mouth and by writing." When asked if he had anything to say, Neil "broke forth with an oration which was choked off by the court." The jury recommended that he be deported but Judge W. G. Fairfield imposed a sentence of one to ten years and kept him at the county jail pending further inquiry into the possibility of deportation.[26]

In the view of the *Abilene Daily Reflector,* which had no problem with his prosecution, Neil's crime was that he "talked too much," "took too free advantage of America's free speech," "ran down the government," and "admitted being a believer in the principles of Soviet Russia."[27] Neil kept talking in the "bull pen" at the county jail, where, a few days after his conviction, his "incendiary" denunciations of the government that had just condemned him to prison resulted in a "general fight" with other inmates, according to the *Hutchinson News.*[28]

Early the following June, Harold Fiske made himself the last Wobbly that Kansas would try for criminal syndicalism by climbing atop the "high platform" at the Missouri Pacific depot in Geneseo, Kansas, and lecturing "a great many harvest hands" on the principles of industrial unionism. Twenty-six years old and relatively new to the IWW, Fiske had been "doing anything that came along" since leaving the sea two years earlier. "I worked in the harvest fields last summer and in the woods of Washington last winter, and in the harvest fields of Oklahoma this year," he said.[29] As Fiske was preaching that day at the depot, the city marshal walked up, seized him, and took him to jail. When questioned, Fiske confessed to being a Wobbly and admitted recruiting into the AWIU three harvest hands.[30]

The county prosecutor charged Fiske with criminal syndicalism and brought him to trial in nearby Lyons that September. Represented at trial by Kansas lawyer Charles Carroll because Lowe and Mulks were busy with other cases, Fiske took the stand and again admitted to his work with the IWW and the AWIU and his recruitment of the three men, although he said that he had enlisted them a few days earlier, in another county. Fiske defended the IWW while denying that the organization was committed to violence or sabotage. This was intended to counter the prosecution's case, which rested on the introduction in evidence of membership cards and applications, accounting records, bylaws, and other documents pertaining to the AWIU, all of which police had seized from Fiske when he was arrested. Prosecutors also presented the jury with the preamble to the IWW constitution, as well as the lyrics of a song named "Everett's Raid," which Fiske had sung— "purely for pleasure," he said—while in jail. Hearing all this evidence, "twelve good and lawful citizens" took two hours to convict Fiske, and the judge sentenced him to one to ten years in prison.[31]

Fiske remained free while his appeal was pending. In the meantime, most of the Wobblies who had been imprisoned in Kansas were released. William Dilgar and Thomas Paine were discharged in May 1922, after serving legally adequate time under their sentences. Harry Breen was freed in October 1922, after the Kansas Supreme Court grudgingly ruled that the bill of information under which he had been charged was too sloppily composed. With a statute that "stops just short of trespassing on constitutional guarantees, it is not safe to take liberties with phraseology," said that court.[32] William Murphy got out in April 1923, after the court ruled that the decision in Breen's case controlled his. However, Joe Neil remained in prison, partly because, with so many other cases pending, no one had remembered to appeal his conviction.

The union did appeal the vagrancy conviction of John Clancy, and with good reason. Clancy had been arrested in the summer of 1922 in McPherson County, convicted by the justice of the peace of violating a statewide vagrancy law that made it a crime to lack a "lawful calling," to "refuse to work when work at fair wages is to be procured in the community," or to "threaten violence or personal injury to fellow workmen or to employers of labor." Clancy was an organizer and therefore obviously guilty. Indeed, according to the justice of the peace, who sentenced Clancy to thirty days and a one-hundred-dollar fine, merely to be associated with the IWW constituted criminal syndicalism, and criminal syndicalism was itself a form of vagrancy.[33]

The vagrancy statute was a statewide law enacted in 1917 for the express purpose of criminalizing the IWW, alongside a provision requiring police to enforce it. The union therefore took Clancy's appeal seriously and engaged Mulks to handle it. His brief to the Kansas Supreme Court highlighted the statute's broad and constitutionally suspect definition of vagrancy. But the court rejected his arguments, declaring in its 1922 opinion that because Clancy's calling was unlawful, he could make no complaint. It thereby dealt what the state's newspapers hopefully called a "death blow" to the union and, in so doing, endorsed the reasoning used by courts everywhere, even under conventional statutes, to justify equating union membership or activism with vagrancy.[34]

. . .

In Oklahoma, as in Kansas, the persecution of Wobblies continued through 1921 and 1922, accompanied by accusations that they were still practicing destructive sabotage and wantonly assaulting and even killing nonunion men. There were surely a few acts of sabotage, and clashes between Wobblies and "scissorbills" persisted. But charges of destruction were, as always, overblown, and union people seemed at least as likely to be the victims of assaults as they were to be perpetrators or to have killed nonunion men. This last point is underscored by events on June 16, 1922, when a forty-year-old Wobbly named Paul Bernarceck was shot and killed just outside of Cherokee, Oklahoma, in a clash between IWWs and nonunion men working the harvest. The incident led to the arrest of the alleged shooter and, predictably, a "clean up" of Wobblies in the area.[35]

A few months after this affair, on December 27, Arthur Berg was arrested by railroad police in Haileyville, Oklahoma, while waiting to hop a freight train in the yard of the Rock Island railroad. A worker in construction and in the wheat and oil fields, Berg had recently served as a delegate in the OWIU. One of the four railroad police who seized him said, "We ought to shoot you." Instead, they searched Berg, found IWW materials, and handed him over to a deputy sheriff, who took him to jail and booked him on a vagrancy charge. With no viable way of fighting the charge, Berg pleaded guilty and was sentenced to thirty days.[36]

On January 17, while Berg was still in jail, county prosecutor O. H. Whitt charged him with criminal syndicalism and had him held for trial in McAlester, where Berg remained, unable to make bail. However, the union did manage to secure him a lawyer; it engaged the services of John Carney, a former judge whose conversion to socialism almost a decade earlier coincided with the state's emergence as a party stronghold. Like many Oklahoma Socialists, Carney sympathized with the IWW, and he represented radicals there and in Kansas, Louisiana, and Texas. In fact, Carney had represented Joe Neil in Kansas and knew that Oklahoma prosecutors would, one way or another, premise Berg's guilt on IWW membership. So he tried unsuccessfully to disqualify potential jurors who were inclined to believe this premise.[37]

When Berg's trial got underway in February, it revealed how much a half decade of organized, legal persecution had normalized the equation of IWW membership with criminality and reconciled this equation with principles of trial procedure and legal process. Carney argued that at the time of Berg's arrest, his membership had lapsed, that he was no longer an organizer, and that he had the union materials with him in order to return them to OWIU headquarters in Oklahoma City. But these claims went nowhere. Whitt managed during the trial to repeatedly highlight Berg's German ancestry, even though Berg's family had been in the country for many decades. He lined up witnesses, including one of the railroad's men and "some of the boys" at a café where the sheriff had taken Berg, who testified that Berg had admitted being a member and an organizer and had shown them IWW propaganda. And he produced documents found on Berg's person that attested to his work for the union.[38]

During cross examination by Whitt, Berg confirmed his membership in the IWW but adroitly deflected questions designed to elicit some kind of confirmation of the union's seditious character. When asked if he would "rather that your lodge or organization, or whatever you call it, run the Government of the United States," Berg responded, "We, we ain't pertaining to the Government. We are pertaining to the industry only." When asked "What do you mean by stating in your membership book here, 'Instead of the conservative motto, "A fair day's wages for a fair day's work," we must inscribe on our banner the revolutionary watchword, "Abolition of the wage system,"'?" Berg responded, "Abolition of the wage system."[39]

By admitting membership, Berg helped make Whitt's case, which was further bolstered with improbable charges that the IWW had sabotaged a train in the area and was responsible for the destruction of government vehicles at a West Virginia munitions plant where Berg was briefly employed. Indeed, it would have been a minor miracle had Berg been acquitted. Guided by a written instruction from Judge A. C. Brewster that incorporated verbatim the text of the preamble to the IWW's constitution into its definition of criminal syndicalism, the jury convicted Berg of one of two counts.[40] After declaring that Berg bore the "brand of Cain" and expressing his hope that no governor would ever pardon him, Brewster sentenced Berg to ten years in prison and a fine of $5,000. "I cannot say too much for the jurors that have just found you guilty," said Brewster. "They are Americans."[41]

The fate of Wobbly Homer Wear was similar, and similarly revealing. A forty-seven-year-old cook who tried to organize miners in the lead and zinc mining region of northeast Oklahoma and adjoining parts of Kansas and Missouri, Wear was arrested in Quapaw, Oklahoma, on vagrancy charges, apparently while conducting a nighttime meeting among workers there in mid-June 1923. He was still in jail on this charge when, on August 7, he was also charged with criminal syndicalism. Held incommunicado for thirty days, Wear was brought to trial in September. The main evidence against him, besides his membership and recruitment materials, was an inflammatory handbill, likely forged, which called on the miners to kill the mine owners and which Wear was said to have distributed. After a two-day trial, Wear was convicted in less than an hour and sentenced to six years in prison and a $750 fine, despite what one of the local papers called a "strong defense" from "Judge Carney" that appealed to Wear's constitutional rights to organize for the union.[42] Wear remained in prison, along with Berg, until early 1925, when both were freed by the Criminal Court of Appeals on the basis of procedural and evidentiary errors in their cases. Neither was ever retried, apparently because Oklahoma authorities' appetite for prosecution had faded along with the fortunes of the organization that so many of them had committed to destroying.

. . .

On the northern end of the wheat belt, Wobblies who persisted in organizing the "laboring men against accepting the going wage" and distributing literature to "poison the mind of the laboring man," as one of the newspapers in Minot, North Dakota, put it, continued to face arrest in the 1920 harvest season and through the following season as well.[43] Indeed, on occasion, these arrests were for serious charges, especially in South Dakota. For example, on July 14, 1921, authorities in Aberdeen arrested Wobbly Harry "Nuf Sed" Casey—the same man on whom authorities in Tulsa had tried to pin the bombing of the J. Edgar Pew home several years earlier—while he was giving a speech and charged him with criminal syndicalism. The next day, two hundred workers gathered around the jail. Police responded by assembling a large, armed posse and rounding up and deporting a hundred of Casey's supporters to the countryside, with orders not to return. When, back in Aberdeen, IWW Olaf Ellie boldly predicted that Aberdonians would somehow suffer for what they had done, he too was charged with criminal syndicalism.[44]

Nearly three months later, just as trial seemed imminent, the state dismissed charges against Casey, who had remained in jail. Contented, it seems, with having served notice to the Wobblies that they were unwelcome, prosecutors did not try Ellie either.[45] A similar outcome eventually obtained following the July 1921 arrests of George Korski and William Bosinger. The two were charged with criminal syndicalism in Sioux Falls after police found them by the Big Sioux River sermonizing about industrial unionism to a gathering of two dozen men. What the police heard, they said, were speeches promoting the overthrow of the government and the burning of crops.[46] The union sent Harold Mulks to take the case. After two juries in two trials held days apart failed to agree on Bosinger's guilt, prosecutors dismissed charges.[47]

The usual charge for poisoning the mind of the laboring man was vagrancy. And usually this was a prelude to a more common practice, which was simply to run these men out of town. That is how Fargo police dealt with a hundred Wobblies roaming the town and distributing literature in July 1921.[48] Likewise, in Langdon, in late August and early September 1921, Wobblies who attempted to force the release of a fellow worker who had been arrested for fighting with a legionnaire by descending on the town in the hundreds were met by a large armed posse that "deported" most of the men and arrested three of the group's leaders on vagrancy and other charges.[49] That season, police and vigilantes in Fairmont also intercepted a trainload of Wobblies whom they suspected of having ejected nonunion men. They asked the Wobblies what wage they sought and, when it proved too high, ordered them to move on.[50] Also in August, Devils Lake police ran off two hundred IWWs holding out for better wages.[51] Usually this kind of thing occurred without a great deal of fuss. But events sometimes took a more serious turn in North Dakota, as elsewhere. In September, an attempt by Fargo police to deny Wobblies the right to speak on the streets resulted in a confrontation in which the chief of police was "overpowered" by a large crowd of union men and relieved of his sidearm. When order was restored by a large posse of armed citizens, one Wobbly had been beaten up and two were under arrest on minor charges.[52]

There were more episodes like these during the 1922 harvest season, by which time the political situation in North Dakota had changed, to the union's detriment. In October 1921, the state's business and professional interests, organized behind something called the Independent Voters Association, used a recall to drive the Nonpartisan League's Lynn Frazier from the governor's office and replace him with a Republican, Ragnvald Nestos. A lawyer and sometime Progressive who had worked in the Minnesota lumber camps as a young man, Nestos was definitely no friend of the IWW. During the 1922 harvest he issued a proclamation in which he inveighed against the "social parasites who infest street corners, railroad yards and the jungles in our cities." Nestos had "no sympathy" for those who refused the "splendid wages" on offer from the state's farmers and threshermen or who organized others to do so; he urged the state's "sheriffs, constables and police officials" to "rigidly enforce" the vagrancy laws against this element.[53] And they did, and did again the following harvest season, when the arrest of Wobblies, especially if they were suspected of organizing or holding out, remained an everyday thing.[54]

. . .

In Idaho, wartime and Red Scare repression had left the IWW battered and much diminished. In the lumber camps that had been the union's stronghold, its remaining supporters had often been driven underground. And when they did surface, they were liable to be thrown into prison. This was the fate of organizer Reynard Quackenbush, for instance, who was arrested in Boise on January 21, 1921, by an agent of the state constabulary and charged with criminal syndicalism. Back in 1918, "Quack" had spent more than five months in jail in Montana, charged with sedition. He did not go to trial on that charge, and his first trial for criminal syndicalism in Idaho ended in a hung jury. But he faced a jury again in June 1921, was convicted, and got six months to one year in prison.[55]

Quakenbush's criminal syndicalism conviction was one of several in 1921. That spring, Gust Sandee and Gust Haraldson were convicted in Boise County and sentenced to nine months to ten years in prison. Patrick Murphy was convicted in Shoshone County and sentenced to six months to one year. And E. B. Waddell was convicted in Ada County and sentenced to one to ten years. However, other defendants imprisoned earlier, including John Otis Ellis, were also pardoned or paroled around this time.[56] After several unsuccessful petitions, Quackenbush himself was freed in January 1922 but returned to prison a year later, in ill health, after an agent reported that he had violated the terms of his release by remaining active in the IWW.[57]

One of Quackenbush's fellow inmates was A. S. Embree, whose criminal syndicalism case went to trial in the late spring of 1921. Shoshone County prosecutor J. H. McEvers described Embree's activism as proof of his "criminal nature" and declared him among "the most notorious" and "capable of the Criminal Syndicalism advocates in the United States."[58] Embree was "second in importance to none other perhaps than Wm. D. Haywood," he told the jury.[59] Indeed, following the big federal raids of 1917, Embree served for a time as secretary-treasurer of the union and later secretary of the general defense committee. Indicted in Washington in 1918 but never brought to trial, Embree was probably the most important member of the union to remain in the organization and yet escape prosecution on federal conspiracy charges.[60] He would likewise be the most important official to be convicted of criminal syndicalism.

Embree's trial followed the well-established pattern in these cases and showed how futile even the best defenses usually were. The state's case against him rested on the testimony of an IWW turncoat who had to consult repeatedly with the prosecutor between appearances on the stand in order to keep his story straight; another who testified in numerous criminal syndicalism trials in Idaho; a former sheriff who claimed an expertise on IWW methods, developed by his "searching" of camps in northern Idaho; a deputy sheriff whose testimony about IWWs' supposed penchant for sabotage drew on his previous job as foreman at a flour mill and his discovery of IWW books and pamphlets in various lumber camps; and a federal agent who had infiltrated IWW operations in Butte.[61]

Bolstered by the usual quotient of radical texts and union documents, this testimony did little more than confirm that the IWW and Embree were active in Idaho. To the extent that the prosecution's case suggested that either the union or Embree was committed to anything violent or criminal in nature, it was refuted by defense witnesses. Among these was Wobbly Joe Doyle, convicted of criminal syndicalism in Shoshone County a year earlier, who attested to the union's commitment to lawful practices. Another was lawyer J. F. Emigh, now a deputy county attorney in Butte, who explained the IWW's and Embree's peaceful methods and goals. And then there was Embree himself, who took the stand and gave jurors an articulate and compelling account of the IWW's aims and methods and his own doings. Nevertheless, after a week of trial, the jury convicted Embree, who was immediately sentenced to one to ten years.[62]

Embree was, along with Doyle and Quackenbush, among five Wobblies imprisoned on criminal syndicalism charges in Idaho in 1921. Although there were quite a few arrests, no Wobblies were convicted in 1922 and only one was convicted the following year. When Edwin Krier, found guilty of criminal syndicalism in St. Maries in December 1923,

FIGURE 19. A.S. Embree at the Idaho State Penitentiary, June 1921. Old Idaho Penitentiary Collection, Idaho State Archives.

arrived at the Idaho State Penitentiary, he was the last union man to suffer this fate.[63] At that point, Embree and Quackenbush were still in custody. So was Harris Herd, described in his prison record as a Mexican "cowpuncher" and a trained nurse, who had served three years for criminal syndicalism without applying for release.[64] But all these men were set free over the next year or so. When paroled, Embree avowed that, "were it not for my wife and children," whose dire situation had been humiliatingly described a few years earlier in the newspapers in Butte, "the prospect of another three years in prison would not worry me a bit."[65]

. . .

The union's travails in Oregon in the early 1920s were similar to its experience in Idaho, as there, too, continued activism generated persistent though more sporadic acts of repression. In January 1921, police in Portland warned that Wobblies were "laughing at" that state's criminal syndicalism law, claiming with some truth that judges and juries had developed a reluctance, one that aligned with the text of the statute, to condemn defendants unless they had become an IWW while within the jurisdiction where they were charged.[66] The legislature therefore followed Idaho, which had addressed this issue in 1919, and changed the law to make being a member of the IWW just as easy to prosecute as becoming a member.[67] But even before this, authorities had become quicker to arrest for criminal syndicalism than to prosecute on the charge. For instance, on January 23, 1921, thirteen Wobblies were charged with criminal syndicalism in Portland, the result of a raid on a gathering featuring lawyer Elmer Smith to commemorate "Bloody Sunday in Petrograd." But while the mayor used the arrests to justify a ban on further meetings, the defendants were never brought to trial.[68]

Later in the year, there were more criminal syndicalism arrests and yet no felony prosecutions.[69] The next year, 1922, followed the same course, even as an increase in activism among the state's waterfront workers brought a surge in arrests.[70] That October, the IWW joined with American Federation of Labor (AFL) unions in a protest against waterfront hiring practices in Portland that precluded union involvement in job assignments. Over several days near the end of the month, police arrested 450 Wobblies—including 200 on one night—mainly on vagrancy charges. Their aim was to stem an "invasion" of men coming to the city to support striking longshore workers. These arrests accompanied a series of raids that closed the union's hall and prompted demands from the national American Civil Liberties Union (ACLU) that the police relent. And they did, when the tide of waterfront activism receded. Some of these defendants ended up on the "rock pile," but most were run out of town, and the few charged with criminal syndicalism were never brought to trial.[71]

In February 1923, two organizers were arrested and charged with criminal syndicalism in North Bend while trying to handbill for a union meeting, and three Wobblies, including two brothers, were indicted in the Coos Bay area.[72] That month, too, organizer Ole Hendricks was charged in Tillamook with promoting the idea of striking on the job, which was but a "new name for sabotage," according to the *Oregonian*.[73] In May, two other IWWs were arrested on criminal syndicalism charges in Astoria, for no particular reason, it seems, and, in September, another was arrested there.[74] But Hendricks's case ended in a mistrial, and nothing came of any of these other cases, which probably represented the last arrests of Wobblies on criminal syndicalism charges in Oregon. By the end of 1923, the union's decline in the state was confirmed by the nearly complete lack of any vagrancy cases.

. . .

In February 1921, the Washington State Supreme Court upheld the convictions of the seven men found guilty of murder following the Centralia affair. They were transported to the state prison at Walla Walla that June, in chains and with their "long months of confinement in the Grays Harbor county jail," where they had remained since the trial, evident "in their faces."[75] Waiting for these victims of the "iron heel," as the *Industrial Worker* put it, were nearly twenty Wobblies already in prison for violating the state's criminal syndicalism law, whose constitutionality the supreme court had just upheld, along with that of Spokane's misdemeanor criminal syndicalism ordinance.[76]

Enforcement of the felony criminal syndicalism law remained strong across the state throughout 1921.[77] That year, three dozen defendants, most of them convicted that year, were imprisoned for felony criminal syndicalism. There were a fair number of misdemeanor arrests as well. In February, for instance, eight Wobblies who would not "agree to quit" selling the union's newspapers in Spokane, despite assurances that by doing so they could avoid sixty days in jail for vagrancy, were taken into custody.[78] The matter was so threatening to organizing efforts in the city that the union brought in George Vanderveer to take on the case. Nevertheless, the men were convicted and jailed for two months.[79]

There were more arrests of Wobblies in the state in 1922, including a handful, at least, on misdemeanor criminal syndicalism charges, and nearly two dozen for felony criminal syndicalism.[80] By this time, though, the authorities' appetite for arresting people had begun to far outstrip their interest in prosecuting them. Frank Belina, arrested in Spokane in August, was the only defendant charged with felony criminal syndicalism in 1922 to go to trial, and he was acquitted that October.[81] The following year, there were no felony prosecutions at all, and the general trend in Washington was toward a decrease in anti-IWW repression. But Washington authorities still had business with Elmer Smith, he of so many troubles.

On June 1, 1923, just after moving into a new office building in Centralia with space in it reserved for the IWW, Smith received notice that the Washington State Board of Bar Examiners was seeking his disbarment.[82] According to the board, Smith was "guilty of moral turpitude rendering him unfit to longer enjoy the privileges of an attorney." The main basis of this charge was that, knowing the nature of the IWW and being aware of the criminal syndicalism law, Smith "has advocated and approved the principles as announced by the Industrial Workers of the World; has made many public addresses over the country under the auspices of such organization; has urged persons to become members thereof and has used his talents and energies in furtherance of the cause of the Industrial Workers of the World, and other similar organizations."[83]

The complaint was upheld and Smith lost his license early in February 1925. Turning down his appeal, the Washington State Supreme Court observed that Smith had "advocated and approved sabotage and criminal syndicalism as a means of accomplishing social and industrial changes in our form of government" and had suffered the distribution of "vile" IWW literature. The court concluded that "any person who advocates such general principles is unworthy of the office of attorney at law." It also condemned Smith's "criminal incitement" to secure the release of people imprisoned for criminal syndicalism.[84] As the IWW's *Industrial Solidarity* saw it, this was all confirmation that their "fighting" lawyer had been disbarred by the "lumber lords."[85] And the newspaper was not wrong. Smith would get his license back, but not till 1930, two years prior to his death at age forty-four.[86] By that time, he reckoned, he had spent "over $20,000 of my own money" fighting for the IWW, and by that time there was not much of a union left to benefit from this fight.[87]

. . .

For about a year following the end of the Red Scare, the IWW had experienced something of a reprieve in California. However, by the fall of 1921, repression was on the upsurge. This was evident in the November 1921 bulletin of the California branch of the general defense committee, which reported the conviction on criminal syndicalism charges of nine men in Los Angeles and trials underway in Alameda, Yolo, Imperial, and Sacramento counties.[88] Among those convicted was James Roe. Sixty-six years old and rheumatic, Roe spent three months hobbling around the Sacramento County jail leaning on two canes before his case was called in October 1921, only to then face a second trial after the jury deadlocked. At the second trial, the judge nearly made Roe represent himself when his attorney could not make it to court. Upon being convicted and sentenced to prison, Roe asked that no more money be spent on his case, as he was "too old to be of much use if I were out" and preferred that resources be used to defend "the younger fellows."[89]

Indeed, there were plenty of young fellows to defend and insufficient money to fund the work. Two dozen IWWs were convicted of felony criminal syndicalism in California in 1921, on the heels of a series of state appellate court decisions upholding earlier convictions and alongside a stream of vagrancy arrests.[90] Among these defendants were Howard Welton, whose contempt for a judge's offer of clemency we saw in the opening pages, and five others who were brought to trial in Oakland in October. The trial featured the testimony of another familiar figure, Elbert Coutts, as well as federal agent John Vail, who beat up an IWW supporter outside the courthouse. Welton had been arrested with his codefendants in late June at a lecture infiltrated by "Confidential Informant V-1," who was happy to report how all the criminal syndicalism cases had left IWWs in the area "demoralized" and "practically out of funds."[91] Because of this lack of funds, the defendants represented themselves. They did reasonably well, according to observers, but were convicted and sentenced to one to fourteen years.[92]

The IWW's troubles in California continued to increase through 1922 and into 1923, in concert with a surge in union activism. Inaugurating this increased activism was organizing at two massive construction works: the Hetch-Hetchy Project, which involved the construction of a large dam on the Tuolumne River and a giant aqueduct leading all the way to San Francisco, and California Edison's Big Creek Project, a massive hydroelectric and irrigation undertaking in the mountains east of Fresno. Pay on these jobs was reasonably good, but rates varied, job security was minimal, supervision was abusive, and the work, which claimed the lives of at least two IWWs, was difficult and dangerous.[93]

Delegates with the IWW's Construction Workers Industrial Union infiltrated construction camps on both projects and, in October and November 1922, led several thousand men out on strike, first at Hetch-Hetchy and then at Big Creek. The strikes sought better working conditions and the repeal of the state's criminal syndicalism laws. They began with promise, as pickets in Fresno, Los Angeles, Sacramento, and San Francisco successfully blocked the recruitment of scabs and labor shortages slowed progress on the jobs. But authorities responded by arresting Wobblies on vagrancy charges and, in about two dozen instances, for criminal syndicalism. When the walkouts began to falter under this pressure, the Mine, Mill and Smelter Workers Union, which had lost recognition on Hetch-Hetchy three years earlier, saw an opportunity to regain influence and "ordered" the strikers back to work. These developments compelled IWW organizers to take the strikes back "to the job," which they did in December.[94]

The decision led to a decline in arrests connected with Hetch-Hetchy and Big Creek. However, IWW organizing efforts that summer and fall extended into the state's agricultural and lumber districts, oil fields, and ports, and trouble followed.[95] This expanding activism gained impetus from a decision made by the IWW's general executive board at the annual convention in the fall of 1922 to reinvigorate the union and to compel the release of political prisoners, not only in California but across the country. The idea was an escalating program of organizing and direct action that would culminate, in the minds of the most ambitious Wobblies, anyway, in a nationwide general strike. Although the strike was initially supposed to begin on May Day, 1923, it was eventually called on April 25, days after the union launched, without much effect, a nationwide boycott of California products.[96]

Within a few days, the strike brought out as many as 10,000 workers scattered about in the lumber mills and camps of the Pacific Northwest. In Aberdeen, Washington, it claimed the life of forty-year-old Wobbly William McKay. On the morning of May 3, McKay was shot dead by company guard E.I. Green at the gates of the Bay City Lumber Mill during a fracas that grew out of the union's attempt to spread the strike. Although accounts differed on what initially happened between McKay and Green, what is clear is that McKay was shot from behind as he fled along a railroad track. Initially charged with murder, Green was never brought to trial.[97]

In the meantime, thousands of sailors and longshoremen, mainly at West Coast ports, also struck, along with a fair number of construction, oil, and agricultural workers, particularly in California. Nevertheless, this "general strike" was destined never to become anything of the sort and never to accomplish its primary purposes.[98] Instead, it offered welcome proof of decline. Four days into the walkout, the *Oakland Tribune* announced that, rather than proving the IWW's strength, it showed that the Wobblies were "no longer feared by employers."[99] After a week or so, most of the strikers had taken their protests back "to the job."

FIGURE 20. Funeral procession for slain IWW striker William McKay in Aberdeen, Washington, May 8, 1923. Edward Nolan Collection, Washington State Historical Society, Tacoma.

The only place the strike threatened to be particularly effective was on the waterfronts, and especially at San Pedro, the sprawling district that was the center of the Los Angeles shipping industry. The port was the domain of the IWW's Marine Transport Workers Industrial Union No. 510 (MTW), but it had been mostly an open shop since the defeat of a strike by the AFL's International Longshoremen's Association (ILA) in 1916. The war had improved working conditions and allowed both ILA and MTW locals to regain some job control at other West Coast ports. But after the armistice, the San Pedro Chamber of Commerce reaffirmed its support for the open shop by issuing a resolution to that effect and overseeing the defeat of another strike.[100]

The lack of union representation meant that the majority of cargo was typically handled by labor assembled via a daily "shape up," whereby dockworkers lined up each morning to inveigle, beg, or bribe gang bosses to pick them for the difficult work of moving enormous cargoes by semimechanized means. The "speedup," which involved driving the men at a breakneck rate, was also a common management practice. So was making them compete against each other or against other gangs. And so was working the men for as long as twenty or thirty hours at a stretch. But during slack periods it was common for dockworkers to go weeks without work or pay. Adding to workers' woes was San Pedro's adoption of a "fink hall," an employer-controlled hiring hall that functioned less as a means of rationalizing employment than as a blacklisting device and a method for administering the speedup.[101]

Although the ILA and the International Seaman's Union, the AFL's main affiliate for shipboard labor, had not simply acquiesced in these developments, their relative lack of militancy and penchant for corruption allowed the MTW to gradually expand its influence in San Pedro, to the point that, by 1922, it was able to lead a great number of brief, localized strikes on the waterfront. The ship owners and stevedore companies, backed by lumber interests and the state's powerful open shop consortium, the Merchants and Manufacturers Association, responded by "declaring war" on the IWW. Not content with merely blacklisting all IWW members and supporters, this coalition enlisted police in a program of arresting large numbers of union men on charges of criminal syndicalism and vagrancy, a practice that extended into 1923.[102] According to Kate Crane Gartz, a wealthy "parlor provocateur" who provided California Wobblies with much financial and political assistance, on a single day in early February 1923, more than 140 Wobblies were in the Los Angeles County jail on criminal syndicalism charges; according to the union, by the end of that month, around 1,000 had recently been arrested on vagrancy charges in Southern California.[103]

When the "general strike" began on April 25, the MTW led a walkout in San Pedro, demanding higher wages and the abolition of the fink hall, as well as the release of political prisoners and the repeal of California's criminal syndicalism statute. The strike brought out about 3,000 workers, tied up as many as ninety ships, and was met with an extraordinary upwelling of repression. As soon as it began, strikebreakers and Ku Klux Klansmen descended on San Pedro, where they worked with police to provoke and assault the strikers and raid their gatherings and halls. On May 14 alone, police seized between 300 and 600 union men and then announced that about 100 of their captives were facing criminal syndicalism charges and the rest would be prosecuted for vagrancy.[104] With smaller "hauls" adding to the toll of arrests and Wobblies descending on the scene from elsewhere, the struggle became a kind of free-speech fight, complete with a stockade in Griffith Park where hundreds of captives were penned up. Indeed, it is likely that more Wobblies were detained in this struggle than in any of the other free-speech fights. No one was killed. But unlike those earlier affairs, this one was shaped by the prospect that quite a few of these men would serve lengthy prison sentences.[105]

It was when the arrests reached their peak that this trouble briefly ensnared Upton Sinclair, arrested May 15 at a place called "Liberty

Hill," where days earlier twenty union people had been taken into custody during a gathering of 5,000 strikers and supporters.[106] In an attempt to support the strikers, Sinclair and a group of well-heeled friends had dared Chief of Police Louis Oaks to have them arrested for speaking there. The chief readily obliged. As soon as the three men in the group began to speak, before an audience composed only of police, they were arrested—Sinclair when midway through his recitation of the First Amendment.[107]

Although first threatened with criminal syndicalism charges and then released the following afternoon in anticipation of facing a host of misdemeanor charges, the three were never prosecuted.[108] Hundreds of workers arrested during the strike were also released without charge or pending minor charges like blocking the street. But they generally fared much worse than Sinclair and his friends. Even those who were never charged endured horrendous conditions in jail or the stockade before they got out. And an undetermined number, possibly running into the hundreds, were actually prosecuted, mainly on vagrancy charges. Over thirty were sent to prison, convicted of criminal syndicalism in a series of trials later that spring and into the summer. Among these was a group of twenty-seven, convicted July 11. The men represented themselves in the five-week trial and refused the offer of probation if they renounced the IWW.[109]

A week after his arrest, Sinclair addressed a crowd of 8,000 strikers and supporters at San Pedro without incident. For some time, he continued to agitate for the release of those imprisoned under California's criminal syndicalism law and lent his support to a fruitless campaign to repeal the statute. He was a principal founder of the Los Angeles affiliate of the ACLU. He also made the persecution of Wobblies under criminal syndicalism laws a recurrent theme in his writing, including his 1927 novel *Oil* and his 1934 play *Singing Jailbirds,* which is based on the IWW's struggle at San Pedro. But Sinclair's sympathy and support could do nothing to save the strike, which was called off on May 24.[110]

. . .

By this time, felony criminal syndicalism trials in California had become such exercises in summary condemnation that lawyers like Elmer Smith were reduced to begging jurors to show their clients compassion. In the trial of J. A. Casdorf, a twenty-one-year-old laborer, and Earl Firey, a twenty-seven-year-old carpenter, who were prosecuted in Sacramento in the spring of 1922, Smith, aided by R. W. Henderson, openly identified with his clients, compared them to Christian heretics, and invited jurors to reflect on "the terrorism of the owners of industry" and the "violence of the master class." Smith ended his statement by pleading with them to "close your eyes" and imagine "these innocent boys" sitting at San Quentin, and asking them to think of what it would be like to be "haunted by a guilty conscience to the day you die."[111]

If the jurors were worried about their consciences, it did not show in the verdict. Plied with testimony from professional witnesses Coutts and Dymond, they quickly convicted Casdorf and Firey, and Judge Malcolm Glenn gave the men the usual one to fourteen years. More remarkable than the verdict were Glenn's decision to bar all defense witnesses who were not IWW members from testifying about the union's purposes and the consequences of this remarkable edict. Perceiving Glenn's ruling as a challenge they could not fail to answer, what the *Sacramento Union* called a "small army" of Wobblies arrived at the courthouse to testify on behalf of Casdorf and Firey.[112] And as each of eleven witnesses from this group left the stand he was arrested and charged with criminal syndicalism.[113]

Prosecutors had no compunction about bringing these men to trial, even if doing so did not seem to sit well with some jurors. One of the eleven accused fled and was never found, but the first trial of the other ten, in June 1922, ended in a hung jury. They were tried again that fall, and again the result was a hung jury. Undeterred, prosecutors indicted—but never tried—two of the defendants on dubious charges of jury tampering and then prepared a third prosecution. The defendants were tried again in December 1922. This time all were convicted and sentenced to prison. When their appeals failed, four rendered a judgment of their own about these proceedings, jumped bail, and were never apprehended. Among those who went to prison was Hagbard Edwards, the man who years earlier had studied alongside "Pork Chop" in the Seattle public library and had been tried and acquitted of criminal syndicalism in Humboldt County in the summer of 1921.[114]

In fact, this was not the only occasion when appearing in court got Wobblies prosecuted. As we saw earlier, A. S. Embree's arrest in Idaho in 1920 came after he testified on behalf of a fellow worker. In November 1921, three Wobblies were charged with criminal syndicalism because of their connections to the Los Angeles trial of a dozen other IWWs: James Fink was arrested as he left the witness stand, Daniel Stevens while observing the trial, and Daniel Duffy because his involvement with that trial somehow brought to light his earlier indictment on the same charge.[115] Three different indictments were dismissed, but the three were indicted yet again in the fall of 1922, this time with twelve other Wobblies.

Several of these defendants absconded before trial, and a couple of others had cases against them dismissed. Among the eight defendants finally prosecuted were Duffy, Fink, and Roy Leonard, who was first arrested when he went to Sacramento to testify in the Casdorf and Firey trial. After a seven-week hearing in which they served as their own lawyers, the defendants were all convicted.[116] When it came time for sentencing, they were defiant. "I expect no leniency from the court or the Prison Board, go ahead and do your damndest," said defendant William Allen to Judge John Shenk—who indeed did his damndest. Shenk sentenced Duffy and two others, who had been convicted on one count, to one to fourteen years and then sentenced Allen, Leonard, Fink, and the remaining two defendants, who had all been convicted on two counts, to two to twenty-eight years.[117]

In a similar case in September 1923, five IWWs were convicted and sentenced to prison after being arrested as they left the witness stand during a criminal syndicalism trial in Sacramento that June.[118] The judge who presided over both trials, Charles Busick, was fully committed to the idea that merely being an IWW made one a criminal. Besides imprisoning IWW witnesses, he also threw union lawyer T. F. Allen in jail for contempt for protesting when Busick essentially ordered a reluctant jury to convict a group of criminal-syndicalism defendants.[119] So it was no surprise when, that summer, Busick issued an injunction which declared membership in the IWW unlawful. As he told an interviewer years later, he agreed with the Sacramento district attorney who petitioned for the order that "sentencing these defendants to San Quentin Prison was not accomplishing the purposes for which the act was designed" and that prosecuting Wobblies piecemeal "was having the same effect as killing one fly in the summer time, namely, a hundred would come to its funeral."[120]

When Busick set out to proscribe the union, he had at his disposal examples of how this might be done. There was the injunction against IWW membership adopted in Kansas in the summer of 1920. There was also an order issued January 5 of that year by Spokane judge R. M. Webster, which prohibited anyone who could conceivably be deemed a Wobbly from "associating, confederating, affiliating, and acting in concert," barred anyone from remaining a member of the organization, and enjoined anyone from "advocating, advising, teaching, or promulgating the said theories, doctrines, practices, and alleged principles" of the IWW.[121] An indeterminate number of Wobblies were jailed for contempt of Webster's edict. But Webster himself paid a price. He was compelled to go under "constant guard" for a time, after reports surfaced that some Montana Wobblies were seeking revenge.[122]

Busick issued his injunction on August 23, 1923. Drawing on an affidavit by none other than Elbert Coutts, he concocted a breathless record of IWW schemes and outrages, and, on the rationale that all Wobblies were insolvent and immune to conventional civil lawsuits, which was basically true, he enjoined the IWW, its general defense committee, the California branch of the defense committee, the general executive board, and some thirty individual officials as well as "their servants, agents, solicitors and attorneys and all others" from conspiring to damage property; controlling the state's industries; "knowingly circulating, selling, distributing and displaying books, pamphlets, papers or other written or printed matter advocating, teaching or suggesting criminal syndicalism"; or advocating, justifying, teaching, or otherwise promoting criminal syndicalism.[123]

The injunction was initially a temporary order but was later made permanent. In essence it barred the IWW from functioning at all, anywhere in the state. So far did it go, in fact, that the editors of the mainstream *Sacramento Union* recoiled, decrying the measure as an unacceptable threat to rights of free speech and trial by jury.[124] Ed Delaney, secretary of the California branch of the general defense committee, confidently predicted that "public opinion" would restrain enforcement of the injunction and pronounced it a "dead letter."[125] He was too confident, as the injunction stood. In the two years after it was issued, only two people were sentenced for violating the order. Nevertheless, it was apparently the basis for several hundred arrests in the Los Angeles area, and it caused over two thousand IWWs to flee the state, according to police.[126]

. . .

Busick's actions demonstrated how easy it had become to use the law not only to batter the IWW in summary and very practical ways but also to express a broad contempt for the organization. However, by the early 1920s the victims of these proceedings were also well-practiced in using trials to express contempt—in their case, contempt for what was being done to them and their organization. This was the logic of both the silent defense and the more vocal protests that Wobblies engaged in during their trials. When, for instance, six IWW members convicted of criminal syndicalism in Oakland on October 27, 1921, deluged the judge with curses before breaking out in song, they were making a definite statement about the law, the state, and the social order, and not just venting.[127] The same was true when eleven Wobbly defendants hurled invectives at former mayor of Seattle Ole Hanson while he tried to testify in a criminal syndicalism case in Los Angeles in November 1921. "You old skunk!" one of them shouted.[128] Earlier in that trial, spectators fled the courtroom in fear when the defendants verbally attacked another witness they felt was lying. The trial ended with the conviction of nine of these men, who, hearing the verdict, embraced their martyrdom. "Hurrah, hurrah," they said, throwing their hats in the air.[129]

Other displays like this expressed the spirit of solidarity that so defined the organization. After a four-month trial, in May 1923 a Los Angeles jury convicted four of thirteen Wobblies of criminal syndicalism. Warned by the judge not to speak, the convicted men threw their hats in the air when the verdict was announced and silently began gesturing and pantomiming as if they were happy to be going to prison. The acquitted men then demanded, unsuccessfully, that Judge Russell Avery send them, too, to San Quentin.[130]

On rare occasions, courtrooms were the scene of a different kind of performance, one that reflected a sense among other parties to these cases that something very wrong was happening. On October 30, 1923, Judge J. O. Moncur wept as he pronounced sentence on eight Wobblies convicted of criminal syndicalism the previous day in his courtroom in Quincy, California. The jury, which acquitted one of the defendants and recommended leniency for three others, had deliberated twenty-six hours to decide the case. It was handled by a prosecutor sent in from Sacramento when, as happened occasionally, the local district attorney refused to press the case.[131] The sheriff's wife had fed the defendants since they had been arrested in a raid on a Lumber Workers Industrial Union meeting the previous July, and he sent their four-year-old son to console the men before they were sent to prison.[132]

. . .

The IWW's last months as an effective organization in California ended in a final surge of raids and arrests. These were especially common on the San Pedro waterfront, where the union thought it could "hold its own" in the wake of the big strike in the spring of 1923.[133] Instead, by the following spring, police there were arresting members at "a rate of half a dozen a day."[134] And they were aided in their efforts to finally crush the union by legionnaires, college boys, and Klansmen. On March 1, 1924, 3,000 men from these groups formed a threatening cordon around the IWW's San Pedro hall. Two weeks later, they returned in somewhat smaller numbers to sack the place and, working with the police, to arrest several leaders among the union men.[135]

Although the captain of the San Pedro division of the Los Angeles Police Department, W. L. Hagenbaugh, made a show of ordering his men not to confederate with these elements, this made little difference.[136] On June 14, 1924, a mob of about 150 police, Klansmen, AFL unionists, and other "citizens" again raided the IWW hall in San Pedro. The place was packed with 300 people there for an entertainment fundraiser to benefit families of men who had been killed on the railroad. Undeterred by the presence of women and children, and armed with firearms, clubs, and axes, the raiders smashed into the place, burned up furniture and documents, and assaulted the union people. They severely scalded seven children, ages four to thirteen, by dipping them into an urn filled with hot coffee and burned another child with hot grease. The raiders also beat these children, along with women and other children. They beat the men, too, and kidnapped six, taking them forty miles into the hills where they left them, tarred and feathered.[137]

Six weeks after this outrage, Lisa "Lizzie" Sundstedt, the mother of two of the scalded children, died, in part, it seems, because of injuries she sustained in the attack. Nevertheless, the matter was never investigated by the police nor much condemned by the major newspapers, which justified the affair with the absurd and unfounded claim that the victims deserved this treatment because some Wobblies had delighted in the recent death of forty-eight sailors, killed in an accidental explosion off San Pedro aboard the battleship USS *Mississippi*. Nor were the union's adversaries satisfied to see this as the last episode of repression against IWWs in California during this period, as police and vigilantes continued to pressure the union for weeks to come.[138]

Finally, though, the raids and assaults did decline, as the purposes of repression were fully realized. That summer and fall a few Wobblies were prosecuted for vagrancy, and there were still some mass arrests, as on December 3, when police in San Francisco arrested twenty-one Wobblies after hearing that they were distributing their literature to high school students.[139] But such episodes were clearly on the wane, along with criminal syndicalism prosecutions, which by 1924 had suddenly become nearly unheard of anywhere, even in California. Only four criminal syndicalism cases went to trial that year in the state. Two of these resulted in convictions, and ten men received prison sentences. But at least nine other cases involving over three dozen defendants ended in acquittal, mistrial, or dismissal.[140] On the few occasions when criminal syndicalism cases were not dropped by prosecutors, they were dismissed in court, by judges, although sometimes with admonitions to defendants that they must change their ways.[141]

The following year, 1925, there were only a few prosecutions of Wobblies, on charges of vagrancy or other relatively minor crimes, and no serious instances of vigilantism. "The nightmare of persecution and terrorism is passing," said Archie Sinclair in the union's *Industrial Pioneer*.[142] The very last criminal syndicalism conviction of a Wobbly in California occurred late that year, in the small town of Susanville, in the state's far northeast. The historical record does not reveal much about the trial or the defendant. What can be learned is that on November 9, a jury deliberated for five hours before it convicted John Bruns, or Brunes, a native of Germany; that Bruns was sentenced to the usual one to fourteen years and began serving his time at San Quentin three days later; that he would not be released until November 9, 1927; and that his crime, according to his prison record, was "I.W.W."[143]

CHAPTER 6

Between the Drowning and the Broken

Punishment, Law, and the Legacies of Repression

"I simply never can get over seeing these men in the penitentiary," wrote Abby Scott Baker after spending two days in May 1923 visiting political prisoners at the federal penitentiary at Leavenworth, Kansas. A prominent suffragist who had herself been sentenced to jail six years earlier for picketing the White House, Baker declared that the visit to Leavenworth had "put scars on my soul." She did not know which sickened her "with helpless pity most," she wrote of the men she visited, "the ones who are holding out for principles, with anguish in their eyes like that of drowning men, or the ones who have broken, who simply cannot stay in that nightmare of living death."[1]

One of the men Baker visited was Ralph Chaplin. Writing years later, Chaplin recalled Leavenworth as "a feverish world of explosive repression and frustrations," marked by assaults, sexual exploitation, and constant snitching. "Life in prison went on, day by day, relentlessly. We had to harden ourselves to avoid cracking up emotionally," he said. Amid all the dangers and insults, the indignities and boredom, Chaplin found relief from his suffering in letters from his family, from Upton Sinclair, and from his friend George Sterling, a bohemian poet whose photograph, hanging in his cell with that of his wife and child, gave Chaplin "much strength."[2] But when Baker met him, she thought Chaplin had "reached the limits of what he can bear."[3]

Chaplin was among 171 IWWs convicted in the three big federal conspiracy trials in Chicago, Sacramento, and Kansas City. A few other Wob-

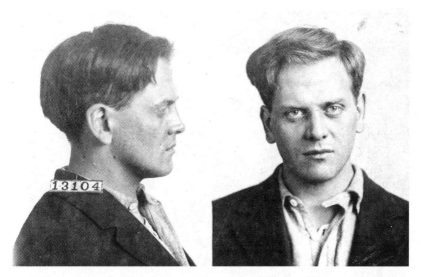

FIGURE 21. Ralph Chaplin at Leavenworth Penitentiary, September 1918. U.S. Bureau of Prisons Records, National Archives.

blies, some also affiliated with the Socialist Party or with tenant-farmer organizations, were convicted on similar charges, either individually or in smaller groups.[4] Among these was one Elmer Kumpula. Convicted in Portland on December 30, 1919, mainly on the basis of having publicly said things like "the United States was not a free country" and the nation was "no good for the workingman," Kumpula was sentenced to a year in the county jail.[5] Unlike hundreds of other defendants who were convicted of violating the Espionage Act and other wartime or state security statutes during this period and who escaped with fines, probation, deportation, or, sometimes, short jail terms, almost all of these IWW defendants were imprisoned, most at Leavenworth.[6] Prison was likewise the most common fate of the 300 Wobblies convicted of felony criminal syndicalism, of whom about 250 were sent to state prisons.[7]

In the eyes of their fellow workers these men were martyrs, not unlike Christ Himself.[8] One of these martyrs was C. E. "Stumpy" Payne, who served ten months and twenty-five days in the Washington State Penitentiary at Walla Walla. Payne was a one-time editor of the IWW's *New Solidarity* newspaper and a member of the union's general defense committee, which was formed in 1917 to meet that period's surge of repression. He was arrested two days before Christmas 1919 and a day after the sheriff entered his small ranch while he was away, without a warrant, and discovered a trove of IWW materials.[9] In a two-part article published by the *Seattle Star,* Payne declared it "very doubtful" that the "citizens of Washington had the faintest suspicion of the villainy being constantly practiced in their name." The prison was ruled by fear, he wrote, administered via a range of penalties from denial of exercise privileges to confinement in the "dark hole" or "Burke's dungeon" or in another place known as "Siberia" or the "slaughter house," in tribute to "the number of men who have been killed in it."[10]

When Baker paid her visit to Leavenworth, Big Bill Haywood had traded prison for exile. His physical and mental health compromised and his faith in how revolution might be accomplished transferred to the communist movement, Haywood apparently worried that a return to prison would amount to a death sentence. In April 1921 he, along with eight others convicted in the Chicago conspiracy trial, jumped bail and never returned to serve their sentences. But in the six months he spent there before getting out on bail, Haywood had time to formulate an opinion about Leavenworth. In his estimation, "like all prisons, it was a vicious place."[11]

So was San Quentin, where roughly one third of all Wobblies who went to prison were incarcerated. If their hunger for the works of Jack London had led them, as it did Haywood, to read his 1915 novel *The Star Rover,* they knew from this story what horrors awaited them there, especially in the prison's "dungeon." The novel's main character, Darrell Standing, "rotted for five years" in that underground vault, where he heard men "rave and howl in the darkness" and where he learned to flee his own thoughts, for in those thoughts "lay madness."[12] Indeed, to be locked up in San Quentin's dungeon meant weeks in darkness, on bread and water, with no bed or chair, only rags or straw on a wet floor. There inmates really did discover, like Standing, that unless they could find and hold to something transcendent in their suffering, they would be destroyed.

Dozens of Wobblies confined at San Quentin, perhaps even a majority, served time in one of the dungeon's 150 cells. Some who did, like Abe Shocker, were destroyed. One of ten Wobblies convicted of criminal syndicalism in a trial in Los Angeles in December 1921, after they declined an offer to escape prosecution by leaving town and renouncing the IWW, Shocker was cast into San Quentin's dungeon in the summer of 1923 because he refused to work in the prison's jute mill. After forty-two days he suffered a breakdown, was hospitalized for a few days, and ordered back to work. He refused again and was again thrown in the dungeon. Shocker suffered another breakdown and this cycle was repeated with another stay in the prison hospital and another consignment to the dungeon. Finally, Shocker's "mind gave way," as his fellow Wobblies put it, and on August 9, 1923, he hanged himself.[13]

The dungeon was commonly used, along with solitary confinement in more conventional cells, to punish Wobblies for engaging in organized protests. The most frequent protests concerned work in the jute mill, where, these defendants said, the dust sickened a man and shortened his life; where, with the machinery unguarded, "not a week passes" without men being "maimed or crippled for life" or developing "blood-poisoning or lockjaw."[14] There were approximately ten major protests by Wobblies over work in the jute mill. The largest occurred in June 1924, when nearly all the Wobblies at San Quentin, about ninety, struck in support of two fellow workers who could no longer bear the work. They marched in formation to the office of the warden, who dismissed their complaint; so they marched back to the mill and stood with arms folded. For this, they were put on bread and water and given twelve days in solitary.[15]

There were protests like these elsewhere. In the spring of 1919, Wobbly inmates in Idaho struck over living conditions at a prison farm where they had been sent.[16] This followed a more serious episode at Leavenworth in December 1918, when some twenty "mutinied" in protest of being put to work loading coal during what was usually a rest period. In punishment, some of the men were chained seven hours a day for days on end to the doors of the isolation cells, their arms pulled up over their heads. In another episode at Leavenworth, in April 1919, a number of Wobbly inmates were charged with instigating a riot in the cafeteria. For this, they were thrown into the "dark hole," where, in a ruthless test of their racial tolerance, they were beaten senseless by black trustees armed with clubs.[17]

Prisoners were often beaten, and sometimes these beatings were also the impetus to protest. In October 1923, for instance, fifty-eight Wobblies at San Quentin were briefly put in solitary after striking to protest the beating of one of their men by a guard and that man's confinement in the dungeon.[18] The next month, seventy-one Wobblies struck over another beating and were placed in the dungeon and in solitary.[19] That fall, officers with the California branch of the general defense committee filed charges with the prison board, asserting that the warden at California's Folsom State Prison, where most other Wobbly defendants in the state were confined, was responsible for the "unmerciful" beating of a Wobbly named Louis Allen. Already in solitary, Allen had inquired about another inmate who had been sent to "the hole," and so the guards wrapped him in a blanket, dragged him to a secluded place, and pummeled him.[20]

Overcrowding was common in prisons in the early twentieth century, and Wobbly inmates suffered from this too. When not working or in isolation, they were often jammed together with two or three other prisoners in the small cells. On occasion, the overcrowding reached outrageous levels. In 1922, Warden James Johnston at San Quentin reported that "every possible expedient" was being employed to accommodate the institution's swollen population.[21] Walter Wismer experienced these expedients, sleeping with forty other men on the floor under other inmates' beds. On April 22 of that year he therefore went "to the office" and announced that he would do no more work in the jute mill until this situation was redressed. Wismer and his fellow inmates got their beds, but first they paid a price: The authorities threw him and thirteen other Wobblies who had joined his protest into the dungeon.[22]

Wobblies at Leavenworth were able to consort with other leftists, forming a kind of "revolutionary university" behind bars, wherein ideas were debated and exchanged.[23] Their large numbers likewise made it easy for Wobblies to convene at San Quentin and Walla Walla. No doubt they found comfort and support and sometimes enlightenment in each other's company and in conversation with other leftists. But a prison is not a university, let alone a welcoming place for radical ideas, and Wobblies complained everywhere of being singled out for additional mistreatment: of having their mail censored, being denied visiting privileges, and being surveilled by special details of guards. As their prison records reveal, it was easy for men such as these, in turn, to accumulate a great number of infractions for violating the institutions' oppressive controls. The record of Richard Brazier, a member of the union's general executive board and a Chicago defendant who was confined at Leavenworth, is fairly typical. It lists, among other violations, "insolence" and "raising hell in general," saying "hello" to other inmates, being late for bugle call, and refusing to break rocks, as many inmates were required to do, day after day.[24] Joe Neil was another "confirmed disturber" and was punished with "solitary" and "bread and water" for infractions that ranged from fighting, to "smoking cigarettes," to "having cigarette papers in his possession," to backtalk and "insolence."[25]

Neil seems to have had a knack for escaping. At some point while serving his time in Wisconsin for throwing rocks at a brakeman, he escaped. Eight years later, during the war, Neil was arrested in Arizona for distributing IWW literature and escaped again, only to be recaptured in Los Angeles eight weeks after, and then paroled in April 1920.[26] Neil did not escape once he was arrested for criminal syndicalism. But others did. In July 1920, Wobblies Fred Morgan, William Nelson, and Joe Martin were among a group of defendants who escaped the Idaho State Penitentiary, later to be tracked down with bloodhounds. Two months later, Leo Brookshire briefly escaped from Walla Walla while serving a criminal syndicalism sentence.[27] With two other inmates, Leo Ellis sawed through the bars at the Stockton, California, jail in May 1920, after being sentenced to one to four years for criminal syndicalism. Ellis was captured in Texas six years later, returned to California, and ordered to serve two years. Freed in September 1928, he was the last IWW criminal syndicalism defendant to leave prison.[28]

Like Abe Shocker, Frank Hastings was never to leave prison alive. Convicted of criminal syndicalism in Olympia in January 1920, he died three years later at Walla Walla of "chronic intestinal nephritis," age fifty.[29] Still other union men made it out of prison only to die soon afterward. Three, we know, died within two and a half years of their release from federal custody of tuberculosis either contracted in prison or aggravated by their time in custody: Tomas Martinez, a Mexican national convicted of violating the Espionage Act in Tucson in June 1918, both an IWW and a follower of Ricardo Flores Magón; William Weyh, convicted in the Chicago conspiracy case; and James Mulrooney, one of the silent defenders in the Sacramento case.[30] R. V. Lewis survived his time behind bars, but when he was released from San Quentin in 1922, it was without one of his legs, which had been amputated because authorities "waited until too late" to treat an abscess he had developed.[31]

Some left prison with devastating injuries to their minds. Among these was criminal syndicalism defendant John "Jack" Beavert, who lost his mind three years into his sentence at San Quentin. Beavert was transferred to the state asylum at Talmadge in March 1928, released two months later, and then recommitted a month after that.[32] Olin Anderson, who suffered some kind of collapse in the Cook County jail, where he also developed tuberculosis, and then went to Leavenworth, died within two years of his release at the State Hospital for the Insane in his native Montana.[33] And then there was Fred Esmond, the silent defender who had so courageously told Judge Frank Rudkin he would accept neither mercy nor pity. Before being prosecuted in Sacramento, Esmond was among the union's most militant voices. Two years into a ten-year sentence at Leavenworth, Esmond began to speak incoherently and incessantly and could not stop rubbing his face, which was soon covered in sores. After medical examinations prompted by Caroline Lowe, Esmond was declared by the warden "a fit subject for the asylum." And, in the summer of 1921, he was removed to the grim confines of St. Elizabeth's Hospital in Washington, D.C., where he remained for two more years.[34]

Esmond's wife, Leone, suffered her own breakdown. According to the newspapers, she responded to his crisis by sending threatening letters to several prominent people in California, including a former U.S. attorney, and for a time faced criminal syndicalism charges herself.[35] Other families caught up in these cases endured in less dramatic but still heartrending ways. Chicago defendant E. F. Doree, a compliant inmate, was twice given leave from Leavenworth to visit his ill son back in Philadelphia. But this kind of accommodation was not typical. Doree's fellow defendant, Luigi, or Louis, Parenti, went fifteen months at Leavenworth before the warden allowed him to contact his wife and three children.[36] Joseph Gresbach was one of three married men convicted in the Kansas conspiracy case. At sentencing, his lawyers reminded the court that Gresbach's wife "was not strong, and has no funds." After going on about how punishment "falls more heavily on the innocent than the guilty," Judge John Pollock sent all the married defendants to prison and gave Gresbach three and a half years.[37]

Indeed the weight of punishment fell very heavily on the families of these men, often in very telling ways. A. S. Embree's family suffered during his time in the Idaho State Penitentiary, as we have seen. Three years into a five-year term in that prison, Wobbly Harris Herd asked the parole board to consider what his incarceration was doing to his wife and child. They were in Kansas living "in very moderate circumstances" with relatives who could not afford to provide "even the most plain necessities of life." The wife was performing farm work, which was bound to "bring her health down," he said, "and was unable to provide suitable clothing for her self [sic] and the child."[38]

On April 9, 1920, Nicholaas Steelink wrote to his wife, Fannia, from the Alameda County jail in Oakland. "I cried a little last week, the day I was sentenced," he confessed. Days later, his words weighted with intimations of grief and apprehension, Steelink tried to remind himself that his situation was not so bad as he gazed upon a black murder defendant at the jail who worriedly awaited his fate. Steelink tried to reassure Fannia and probably himself about what he would face at San Quentin. "Not that I'm afraid to go, for they all tell me it's not so terrible up there after all." But two years of prison were terrible for Steelink,

FIGURE 22. Unnamed IWW inmate, date and location also unknown. The book above the latch is *The Pinkerton Labor Spy*, an exposé of the agency, by Morris Friedman. Walter P. Reuther Library, Archives of Labor and Urban Affairs, Wayne State University.

as they would have been for any decent person. His letters to Fannia confirm this, detailing worries about her health, about whether she could find work and keep up with living expenses, about his own health, as he seemed worn down and was chronically ill, about his prospects for bail, and, later, about when he might finally be released.[39] Most of all, it seems, Steelink missed his wife.

. . .

In 1921, the California Supreme Court decided Steelink's appeal of his criminal syndicalism conviction. His lawyers had raised a range of objections, including claims that both the statute and the indictment under which Steelink was charged were too ambiguous and that the prosecution infringed his rights of free speech. Although the court complimented the "great learning" with which Steelink's lawyers framed these arguments, it rejected every one of them, waiting till the end of its opinion to conclude, with no regard for whether Steelink himself had done any of these things, that the "right of free speech does not include the right to advocate the destruction or overthrow of the government or the criminal destruction of property."[40]

IWW lawyers filed dozens of appeals in both state and federal court, trying to get men like Steelink released. Some courts, especially at the state level, obliged, throwing out convictions of Wobblies because juries were biased, improperly composed, guided by incorrect jury instructions, or influenced by improperly admitted hearsay testimony.[41] Occasionally, a state court took the view that mere possession of radical documents did not justify conviction for criminal syndicalism.[42] And in 1924, the Idaho Supreme Court ruled that the state's criminal syndicalism statute did not criminalize advocacy of slowdowns and similar protests on the job.[43] But in line with nearly everything the union said about law and the legal system, such favorable decisions were uncommon, and they mostly came after the union was in decline.

It was far more common for appellate courts to uphold the convictions of Wobblies. Like the one that heard Steelink's case, most courts, if they considered it, rejected the argument that key terms in these statutes, particularly *sabotage*, *terrorism*, and *syndicalism*, were so indefinite or vague as to make these laws and the defendants' convictions unconstitutional. Usually, they held that the meanings of these words were simply "matters of common knowledge."[44] Or they decided that the argument proved too much. "It would be easy," said the Washington State Supreme Court in 1921, "to find many statutes now on the books which are open to the objection of uncertainty, but which have heretofore never been suspected of that fault"—like those concerning vagrancy, it noted, without irony.[45] At least one court also rejected the claim that criminal syndicalism defendants were entitled to instructions directing the jury that a conviction required a finding that the IWW was actually committed to criminal means of industrial or political change.[46]

Consistent with the way these statutes were written, the courts routinely upheld the idea of convicting people of criminal syndicalism based on union membership, even when that membership predated the enactment of the criminal syndicalism statute.[47] They approved the use of IWW literature, songs, and propaganda as evidence of the organization's criminality and, therefore, the guilt of individual defendants.[48] They endorsed convictions based on the testimony of professional witnesses and witnesses who had been intimidated, and they were also indifferent to unethical prosecutorial practices.[49] They likewise rejected the argument that by levying such stiff penalties for speech and association, the statutes imposed cruel and unusual punishment, in violation of the Eighth Amendment to the U.S. Constitution.[50]

The courts were equally unmoved by the argument that criminal syndicalism prosecutions violated any provisions of the U.S. Constitution or of any state constitutions by constituting a kind of "class legislation" that singled out for punishment radicals while failing to criminalize the actions of businessmen, vigilantes, police, and others who used such means to preserve the social order. They either dismissed this argument by declaring that the distinction between revolutionaries and reactionaries was a rational one and therefore constitutional,[51] or they adverted to an important premise of Progressivism to subvert the claim, asserting that because states could regulate employment relations in reformist ways, there could be no basis for claiming that to do so in punitive ways was unconstitutional.[52]

Of course, courts have never been overly generous to criminal defendants, whatever their crime. But their hostility to these defendants seems to have been especially acute and their dislike for what they stood for evident in how consistently they rejected defendants' claims that convicting them of criminal syndicalism based on membership in the IWW or advocacy of its doctrines violated rights of free speech and association. Some dismissed these arguments out of hand.[53] Others reached the same conclusion in more considered ways. This is how the California Supreme Court decided the issue in Steelink's appeal. It is also how that court ruled in the case of John Taylor, Communist Labor Party member, former Wobbly, and former state secretary of the Socialist Party, who was convicted of two counts of criminal syndicalism in Oakland in May 1920. The court declared that the case law on free speech had "no application to a statute such as ours, which denounces organizations formed for the purpose of committing crimes against persons and property in furtherance of political or industrial changes."[54]

These state cases unfolded in concert with the rapid development in the U.S. Supreme Court of a body of law that seemed to limit the author-

ity of governments to infringe constitutional rights of speech and association. This change in the law was of little benefit, however, partly
because it would be several years before the Supreme Court allowed
convictions under state and local law to be challenged under the First
Amendment to the U.S. Constitution, as opposed to state constitutions,
and partly because the law's main thrust was actually to justify these
convictions anyway. The key decision in the latter regard was *Schenck
v. United States,* in which the court in 1919 upheld the conviction of
two Socialists for violating the Espionage Act. Invoking the "clear
and present danger" test for the first time, the court ruled that these
defendants' conduct, which consisted only of agitating peacefully
against war and conscription, was sufficiently dangerous to warrant
conviction.[55]

The court's two most Progressive justices, Oliver Wendell Holmes and
Louis Brandeis, fully supported this ruling. Indeed, Holmes, whose Social
Darwinist views served a very different purpose than they did for Jack
London or any Wobblies, devised the "clear and present danger" test and
authored the opinion in *Schenck.* As Holmes conceived of it, the test
required that the danger posed by defendants be neither particularly imminent nor very probable to justify a conviction.[56] Ten months later, in
Abrams v. United States, the court upheld the conviction of another group
of radicals engaged in peaceful protest, reverting to the older and, for
defendants, less favorable "bad tendency" test, which justified convictions
whenever speech or actions tended to produce the harm the government
legitimately sought to prevent. This time, Holmes and Brandeis parted
company with their colleagues and dissented, giving expression to a tolerant side of their Progressivism. But in so doing they offered a more refined
way to justify the continued prosecution of radicals, particularly IWWs,
while pretending to honor the principles of free speech and association.

Holmes's dissent in *Abrams* questioned the notion, which had influenced the court's decision in *Schenck* and several other Espionage Act
cases, that the right to dissent was necessarily more limited in wartime
than in times of peace. He also introduced to this debate the liberal
concept of a "market" of ideas. Indeed, his views on how far the government might go in criminalizing radicalism had shifted, along with
those of Brandeis. But then Holmes suggested how little this all really
meant when dealing with actual radicals, and how little his views would
likely have limited prosecutors and lower courts if they had been readily
adopted, when he cast the defendants in *Abrams* as "poor and puny

anonymities" who had published a "silly leaflet" and whose speech was worth protecting mainly because it was not worth anything.[57]

The IWW might have been worthless in the eyes of many Progressives and conservatives alike, but it hardly fit the image of a poor and puny organization, not in 1917 and not until it had been destroyed. Mindful that any First Amendment claims were therefore destined to fail regardless of the test employed, defense lawyers in the Chicago conspiracy case did not raise any when they appealed to the U.S. Court of Appeals for the Seventh Circuit.[58] Instead, with Otto Christensen in the lead, they set forth an array of "assignments of error," which mainly contended that the convictions were based on illegally seized evidence, improper jury instructions, and a flawed indictment.

In October 1920, the court of appeals overturned the defendants' convictions on counts one and two. It determined that count one, which alleged conspiracy to "prevent, hinder and delay" the execution of a number of federal laws and proclamations, duplicated count three. And count two, conspiring to interfere with rights or privileges secured by federal law to various businesses by preventing them from producing and selling goods to the government, rested on the improper assumption that these rights were guaranteed by federal law. These determinations affected the fines that some defendants owed. But the court let stand the convictions on counts three and four, which had broadly charged the defendants with conspiring to impede the war effort. As a result, the prison sentences remained unchanged and those defendants who had been released on bail were ordered to return to prison.[59]

The appeals in the other two big federal cases raised similar procedural and technical objections while likewise omitting any claims under the First Amendment. The U.S. Court of Appeals for the Ninth Circuit upheld convictions on all counts in the Sacramento conspiracy case.[60] The U.S. Court of Appeals for the Eighth Circuit, which heard the appeal in the Kansas conspiracy case despite Fred Moore's failure to meet a filing deadline, overturned the defendants' conviction on count one, which charged them with seditious conspiracy, a crime that was not actually based on the Espionage Act and which the court decided had never been properly defined. But it upheld their convictions on counts two and three, which charged conspiracy to impede recruitment and the draft and create dissension in the armed forces in violation of the Espionage Act, as well as count four, which charged conspiracy to violate the Lever Act. Because of how their sentences had been established, this ruling resulted in the release of nineteen of the defendants, but the others remained in prison.[61] Although the union's lawyers appealed these cases to the Supreme Court, the court declined to review any of them.

. . .

Most federal inmates' only hope for early release lay with the success of a campaign to secure "amnesty" on behalf of political prisoners. This effort was focused on the plight of not only IWWs but also several hundred socialists, anarchists, pacifists, religious objectors, black nationalists, and others who had been convicted of violating the Espionage Act and other state security measures during and just after the war.[62] Wobblies were the largest contingent of those imprisoned and, as William Preston puts it, "the most detested by the government authorities."[63] This put the IWW defendants very much at the center of the amnesty campaign.

An important leader in this campaign was U.S. Senator William Borah, who had unsuccessfully prosecuted Haywood for the murder of Frank Steunenberg. An independent Progressive with civil-libertarian tendencies, Borah had opposed the Espionage Act and worked hard on behalf of the prisoners, including the IWWs. Borah promised Ralph Chaplin that he would hold what Chaplin called a "one-man sitdown strike on the White House steps" to get the prisoners released.[64] The amnesty campaign was also backed by fifty other members of Congress, some progressive in their views, others conservative; by activists like Jane Addams and Mary La Follette, the daughter of Senator Robert La Follette Sr., who had joined Borah in voting against the Espionage Act; by the IWW's fellow unionists in the United Mine Workers, the International Association of Machinists, and dozens of local labor federations, besides the American Federation of Labor (AFL) itself; and by liberal churchmen, especially those associated with the Federal Council of Churches.[65]

Most important was the work of the American Civil Liberties Union (ACLU), which was founded in 1920 by Roger Baldwin, two years after he briefly joined the IWW himself.[66] Baldwin constructed the ACLU from the National Civil Liberties Bureau, which he and Chrystal Eastman, Socialist and feminist, had established in 1917. The Bureau was involved in defending leftists and included an entity called the Workers Defense Union, which assisted with the representation of hundreds of radicals, including many IWWs.[67] The ACLU inherited that concern for the interests of radicals and took the lead in organizing the campaign to secure amnesty for political prisoners.

The campaign met considerable resistance from American Legion-naires, right-wing clergy, government officials, and many mainstream newspapermen.[68] But it benefited from the diversity of the political pris-oners, who could not all so easily be dismissed as dangerous radicals; from its organizers' success in highlighting the egregious circumstances under which many defendants were convicted and the hardships that they and their families endured; and from the support of some newspa-permen who questioned Congress's failure to repeal the Espionage Act after the war and wondered, if all the repression was really justified by the war, why people were still locked up so long after the fighting had ended.[69] Then, too, there was the benign indifference of many main-stream Progressives, who did nothing to help the defendants but found it easier to tolerate the radicals among them, and countenance their freedom, as they descended into irrelevance.

Two years after the armistice, almost half the people imprisoned for violating the Espionage Act had been released.[70] Within another year, dozens more gained their freedom, including Eugene Debs, the most famous. Convicted in September 1918 for giving an antiwar speech in Canton, Ohio, three months earlier, Debs was released on Christmas Day, 1921, two years and nine months after the Supreme Court, in a decision written by Holmes, unanimously rejected his appeal.[71] When Debs walked free, besides a relatively small number whose terms had expired, only a few Wobblies had gotten out. This was partly because the Warren Harding and Woodrow Wilson administrations did not want them released and partly because they rejected the terms on offer. A few stood fast because they were hoping somehow to avoid deporta-tion. Others objected to the way clemency was being granted on an individual basis. They wanted to be released en masse, on the theory that their collective convictions on conspiracy charges logically demanded this, as did the principle of solidarity. Many also considered anything but a pardon an unacceptable admission of guilt. As one Wob-bly put it, "Parole is for those who are guilty."[72]

However, quite a number of these men soon came to realize how much truth inhered in Jack London's observation in *The Star Rover*, that prison is a "training school for philosophy," one that bursts inmates' "fondest illusions and fairest metaphysical bubbles."[73] In the fall of 1921 and through 1922, a number of defendants broke ranks and applied for, and in many cases were granted, release from prison on the condition that they renounce the IWW. The union's general defense committee responded with a policy that withheld from these defendants and their families any relief benefits; later, toward the end of 1922, delegates to the union's convention also voted to expel such men from the union.

In the summer of that year, there were still ninety-five Wobblies in federal custody, divided between those who favored clemency and those who continued to oppose it. Fifty-two of the latter group dispatched a letter to President Harding explaining why it remained "impossible" for them to apply for release. They "were not criminals" but prisoners in a class struggle whose views remained "unchanged." They pointed out the flaws in the cases against them, the unequal treatment they had received, and the hardships they had endured. They reiterated that because they had been convicted all together of the same basic conspiracies, and not for their individual acts, it would be wrong to say that if some deserved clemency others somehow did not. For these reasons, they "refused to beg" for their freedom and were prepared to remain behind bars, confident "that history will some day [*sic*] vindicate our stand."[74]

In the summer of 1923, the administration set forth broader conditions for clemency that nonetheless required that recipients pledge "to be law-abiding and loyal to the Government of the United States" and not "encourage, advocate or become willfully connected with lawlessness in any form," which could be construed as a renunciation of the IWW.[75] The offer also excluded nearly all the defendants from the Sacramento conspiracy case as the administration decided they were more dangerous. But now the union's leadership quietly withdrew its objections to clemency, clearing the way for a majority of defendants to accept the offer. Among those who left prison on these terms was Ralph Chaplin, who wrote poems in prison about his family and freedom and the smell of grass and flowers and told Roger Baldwin that he cried for two weeks after his release.[76]

As with earlier offers of clemency, fines that had been levied, which had generally remained unpaid, were remitted. Nevertheless, eleven defendants who were eligible for release continued to hold out, contending, quite correctly, that the government was using the process to divide the Wobblies and undermine their organization. Ten days before Christmas 1923, facing pressure from Borah and others and knowing that these men probably would never concede, the new president, Calvin Coolidge, unconditionally commuted the sentences of all thirty-one IWWs still in custody to time served.[77] Among the holdouts who finally walked free was James Rowan, telling Warden W. I. Biddle, "I have always been law-abiding in the past and don't expect to change now." Biddle, in turn, seemed confident that this "considerable of a disturber" would make more trouble.[78]

. . .

Release did not bring an end to punishment, as Lois Phillips Hudson understood when she wrote *The Bones of Plenty,* a disconsolate but remarkably sympathetic novel about a North Dakota farm family and its struggles in the Great Depression. A character in the novel is a destitute old Wobbly named Oblonsky who cannot stop talking as he lay dying in the hospital. Oblonsky muses, without self-pity, about how lucky his roommate is to have a place of his own to go and die. Although his hatred of capitalism seems intact, Oblonsky does not "feel too bad about the way our great country is going." As he sees it, "The Wilson Democrats put me in jail and took away my citizenship because I did not believe in war, but two days ago the Roosevelt Democrats gave me back my citizenship. Now I can have a citizen's burial."[79]

The federal defendants who were citizens were not restored their full rights of citizenship until 1933. About two dozen who were not citizens were subject to deportation, although extended litigation and political agitation limited the number who, like Luigi Parenti and Charles Ashleigh, were actually removed from the country.[80] Defendants who had been naturalized had to fight to prevent their citizenship being revoked— among them Rowan, the considerable disturber, who fought a five-year battle on this front.[81] As we shall see, the poverty and isolation that defined Oblonsky's later life were the fate of many after their release.

Nor did the federal amnesty apply to state inmates, many of whom remained in custody long after the last federal defendant walked free. Published during the Depression, John Dos Passos's novel *1919* incorporates much about the IWW's story and drips with contempt for those who engineered the brutal campaign to destroy it. The book notes quite correctly that some IWW defendants were still in prison in the 1930s. In its closing pages, Dos Passos writes that no one knows where Wesley Everest was buried, but the Wobblies convicted of murder in the trial that followed, "they buried in the Walla Walla Penitentiary."[82] After the defendants' appeals were rejected, Elmer Smith made their freedom his primary concern, even after he was disbarred. But release was long in coming. Between 1931 and 1933, five of the defendants finally were paroled, several after Smith himself died in 1932. Raymond Becker, who had insisted he would only leave if granted a full pardon, was released, "almost against his will," in 1939, when his sentence was commuted. James McInereny never did leave prison. Shot at on the *Verona*, maybe wounded that day, wrongly charged with murder in that case, then convicted of murder and nearly lynched along the way, he died of tuberculosis in 1930, only forty-four years old.[83]

Aside from the IWW's own scattered and unsuccessful efforts to secure its members' release with strikes and a few gestures by the ACLU, the state inmates were never the object of a well-organized, nationwide campaign to secure their early release, something made impractical by the fact that they were incarcerated as a result of many different trials and in many different states. Nevertheless, in keeping with the way most prison sentences worked, and despite the lingering hostility of many state officials, the great majority of IWW defendants in state custody got out on parole. Most who went to prison for criminal syndicalism served between one and three years. But like Raymond Becker and so many of the federal inmates, more than a few disdained the idea of parole, at least for a while. Thus Howard Welton's reaction to a California judge's offer of help, for instance. Some defendants in Idaho, including A. S. Embree and Harris Herd, also declined for years to apply for release. For several years, five Wobblies serving prison sentences for criminal syndicalism at Walla Walla refused the governor's offer of parole. The men would only accept a pardon, and only if the Centralia defendants were also released.[84] Likewise, on November 7, 1923, forty-one Wobbly inmates at San Quentin endorsed a resolution "reaffirming" their opposition to parole.[85]

Some who did seek release endeavored to satisfy the requirement that they disclaim violence without denouncing the IWW. The letters that Idaho inmates wrote supporting their applications for relief are revealing. John Shea, for instance, noted, "I am a member of the organization known as the Industrial Workers of the World. I joined the Industrial Workers of the World believing that I was joining a strictly labor organization; and if the said organization was, in reality, a criminal organization, I was not aware of it."[86] Others took pains to affirm the legitimacy of their purpose. "I have always believed and do believe now in the rights of labor to organize by lawfull [*sic*] methods for the purpose of bettering their working conditions where unjust and miserable condition exist," said Idaho inmate Charles Anderson.[87]

Inmates seeking release frequently enjoyed the support of friends and family, who wrote plaintive letters in which they sought to convince the authorities to free their loved ones. A friend of Idaho inmate Joe Martin reminded the warden that Martin "has consumption and is in serious condition," and asked that he be released so that if his friends could not "nurse him back to health again," he might at least die among them. "It grieves me to hear of anyone dying in prison," said the friend.[88] The mother of Bert Banker urged, in her plea to the governor of Idaho, that her son be pardoned in part because he had tuberculosis. She said she would send him "money for clothes and car fare to come home."[89] The brother of defendant Charles Clifford wrote a letter to the Idaho governor in which he pleaded that their mother, who was seriously ill and had not seen Clifford in two years, should see him before she died.[90] The note followed several letters from the mother herself, begging that she be allowed to see her son "once more while on Earth."[91]

These files also contain a surprisingly large number of supportive letters from local sheriffs, judges, and even the occasional businessman, showing that decency and good sense were not unknown among such people. Sheriff W. M. Eller of Idaho County wrote to the pardon board in December 1920 in support of Gust Sandee and Gust Haraldson. He knew "these boys" and thought they were honest and hard-working. He reckoned they were "partly or wholly ignorant of the laws of the state of Idaho" and should be released "providing their conduct has been as excellent during their time at Boise as it was while they were with me in jail in Grangeville."[92] Likewise, on the very day that the IWW's general defense committee dispatched a telegram to Idaho Governor D. W. Davis urging that he free Thomas O'Hara from prison because the man was "breaking down mentally," the trial judge in O'Hara's case, Robert Terrell, also wrote the governor asking that O'Hara be released. Terrell told Davis that he thought O'Hara was "not exactly right mentally." The judge recalled a man who "seemed unduly obsessed with certain ideas with reference to economics and IWWism."[93] An Englishman who had told prison official he had no home, O'Hara was paroled in 1921. More than three decades later, after finding a home in Kenilworth, Illinois, he sent the prison in Idaho $10 for the aid of inmates confined there.[94]

. . .

Chained to the bars of his cell for eight days because of his involvement in the incident in the prison cafeteria at Leavenworth in April 1919, Edward Hamilton spent two and a half years in solitary, despite suffering from an advanced case of tuberculosis. Released the day after Christmas 1921, mainly as a result of the efforts of Caroline Lowe, he announced, "I have not changed my views."[95] Similarly, when Nicholaas Steelink was paroled in March 1922, he viewed himself as a "veteran soldier" and remained committed to the IWW and optimistic that he would continue to advance its cause: "I thought that if we had a hundred individuals like myself, we could make an impact." But he soon discovered otherwise.[96]

Steelink was one of a fair number of Wobblies who resumed the struggle upon leaving prison. Some of these men suffered an extra measure of punishment as a result. James Price was not locked up as long as the Centralia defendants. Nor did he serve as long as Blackie Ford and Herman Suhr. They spent twelve years behind bars, and Ford narrowly avoided another term when, upon his release, the son of the district attorney killed at Wheatland, now the district attorney himself, tried him in Charles Busick's court for the murder of the deputy sheriff killed that day.[97] Nevertheless, Price's refusal to abandon the struggle put him behind bars longer than most. He spent thirteen months in jail in Sacramento awaiting trial before being convicted with the other silent defenders and sentenced to four years. After nineteen months at Leavenworth, he was released on bail and then arrested in Los Angeles while trying to raise money for criminal syndicalism defendants. Charged with criminal syndicalism himself, Price was convicted in June 1921 and sent to Folsom, where he remained until March 1926.[98] Similar was the fate of Leo Stark, who had organized all over the country and briefly faced murder charges in the Mesabi case in 1916 before being prosecuted on federal charges in Kansas. Released from Leavenworth in 1921, Stark was convicted of criminal syndicalism in Los Angeles in 1923. One of the twenty-seven convicted together of that charge after the San Pedro waterfront strike, he spent four years at San Quentin and Folsom.[99]

When Steelink was released, thinking about making an impact, it is not clear how many members the IWW had on its rolls. Even before the tide of repression broke over the union, its rolls were fluid and record-keeping was deficient and sometimes misleading, and estimates of membership from this period are altogether inconsistent and unreliable. These problems were compounded by the seizure and destruction of union records, the spread of a culture of secrecy and paranoia, and a state of disorder manifested, among other ways, in the union's failure even to hold an annual convention in 1917 and 1918. Not only did repression make it perilous to belong to the IWW, it also made it difficult for people involved with the organization to collect and pay the dues on which researchers have had to rely in estimating membership.[100]

For all these reasons, only the roughest estimates can be made of the union's size in the late 1910s and 1920s without entering the realm of conjecture and pointless contestation. It is safe to say, however, that in the early 1920s, dues-paying membership was much less than in 1917 and probably did not exceed 30,000 in any given year after 1919. As in earlier years, the IWW had the allegiance or sympathy of many who were not paid-up members. But repression clearly diminished support for the union at every level and drove much of that support underground. The union did not become stronger than ever after the war and the Red Scare as the union's own historian, Fred Thomson, improbably claims. But neither was it already finished at the beginning of the new decade, as the leading academic historian of the IWW, Melvyn Dubofsky, seems to suggest.[101]

Ironically, perhaps the best measure of the IWW's continued vitality in the years after the war and the Red Scare is the fact that its members continued to be persecuted so relentlessly. The fortitude shown by these men was impressive and, at times, simply astonishing. But as repression took its toll on them, the organization foundered. In 1920, the *Los Angeles Times* applauded Steelink's prison sentence as a "harsh happening" that "throws scare into Wobblies" and had caused a number of IWWs "to fold their tents."[102] Indeed, in confirmation of what scholars call the "demonstrative" or "general deterrent" effect of criminal punishment, many Wobblies simply left the IWW to avoid persecution; countless other workers who might have been recruited never deigned to join an organization whose membership card was so obviously a ticket to prison or jail and an invitation to be beaten or even killed.

For those Wobblies who experienced the worst of this repression, continuing with the union sometimes became unthinkable. While slowly dying at Leavenworth, Olin Anderson confessed his "shocking disillusionment" and his sense that further sacrifice would be futile; he was among a few dozen federal defendants who explicitly renounced the IWW.[103] According to Eric Thomas Chester, even those Wobblies who held out longest for unconditional release from that institution nonetheless emerged "demoralized and defeated" and often moved on to other callings.[104] This was true of Wencil Francik, for instance, convicted in the Kansas conspiracy case. One of the staunchest of these defendants, Francik said he had done nothing but work for the IWW for a decade prior to his arrest. After his release, he spent his remaining days farming in Iowa, never bothering much with life's comforts, even a decent suit of clothing, and never speaking much about unionism.[105] Vincent St. John's course was similar. Having left the IWW for a simpler existence after being shot in Goldfield, only to be thrown in Leavenworth, St. John may have briefly rejoined the union after his release in 1922, but he soon drifted into a life of "obscurity" and died in poverty in 1929.[106]

Although he is wrong to say that the IWW was destroyed by wartime repression, Melvyn Dubofsky is no doubt at least partly right when he suggests that a number of federal defendants who returned to the IWW did so only because "they had no place else to go."[107] Even those, like Steelink, who remained earnestly committed to the organization found themselves diminished by what they had experienced. Reflecting on his own situation later in life, Steelink recalled his state when he got out of prison: "I could not be the same IWW that I was before."[108]

The organization to which Wobblies like Steelink returned was not the same, either. Repression prevented the IWW from engaging freely in its most essential functions: organizing and striking. Beyond this, it also damaged the union internally. Federal law enforcement, which has preoccupied those interested in this issue, resulted in the extended occupation of union offices; the seizure of huge amounts of essential documents; the banning from the mail of union correspondence, including fundraising and defense materials and anything containing the word *sabotage*; and the "decapitation" of the union, accomplished by the incarceration of nearly all of its top leadership.[109] But just as devastating were the countless arrests, raids, deportations, and prosecutions authored by state and local officials, as well as the many acts of vigilantism that Wobblies faced. These depredations were also conceived, in part, for the purpose of making union business impossible to conduct. And that is what they did.

Repression took its toll, as well, by turning the IWW into a legal defense organization, which meant that, against many of the values on which it was founded, and to the disgust of many members, it had to become a fundraising organization.[110] The IWW's financial records are as messy and incomplete as its membership figures. It seems certain, for instance, that many expenses related to legal defense were handled informally or at the local level and never made it into the union's records. But what records do exist aptly confirm how this work utterly consumed the union. The IWW probably raised nearly $1 million—about $18 million in today's money—to cover legal expenses related to wartime persecution.[111] And the end of the war brought only partial relief from this obligation. In the calendar year of 1920, the IWW reported spending about $100,000 on defense-related expenses—including legal services, relief of prisoners, and bail—which probably equals about half its total operating expenses.[112] Nor did the passing of the Red Scare eliminate the need to raise large sums of money. During the fiscal year that ended October 1, 1924, the union's records show it still spent at least $56,000 dealing with legal repression. This amounts to more than its reported income in 1916, the year it really found its footing.[113]

The support that the ACLU gave to IWW defense efforts was significant and constitutes an important chapter in the history of that organization.[114] But the Wobblies bore primary responsibility for their defense and relief. The union's records and publications document thousands of small donations and are littered with pleas to members to dig deep to aid this cause.[115] And those trying to raise money encountered many problems. Defense offices were repeatedly raided, as we have seen, and to be arrested and prosecuted for doing this work, as happened to Theodora Pollok, Fred Esmond, and John Price, was not at all uncommon.[116] Picked up while raising money in Marshfield, Oregon, in April 1918, Wobbly Nestor Junkala may have been subjected to something much worse. While serving a ten-day sentence, likely for vagrancy, Junkala was found dead in his jail cell, supposedly a victim of suicide. "Necktie performs a patriotic service," said the *News-Review* of Roseburg, Oregon.[117]

On a mission to raise funds while out on bail after his conviction in Chicago, Ralph Chaplin did well here and there. But he was routinely denied meeting space and threatened with arrest and physical violence, and his efforts were not always rewarded with much money.[118] Caroline Lowe's fundraising work was similarly frustrating. "Money cannot be obtained here," she informed Roger Baldwin while trying to raise funds in Kansas in the summer of 1919. "We cannot get bond for the boys even after it is reduced to $250." Lowe had sent out 250 letters to "warm friends" who three years earlier "would have rallied promptly to any reasonable request [she] might have made." She got only one reply.[119]

Lawyers who aided the IWW frequently waived their fees or worked at reduced rates. But they still needed money for expenses, including court costs. This was the issue when Caroline Lowe and a colleague, Philip Callery, represented Joe Neil for no charge after his conviction. But they needed over $600 in relief funds just to get Neil out of the asylum so that he might apply for parole.[120] Money was also needed for bail. It is impossible to produce comprehensive totals of any kind, given both the nature of this expense and the thousands of cases involved. But the funds required in individual cases were substantial: usually several thousand dollars in criminal syndicalism cases and even more in the federal conspiracy cases. In this light, it seems probable that total expenses for bail exceeded $1 million and may have far surpassed that amount, and that is without any consideration of vagrancy and other misdemeanor cases.[121]

The inability to raise the necessary funds, whether for legal representation or bail, contributed to problems like the messy settlement of the murder case in the 1916 Mesabi strike. It is the reason some defendants represented themselves and others, if they trusted the attorneys and were offered their services, relied on court-appointed lawyers. In the case of bail, the shortage of funds left many defendants to languish, punished without yet being convicted of anything; vulnerable to the entreaties of prosecutors looking for turncoats; or, in the vagrancy cases, forced to submit themselves to the rock pile or weeks in jail.[122]

How this constant struggle to cover costs converged with the more immediate effects of all the arrests and convictions to drive the union into crisis can be seen in the series of reports that federal agent Edward Morse filed in 1921 concerning the "IWW situation" in the Bay Area. Quoting "Agent V-14," Morse was satisfied to report a long string of accomplishments that summer and fall: how the union struggled to gather a quorum at its meetings and recruit new members; how it was unable to muster the $10,000 needed to bail out five of seven members arrested in Oakland; how, of that group, which included Howard Welton, only one could be bailed because the local defense committee "is practically out of funds"; how the Wobblies were "very much demoralized" and how more arrests would "no doubt materially increase their discomfort"; and how V-14 found the members in "a very confused condition, as the Defense Treasury is nearly exhausted and they are at a loss where to turn for funds to defend the men who are now in jail."[123]

. . .

It is difficult to imagine how the IWW could have continued to function, let alone grow and prosper, in the face of all the repression that the organization and its members endured. Repression was indeed a death blow. But just as it is possible to murder a man who is already unwell or dying, so repression was not the only serious problem the IWW faced in the 1920s. During this, the "open shop decade," many employers discovered the value of constructing paternalistic relationships with their workers of the sort that blunted the appeal to a class struggle, including "employee welfare" programs and "representation plans" not entirely unlike the Loyal Legion of Loggers and Lumbermen. Progressive reforms legislated by the state, like health and safety schemes and, in some industries, wage and hour regulations, were also increasingly on offer. And for many workers, these reforms and their promise of a more humane capitalism, increasingly defined by a culture of consumption and distraction, were simply more appealing than the disruptions and uncertainties of revolutionary unionism. In similar ways, so was the more conservative brand of unionism afforded by the AFL.

The IWW also had to reckon with broad changes in work itself, including the consequences of having so successfully built itself around lower-skilled, migratory workers. In wheat and other grain agriculture, for instance, the adoption of the combine accelerated through the 1920s. Labor demand remained strong in many places into the 1930s, but the new machinery increased the competitive advantage of larger, more "progressive" farms, as they were called, and, in a time of steeply declining prices, reduced the prevalence of smaller farmers who had been more likely to accommodate the Wobblies. In lumber, oil, construction, mining, and maritime shipping, the effects of technological change were often even more immediate, as the proliferation of machinery driven by electrical motors and internal combustion engines simply eliminated many jobs that were the union's mainstay and made its strikes less effective. There was also the fact that transient workers in all these industries increasingly traveled by automobile. This changed the kinds of workers who labored in these industries, replacing the footloose, single men who had been such staples of IWW organizing with married men and families; and it isolated these workers, pulling them away from the IWW's traditional recruiting grounds in the boxcars, jungles, and labor camps.[124]

In light of all of this, it seems clear that while repression sealed the IWW's fate, it is not clear how viable the union would otherwise have been, at least without becoming a very different organization. As former Wobblies James P. Cannon and Elizabeth Gurley Flynn both noted, when each looked back on the IWW a half century after its founding, the organization was always characterized by a tension inherent in its "dual identity" as both a democratic labor union open to all workers, defined by their views and interests, and shaped around a syndicalist vision, and a vanguard party with a particular revolutionary aspiration entwined with the broader currents of revolution in its age, which were increasingly political in form.[125] Evident in earlier conflicts in the union about parliamentary socialism, this tension was heightened by the rise of the Bolsheviks, who, as they consolidated power in the aftermath of the October Revolution, called for a Third Communist International to convene in Moscow in the spring of 1919.

A great number of socialist parties and movements from around the world, including the IWW, were invited to these proceedings, which were very much intended to shape the future of world socialism around the Bolsheviks' revolutionary vision and their interests. The IWW sent no delegates to the inaugural World Congress of the Comintern, as it was called. But a sizeable number of IWWs, including many in the union's leadership, sympathized with the Bolsheviks and their program. In fact, in 1919, the general executive board essentially endorsed the Comintern by supporting a motion on the principle of leftist unity. But that decision was reversed in 1920 by a new board, and the union declined to send delegates to the Second World Congress of the Comintern that summer.[126]

Underlying the IWW's circumspection was the Communists' commitment to capturing the power of the state and putting it behind their revolutionary aims, which clashed with the IWW's syndicalism and its anarchist tendencies, replicated its earlier conflict with the Socialist Party, and threatened its identity as a union. Indeed, with no inherent faith in the revolutionary value of unions, the Communists were bound to treat such organizations as mere instruments in their schemes. The union's new leadership and most of its members knew this and anticipated that the Comintern would demand that leftist unionists in America abandon their organizations and "bore into" conventional AFL unions. This concern was soon borne out. In early 1921, the Bolsheviks created the Red International of Labor Unions, or Profintern, to coordinate the relationship between Communists and the labor movement. An IWW who attended the Profintern's founding conference that summer in Moscow confirmed that affiliating with the Bolsheviks would indeed mean the end of the union's tenure as an independent industrial union.

As the IWW and the Communist Party moved apart, and as the union shuddered under the weight of repression, perhaps 2,000 Wobblies enlisted with the party. Among them were James P. Cannon, who later became a prominent Trotskyist; Roy Brown, who had done crucial work organizing in lumber; George Hardy, the union's secretary-treasurer in 1920 and 1921; and Charles Ashleigh. There was also George Andreytchine, who had headed the union's publicity bureau, been charged with murder in the Mesabi Strike in 1916, was convicted in Chicago, and jumped bail with Haywood. Like Haywood, Andreytchine sought refuge in Russia, where he regaled his new comrades with stories about the twelve jails he had been thrown in during his time in the United States and about being arrested every harvest season. But as a sympathizer of Trotsky, he was jailed in the Soviet Union, too, and executed there in 1950.[127]

Then there is Haywood himself, whose flight to Russia proved especially costly, and not only in terms of lost leadership. Some of Haywood's bail had been provided by journalist Mary Marcy, who had put up her home. Despite the Bolsheviks' promise to indemnify the bondsmen, Haywood's flight caused her to lose the property and contributed to her suicide in 1922. Among ten others who had signed a writ of indemnity on Haywood's $15,000 bond were George Vanderveer, Otto Christensen, and C. E. Payne. Altogether, about $75,000 in bond money was lost when Haywood, Andreytchine, and the other seven defendants jumped bail.[128]

As damaging as these departures were, even more destructive was the conflict that communism created within the IWW. There remained in the union a large faction whose stance on Bolshevism was open and pragmatic. They existed alongside another that strongly opposed Bolshevism. Prominent in Chicago and on the Great Plains and strongly associated with the Agricultural Workers Industrial Union (AWIU), which had always aspired to running things in well-structured fashion, the former faction tended to favor centralized and pragmatic management of the union's affairs. The latter faction, in contrast, was strong in California and the Northwest and associated with the Lumber Workers Industrial Union (LWIU); it consisted of "decentralizers" who embraced the organization's antistatist traditions, resented the authority of the national office and the influence of the AWIU, and considered their rivals to have betrayed the union's founding principles.[129]

Aggravating this conflict were repression and the matter of defense work. A major point of disagreement was the decentralizers' charge that the union's top leadership had been too tolerant of members who sought clemency. Beyond this, the schism was informed by the belief of many decentralizers that their fellow Wobblies, many of them now largely safe from persecution in Chicago or other eastern cities, were indifferent to what they, in the early 1920s, still faced in the way of arrests, imprisonment, and vigilantism out West.[130] The conflict was also framed by specific disagreements about how defense funds were raised and spent, as well as the more fundamental question, which the decentralizers had come to press with increasing force over the years, as to whether legal defense was a worthwhile alternative to organizing and direct action, when almost every serious case ended in conviction anyway.[131]

The schism highlights how repression tended to be integrated with all the other problems the IWW faced. It was also the defining issue at the union's 1924 convention, where it tore the IWW apart. Poorly attended, the proceedings were as ridiculous as they were chaotic and pathetic, marked by opposing sessions, fistfights, and various attempts by the factions to oust each other. The convention ended with the "centralizers" in control of the union's headquarters and finances and most of the decentralizers expelled. In this latter category was James Rowan, who, in foolish and mercenary defiance of IWW values, resorted to a court injunction in a bid to regain control of union property. While Rowan's faction went on to form a rival IWW that never amounted to anything, the centralizers emerged as the main legatees of the original IWW. But they inherited an organization that was collapsing.[132]

The IWW had never been a model of effective internal organization, even in its strongest days. There were always plenty of disagreements about strategy and tactics and plenty of destructive rifts and rivalries. Some of the issues that underlay the schism were not new, having emerged, as we have seen, early in the union's history. Nevertheless, the schism that erupted in the early 1920s is a crucial event in the IWW's demise, not only because it fractured the union structurally but also because, having been shaped by repression, it aggravated repression's consequences. It is easy to imagine how people who had been so battered because of their commitments to industrial unionism were, precisely for this reason, unable to support an organization that was in such a shameful state of disarray. It is just as easy to see how all this trouble worsened the problems the union faced in recruiting new members, let alone organizing the strikes and protests that had once made it so substantial.

By 1925, the IWW was largely destroyed, its demise evident in and driven by the collapse of its most important local, the AWIU. In 1922, the harvest workers union raised $85,000 in funds to support other IWW strikes and the defense of Wobblies on the West Coast.[133] And in the 1923 harvest season, despite everything, the AWIU enlisted some 15,000 members nationwide. The following season it signed up only 10,000. It then began the summer of 1925 with a conference in Omaha, where its delegates vowed they were ready to reap a great harvest of workers. But that season brought increasing frustration, with a total enlistment of maybe 8,500. Especially disappointing was its failure to regain any ground in its old stronghold of North Dakota, where continuing declines in arrests and prosecutions for vagrancy gave ironic but irrefutable proof of the union's demise. In August, the AWIU found it could not even organize a free-speech fight anymore, as police in Fargo found plenty of room in the jail to blunt the union's efforts.[134]

The following year, AWIU recruitment faltered completely, never to recover. It signed up only 1,538; in 1927, only 783 new members were enlisted; in 1928, only 1,051; and the following year, 639. By then total AWIU membership was almost certainly less than 3,000, far too small to exert much influence in the field, and it was practically defunct. Already lifeless by this point were the LWIU, still dominated by decentralizers, and the IWW's unions in oil, mining, construction, and maritime.[135] These organizations collapsed very quickly, a result in no small part of how heavily their ranks had been filled with transient workers and had to be constantly refilled. As these key constituents faded into irrelevance, the IWW's reign as a functional organization came to an end. There would be no workers' commonwealth, no rising of the working class in unvanquishable numbers. Only defeat. The IWW held only two more conventions in the decade, both of them very poorly attended and already pervaded more by nostalgia, illusions, and recriminations than realistic hopes and effective planning.

. . .

In May 1927, the U.S. Supreme Court finally decided the constitutionality of prosecuting people for criminal syndicalism. By then, the prisons and jails were nearly empty of Wobblies, and the union was no longer under the iron heel, thanks to its irrelevance. But the Wobblies were not done receiving lessons about the propriety of what had been done to them. In *Fiske v. Kansas*, the court threw out Harold Fiske's conviction, primarily on the grounds that evidence of his guilt was inadequate and that Fiske's conviction was therefore a denial of due process.[136] But the justices came to a very different conclusion in two other criminal syndicalism cases decided that same day.

The facts behind *Burns v. United States* read like a parable of the union's final days of relevance, inscribed in legal process. In April 1923, William Burns was walking along a railroad track in Yosemite National Park, on his way to a lumber job, when police arrested him and found IWW literature and credentials on his person. Burns was one of three Wobblies arrested within park boundaries that year, amid union attempts to organize lumber and construction workers there, and charged with criminal syndicalism. The men were charged under a federal statute that imported to federal lands state criminal laws that regulated conduct not addressed by federal statute.[137] But Burns, who declined an offer to walk free if he renounced the IWW, was the only one brought to trial.[138]

Convicted in December despite a strong defense from R. W. Henderson, Burns was sentenced to fifteen months at Leavenworth. The main issue in his appeal was whether the jury instructions defined sabotage too broadly. For Justice Pierce Butler, this objection was negated by all the evidence showing that Burns was a member and organizer in the IWW and the fact, which needed no evidence, that the IWW was committed to sabotage, never mind that the statute itself limited the meaning of sabotage to the "willful and malicious physical damage or injury to physical property." As for the contention of Burns's lawyers that the statute was "void for uncertainty," Butler pointed to the court's decision that day in *Whitney v. California*.[139]

Born in California just two years after the end of the Civil War, Charlotte Anita Whitney was a child of privilege who had lived much of her life as a Progressive before moving further to the left and passing "over the line, the invisible line," as she put it, "which divides mankind into two different groups."[140] During the early 1910s, Whitney supported the Wobblies implicated in the Wheatland affair. She was a friend of the not-so-silent defender Theodora Pollok and aided the legal defense of Tom Mooney and Warren Billings. A leader in the Socialist Party in the Bay Area, Whitney was one of many left-wing party members who reformed the state Socialist Party into a chapter of the Communist Labor Party (CLP)—an event ratified at a convention in Oakland on November 9, 1919, which Whitney attended.[141]

On the evening of November 28, 1919, Whitney delivered a speech in Oakland before an audience of 150, "The Negro Problem in the United States." Arrested that night, she was convicted the following February after a three-week trial. The prosecution's theory was that Whitney's membership in the CLP made her guilty of criminal syndicalism, in part because of the CLP's ties to the Comintern and in part because the CLP was but a "political adjunct of the I.W.W."[142] To prove its case, the prosecution relied on Coutts and Dymond, who linked Whitney to the sensational story about Dublin Bob and the bomb-making laboratory on a houseboat in Stockton. Several days after her conviction, in a courtroom again packed with legions of supporters—and a number of American Legionnaires—the judge sentenced Whitney to one to fourteen years in prison. She was jailed for eleven days and then freed while awaiting the results of her appeal.[143]

Now, seven years later, the Supreme Court also ruled against Whitney. Writing for the majority, Justice Edward Sanford dismissed the arguments advanced by Whitney's lawyers. Citing his own majority opinion in *Gitlow v. New York*, a 1925 decision that established that the First Amendment governed the actions of states and local governments but upheld the conviction under New York's criminal anarchy law of another Socialist turned Communist, Sanford averred that a state was permitted to "punish those who abuse this freedom by utterances inimical to the public welfare, tending to incite to crime, disturb the public peace or endanger the foundations of organized government and threaten its overthrow by unlawful means."[144] Nor was the law "void for uncertainty," when, like many other statutes, it was open to clear and definite interpretation by "men desirous of observing the law." It was not a violation of equal protection, either, since it was not "purely arbitrary."[145] In all these ways, Sanford confirmed that the statute and the prosecution were sound. Whitney avoided being imprisoned only because, encouraged by her powerful friends, California Governor C. C. Young granted her an unconditional pardon.

If Sanford's opinion made clear where the law stood on the question of prosecuting Wobblies, the opinion that Justice Louis Brandeis wrote in the case made very clear what a great many Progressives generally thought about the Wobblies and what had been done to them. A mentor to a young Roger Baldwin, Brandeis accepted that capitalism had faults and needed to be managed for its own sake. But he also believed capitalism to be a font of freedom, economic advancement, and individual self-fulfillment, and he had little truck with radicalism, least of all the kind promoted by the IWW. As legal historian David Rabban points out, although Brandeis sometimes supported conventional unions, he feared the IWW and saw in the rise of the union and the disorder it sowed justifications for both ameliorative social reforms and antiradical repression.[146]

Often lauded as a masterpiece of judicial rhetoric and a paean to the virtues of free speech and association in a liberal, democratic society, Brandeis's opinion restated the clear and present danger test that Justice Holmes had developed a few years earlier. In it he took the view, which paralleled Holmes's own, later perspective, that the test protected the rights of individuals unless the harm they portended was imminent or unless impinging on those rights was essential to preserving the state against "destruction or from serious injury, political, economic, or moral." He recognized that the California statute did not merely criminalize "the practice of criminal syndicalism," or even just "the preaching of it," but extended beyond this to prohibit "association with those who propose to preach it." He affirmed that "the right of free speech, the right to teach and the right of assembly are . . . fundamental rights."[147] He lionized those who "won our independence": they "were not cowards," he said; they sought to preserve liberty "unless the incidence of evil apprehended is so imminent that it may befall before there is opportunity for full discussion." And the "evil apprehended," he said, "must be severe." Therefore, Brandeis concluded, "it must remain open to a defendant to present the issue whether there did exist at the time a clear danger, whether the danger, if any, was imminent, and whether the evil apprehended was one so substantial as to justify the stringent restriction imposed by the Legislature."[148]

But this was not all that Brandeis said. In a telling qualification of all the fulsome endorsements of liberty that went before, he noted that "Miss Whitney" had not properly invoked the clear and present danger test. Although she claimed "that the statute as applied to her violated the federal Constitution," she had not put the test, or the evidence to support her claims under the test, before the jury and the trial court. Moreover, Brandeis concluded, "there was evidence on which the court or jury might have found that such a danger existed." In the appeal of a prominent Communist named C. E. Ruthenberg, who died just before the case appealing his conviction for criminal syndicalism could be decided, Brandeis had been prepared to dissent in support of free speech, but he did not for Whitney, whose CLP membership and ties to the IWW were disqualifying. As Brandeis put it, "there was other testimony which tended to establish the existence of a conspiracy on the part of members of the Industrial Workers of the World to commit present serious crimes, and likewise to show that such a conspiracy would be furthered by the activity of the society of which Miss Whitney was a member." Therefore, "the judgment of the State court cannot be disturbed," Brandeis concluded, concurring with the majority and giving his own endorsement to the idea that measures such as these, which had left so many men drowning and broken, were as appropriate in the world he idealized as they were in the one that he, in the name of progress, sometimes purported to reject.[149]

. . .

A few months later and 1,500 miles away from the justices' chambers, the IWW fought a last, heroic and tragic battle, one that confirmed what it likely would have continued to face everywhere, were the union still as relevant as it had once been. In the summer of 1927, enterprising Wobblies under the leadership of the redoubtable A. S. Embree organized Colorado

FIGURE 23. State policeman threatening a journalist, Walsenburg, Colorado, January 12, 1928. Shortly before this photograph was taken, state police shot and killed a bystander and, moments later, an IWW striker at the building in the background, which is the IWW hall. Walter P. Reuther Library, Archives of Labor and Urban Affairs, Wayne State University.

coal miners and, that fall, brought 12,000 out in a statewide strike. They sought better wages and working conditions and to protest the execution of Sacco and Vanzetti, who were put to death in August, after Justices Holmes, Brandeis, and Harlan Fiske Stone each in turn denied their last petitions for a stay of execution.

For weeks the strike crippled coal production in the state. It was met with a surge of arrests and assaults on union men and IWW property and a massacre. On November 21, 1927, state police "rangers" responded to a picket line fracas at the Columbine Mine in Boulder County by shooting and killing six strikers. "We're all leaders," said picketers at the Columbine, just like their fellow workers on the *Verona* a decade earlier, when, moments before the standoff exploded in violence, they too were challenged to name those in charge. The strike extended into the following year but it was doomed by continued repression, the workers' exhaustion, and the shrewd machinations of the coal companies. Under the influence of Progressive managers, the leading producers provided workers with modest, mainly short-lived concessions and also extended union recognition, not to the IWW, but to the United Mine Workers, which had failed to support the walkout. But this last great strike in the IWW's tragic history did not end without a final upwelling of violence. On January 12, state police in Walsenberg, in the southern part of the state, confronted a parade of 500 strikers heading to a meeting of the Colorado Industrial Commission in Walsenberg. After putting the men to flight, the heavily armed police opened fire, killing with impunity a sixteen-year-old bystander named Celestino Martinez and, moments later, at the union hall, a striker named Clemente Chavez.[150]

Conclusion

A Vision We Don't Possess

The writer James Jones never laid pipeline in Oklahoma, felled trees in Oregon, or loaded ships in San Pedro; he never worked in a mine, carried a red card, or served time at Leavenworth or San Quentin. But like Jack London, a crucial influence he shared with the Wobblies, Jones saw plenty of hardship and brutality in his life. Foremost were merciless experiences in the Battle of Guadalcanal that attuned him to the importance of always telling the truth.[1] And there is truth aplenty in his debut novel, *From Here to Eternity,* about an army unit in Hawaii around the time of America's entry into the Second World War. Published in 1951 and partly autobiographical, this book is one of the greatest novels of the twentieth century, and it stands out among a multitude of other reflections on the IWW, both literary and academic, for its remarkable grasp of the Wobblies' situation and their destiny.

These reflections center on a character named Jack Malloy. "Born the son of a county sheriff in Montana," Malloy, Jones tells us, was "13 in 1917 when his father started jailing the IWWs in earnest. That was what started Malloy off: The Wobblies had taught him to read. He started his reading in his father's jail with the books they always carried with them." The "second thing he bought" after Walt Whitman's *Leaves of Grass,* with the "first money from his first job" was "the Red Card and his membership dues in the IWW." As a Wobbly, Malloy "learned to know jails from the prisoners' side." A "veteran of Centralia," he also "learned to worship" Big Bill Haywood, Ralph Chaplin, Charles Ashleigh, and the others locked up at Leavenworth and gave "most of his money" to helping their defense. Through all of this, Malloy "went on reading," always reading, he "wanted to be ready." He read Upton Sinclair and George Sterling and he "studied, and came to love, the memory of Jack London." He worked hard and he sacrificed, waiting like this until the union's bottom "finally fell clear out." Only weeks before the Pearl Harbor attack, Malloy, a dreamer, a tough apostle of a better world who had been "born in the wrong time," found himself locked up in the army's most brutal stockade.[2]

A key scene has Malloy in quiet conversation with a fellow dreamer, Robert E. Lee Prewitt, one of the novel's leading characters. "On the bum" as a mere child, where he suffered the kinds of assaults and imprisonment that would have been familiar to so many who joined the IWW, Prewitt is locked up alongside Malloy, who tries to impress on the younger man who these Wobblies were and what they meant for the world. Malloy spent two decades wandering about, working as a harvest hand, seaman, and longshoreman, but feels that his past membership no longer qualifies him to speak of the IWW in the first person. So he interrupts himself, describing it with detached reverence: "You dont remember the Wobblies. You were too young. Or else not even born yet. There has never been anything like them, before or since. They called themselves materialist-economists, but what they really were was a religion. They were workstiffs and bindlebums like you and me, but they were welded together by a vision we dont possess."[3]

Malloy's haunting memories of industrial unionists in his father's Montana jail are an essential backdrop against which to highlight the promises of a better world, the "new religion," as Malloy describes it, misspent and shattered in concert with the crumbling of these soldiers' own lives. The men in the stockade with Malloy and Prewitt are equally relevant in this regard. They had "cut timber up in Washington, . . . worked in the Indiana mines, poured steel in Pennsylvania, followed the wheat harvest in Kansas and the fruit harvest in California, loaded cargoes at the docks in Frisco and Dago and Seattle and N.O. La."; they had tried to change the country "and been defeated." Deprived of "organization," these men "graduated into the Army," a dead end where their lives and destinies came to reflect the broader tragedy of the working class and its political aspirations and the tragic course of America itself.[4]

And then there is Prewitt. Adjudged a "Bolshevik" by his commanding officers because he would not let them exploit his skills as a boxer, he is much more Wobbly than Communist. But Jones, who has Prewitt

FIGURE 24. Funeral of Hugo Gerlot, Felix Baran, and John Looney, victims of the Everett massacre, at Mount Pleasant Cemetery, Seattle, Washington, November 18, 1916. University of Washington Libraries, Special Collections, SOC 3841.

become a voracious reader and a student of Jack London, no doubt understood this. He assigns him a transcendent abhorrence of the powerful, one that suffices to oppose any social order in which authority and violence have fully converged, as Jones elsewhere makes very clear, with "property." In this vein, Prewitt's bolshevism consists not in a depraved ego, as his officers saw things, let alone in any connection to the Communist Party, but in some things they, by dint of their own self-annulling faith in the world as they found it, could not appreciate: a consuming affinity with the underdog and an antipathy to inequity so complete and so uncompromising as to bring Prewitt to the point of self-destruction. So armed, he would not be broken. But as one officer insists, to kill a man is the same thing as to break him.[5]

. . .

Prewitt's full name is an obvious allusion to a lost cause. He is a refugee from Harlan County, Kentucky, where, Jones tells us, his mother had died of consumption during a big coal strike, when blood "actually ran like rainwater in the gutters" the day his uncle was killed in a shootout with "several deputies." And Prewitt "saw that battle, at least as near as any man can ever come to seeing any battle."[6] As Jones surely knew, in 1931, amid just such a strike, a delegation of intellectuals led by Theodore Dreiser and John Dos Passos went to Harlan and neighboring

Bell counties to investigate the extraordinary repression visited on impoverished miners associated with a Communist union. For their troubles, they were indicted on criminal syndicalism charges.

It was in Harlan County, too, several months later, that Wobbly Tom Connors, among a contingent of Wobblies who futilely attempted to gain control of the struggle in that area, nearly gave his life to a very different lost cause. Twice arrested in California for criminal syndicalism, once after testifying on behalf of other Wobblies, Connors had been imprisoned in San Quentin in 1924 on charges of attempting to influence a juror after a pamphlet he had written on behalf of criminal syndicalism defendants ended up in the hands of someone called to jury duty. He had been active in Colorado during the coal strike in 1927 and 1928. Now, in Harlan, where a union lawyer was whipped, Connors was nearly beaten to death by the sheriff's men.[7]

What happened in southeastern Kentucky in those years reflected in many ways the changing course of industrial unionism and antiradicalism in the wake of the IWW's collapse. In 1928, the Communist Party occupied the space created by the union's demise and embarked on a campaign to build its own industrial unions. Over the next seven years, several hundred party organizers and activists were arrested, and several dozen people were sentenced to prison on criminal syndicalism charges in California, Kentucky, Ohio, and Oregon. More than a few served significant time behind bars. Although the U.S. Supreme Court had signaled in a 1931 decision, *Stromberg v. California,* in which it invalidated the conviction of a young Communist woman for violating a 1919 California law barring the display of radical flags, that it was no longer prepared to enforce without much qualification antiradical laws, the courts continued to uphold these criminal syndicalism prosecutions when they deemed them procedurally sound and backed by sufficient evidence.[8] As in the IWW cases, it did not matter that the defendants had engaged in no violence and were not about to do so. Nor did the law do anything to stem a tide of vigilantism that accompanied this surge in Communist labor unionism and the flurry of strikes that the party's unions led.

In 1935, the party reverted to its earlier strategy of "boring into" existing unions, the one Wobblies correctly foresaw would have spelled the end of their own union had they joined with the Communists. The strategy's main manifestation was the party's "Popular Front" alliance with the Committee for Industrial Organization, or CIO, and other reformist elements of the New Deal coalition. Repression was hardly the only impetus for this development, which was much dictated by Moscow and the Soviet state's own interests. At the same time, there can be no doubt that the Popular Front gave the party a semi-legitimacy it never before enjoyed, one that corresponded with a dramatic decrease in the kinds of prosecution that its activists faced earlier in the decade. In turn, the party's support was essential to the success of the CIO and, in this way, the triumph of the New Deal and the real improvements this brought for millions of workers. But allying with the CIO meant that the party had to abandon its commitment to building its own radical industrial unions and accede to an unequal partnership that, beginning in the late 1930s, culminated in the CIO's eventual purge of Communists from the unions they had helped to found.

If this compromise did not produce a further revision of the Supreme Court's stance on antiradical laws, it at least underlay this revision. In 1937, the court reversed the conviction of Communist Dirk De Jonge, arrested in Portland, Oregon, in 1934 for giving a speech at a meeting in the midst of the wide-ranging West Coast maritime strike that year. For the first time, the court stated unequivocally that the First Amendment protected freedom of assembly against intrusions by the state, declaring that "peaceable assembly for lawful discussion cannot be made a crime. The holding of meetings for peaceable political action cannot be proscribed."[9] Although this language seems to certify *De Jonge v. Oregon* as a leap forward for civil liberties and rights of dissent, it also reflects the limits of the court's decision, as it was exactly a rather dubious contrast of the "peaceful" nature of De Jonge's activity with the ostensibly unpeaceful conduct involved in *Whitney v. California* and *Gitlow v. New York* that allowed the court to leave those precedents intact.[10] Such was the logic, too, of the court's decision that same year in the case of Angelo Herndon, a young black Communist convicted in early 1933 of violating Georgia's insurrection statute by organizing a large protest against inadequate relief policies. A narrowly divided court ruled that this statute, as construed in Herndon's trial, was too broad and did not survive application of the clear and present danger test. But as it did in *De Jonge,* the court left in place earlier precedents holding that the advocacy of social change by radical means, or the participation in organizations committed to such a cause, could still be criminalized if such advocacy or participation could be cast as portending criminality or violence.[11]

The implications of the Supreme Court's position became evident in the 1940s and 1950s, when that court joined with lesser courts in endorsing a new wave of antiradical prosecution. This time, the defendants were members of the Communist Party, who found themselves without a home in postwar liberalism.[12] In a series of trials, over a hundred party members were convicted of violating the 1940 Smith Act—a statute that was premised on, and understood as a federal version of, the state criminal syndicalism laws.[13] Most were imprisoned, among them Elizabeth Gurley Flynn, who had escaped this fate more than three decades earlier but was convicted this time, she recalled, by a jury that included a nephew of Judge Kenesaw Mountain Landis and that was plied with a copy of her pamphlet on sabotage, the one that had helped convict many Wobblies. Most of these Communists lost their appeals, on the grounds that the prosecutions were essentially consistent with the clear and present danger test, even as envisaged by Holmes and Brandeis.[14]

Among the judges who let these convictions stand was Supreme Court Justice Felix Frankfurter, the man who more than three decades earlier had helped fashion the President's Mediation Commission as a way of suppressing the IWW. Only toward the end of the 1950s did the Supreme Court adopt a more circumspect view of the Smith Act and the business of antiradical repression in general. It was by then under the leadership of Chief Justice Earl Warren, who had been the district attorney of Alameda County, California, home to Oakland. Warren claimed that on his "starting day" as an assistant in that office he was made to sit in on a criminal syndicalism trial. Although Warren does not specify, it is clear he had in mind the 1920 trial of John Taylor, the former Wobbly and Communist Labor Party supporter who was the defendant in the important California Supreme Court case *People v. Taylor.* The trial ended with Taylor, who represented himself, convicted, sentenced to one to fourteen years in prison, and on his way to San Quentin.[15]

Although Warren claimed to have found these criminal syndicalism cases replete with "repulsive informers," said that he "never liked" the statute and never used it when he was the district attorney, and did not imprison Anita Whitney in the time between her lost appeal and pardon, his opposition to such laws otherwise amounted to very little until he became a Supreme Court justice.[16] Even then, the court was equivocal about reining in the prosecution of radicals until Warren's last term. In the 1969 criminal syndicalism case *Brandenburg v. Ohio,* which involved the conviction of a publicity-hungry Klansman who arranged to be filmed delivering two speeches in which he propounded his belief in white supremacy and denigrated Jews and blacks, the court held that neither the statute nor the judge's instruction sufficiently distinguished "mere advocacy," which could not be prosecuted, from "incitement to imminent lawless action." Going beyond what Louis Brandeis had conceived with his concurring opinion in *Whitney,* the court now required prosecutors to prove that defendants intended their words to cause imminent disorder or crime and to show that the words were likely to cause such disorder or crime. The case explicitly overruled *Whitney* and, a half century too late to matter, condemned the premise on which the felony prosecutions of nearly all Wobblies had been based.[17]

It fell, though, to Justice William O. Douglas, whose dissents in the many decisions upholding Smith Act convictions were rewarded with years of surveillance by J. Edgar Hoover's Federal Bureau of Investigation, to render final judgment on this business of legal repression.[18] Douglas was not a typical Supreme Court justice. As a young man, he had picked cherries, waited tables, and hoboed across the country; he recalled how he had "worked among the very, very poor, the migrant laborers, the Chicanos and the I.W.Ws who I saw being shot at by the police."[19] He remembered seeing "roundups" of Wobblies and hearing from "their lips unvarnished stories of privations and sufferings." He recollected walking home as a teenager in 1917 "with tears in [his] eyes" after watching authorities in North Yakima arrest dozens of Wobblies and seal them up in boxcars with no food, water, or sanitary facilities. Douglas was prone to distorting his life story, but if he did not actually see these things, he managed to feel for those who had endured them. He respected the work the IWW had done among migrant workers, miners, lumberjacks, and the like; he admired the Wobblies' resolve to organize workers without discrimination; and he recognized how the criminal syndicalism laws had subjected the union to "the full force of governmental prosecution." From the vantage of the 1970s, Douglas attested that "I thought then, and I still think, that our record as a nation against the IWWs was disgraceful."[20]

Douglas wrote a concurring opinion in *Brandenburg* which is no less than a comprehensive exposé of the clear and present danger test and all it purports to represent. For Douglas, the test was simply too malleable to constrain the state. Under it, the threats being tested were easily exaggerated "by judges so wedded to the status quo that critical analysis made them nervous." Indeed, he said, the test was a license for judges to conduct or endorse "political trials" while posing as champions of liberty and to destroy the First Amendment while pretending to honor it. Instead, he preferred that there be almost no permissible limits on rights of free speech and association.[21]

Three years later, Douglas authored the court's opinion in *Papachris-tou v. Jacksonville,* a decision that substantially limited the ways vagrancy laws could be enforced. Here, in another case whose facts were far removed from the doings of radical industrial unionists, Douglas also left his unique mark. Crowning a constitutional campaign against these laws that had far more to do with validating civil rights and New Left politics and the countercultural values of the 1960s than with ratifying the principles of labor solidarity and class struggle that defined the 1910s or 1920s, he avowed these laws contrary to basic American values of tolerance and due process. He specifically invoked "poor people, nonconformists, dissenters, idlers" as those whose inter-ests stood to be compromised by these laws if they were not reined in. And to bring home this point, Douglas alluded, not to the wanderings of the Wobblies but to the somewhat less worrying examples of Walt Whitman, Vachel Lindsay, and Henry David Thoreau.[22]

A true if uneasy liberal, Douglas was not prepared to cross the invis-ible line that brought Anita Whitney so close to the prison's gates. Closer in thought and sensibility to Thoreau, or maybe Burton Wheeler or William Borah, than to Jack London, James Jones, or Big Bill Hay-wood, his concern was to defend freedom of expression, conscience, and belief, to manage society in more reasonable and humane ways, not to abet the latter's concept of revolution or their contempt for the social order. Similar to Holmes's dissent in *Abrams v. United States,* which defended the rights of "poor and puny anonymities," Douglas's concur-rence in *Brandenburg* cast the "threats" presented in all the court's most notorious civil liberties cases as "always puny."[23] Nevertheless, his opinions in *Brandenburg* and *Papachristou* stand as frank indictments of an earlier liberalism's role in building upon both law and lawlessness a legacy of malice, violence, and class conflict disguised as a defense of freedom—a kind of judicial masque of anarchy.

. . .

Unlike Big Bill Haywood, who died lonely in Moscow in 1928, just as Joseph Stalin turned a revolution into a nightmare not unlike the one depicted in *The Iron Heel,* Charles Ashleigh's shifted allegiance to the Communist cause unfolded in his native England, to which he had been deported upon his release from Leavenworth in 1921. From that vantage, Ashleigh described his old union as a guerilla force, spirited but undisci-plined, in contrast to the disciplined army of class warriors he imagined himself to have joined when he became a Communist. And what became of that army, heir to the IWW's push for radical industrial unions? Convicted in 1949 of violating the Smith Act, Henry Winston, a black man, was one of several party leaders who jumped bail before he could be imprisoned. Captured, Winston was crippled and permanently blinded by a brain tumor which prison officials waited two years to adequately treat. "They took my sight but my vision remains," said Winston.[24]

Winston's courage was undeniable. But whatever vision he retained was hard to find in the party he served. Long before he was convicted, the party's interest in radical industrial unionism had withered. Moreover, its membership never recovered from the repression it endured or the compromises it made. It is now embalmed, not in sectarian rigidities or archaic, radical delusions, as some distant critics are wont to think, but in exactly the opposite. Even before the demise of the Soviet Union and other socialist regimes in the late 1980s and early 1990s turned its world upside down, the party had subordinated its radical aspirations to conformism and opportunism. And so, as if to give added proof to Marx's point about history repeating itself first as tragedy and then as farce, it pretends to do battle with capitalism and yet tethers itself to a Democratic Party that is reconciled to the existing social order. Almost nothing remains of the communist movement, least of all the kind of romance that has always been more the legacy of insurgents than soldiers.

There are other political successors to the anticapitalist upsurge of a century ago that gave rise to the IWW. They range from various Trotskyist groups to legatees of Debs's old Socialist Party, and although they have done a good job of sustaining debates about socialism and alternatives to capitalism, they have no mass support and few resources. The largest of these, the Democratic Socialists of America (DSA), is conspicuously among the least radical. In recent years, the DSA has found a measure of electoral success by making impassive suggestions that this or that industry be nationalized while actually embracing the spirits of New Deal and Great Society liberalism and putting these notions behind an agenda that consists mainly of welfare-state paternalism and Keynesianism, seasoned with identity politics. In all these ways, it is less the descendant of Debs than of the Progressives who put him in prison, and less a proponent of revolution than a champion, unwitting or otherwise, of what Jack London called a "fairer, juster form of slavery than any the world has yet seen."[25]

To be sure, in the fashion of some of these Progressives of yesteryear, the DSA has, along with some of these other groups, opposed the recent persecution of whistleblowers and antiwar activists for violating the

Espionage Act, which remains on the books. Over the years, such organizations have also condemned the infrequent prosecution of civil rights and New Left activists under state criminal syndicalism laws, which also remain on the books. And they have usually stood apart from today's mainstream Progressives who attack cases like *Brandenburg* as too protective of "dangerous" speech and "threatening" organizations. But as the ACLU's evolution likewise makes clear, it is one thing to support democratic rights and civil liberties and quite another to advance the cause of labor radicalism.[26]

In the end, none of these groups really offers a vision of a workers' commonwealth of the kind that had such a hold on Jack Malloy and that drove so many real Wobblies to such remarkable levels of sacrifice. And neither does the labor movement itself, or what remains of it. In the postwar period, the mainstream labor movement fully resigned itself to the sovereignty of capitalism, focused workers' attentions on bread-and-butter issues, embraced the state as a legitimate arbiter of workers' rights and interests, and so became, as London also forecast, an accomplice of oligarchy in the construction of "an age of selfishness." Now, two decades into a new century, with that oligarchy more powerful than ever and the movement's membership rolls and influence in a state of inexorable decline, it is hard not to see in the recent increase in professed support for organized labor among some elements of liberal society a cheap and harmless indulgence of something that no longer matters.[27]

As James Jones understood, by the time the Second World War began, the IWW was finished, an entity composed mainly of aging men and their memories. What activism the union mustered during the New Deal and postwar periods consisted mainly of the vehement promotion of a syndicalism often shorn of much of its radicalism, which occasionally justified attacks on communism or alliances with anticommunists important enough to register in Cold War America. In recent decades the IWW has managed a comeback on the strength of earnest organizing and principled activism. But it remains a small organization. And although it is probably the country's most radical union, its radicalism is quite subdued compared to a century ago. Indeed, as even the most ardent Wobblies must admit, whatever its virtues, today's IWW is not the union it once was, which is a major reason its members suffer so little of what their forbearers endured.[28]

. . .

Like every part of this story, the union's decline into irrelevancy a hundred years ago is, above all, a human tale. The men who endured the repression that helped break the IWW sometimes managed to build for themselves meaningful lives, even as the union collapsed beneath them. Nicholaas Steelink, for example, dusted himself off and struggled onward with the IWW. So did Jack London's old friend George Speed, who, well into his sixties, hoboed his way across the Rocky Mountains to join the Colorado coal strike in 1927. In a quieter way, so did Ralph Chaplin, who around that time received a "farewell visit" from Speed and Vincent St. John. That same year, 1927, just before the building was torn down, Chaplin paid twenty-five cents to tour the ruins of the old Cook County jail. There he had written "Prison Song," a number in the union's songbook, in which he spoke of being "defiant 'neath the Iron Heel." And there he found above the door of cell number 125, still legible ten years after he had put it there, the inscription "Non Sum Qualis Eram Bonae Sub Regno Cynrae," or "I am not such, as in the reign of the good Cynara I was." The line is the title of a poem about lost love by Ernest Dowson, taken from book 4 of Horace's *Odes,* wherein the speaker, fifty years old, implores the goddess Venus to find someone younger to worship at her shrine. The discovery seemed to deeply affect Chaplin, who wrote how the "ghosts of that horrible place haunted me for many a day" after his visit.[29]

In the 1930s, Chaplin drifted away from what remained of the IWW. While he always defended the union's program, he spent his last years devoted to left-wing Roman Catholicism, warning of the dangers of communism, business unionism, and the "uneasy rocking chair of the welfare state," while curating the archives of the Washington State Historical Society.[30] Quite a few Wobblies followed a different course, falling in with leftist, sometimes Communist-influenced unions in the 1930s and 1940s. Among these was Embree, who by the late 1930s was organizing with the Mine, Mill, and Smelter Workers Union, by then on the left wing of the labor movement. But the prison records of Wobblies incarcerated in Idaho alongside Embree contain a good number of inquiries, written years later, about the pasts of men whose lives had turned out a lot more like Jack Malloy's or Robert Prewitt's. Some are from relief agencies, others from police. Among the most tragic of these are requests for information about John Shea, imprisoned in 1918, released three years later, and found dead in 1936 in Portland, destitute and calling himself Fred Briggs. The prison was able to confirm Shea's identity. But it could provide no information on next of kin, as Shea, who had left home at nine and was about sixty-nine

years old, had none and had given no home address besides IWW headquarters.[31]

Shea's fate was not uncommon, as researcher Earl Bruce White found
in the 1970s when he investigated the fortunes of the defendants in the
Kansas conspiracy case and discovered how several defendants had
been found dead in just this way and how others struggled with alcoholism and troubles with the law.[32] Especially common, it seems, were
cases where these men resumed their lives as low-paid industrial workers, with all the usual frustrations and hardships that this entailed, but
now without much promise of building from their circumstances a revolution. Typical in this regard was Hagbard Edwards, who became the
kind of revolutionary that Jack London envied and served two and a
half years at San Quentin as a result, several years after spending time
with "Pork Chop" at the Seattle Public Library, where he devoured
London's writings. In his youth, London himself read voraciously at the
public library, hiding this from his streetwise associates while also
working for a time as a janitor at the high school he attended, before he
became wealthy and famous.[33] Thirteen years after his release, Edwards
was working as a janitor in a theater in Seattle, making about $1,400 a
year and paying $25 a month in rent. This was thirty-eight years before
he died in obscurity and was buried without a funeral, long after he had
risen to some prominence in a union that had tried to deliver the whole
world from such a fate.[34]

When Jack London died, about two weeks after the Everett massacre
and just as the IWW was really beginning to surge toward its main
appointments with the iron heel, he had abandoned his membership in
the Socialist Party because of its "lack of fire and fight[,] . . . its loss of
emphasis on the class struggle," and its commitment to "peaceableness
and compromise." This was three years after he had affirmed his support for "direct action" and "syndicalism" in opposition to a party that
"was doomed to become a bulwark of conservatism."[35] News of the
death of this "I.W.W. man," this "genius" and friend, broke just as the
IWW was holding its tenth convention, where it plotted a year of
unprecedented gains while already reckoning that *The Iron Heel* was
"not fiction but fact," and it promptly dispatched a "telegram of con-
dolence" to his widow, Charmain.[36] Many years later, the critic Alfred
Kazin proposed that "the greatest story Jack London ever wrote was
the story he lived."[37] Something very similar can be said of forgotten
men like Edwards, whose experiences offer a stronger confirmation
than anything they ever preached of the essential validity of the premises

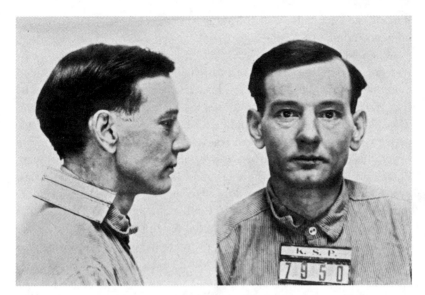

FIGURE 25. Joe Neil at the Kansas State Penitentiary, January 1923. Kansas State Archives.

upon which their union was founded. Foremost among these are the beliefs, which they shared with London himself and with James Jones as well, that in this world the ultimate arbiter of things is power; that power implies violence, of one kind or another; and that whatever the law should or pretends to be, it is never much more than the prerogative of men with power to do this violence, in one way or another as they inevitably bow down before social laws far mightier than legal texts or moral pretense.

A close confidant of both London and Ralph Chaplin, George Sterling once wrote of a "pathway traced with blood and tears, / and dust of all our father's dead, / Whose backward footsteps, wandering, red, / Fade to the mist of nameless years."[38] Among the many Wobblies who gave content to these verses, their lives a study in the realities of law, power, and capitalism and proof of their own unsparing theories about the world, was Joe Neil himself. When Marcet Haldeman-Julius met Neil behind bars, she found a man "full of genuine courage" who was "as interested in the fate of some of his fellow prisoners as in his own."[39] These were Caroline Lowe's impressions, too, as she bore witness to Neil's preoccupation with the welfare of Wobbly John Caffrey and told of how he listened in on Caffrey talking "all the time" about the IWW, while Caffrey himself, a defendant in the Kansas conspiracy case who had been adjudged criminally insane before trial, wasted away in the asylum.[40]

When Neil was paroled he expressed some disappointment that he had not received more mail from his fellow Wobblies while incarcerated. He probably did not realize how few remained to write letters by that time. When released, he folded his tent, just as the *Los Angeles Times* had prayed his kind would do when, six years earlier, the newspaper reveled in Steelink's incarceration. Pushed along by a deportation order, this confirmed disturber, as prison officials called him, this wanderer and searcher after the truth, in Haldeman-Julius's words, last appears in the historical record in 1930, in Skeena Crossing, a remote native village in northern British Columbia also called Gitsegukla. That is where Kansas authorities mailed Neil his full pardon. And there he faded to the mist of nameless years, proud to have suffered so much for the cause of radical industrial unionism.[41]

Acknowledgments

A book like this can hardly be written without the help of a great number of relatives, friends, colleagues, and institutions. In fact, so lengthy is the list of contributors to this one that I cannot reasonably mention every person or place that deserves acknowledgment. At the risk of an embarrassing omission, and with the important caveat that any shortcomings in the book are my responsibility and mine alone, I must therefore content myself to name only those whose help was most significant.

Near the top of this list are David Hill, Vildja Hulden, Ben Levin, Chad Pearson, and Tilman Wuerschmidt, who generously reviewed drafts of the book, in some instances multiple times, and provided me with immensely helpful criticisms and suggestions. I also benefited enormously from the careful attention of the four scholars who reviewed the manuscript at the behest of the University of California Press. I am very much in their debt as well. Others deserve my thanks for reading components of the book, offering important advice about the overall contours of the project as it evolved, helping with the publication process, or encouraging me to take on the subject in the first place. Among these are Paul Campos, John Carlson, Peter Cole, Victor Devintaz, Toni Gilpin, Aya Gruber, Lakshman Guruswamy, Jennifer Hendricks, Tobie Higbie, Mark Linder, Jim Pope, Carolyn Ramsey, and Niles Utlaut.

The greater part of the book is based in original research completed over the last few years, and all of its text is original as well. However, some elements of it derived from, were inspired by, or are consistent with work that I previously published in the *Berkeley Journal of Employment and Labor Law*, the *University of Colorado Law Review*, the *University of Oregon Law Review*, and the *Journal of Employee Rights and Responsibilities*, as well as online with *Jacobin*. I sincerely thank the editors of those publications.

I received a great deal of encouragement and support for this project when I presented parts of it in 2017 at an event sponsored by the Labor Education and Arts Project in Cleveland, Ohio, organized by my friend Tom Sodders. I likewise benefited from presentations to academic colleagues here at the University of Colorado School of Law, and, some years ago, the University of Arizona Law School, Hofstra University School of Law, and the University of Minnesota Law School.

In the course of my travels to conduct research, I enjoyed the generous hospitality of my friends Kevin and Ellen Baker and Carolyn Buppert and the support of the Baldy Center for Law and Social Policy at the SUNY Buffalo. My work was also aided by my receipt of Colorado Law's Gilbert Goldstein Award, which facilitated travel, as well as the school's Gordon Gamm Award, which defrayed costs. For these awards I thank the donors and James Anaya, then dean of the law school. Most of the expenses incurred in writing this book, however, were covered by funds normally available to faculty here at the University of Colorado. I therefore express my sincere appreciation to the students and graduates of the university and to the people of the state of Colorado, who are ultimately responsible for providing those resources.

The many libraries and archives that assisted me are listed in the bibliography. A few warrant special mention because of their contributions. In this category are the University of Colorado Library and University of Colorado Law Library, the Idaho State Archives, the Kansas State Historical Society and State Archives, the Oregon Historical Society, the Walter Reuther Library at Wayne State University, the University of Washington Library, and the Washington State Historical Society. Every institution treated me with abundant courtesy and professionalism. This was likewise the case during the process of obtaining the images used in the book, as a number of institutions waived their fees or went out of the way to accommodate my requests.

I was fortunate to have the assistance of two exceptional students, Kaitlin DeWulf and Sarah Thomas, who helped with organizing the research, developing the manuscript, and obtaining sources. I am similarly grateful to my coworkers Kelly Ilseng and Nicole Drane for their help in preparing the manuscript for publication, arranging travel, obtaining images, and other important matters, and to Jane Thompson and Matt Zafiratos for their help in securing sources. And I am greatly indebted, as well, to the editors and staff at the University of California Press for their faith in the book and the patience they showed as I prepared it for publication. This is the second book I have published with the press and my dealings with the organization and its people have been unfailingly positive and rewarding at every turn. In this regard, I am happy to acknowledge a special debt of gratitude to Niels Hooper, Julie Van Pelt, and Naja Pulliam Collins.

My interest in the Industrial Workers of the World has always been entwined with an appreciation for the working lives of its members, an intimate sense of all the ways in which the kind of labor they did and that many people still do is both dignifying and degrading, and an understanding of how the resulting contradictions define the human experience. To this, I owe my extended family and the people I grew up among in Plaisance, Louisiana. And I am especially beholden to my late father, Marion Overton White, who knew quite a lot about hard work and repression, and to my mother, Doris Morein White, a great teacher whose love and support are essential to me.

Speaking of love, support, and people who are essential, I must, of course, acknowledge my wife, Teresa Bruce. A colleague and a scholar as well, she read multiple drafts of the manuscript, assisted with the research, suffered my innumerable questions, and offered a great number of suggestions and encouragements about how best to bring this book to fruition. Without Teresa, it would never have been written. And without her, I hasten to add, my life would be unimaginably less rewarding.

Abbreviations

WCU	Working Class Union
WFM	Western Federation of Miners

IN NOTES

ACLU Records	Records of the National Office of the American Civil Liberties Union
CDDC	California District Defense Committee
DOJ-CP	Department of Justice Investigative Files: Communist Party
DOJ-IWW	Department of Justice Investigative Files: Industrial Workers of the World
DOJ-MF	Department of Justice Investigative Files: The Use of Military Force by the Federal Government in Domestic Disturbances, 1900-1938
ISA	Idaho State Archives and Idaho Historical Society
KSA	Kansas State Archives and Kansas Historical Society
MHS	Minnesota Historical Society
MIR	U.S. Military Intelligence Reports: Surveillance of Radicals, 1917–1941
OHS	Oregon Historical Society
UKSC	University of Kansas Special Collections
UMSC	University of Michigan Special Collections
UWSC	University of Washington Special Collections
WRML	Walter Reuther Memorial Library
WSHS	Washington State Historical Society

Notes

INTRODUCTION

1. "Joe Neil Released, Rearrested," *Industrial Worker,* June 30, 1928, 1.

2. Marcet Haldeman-Julius, "Joe Neil, Victim of a Great State's Bigotry," Clippings-Georgia, Records of the National Office of the American Civil Liberties Union (ACLU Records), vol. 352, pp. 54–70. According to his Kansas prison record, Neil had several "aliases": Joe Niel, Andy McDonald, Jack Neall, Johnann Diermeyer, Peter Murphy, and John Deermeyer. "Niel" is the primary name used in these records but "Neil" otherwise predominates. See also Records of Joe Neil, No. 7950, Kansas State Penitentiary at Lansing Records, KSA.

3. Correspondence Cases–Kansas, ACLU Records, Volume 286, pp. 5–8.

4. Prisoner Interview, Joe Neil, No. 7950, Kansas State Penitentiary at Lansing Records, Kansas State Archives and Kansas Historical Society.

5. The origin of the practice of referring to IWW members as "Wobblies" has been the subject of much speculation and yet remains unclear. "What Is the Origin of the Term 'Wobbly'?," https://archive.iww.org/history/icons/wobbly/.

6. Michael Cohen, "'The Ku Klux Government': Vigilantism, Lynching, and the Repression of the IWW," *Journal for the Study of Radicalism* 1 (2006): 32, 35.

7. Sebastião Salgado, *An Uncertain Grace* (New York: Aperture, 2005), 7.

8. See also Haldeman-Julius, "Joe Neil," 54–70.

9. "Oakland I.W.W. Spurns Judge's Offer to Pardon," *Industrial Solidarity,* Dec. 31, 1921, 5; "Pardon, Never Offered, Refused," *Oakland Tribune,* Dec. 23, 1921, 2. See also "The Shadow on Sunny California," Correspondence Cases–California, ACLU Records, Volume 214, p. 93; Clippings-Alabama, ACLU Records, Volume 208, pp. 76–77; Clippings-Alabama, ACLU Records, Volume 175, pp. 18–19.

10. "Joe Neil Thanks Fellow Workers," *Industrial Worker,* July 14, 1928, 1.

11. Haldeman-Julius, "Joe Neil," 4.

12. "Joe Neil Released, Rearrested," *Industrial Worker,* June 30, 1928, 1. Although some records suggest Neil did suffer a breakdown, he claimed that he "pretended" insanity to get better food. Letter from Caroline Lowe to Roger Baldwin, June 3, 1925, Correspondence Cases–Kansas, ACLU Records, Volume 286, pp. 22–23; Haldeman-Julius, "Joe Neil," 33–37, 43, 54–70.

13. The IWW was remarkable for its defiance of prevailing sexual norms and its openness to the recruitment of women. These aspects of the union's history have recently received very worthy and overdue attention from scholars. See Heather Mayer, *Beyond the Rebel Girl: Women and the Industrial Workers of the World in the Pacific Northwest,* 1905–1924 (Corvallis: Oregon State University Press, 2018); Laura Vapnek, *Elizabeth Gurley Flynn: Modern American Revolutionary* (New York: Taylor and Francis, 2015); Jane Little Botkin, *The Girl Who Dared to Defy: Jane Street and the Rebel Maids of Denver* (Norman: University of Oklahoma Press, 2021). At times, especially in its early years, women were recruited into the IWW in significant numbers and, as Mayer points out, were integrated into IWW organizations even in later years and in places, like the Pacific Northwest, where membership was otherwise dominated by men. Nevertheless, men comprised the overwhelming majority of the union's leadership and a great majority of its membership, particularly in the late 1910s and early 1920s and in the industries and places were organizing was most extensive and generated the most sustained and intensive repression. It is primarily for these reasons that the overwhelming majority of union people who were jailed, imprisoned, beaten, and killed were men, and that terms like *men* and pronouns like *he* and *him* are used freely in the pages that follow.

14. Lowell S. Hawley and Ralph Bushnell Potts, *Counsel for the Damned: A Biography of George Francis Vanderveer* (Philadelphia: J.B. Lippincott, 1953), 244.

15. Jack London, *The Iron Heel* (Orinda, CA: SeaWolf Press, 2017), 80, 81.

CHAPTER 1. SOCIALISM WITH ITS WORKING CLOTHES ON

1. Melvyn Dubofsky, *We Shall Be All: A History of the Industrial Workers of the World* (Urbana: University of Illinois Press, 1969), 81; *The Autobiography of Big Bill Haywood* (New York: International Publishers, 1977), 180–81.

2. *Big Bill Haywood,* 7, 11, 13–14, 33–37.

3. Liesl Miller Orenic, "The Base of the Empire: Teamsters Local 743 and Montgomery Ward," *Labor* 15, no. 2 (2018): 49, 57. See also Robert Leiter, *The Teamsters Union: A Study of Its Economic Impact* (New York: Bookman Associates, 1957), 24–26.

4. "Forming a Labor Trust," *Chicago Daily Tribune,* June 27, 1905, 2.

5. *Founding Convention of the IWW: Proceedings* (New York: Merit Publishers, 1969), 247–48.

6. *Big Bill Haywood,* 158. On the formation of the IWW, see also Paul F. Brissenden, *The Launching of the Industrial Workers of the World* (New York: Johnson Reprint Group, 1966).

7. U.S. Bureau of the Census, *Historical Statistics of the United States, Colonial Times to 1970* (Washington, D.C.: GPO, 1975), A6–A8, A57–A81, C76–C80, D152–D166, D181, K17–K81, K162–K173, K184–K191.

8. See, for example, "The Ownerless Slaves," *Industrial Pioneer,* June 1921, 46.

9. James D. Schmidt, *Industrial Violence and the Legal Origins of Child Labor* (New York: Cambridge University Press, 2010); "Improvements in Workplace Safety—United States, 1900–1999," *Morbidity and Mortality Weekly Report* 48, no. 22 (1999): 461; Gustavas Myers, "A Study of the Causes of Industrial Accidents," *Publication of the American Statistical Association* 14, no. 111 (1915): 672, 673–74.

10. J. Anthony Lukas, *Big Trouble: A Murder in a Small Town Sets Off a Struggle for the Soul of America* (New York: Simon and Schuster, 1997), 233.

11. See, for example, Description List of the Convict, J. A. Griffith, Montana State Prison, Montana Historical Society Research Center; Description of the Convict, Thomas Burans, Montana State Prison, Montana Historical Society Research Center.

12. Prosecutor's Statement to the Warden, June 1, 1921, Record of Patrick J. Murphy, No. 2993, Inmate Records, Idaho State Archives and Idaho Historical Society (ISA).

13. Letter from Fred Miller to Board of Pardons, Oct. 28, 1921, Record of Patrick J. Murphy, No. 2993, Inmate Records, ISA.

14. Herbert G. Gutman, *Work, Culture, and Society in Industrializing America* (New York: Vintage, 1977), 19–26; David Brody, *Workers in Industrial America: Essays on the Twentieth Century Struggle* (New York: Oxford University Press, 1980), 13–14.

15. E. P. Thompson, "Time, Work-Discipline, and Industrial Capitalism," *Past and Present* 38 (1967): 56, 61.

16. Melvyn Dubofsky, *Industrialism and the American Worker, 1865–1920* (Arlington Heights, IL: H. Davidson, 1985), 20–23; Richard Steckel, "Stature and the Standard of Living," *Journal of Economic History* 33, no. 4 (1995): 1903; *Historical Statistics of the United States, Colonial Times to 1970,* series B107–B115, B136–B148.

17. Theodore Dreiser, *Sister Carrie* (New York: B. W. Dodge, 1907), 83.

18. Michael McGerr, *A Fierce Discontent: The Rise and Fall of the Progressive Movement in America* (New York: Oxford University Press, 2003), 6–8, 16; U.S. Bureau of the Census, *Historical Statistics of the United States, Colonial Times to 1957* (Washington, D.C.: GPO, 1960), D722–D727.

19. Selig Perlman, *A Theory of the Labor Movement* (New York: Macmillan, 1928), 4–5.

20. Peter Carlson, *Roughneck: The Life and Times of Big Bill Haywood* (New York: W. W. Norton, 1983), 146.

21. Dubofsky, *Industrialism and the American Worker,* 16–19. See also Jeremy Atack et al., "Skill Intensity and Rising Wage Dispersion in Nineteenth-Century American Manufacturing," *Journal of Economic History* 64, no. 1 (2004): 172; "Wages in the United States and Europe, 1870–1898," *U.S. Bureau*

of Labor, Bulletin No. 18 (Washington, D.C.: GPO, 1898), 665–93; *Historical Statistics of the United States, Colonial Times to 1970*, D728–D738.

22. Charles Ashleigh, *The Rambling Kid: A Novel about the IWW* (New York: Charles H. Kerr, 2004), 8.

23. *Big Bill Haywood*, 80–81.

24. Letter from Unidentified to Fred Thompson, Oct. 6, 1973, Box 11, File 16, Frederick Thompson Papers, Walter Reuther Memorial Library (WRML).

25. Kim Voss, *The Making of American Exceptionalism: The Knights of Labor and Class Formation in the Nineteenth Century* (Ithaca, NY: Cornell University Press, 1994); Kim Voss, "Disposition Is Not Action: The Rise and Demise of the Knights of Labor," *Studies in American Political Development* 6, no. 2 (1992): 272.

26. *Historical Statistics of the United States, Colonial Times to 1957*, D940–D955.

27. See Julie Greene, *Pure and Simple Politics: The American Federation of Labor and Political Activism, 1881–1917* (New York: Cambridge University Press, 1998). On the debate about the AFL's degree of conservatism, see, for example, Dorothy Sue Cobble, "Pure and Simple Radicalism: Putting the Progressive AFL in its Time," *Labor* 10, no. 4 (2013): 61; Julie Greene, "Not So Simple: Reassessing the Politics of the Progressive Era AFL," *Labor* 10, no. 4 (2013): 105.

28. Dubofsky, *We Shall Be All*, 60.

29. Ralph Chaplin, *Wobbly: The Rough-and-Tumble Story of an American Radical* (Chicago: University of Chicago Press, 1948), 4, 8, 66.

30. Harry W. Laidler, *History of Socialism* (New York: Crowell, 1968), 587–88; James Weinstein, *The Decline of Socialism in America, 1912–1925* (New York: Vintage, 1967), 93, 103; Jack Ross, *The Socialist Party of America: A Complete History* (Lincoln, NE: Potomac Books, 2015), 117–27, 603–58.

31. Ashleigh, *Rambling Kid*, 5.

32. Stewart Bird et al., eds., *Solidarity Forever: An Oral History of the IWW* (Chicago: Lake View Press, 1985), 199. Steelink's name is also spelled *Nicholas*.

33. Chaplin, *Wobbly*, 9–13, 29.

34. Jack London, "What Life Means to Me," in *Revolution* (Orinda, CA: SeaWolf Press, 2018), 237–39.

35. Leigh Campbell-Hale, "Remembering Ludlow but Forgetting the Columbine: The 1927–1928 Colorado Coal Strike," PhD diss., University of Colorado-Boulder, 2013, p. 35.

36. Earl Bruce White, "The Wichita Indictments and Trial of the Industrial Workers of the World, 1917–1919," PhD Dissertation, University of Colorado-Boulder, 1980, p. 190.

37. William M. Adler, *The Man Who Never Died: The Life, Times, and Legacy of Joe Hill, American Labor Icon* (New York: Bloomsbury Press, 2011), 170–80; Shawn L. England, "Anarchy, Anarcho-Magonismo, and the Mexican Peasant: The Evolution of Ricardo Flores Magon's Revolutionary Philosophy," MA thesis, University of Calgary, 1995, pp. 52–58; Hyman Weintraub, "The I.W.W. in California: 1905–1931," MA thesis, University of California, Los Angeles, 1947, pp. 50–57, 273–74.

38. B. Traven, *The Cotton-Pickers* (Chicago: Ivan R. Dee, 1995), 68.

39. Traven, *Cotton-Pickers,* 120–21, 132, 200.

40. Ralph Chaplin, "The West Is Dead," in *The Prison Poems* (New York: Leonard Press, 1922), 29; Chaplin, *Wobbly,* 91.

41. Nels Anderson, *The Hobo: The Sociology of the Homeless Man* (Chicago: University of Chicago Press, 1922), 3–10, 14, 105–7. See also Mark Wyman, *Hoboes: Bindlestiffs, Fruit Tramps, and the Harvesting of the West* (New York: Hill and Wang, 2010), 36–39; D.D. Lescohier, *The Labor Market* (New York: Macmillan, 1919), 18, 271–74.

42. U.S. Commission on Industrial Relations, *Final Report* (Washington, D.C.: GPO, 1916), 68–69, 300.

43. See Appellant's Brief, State v. Sorllie, Oregon Supreme Court, p. 3, Box 1, IWW Seattle Joint Branches Collection, University of Washington Special Collections (UWSC).

44. U.S. Commission on Industrial Relations, *Final Report,* 101–3; Lescohier, *Labor Market,* 271–74. See also Desmond Kelly, *The Elimination of the Tramp* (New York: Putnam, 1908); Frank C. Laubach, *Why There Are Vagrants* (New York: Columbia University Press, 1916); Josiah Flynt, *Tramping with Tramps* (New York: Century, 1899); Benjamin C. Marsh, "Causes of Vagrancy and Methods of Eradication," *Annals of the American Academy of Political and Social Science* 23, no. 3 (1904): 445.

45. Prisoner Interview, Joe Neil, No. 7950, Kansas State Penitentiary at Lansing Records, Kansas State Archives and Kansas Historical Society (KSA).

46. Description of Convict, Records of John O'Hara, No. 3039, Inmate Records, ISA. The average age of defendants in the prosecution of several dozen Wobblies for conspiracy in Kansas was also about thirty-five. White, "Wichita Indictments," 188. Likewise, the twenty-three Wobblies who served time for criminal syndicalism in Washington State and whose records list a place of nativity hailed from twelve different states and three foreign countries. Washington State Archive, Washington State Penitentiary, Commitment Registers, https://www.digitalarchives.wa.gov.

47. Florence Peterson, "Review of Strikes in the United States," *Monthly Labor Review,* 46, no. 5 (1938): 1047, 1054, 1066. See also Gutman, *Work, Culture, and Society,* 48–50.

48. Florence Peterson, "Strikes in the United States, 1880–1936," in *U.S. Bureau of Labor Statistics, Bulletin No. 651* (Washington, D.C.: GPO, 1938), 32–34. See also Michael Biggs, "Strikes as Sequences of Interaction: The American Strike Wave of 1886," *Social Science History* 26, no. 3 (2002): 583.

49. U.S. Senate, Committee on Education and Labor, *Violations of Free Speech and the Rights of Labor: Private Police Systems,* Report No. 6, pt. 2, 76th Congress, 1st Session (Washington, D.C.: GPO, 1939), 4–11; U.S. Senate, Committee on Education and Labor, *Violations of Free Speech and the Rights of Labor: Strikebreaking Services,* Report No. 6, pt. 1, 76th Congress, 1st Session (Washington, D.C.: GPO, 1939), 1–13.

50. Chad Pearson, *Reform or Repression: Organizing America's Anti-Union Movement* (Philadelphia: University of Pennsylvania Press, 2016). On the class politics of Progressivism, see also McGerr, *A Fierce Discontent,* xiv-xv, 70–71,

124–25; Shelton Stormquist, *Re-Inventing "The People": The Progressive Movement, the Class Problem, and the Origin of Modern Liberalism* (Urbana: University of Illinois Press, 2006), 2–11. On the open-shop movement, see Allen Wakstein, "The Origins of the Open-Shop Movement, 1919–1920," *Journal of American History* 51, no. 3 (1964): 460. On Progressivism and vigilantism, see Michael Cohen, "'The Ku Klux Government': Vigilantism, Lynching, and the Repression of the IWW," *Journal for the Study of Radicalism* 1, no. 1 (2006): 32.

51. See, for example, Stormquist, *Re-inventing "The People,"* 71–76. See also Christopher Tomlins, "Necessities of State: Police, Sovereignty, and the Constitution," *Journal of Police History* 20, no. 1 (2008): 47, 60; Michael R. Johnson, "The I.W.W. and Wilsonian Democracy," *Science and Society* 28, no. 3 (1964): 257.

52. Dubofsky, *We Shall Be All*, 95–96, 106, 115–19, 168–69; Philip S. Foner, *The Industrial Workers of the World* (New York: International, 1965), 77–80.

53. Dubofsky, *We Shall Be All*, 156–60.

54. Francis Shor, "The Iron Heel's Marginal(ized) Utopia," *Extrapolation* 35, no. 3 (1994): 211, 217.

55. On London's place in the intellectual life of the IWW, see Larry Peterson, "The Intellectual World of the IWW: An American Worker's Library in the First Half of the 20th Century," *History Workshop Journal* 22, no. 2 (1986): 153; Nicholas Peterson, "A Rip in the Social Fabric: Revolution, Industrial Workers of the World, and the Paterson Silk Strike of 1913 in American Literature, 1908–1927," PhD diss., Temple University, 2011, passim; Michael Cohen, *The Conspiracy of Capital: Law, Violence, and American Popular Radicalism in the Age of Monopoly* (Amherst: University of Massachusetts Press, 2019), passim. On his popularity among transients, see Anderson, *The Hobo*, 185; Todd Depastino, *Citizen Hobo: How a Century of Homelessness Shaped America* (Chicago: University of Chicago Press, 2003), 99. On his political philosophy, see Alex Kershaw, *Jack London: A Life* (New York: St. Martin's Press), passim; Jonathan Berliner, "Jack London's Socialistic Social Darwinism," *American Literary Realism* 41, no. 1 (2008): 52; Jonah Raskin, "Jack London, Burning Man: Portrait of an American Socialist," *Socialism and Democracy* 19, no. 2 (2005): 57. On his admiration of the IWW, see also Joan London, *Jack London and His Times* (New York: Doubleday, 1939), 294–95.

56. Jack London, "Preface," in *War of the Classes* (Orinda, CA: SeaWolf Press, 2018), vii, xiii–xiv. Among many other examples of this line in London's thought, see "A New Law of Development," ibid., 135–62.

57. Dubofsky, *We Shall Be All*, 147.

58. Bryan D. Palmer, *James P. Cannon and the Origins of the American Revolutionary Left, 1890–1928* (Urbana: University of Illinois Press, 2010), 43.

59. Chaplin, *Wobbly*, 84, 90–91; *Big Bill Haywood*, 256.

60. "Jack London, in Memoriam," *International Socialist Review* 17, no. 10 (1917): 624; "Life Meant Struggle and Revolt to Jack London," *Industrial Worker*, Mar. 3, 1917, 6; "Helping Hand" or "Iron Heel"?, *Solidarity*, Dec. 2, 1916, 2.

61. Joan London, *Jack London*, 181–83.

62. Walker C. Smith, *Sabotage: Its History, Philosophy, and Function* (Chicago: Solidarity Bookshop, 1947), 32.

63. Joan London, *Jack London*, 305.

64. Nicholas Peterson, "Rip in the Social Fabric," passim; Shor, "Iron Heel's Marginal(ized) Utopia," passim. London's conception of the state and the legal system and their subservience to the power of capital perhaps best resembles that of Marxist lawyers and political scientists Franz L. Neumann and Otto Kirchheimer. See Franz L. Neumann, *Behemoth: The Structure and Practice of National Socialism, 1933–1944* (Chicago: Ivan R. Dee, 2009); Otto Kirchheimer, *Political Justice: The Use of Legal Procedure for Political Ends* (Princeton, NJ: Princeton University Press, 1961); William E. Scheuerman, ed., *The Rule of Law Under Siege: Selected Essays of Franz L. Neumann and Otto Kirchheimer* (Berkeley: University of California Press, 1996).

65. *Big Bill Haywood*, 181.

66. Jack London, *The Iron Heel* (Orinda, CA: SeaWolf Press, 2017), 245–46.

67. On the role of anarchist and syndicalist ideas in shaping the IWW, see Salvatore Salerno, *Red November, Black November: Culture and Community in the Industrial Workers of the World* (Albany: SUNY Press, 1989). See also Paul F. Brissenden, *The I.W.W.: A Study of American Syndicalism* (New York: Columbia University Press, 1919), 53, 272–74.

68. Michael Mark Cohen, "'The Conspiracy of Capital': American Popular Radicalism and the Politics of Conspiracy," PhD diss., Yale University, 2004, pp. 183–84.

69. Goffredo Fofi, quoted in Alessandro Portelli, "Jack London's Missing Revolution: Notes on 'The Iron Heel,'" *Science Fiction Studies* 9, no. 2 (1982): 180.

70. "'Helping Hand' or 'Iron Heel'?," *Solidarity*, Dec. 2, 1916, 2.

71. Quoted in Foner, *Industrial Workers of the World*, 53.

72. Jeffory A. Clymer, *America's Culture of Terrorism: Violence, Capitalism, and the Written Word* (Chapel Hill: University of North Carolina Press, 2003), 134–70.

73. "Greatest Battle Ever Waged," *Industrial Worker*, June 1907, 1.

74. Eugene Debs, "Arouse, Ye Slaves," in *Debs: His Life, Writings and Speeches* (Chicago: Charles H. Kerr, 1908), 309–11; Dubofsky, *We Shall Be All*, 122, 124.

75. Foner, *Industrial Workers of the World*, 178–92, 197–99, 201–2; Dubofsky, *We Shall Be All*, 173–97; Mathew May, *Soapbox Rebellion: The Hobo Orator Union and the Free Speech Fights of the Industrial Workers of the World, 1909–1916* (Tuscaloosa: University of Alabama Press, 2013). For eyewitness and first-hand accounts of the free-speech fights, see Philip Foner, *Fellow Workers and Friends: IWW Free Speech Fights as Told by Participants* (Westport, CT: Greenwood, 1981); H. Minderman, Fresno Free Speech Fight, 002117-009-0544, Department of Justice Investigative Files: Industrial Workers of the World (DOJ-IWW); Interview of Harry Jenkins, Meridel Le Sueur Papers, Audio Recordings, Box 37, Tape 42, Sides 1–2, Minnesota Historical Society.

76. Weintraub, "I.W.W. in California," 37–48.

77. Foner, *Industrial Workers of the World*, 210–12; Dubofsky, *We Shall Be All*, 196–97.

78. Bird et al., *Solidarity Forever*, 147–48.

79. Hagbard Edwards Autobiographical Manuscript, pp. 261–62, in Hagbard Edwards Papers, Box 1, Files 1–7, WRML.

80. See, for example, Library List, Box 1, File 9, IWW Seattle Joint Branches Collection, UWSC. See also various files in Box 153, IWW Collection, WRML. On the culture of IWW halls, see Carlton Parker, *The Casual Laborer and Other Essays* (New York: Harcourt, Brace and Howe, 1920), 115–16; Larry Peterson, "Intellectual World of the IWW," passim.

81. When asked by federal agents how much of the union's materials they had read, a group of Wobblies arrested in 1917 gave a range of answers, from none at all, sometimes with the explanation that the defendant was not a good reader, to "all of it." IWW Activities in Omaha, Nebraska, 002371-003-0468, DOJ-IWW.

82. Mark Leier, "Kipling Gets a Red Card," *Labour/Le Travail* 30 (1992): 163.

83. See, for example, Carleton Parker, *The California Casual* (New York: Harcourt, Brace and Howe, 1920), 6–24; Donald D. Lescohier, "With the I.W.W. in the Wheat Lands," *Harper's Monthly Magazine*, Aug. 1923, 371.

84. R. F. Hoxie, "The Truth about the IWW," *Journal of Political Economy* 21 (1913): 785, 792–93, 797; Parker, *Casual Laborer*; Carlton Parker, "The I.W.W.," *Atlantic Monthly*, Nov. 1917, 651.

85. Parker, *Casual Laborer*, 103–7. See also Frank Tobias Higbie, *Indispensable Outcasts: Hobo Workers and Community in the American Midwest, 1880–1930* (Urbana: University of Illinois Press, 2003), 87–89; "Organization or Anarchy," *New Republic*, July 21, 1917, 320.

86. Transcript of Record, State v. Berg, Pittsburg County District Court, No. 2146, pp. 194–95, Box 127, File 10, IWW Collection, WRML.

87. Ashleigh, *Rambling Kid*, 111.

88. Elizabeth Gurley Flynn, *Memories of the Industrial Workers of the World* (New York: Institute for Marxist Studies, 1977), 4–7.

89. See also Marcet Haldeman-Julius, "Joe Neil, Victim of a Great State's Bigotry," Clippings-Georgia, American Civil Liberties Union Records, Volume 352, pp. 54–70; Records of Joe Neil, No. 7950, Kansas State Penitentiary at Lansing Records, KSA.

90. Archie Sinclair, "A Visit to San Quentin," *Industrial Pioneer*, Oct. 1923, 27.

91. Bird et al., *Solidarity Forever*, 40.

92. Russell Elliott, "Labor Troubles in the Mining Camps at Goldfield, Nevada, 1906–1908," *Pacific Historical Review* 19, no. 4 (1950): 369, 370, 380; Fred Thompson, *The I.W.W.: Its First Fifty Years* (Chicago: IWW, 1955), 23–52; Sally Zanjani and Guy Louis Rocha, *The Ignoble Conspiracy: Radicalism on Trial in Nevada* (Reno: University of Nevada Press, 1986), passim; Dubofsky, *We Shall Be All*, 120–24.

93. U.S. House of Representatives, Committee on Labor, *Hearings on Peonage in Western Pennsylvania*, 62nd Cong., 1st Session, 1911; Foner, *Industrial Workers of the World*, 282–83.

94. John N. Ingham, "A Strike in the Progressive Era: McKees Rocks, 1909," *Pennsylvania Magazine of History and Biography* 90, no. 3 (1966): 353; Dubofsky, *We Shall Be All*, 205–7.

95. Weintraub, "I.W.W. in California," 16–94, 116–17, 120–23, 216; Eldridge Foster Dowell, "A History of the Enactment of Criminal Syndicalism Legislation in the United States," PhD diss., Johns Hopkins University, 1936, p. 322. On the broader radical impulses in the state, see David M. Struthers, *The World in a City: Multiethnic Radicalism in Early Twentieth-Century Los Angeles* (Urbana: University of Illinois Press, 2019).

96. On several of these strikes, see Joseph R. Conlin, ed., *At the Point of Production: The Local History of the I.W.W.* (Westport, CT: Greenwood, 1981). The most comprehensive catalogue of these struggles is an online database developed by the University of Washington's IWW History Projects: https://depts.washington.edu/iww/strikes.shtml.

97. Dubofsky, *We Shall Be All*, 235–83; Fred Thompson, *The I.W.W.*, 62–63. On the course of these strikes, see generally Robert Forrant and Jurg Siegenthaler, eds., *The Great Lawrence Textile Strike of 1912: New Scholarship on the Bread and Roses Strike* (New York: Routledge, 2016); U.S. Senate, *Report on Strike of Textile Workers in Lawrence, Massachusetts* in 1912, 62nd Congress, 2nd Session (Washington, D.C.: GPO, 1912); Steve Golin, *The Fragile Bridge: The Paterson Silk Strike, 1913* (Philadelphia: Temple University Press, 1992); Anne Huber Tripp, *The I.W.W. and the Paterson Silk Strike of 1913* (Urbana: University of Illinois Press, 1987). On the prosecution of Boyd, see State v. Boyd, 91 A. 586 (N.J. 1914).

98. Leon Trotsky, *My Life* (London: Scribner, 1930), 235–36.

99. Carlson, *Roughneck*, 158.

100. *Proceedings of the National Convention of the Socialist Party, 1912* (Chicago: Socialist Party, 1912), 126–43, 209. On the split between the IWW and the party, see also Joseph Conlin, "The I.W.W. and the Socialist Party," *Science and Society* 31, no. 1 (1967): 22.

101. Conlin, "The I.W.W.," 28–29.

102. Foner, *Industrial Workers of the World*, 160–61; Dubofsky, *We Shall Be All*, 160–64.

103. On debates about the origin of the term, see Rebecca Lossin, "The Point of Destruction: Sabotage, Speech, and Progressive-Era Politics," PhD diss., Columbia University, 2020, pp. 23–34, n. 24; Dominque Pinsolle, "Sabotage, the IWW, and Repression," in Peter Cole et al., *Wobblies of the World: A Global History of the IWW* (London: Pluto, 2017), 44.

104. Dubofsky, *We Shall Be All*, 162–64; Foner, *Industrial Workers of the World*, 160–64; Fred Thompson, *The I.W.W.*, 81–88.

105. Louis Adamic, "Sabotage," *Harper's Monthly Magazine*, Jan. 1931, 216.

106. For a discussion of this issue in the context of lumber, see Erik Loomis, *Empire of Timber: Labor Unions and the Pacific Northwest Forests* (New York: Cambridge University Press, 2015), 59–61.

107. Bird et al., *Solidarity Forever*, 39–40. On debates about the prevalence of destructive sabotage among Wobblies, see Lossin, "Point of Destruction,"

5–6; Dowell, "Criminal Syndicalism," 53–62. The point about no Wobblies ever being proved culpable of destructive sabotage is debatable, partly because such charges were often introduced to help convict Wobblies of crimes, like conspiracy, that did not require proof that such destruction occurred. Among cases that at least suggested actual destruction by Wobblies, see for instance the December 1918 conviction of three Wobblies, Thomas Nolan, E. A. Matson, and Robert Solen, for conspiring to organize a strike among firefighters while a blaze raged in the Olympic National Forest. Although the facts remain unclear, the men were also alleged to have set the fire. "I.W.W. Firebugs Are Sentenced," *Everett Labor Journal,* Jan. 4, 1918, 1. See also Cloice R. Howd, "Industrial Relations in the West Coast Lumber Industry," *U.S. Bureau of Labor Statistics Bulletin No. 349* (Washington, D.C.: GPO, 1923), 76; IWW Cases and Activities-Western Washington, 002366-005-0968, DOJ-IWW.

108. Smith, *Sabotage,* 32. See also Émile Pouget, *Sabotage* (Chicago: Charles H. Kerr, 1913); Lossin, "Point of Destruction," passim; Mike Davis, "The Stopwatch and the Wooden Shoe: Scientific Management and the Industrial Workers of the World," *Radical America* 9, no. 1 (1975): 84; White, "Wichita Indictments," 46–60.

109. Cletus E. Daniel, "In Defense of the Wheatland Wobblies: A Critical Analysis of the IWW in California," *Labor History* 19, no. 4 (1978): 485, 489–90; Dubofsky, *We Shall Be All,* 294–99.

110. Greg Hall, *Harvest Wobblies: The Industrial Workers of the World and Agricultural Laborers in the American West, 1905–1930* (Corvallis: Oregon State University Press, 2001), 49–53; Daniel, "Wheatland Wobblies," 490–91.

111. Daniel, "Wheatland Wobblies," 495.

112. Eric Thomas Chester, *The Wobblies in Their Heyday* (Santa Barbara, CA: Praeger, 2014), 11, 15, 133. See also Hall, *Harvest Wobblies,* 48–54.

113. Daniel, "Wheatland Wobblies," 496–99, 501–4.

114. Chester, *The Wobblies,* 12–27; IWW Cases and Activities-California and the Pacific Northwest, 002366-001-1132, DOJ-IWW.

115. See, for example, "Fire Bugs Set Great Blazes," *L.A. Times,* June 15, 1915, 1; "Armed Deputies Guard Hop Crops," *Atwater Signal,* Sept. 17, 1915, 1; "I.W.W. Plots Told," *Sacramento Bee,* Sept. 25, 1915, 1; "The I.W.W. Criminals," *Modesto Bee,* Sept. 17, 1915, 4; "James McGill Anxious for Sentence," *Sacramento Bee,* Sept. 28, 1915, 1; "Fire Buildings on Hop Ranch," *Fresno Morning Republican,* Oct. 23, 1915, 1.

116. Chester, *The Wobblies,* 20–23.

117. "I.W.W. Threats of Devastation Arouse Governor Johnson," *Fresno Morning Republican,* Sept. 12, 1915, 1; Daniel, "Wheatland Wobblies," 501–2.

118. Chester, *The Wobblies,* 19–20, 23–26, 151; Daniel, "Wheatland Wobblies," 502.

119. Michael Belknap, "Uncooperative Federalism: The Failure of the Bureau of Investigation's Intergovernmental Attack on Radicalism," *Publius* 12, no. 2 (1982): 25, 26.

120. Dubofsky, *We Shall Be All,* 287.

121. Eric Chester, "The Rise and Fall of the IWW: As Viewed through Membership Figures," *Anarcho-Syndicalist Review* 55 (2011): 13; Frank Tobias

Higbie, "Indispensable Outcasts: Seasonal Laborers and Community in the Upper Midwest, 1880–1930," PhD diss., University of Illinois, Urbana-Champaign, 2000, pp. 295, 254; Dubofsky, *We Shall Be All*, 106, 131–33; Foner, *Industrial Workers of the World*, 81, 98, 113, 462. See also Data from Taft: Federal Trials, Box 25, File 15, Frederick Thompson Papers, WRML.

122. Jack London, "The Dream of Debs," *International Socialist Review* 9, nos. 7–8 (1909): 481, 561, 570.

CHAPTER 2. PROTECTING THE BUSINESS PEOPLE

1. Melvyn Dubofsky, *We Shall Be All: A History of the Industrial Workers of the World* (Urbana: University of Illinois Press, 1969), 338–39; Robert L. Tyler, *Rebels of the Woods: The IWW in the Pacific Northwest* (Eugene: University of Oregon Press, 1967), 65–71.

2. Tyler, *Rebels of the Woods*, 64–70; Dubofsky, *We Shall Be All*, 338–39.

3. Robert L. Tyler, "The I.W.W. in the Pacific N.W.: Rebels of the Woods," *Oregon Historical Quarterly* 55, no. 1 (1954): 3, 14–15; Walker C. Smith, *The Everett Massacre: A History of the Class Struggle in the Lumber Industry* (Chicago: IWW, 1917), 69–80.

4. Smith, *Everett Massacre*, 88–96.

5. Tyler, *Rebels of the Woods*, 73–77; Smith, *Everett Massacre*, 95–100; "1,300 March in Cortege," *Seattle Star*, July 10, 1919, 1. The known dead Wobblies were Felix Baran, Hugo Gerlot, Gus Johnson, John Looney, and Abraham Rabinowitz.

6. Charles Ashleigh, "Everett, November Fifth," song), *Industrial Pioneer*, July 1921, 35.

7. Smith, *Everett Massacre*, 40.

8. Amy Dru Stanley, "Beggars Can't Be Choosers: Compulsion and Contract in Postbellum America," *Journal of American History* 78, no. 4 (1992): 1265; Sidney Harring, "Class Conflict and the Suppression of Tramps in Buffalo, 1892–1894," *Law and Society Review* 11, no. 5 (1977): 873, 879–82.

9. Stanley, "Beggars," 1266–68, 1275.

10. Fargo, North Dakota, Charter and Ordinances, Title I, § 23 (1908).

11. Jack London, *The Road* (New Brunswick, NJ: Rutgers University Press, 2006), 68–71.

12. London, *The Road*, 71–72.

13. Stanley, "Beggars," 1278; Ahmed A. White, "A Different Kind of Labor Law: Vagrancy Law and the Regulation of Harvest Labor, 1913–1924," *University of Colorado Law Review* 75, no. 3 (2004): 668, 683–84.

14. Alfred Queen, *The Passing of the County Jail* (Menasha, WI: Banta, 1920), 3–19. See also, for example, Joseph F. Fishman, *Crucibles of Crime: The Shocking Story of the American Jail* (New York: Cosmopolis, 1923); *The Cook County Jail Survey* (Chicago: Chicago Community Trust, 1922).

15. Smith, *Everett Massacre*, 64–65.

16. D.D. Leschier, "Harvest Labor Problems in the Wheat Belt," in *U.S. Department of Agriculture Bulletin No. 1020* (Washington, D.C.: GPO, 1922), 4–5.

17. Thomas D. Isern, *Bull Threshers and Bindlestiffs: Harvesting and Threshing on the North American Plains* (Lawrence: University of Kansas Press, 1990), 24–45, 57–62, 68–102; Don D. Lescohier, "Conditions Affecting the Demand for Harvest Labor in the Wheat Belt," in *U.S. Department of Agriculture Bulletin No. 1230* (Washington, D.C.: GPO, 1924), 14–21; Greg Hall, *Harvest Wobblies: The Industrial Workers of the World and Agricultural Laborers in the American West, 1905–1930* (Corvallis: Oregon State University Press, 2001), 18–20.

18. Don D. Lescohier, "Sources of Supply and Conditions of Employment of Harvest Labor in the Wheat Belt," in *U.S. Department of Agriculture Bulletin No. 1211* (Washington, D.C.: GPO, 1924), 1, 5–9; Lescohier, "Harvest Labor Problems," 1; Hall, *Harvest Wobblies*, 20–22.

19. Lescohier, "Harvest Labor Problems," 15; Lescohier, "Sources of Supply," 16–19.

20. Ralph Chaplin, *Wobbly: The Rough-and-Tumble Story of an American Radical* (Chicago: University of Chicago Press, 1948), 87–90.

21. Lescohier, "Sources of Supply," 12.

22. Interstate Commerce Commission, "Accident Bulletins," *Railway Age*, Mar. 7, 1919, 10; Hall, *Harvest Wobblies*, 23–24; Frank Tobias Higbie, *Indispensable Outcasts: Hobo Workers and Community in the American Midwest, 1880–1930* (Urbana: University of Chicago, 2003), 52.

23. Higbie, *Indispensable Outcasts*, 153–54, 184–85; Stewart Bird et al., eds., *Solidarity Forever: An Oral History of the IWW* (Chicago: Lake View Press, 1985), 38–39, 46; David Wagaman, "The Industrial Workers of the World in Nebraska, 1914–1920," *Nebraska History* 56 (1975): 295, 296.

24. Marcet Haldeman-Julius, "Joe Neil, Victim of a Great State's Bigotry," Clippings-Georgia, American Civil Liberties Union Records, Volume 352, pp. 54–70.

25. See, for example, "Fear Lynching of I.W.W.," *Spearfish Queen City Mail*, July, 27, 1921, 1; "I.W.W. Leader Held at Lakota for Shooting at Railroad Men," *Fargo Forum and Daily Republican*, Sept. 3, 1919, 1; "Night Marshal at Stanley Shot and Killed by I.W.W.," *Ward County Independent*, Aug. 24, 1922, 4; "Wobbly Pleads Guilty: Pulled Gun on Detective," *Ward County Independent*, Sept. 29, 1921, 1.

26. "Harvest Hands Must Protect Themselves," *Solidarity*, Oct. 9, 1915, 1; "Schmidt Jury Disagrees," *Sioux Falls Argus-Leader*, Nov. 1, 1915, 1. See also Higbie, *Indispensable Outcasts*, 153–54.

27. See, for example, "Free Ride on the Top of Cars," *Fargo Forum and Daily Republican*, July 25, 1921, 7; "Transients Freely Beat Passage on Railroad Trains," *Minot Daily News*, July 22, 1921, 1.

28. Hall, *Harvest Wobblies*, 78; Lescohier, "Sources of Supply," 11–14.

29. Len De Caux, *Labor Radical: From the Wobblies to the CIO* (New York: Beacon, 1970), 58–59.

30. Hall, *Harvest Wobblies*, 220.

31. Police Magistrate Court Docket, Justice of the Peace Records, File 116, Box 6, Institute for Regional Studies, North Dakota State University.

32. Nigel Anthony Sellars, *Oil, Wheat and Wobblies: The Industrial Workers of the World in Oklahoma, 1905–1930* (Norman: University of Oklahoma Press, 1998), 37–39; Higbie, *Indispensable Outcasts*, 48–52.

33. E. F. Doree, "Gathering in the Grain," *International Socialist Review* 15, no. 12 (1915): 740.

34. Doree, "Gathering in the Grain," 740.

35. *Solidarity Forever*, 37.

36. Isern, *Bull Threshers*, 103–4; "Dust Explosions and Fires in Grain Separators in the Pacific Northwest," in *U.S. Department of Agriculture, Bulletin No. 379* (Washington, D.C.: GPO, 1916); "Harvest Fatality," *Alton Empire*, July 6, 1922, 1; "Died from Heat Stroke," *Sterling Kansas Bulletin*, June 25, 1914, 1; "Boy Harvest Hand Killed by Lightning," *Wichita Daily Eagle*, June 7, 1912, 1; "Texas Harvest Hand Killed under Wagon," *Kingman Journal*, July 28, 1918, 1; "Many Accidents the Past Week," *Norwich Herald*, July 7, 1921, 1.

37. Chaplin, *Wobbly*, 89–90. On the "transient mutuality" among these men, see Higbie, *Indispensable Outcasts*, 175–76.

38. Philip Taft, "The I.W.W. in the Grain Belt," *Labor History* 1, no. 1 (1960): 53, 58.

39. Dubofsky, *We Shall Be All*, 343–45.

40. Cloice R. Howd, "Industrial Relations in the West Coast Lumber Industry," *U.S. Bureau of Labor Statistics Bulletin No. 349* (Washington, D.C.: GPO, 1923), 26, 67–68; Wagaman, "Industrial Workers of the World in Nebraska," 298–99. See also Tyler, "I.W.W. in the Pacific N.W.," 7; Hall, *Harvest Wobblies*, 71.

41. Dubofsky, *We Shall Be All*, 314–15. See also Minutes of Conference of Harvest Workers, Apr. 15, 1915, in E. W. Latchem Papers, Walter Reuther Memorial Library (WRML); Fred Thompson, *The I.W.W.: Its First Fifty Years* (Chicago: IWW, 1955), 93; Hall, *Harvest Wobblies*, 81–91.

42. "I.W.W. Carry on Industrial War," *Abilene Daily Reflector*, July 12, 1916, 1; "Thinklets," *Hays Free Press*, July 22, 1916, supplement.

43. "I.W.W.s Raise Cain," *Trego County Reporter*, July 13, 1916, 1; "A Kansas Town Is Menaced by an I.W.W. Mob," *Hutchinson Gazette*, July 9, 1916, 1.

44. "'Burn Wakeeney,' Cry I.W.W. as Citizens Arm," *Salina Evening Journal*, July 10, 1916, 1.

45. "Detectives in Pistol Fight with 50 I.W.W.s," *St. Louis Post-Dispatch*, July 14, 1916, 10; "I.W.W. Burn Wheat Stacks Near Salina," *Hutchinson Gazette*, July 16, 1919, 1; "Guard Salina Jail," *Westphalia Times*, July 20, 1916, 1.

46. Wagaman, "Industrial Workers of the World in Nebraska," 299–301.

47. "Pitched Battles in S.D. Towns with I.W.W. Armies," *Sioux Falls Argus-Leader*, July 28, 1916, 1; "Mitchell Asks Troops Sent from Redfield," *Sioux Falls Argus-Leader*, July 27, 1916, 1; Wagaman, "Industrial Workers of the World in Nebraska," 305.

48. Higbie, *Indispensable Outcasts*, 155–60. See also Hall, *Harvest Wobblies*, 101.

49. "Pep Is Walked out of I.W.W. Leaders," *Fargo Forum and Daily Republican*, Aug. 17, 1916, 1.

50. White, "Vagrancy Law," 716–26.

51. "I.W.W.'s Have Reached Minot," *Ward County Independent,* Aug. 3, 1916, 1.

52. Taft, "I.W.W. in the Grain Belt," 59, 62; Higbie, *Indispensable Outcasts,* 155.

53. IWW in Omaha, Nebraska, 002371-003-0468, Department of Justice Investigative Files: Industrial Workers of the World (DOJ-IWW).

54. Wagaman, "Industrial Workers of the World in Nebraska," 298–99.

55. William Dimmit, "An Organized Harvest," *Industrial Pioneer,* Sept. 1921, 1, 4.

56. De Caux, *Labor Radical,* 60–61, 68–69.

57. Thompson, *The I.W.W.,* 94. See also Higbie, *Indispensable Outcasts,* 153–54, 184–90.

58. "I.W.W.'s in Command of N.P. Freight," *Fargo Forum and Daily Republican,* Aug. 1, 1916, 2.

59. For a reflection on this aspect of union membership, see interview of Harry Jenkins, Meridel Le Sueur Papers, Audio Recordings, Box 37, Tape 37, Side 1, Minnesota Historical Society.

60. Howd, "West Coast Lumber Industry," 50–54.

61. *Report of the President's Mediation Commission to the President of the United States* (Washington, D.C.: GPO, 1918), 13–15. See also Benjamin G. Rader, "The Montana Lumber Strike of 1917," *Pacific Historical Review* 36, no. 4 (1967): 189, 192–95.

62. Howd, "West Coast Lumber Industry," 38–39.

63. For instance, in Oregon, in the year ending June 30, 1920, there were 81 deaths in logging, 2 cases of "permanent total disability," 176 cases of "permanent partial disability," and 2,215 cases of "temporary partial disability" among a workforce of about 12,000. "Accidents in the Logging Industry of Oregon," *Monthly Labor Review* 15 (1922): 148–49.

64. Industrial Workers of the World, *The Lumber Industry and Its Workers,* 3d ed. (Chicago: IWW, 1921), 58. On accidents in the South, see Ruth A. Allen, *East Texas Lumber Workers: An Economic and Social Picture, 1870–1950* (Austin: University of Texas Press, 1961), 107–15.

65. Aaron Goings, *The Port of Missing Men: Billy Gohl, Labor, and Brutal Times in the Pacific Northwest* (Seattle: University of Washington Press, 2020).

66. Howd, "West Coast Lumber Industry," 6; Rader, "Montana Lumber Strike," 190.

67. Howd, "West Coast Lumber Industry," 41–43. On conditions in the South, see Allen, *East Texas Lumber Workers,* passim.

68. Hagbard Edwards Autobiographical Manuscript, pp. 135–38, in Hagbard Edwards Papers, Box 1, Files 1–7, WRML.

69. Edward B. Mittelman, "The Loyal Legion of Loggers and Lumbermen: An Experiment in Industrial Relations," *Journal of Political Economy* 31, no. 3 (1923): 313, 320.

70. On industry demographics, see Howd, "West Coast Lumber Industry," 45; Allen, *East Texas Lumber Workers,* 52–60, passim.

71. Dubofsky, *We Shall Be All*, 128–29; Roy Appleman, "Timber Empire from the Public Domain," *Mississippi Valley Historical Review* 26, no. 2 (1939): 193–97, 203–4; *The Lumber Industry: Part 1, Standing Timber* (Washington, D.C.: GPO, 1913), 6–40; John Fahey, "Big Lumber in the Inland Empire: The Early Years, 1900–1930," *The Pacific Northwest Quarterly* 76, no. 3 (1985): 95.

72. Howd, "West Coast Lumber Industry," 41. Wages and working conditions were generally less favorable in the South. Allen, *East Texas Lumber Workers*, 69–80, 106–7. See also John E. Haynes, "Revolt of the 'Timber Beasts': IWW Lumber Strike in Minnesota," *Minnesota History* 42 (1971): 162, 164.

73. Howd, "West Coast Lumber Industry," 39, 44.

74. Howd, "West Coast Lumber Industry," 64–65; Thompson, *The I.W.W.*, 34–35.

75. "Officers Use Clubs upon Strikers," *Missoulian*, June 10, 1909, 1. See also "Thirty I.W.W. Orators Arrested," *Butte Miner*, Oct. 7, 1909, 1; "Woman Would Fill City's Prisons," *Missoulian*, Oct. 3, 1909, 10; "First Arrest in Labor Troubles at Kalispell," *Butte Miner*, June 19, 1909, 1.

76. "I.W.W. Orators Thrown into the Dungeon," *Butte Miner*, Oct. 2, 1909, 10.

77. Chaplin, *Wobbly*, 150; James R. Barrett, *William Z. Foster and the Tragedy of American Radicalism* (Urbana: University of Illinois Press, 1999), 40–41.

78. Tyler, *Rebels of the Woods*, 35–39; Dubofsky, *We Shall Be All*, 175–84.

79. Aaron Goings, "Red Harbor: Class, Violence, and Community in Grays Harbor, Washington," PhD diss., Simon Fraser University, 2011, pp. 205–35; Philip Jacques Dreyfus, "Toward Industrial Organization: Timber Workers, Unionism and Syndicalism in the Pacific Northwest, 1900–1917," PhD diss., CUNY, 1993, pp. 121–73; Howd, "West Coast Lumber Industry," 65–66.

80. Tyler, "I.W.W. in the Pacific N.W.," 3, 11, 12; Howd, "West Coast Lumber Industry," 67; Dennis E. Hoffman and Vincent J. Webb, "Police Response to Labor Radicalism in Portland and Seattle, 1913–19," *Oregon Historical Quarterly* 87, no. 4 (1986): 341, 345–49.

81. James R. Green, "The Brotherhood of Timber Workers, 1910–1913: A Radical Response to Industrial Capitalism in the Southern U.S.A.," *Past and Present*, no. 60 (1973): 161, 185–86.

82. Green, "Brotherhood," 180–82; James F. Fickle, "Race, Class, and Radicalism: The Wobblies in the Southern Lumber Industry, 1900–1916," in Joseph R. Conlin, ed., *At the Point of Production: The Local History of the IWW* (Westport, CT: Greenwood Press, 1981), 97, 106–7. The place was also known as Graybow or Graybeaux.

83. "Iron Heel on Dixie," *Solidarity*, Aug. 17, 1912, 1; Green, "Brotherhood," 180–90; Industrial Workers of the World, *The Lumber Industry*, 75–78; Fickle, "Race, Class, and Radicalism," 107–8.

84. Merl E. Reed, "Lumberjacks and Longshoremen: The I.W.W. in Louisiana," *Labor History* 13, no. 1 (1972): 49, 52–54.

85. Dubofsky, *We Shall Be All*, 216.

86. Minutes of the 10th General Convention of the Industrial Workers of the World, 1916, pp. 32, 36, Box 2, File 2, IWW Collection, WRML.

87. Dubofsky, *We Shall Be All*, 336, 361; Hall, *Harvest Wobblies*, 108. On the financial circumstances of the IWW's agricultural affiliate and their effect on overall union finances, see Monthly Report of Spokane District of I.U. #400 and #573, June 1917–July 1917, Box 28, File 1, IWW Collection, WRML.

88. Howd, "West Coast Lumber Industry," 69.

89. Emil Engstrom, *The Vanishing Logger* (New York: Vantage, 1956), 38.

90. Eldridge Foster Dowell, "A History of the Enactment of Criminal Syndicalism Legislation in the United States," PhD diss., Johns Hopkins University, 1936, p. 141.

91. Oppenheim had worked under the local district attorney and served briefly as an assistant U.S. attorney. Dowell, "Criminal Syndicalism," 142–44; "Brief Local News," *Boise Idaho Statesman*, July 7, 1908, 5; "Attorney's Clerk Appointed Assistant," *Boise Idaho Statesman*, Mar. 20, 1908, 5.

92. Robert C. Sims, "Idaho's Criminal Syndicalism Act: One State's Response to Radical Labor," *Labor History* 15, no. 4 (1975): 511, 512–13. See also Eldridge Foster Dowell, *Criminal Syndicalism in the United States* (Baltimore, MD: Johns Hopkins University Press, 1939), 51, n. 17.

93. Act of March 14, 1917, ch. 145, § 1, Idaho Session Laws 1917.

94. Archibald E. Stevenson, ed., *Revolutionary Radicalism: Its History, Purpose and Tactics with an Exposition and Discussion of the Steps Being Taken and Required to Curb It* (Albany, NY: Lyon, 1920), 872.

95. Act of March 14, 1917, ch. 145, §§ 1–4, Idaho Session Laws 1917.

96. Dowell, "Criminal Syndicalism," 145–46.

97. Dowell, "Criminal Syndicalism," 139–40, 146–48; "To Curb Activities of the Agitators in Northern Idaho," *Boise Evening Capital News*, Mar. 2, 1917, 6. See also Sims, "Idaho's Criminal Syndicalism Act," 512.

98. Dowell, *Criminal Syndicalism*, 18, n. 29. Oppenheim patterned his law directly on Wisconsin's "criminal anarchy" statute, which was in turn based on a law enacted by New York in 1902, seven months after President William McKinley was shot by self-proclaimed anarchist Leon Czolgosz. Like Oppenheim's bill, the New York statute criminalized advocating the overthrow of "organized government" by violence, assassination, or other "unlawful means" and membership in organizations engaged in such advocacy. Act of Apr. 2, 1902, Laws of New York, ch. 371, §468. That statute's enactment was a key event in the "Anarchist Scare" of 1901 to 1903. But until the postwar Red Scare, there were only a few prosecutions. Robert J. Goldstein, "The Anarchist Scare of 1908," *American Studies* 15, no. 2 (1974): 155; Zechariah Chafee Jr., *Free Speech in the United States* (Cambridge, MA: Harvard University Press, 1954), 575–97.

99. Neil Betten, "Riot Revolution, Repression in the Iron Range Strike of 1916," *Minnesota History* 41 (1968): 63, 67.

100. Neil Betten, "Strike on the Mesabi—1907," *Minnesota History* 40 (1967): 340.

101. Gary Kaunonen, *Flames of Discontent: The 1916 Minnesota Iron Ore Strike* (Minneapolis: University of Minnesota Press, 1917), 182–83; Betten, "Riot Revolution," 69–71.

102. Betten, "Riot Revolution," 66–72.

103. Dubofsky, *We Shall Be All*, 326–32; Robert Eleff, "The 1916 Minnesota Miners' Strike against U.S. Steel," *Minnesota History* 51 (1988): 63.

104. Leslie Marcy, "The Iron Heel on the Mesaba [*sic*] Range," *International Socialist Review* 17, no. 2 (1916): 74, 77.

105. Lara Vapnek, *Elizabeth Gurley Flynn: Modern American Revolutionary* (New York: Taylor and Francis, 2015), 63–66; Elizabeth Gurley Flynn, *Memories of the Industrial Workers of the World* (New York: Institute for Marxist Studies, 1977), 13; *Elizabeth Gurley Flynn, the Rebel Girl: An Autobiography* (New York: International, 1955), 207–16; *The Autobiography of Big Bill Haywood* (New York: International Publishers, 1977), 292–93; Peter Carlson, *Roughneck: The Life and Times of Big Bill Haywood* (New York: W. W. Norton, 1983), 237.

106. Dowell, "Criminal Syndicalism," 168–170; IWW Cases and Activities-Minnesota, 002366-004-0747, DOJ-IWW; See also "I.W.W. Inquiry Asked in Senate," *Duluth Labor World*, Jan. 13, 1917, 1; "Woodsmen Return to Work," *Minneapolis Morning Tribune*, Jan. 4, 1917, 2.

107. Dowell, "Criminal Syndicalism," 175.

108. Dowell, "Criminal Syndicalism," 170–80. See also "'Liar' and 'Dynamiter' Shouts Make I.W.W. Inquiry Almost a Riot," *Minneapolis Morning Tribune*, Feb. 3, 1917, 12; "I.W.W. Agitators Make Appearance in Front of Legislators," *Minneapolis Morning Tribune*, Jan. 31, 1917, 1; "Quelling of I.W.W. by Giving Burnquist More Power Planned," *Minneapolis Morning Tribune*, Jan. 12, 1917, 5.

109. Dowell, "Criminal Syndicalism," 181–82; "Criminal Syndicalism Bill Passed by Senate," *Duluth Labor World*, Apr. 14, 1917, 1; Act of Apr. 13, 1917, ch. 215, §§ 1–4, Minnesota Session Laws 1917.

110. Dowell, "Criminal Syndicalism," 189, 191–96.

111. Dowell, *Criminal Syndicalism*, 51, n. 18, 56–58.

112. Tyler, *Rebels of the Woods*, 77–81; Smith, *Everett Massacre*, 142–77.

113. Smith, *Everett Massacre*, 177–289. On the incident and the case, see also IWW Cases and Activities–California and the Pacific Northwest, 002366-001-0000, DOJ-IWW; IWW Cases and Activities–California and the Pacific Northwest, 002366-001-0206, DOJ-IWW.

114. "Governor Lister Vetoes So-Called Sabotage Bill," *Northwest Worker*, Apr. 5, 1917, 1.

115. Dowell, "Criminal Syndicalism," 200; Tyler, *Rebels of the Woods*, 21–22; Robert Evans, "Montana's Role in the Enactment of Legislation Designed to Suppress the Industrial Workers of the World," MA thesis, Montana State University, 1964, p. 42.

116. Paul L. Murphy, *World War I and the Origin of Civil Liberties in the United States* (New York: W. W. Norton, 1978), 57–63; Shelton Stormquist, *Reinventing "The People": The Progressive Movement, the Class Problem, and the Origins of Modern Liberalism* (Urbana: University of Illinois Press, 2006), 198–201; Michael McGerr, *A Fierce Discontent: The Rise and Fall of the Progressive Movement in America* (New York: Oxford University Press, 2003), 281–310.

117. David M. Rabban, "The Emergence of Modern First Amendment Doctrine," *University of Chicago Law Review* 50, no. 4 (1983): 1205, 1217–19; Chafee, *Free Speech in the United States*, 37–38.

118. David M. Rabban, *Free Speech in the Forgotten Years* (New York: Cambridge University Press, 1997), 249–55; Rabban, "Modern First Amendment Doctrine," 1217–27; H.R. 291, 55 Cong. 1917; S.2, 55 Cong. 1917; Murphy, *World War I and the Origin of Civil Liberties*, 78–79; Espionage Act, ch. 30, 40 Stat. 217 (1917); U.S. Senate, *Congressional Record*, 55, 1917, pp. 2270–71, 3498; U.S. House, *Congressional Record* 55, 1917, pp. 1841, 3307.

119. "Espionage Bill Is Signed," *N.Y. Times,* Jun. 16, 1917, 9. On Creel's support for prosecuting the IWW, see Eric Thomas Chester, *The Wobblies in Their Heyday* (Santa Barbara, CA: Praeger, 2014), 179.

120. Michael R. Johnson, "The I.W.W. and Wilsonian Democracy," *Science and Society* 28, no. 3 (1964): 257, 264–66; Chester, *The Wobblies,* 159; Jack Ross, *The Socialist Party of America: A Complete History* (Lincoln, NE: Potomac Books, 2015), 188.

CHAPTER 3. IN THE WAR OF CAPITAL AGAINST LABOR
SOMEONE MUST SUFFER

1. Dashiell Hammett, *Red Harvest* (New York: Vintage, 1989), 3–4.

2. Arnon Gutfeld, "The Murder of Frank Little: Radical Labor Agitation in Butte, Montana, 1917," *Labor History* 10, no. 2 (1969): 177, 179–81.

3. Robert Evans, "Montana's Role in the Enactment of Legislation Designed to Suppress the Industrial Workers of the World," MA thesis, Montana State University, 1964, pp. 45–49.

4. Eric Thomas Chester, *The Wobblies in Their Heyday* (Santa Barbara, CA: Praeger, 2014), 71–82.

5. Melvyn Dubofsky, *We Shall Be All: A History of the Industrial Workers of the World* (Urbana: University of Illinois, 1969), 303–5, 366–68; Chester, *The Wobblies,* 86–88.

6. Gutfeld, "The Murder of Frank Little," 183–84.

7. Todd Depastino, *Citizen Hobo: How a Century of Homelessness Shaped America* (Chicago: University of Chicago Press, 2003), 121.

8. Ralph Chaplin, *Wobbly: The Rough-and-Tumble Story of an American Radical* (Chicago: University of Chicago Press, 1948), 209.

9. Jane Little Botkin, *Frank Little and the IWW: The Blood That Stained an American Family* (Norman: University of Oklahoma Press, 2019), 23, 62, 198–202; Chester, *The Wobblies,* 98–101.

10. Chester, *The Wobblies,* 101–4; Gutfeld, "The Murder of Frank Little," 186, 188–89; Diane Johnson, *Dashiell Hammett: A Life* (New York: Random House, 1983), 18–21.

11. Dubofsky, *We Shall Be All,* 392.

12. Evans, "Montana's Role," 62–63; Arnon Gutfeld, "Years of Hysteria, Montana, 1917–1921: A Study in Local Intolerance," PhD diss., 1971, pp. 41–42.

13. Chaplin, *Wobbly,* 208–9; Chester, *The Wobblies,* 118–24; Francis Shor, "The IWW and Oppositional Politics in World War I: Pushing the System Beyond Its Limits," *Radical History Review* 64 (1996): 74, 78–84.

14. Chester, *The Wobblies,* 117–18, 120–32; Fred Thompson, *The I.W.W.: Its First Fifty Years* (Chicago: IWW, 1955), 113–14.

15. Thompson, *The I.W.W.*, 86–87; Chester, *The Wobblies*, 218; Greg Hall, *Harvest Wobblies: The Industrial Workers of the World and Agricultural Workers in the American West, 1905–1930* (Corvallis: Oregon State University Press, 2001), 71.

16. IWW Activities in Omaha, Nebraska, 002371-003-0468, f. 00583, Department of Justice Investigative Files: Industrial Workers of the World (DOJ-IWW).

17. See, for example, IWW Cases and Activities, California and the Pacific Northwest, 002366-001-1132, DOJ-IWW; Intelligence Report, Jun. 17–30, 1918, in Report on Anarchist Bomb Plot, 002371-014-0715, U.S. Military Intelligence Reports: Surveillance of Radicals, 1917–1941 (MIR).

18. Letter from George Vanderveer to Roger Baldwin, Mar. 25, 1918, Correspondence Cases-Amnesty, American Civil Liberties Union (ACLU) Records, Volume 27, p. 36; Chester, *The Wobblies*, 146–51. See also Dubofsky, *We Shall Be All*, 404–6.

19. See, for example, Howard Blum, *Dark Invasion: 1915: Germany's Secret War and the Hunt for the First Terrorist Cell in America* (New York: Harper, 2014); Jules Witcover, *Sabotage at Black Tom: Imperial Germany's Secret War in America, 1914–1917* (Chapel Hill, NC: Algonquin Books, 1989).

20. Chester, *The Wobblies*, 227; *American Labor Yearbook, 1919–1920* (New York: Rand, 1920), 191. See also *Solidarity Forever*, 120–21; Dubofsky, *We Shall Be All*, 445; Eldridge Foster Dowell, "A History of the Enactment of Criminal Syndicalism Legislation in the United States," PhD diss., Johns Hopkins University, 1936, p. 70.

21. Paul Brissenden determined that while total IWW strength in California in 1914 might have been as much as 5,000, only about half this number could be called "missionary revolutionists," and only about 200 to 300 were substantially involved in organizing. P. F. Brissenden, *Report on the Industrial Workers of the World in California*, 002117-016-0850, DOJ-IWW.

22. On turnover in IWW membership and the large number of people who passed through the organization, see Paul Brissenden, *The I.W.W.: A Study of American Syndicalism* (New York: Columbia University Press, 1919), 352; Robert L. Tyler, *Rebels of the Woods: The IWW in the Pacific Northwest* (Eugene: University of Oregon Press, 1967), 90–91.

23. Meyer H. Fishbein, "The President's Mediation Commission and the Arizona Copper Strike, 1917," *Southwest Social Science Quarterly* 30, no. 3 (1949): 175, 178; Chester, *The Wobblies*, 41–45.

24. "1200 I.W.W. Deported from District by Citizens," *Bisbee Daily Review*, July 13, 1917, 1. On the overall course of events, including Brew's killing, see James Byrkit, "The Bisbee Deportation," in James C. Foster, ed., *American Labor in the Southwest* (Tucson: University of Arizona Press), 86–102.

25. James W. Byrkit, *Forging the Copper Collar: Arizona's Labor-Management War of 1901–1921* (Tucson: University of Arizona Press, 1982), 94.

26. Paul L. Murphy, *World War I and the Origin of Civil Liberties in the United States* (New York: W. W. Norton, 1978), 128–32.

27. Dubofsky, *We Shall Be All*, 382–84.

28. Zechariah Chafee Jr., *Free Speech in the United States* (Cambridge, MA: Harvard University Press, 1954), 41–46.

29. Byrkit, *Forging the Copper Collar*, 265–72.

30. U.S. Commission on Public Information, *Report of President Wilson's Mediation Commission on the Bisbee, Ariz., Deportation*, Bisbee, AZ, Nov. 5, 1917, pp. 2–3; Dubofsky, *We Shall Be All*, 416–22.

31. Byrkit, *Forging the Copper Collar*, 291–94.

32. United States v. Wheeler, 245 U.S. 281 (1920).

33. "The Iron Heel at Work," *Solidarity*, July 21, 1917, 1.

34. Cloice R. Howd, "Industrial Relations in the West Coast Lumber Industry," *U.S. Bureau of Labor Statistics Bulletin No. 349* (Washington, D.C.: GPO, 1923), 6, 70–72; Benjamin G. Rader, "The Montana Lumber Strike of 1917," *Pacific Historical Review* 36, no. 2 (1967): 190.

35. Report of the Montana Department of Labor and Industry, Aug. 25, 1917, in Moses Alexander Papers, Box 1, File 2, Walter Reuther Memorial Library (WRML); Robert L. Tyler, "The United States Government as Union Organizer: The Loyal Legion of Loggers and Lumbermen," *Mississippi Valley Historical Review* 47, no. 3 (1960): 434, 437. See also Evans, "Montana's Role," 33–34.

36. Tyler, *Rebels of the Woods*, 90–91; Rader, "Montana Lumber Strike," 196–99.

37. See, for example, "Alleged I.W.W. Would Close Coal Mines," *Anaconda Standard*, Nov. 15, 1917, 12; "Thompson Falls I.W.W. Is Back in Jail Again," *Missoulian*, Nov. 23, 1917, 4; "I.W.W. Leaders Are Put under Arrest in Anaconda," *Daily Missoulian*, Oct. 25, 1917, 1; "Vagrancy Sentence," *Great Falls Tribune*, Oct. 10, 1917, 3; "Libby Justice Sentences Another IWW Vagrant," *Missoulian*, Aug. 22, 1917, 3; "I.W.W.'s Convicted," *Great Falls Tribune*, Aug. 18, 1917, 3; "Sixty Days for Vagrancy," *Helena Independent Record*, Aug. 18, 1917, 5; "Round-Up of Leaders," *Great Falls Tribune*, June 28, 1917, 3; "Have a Busy Day in Kluge's Court," *Helena Independent Record*, June 23, 1917, 2.

38. Clemens Work, *Darkest before Dawn: Sedition and Free Speech in the American West* (Albuquerque: University of New Mexico Press, 2005), 139.

39. Evans, "Montana's Role," 75; Dowell, "Criminal Syndicalism," 266–67.

40. "Red Lodge Woman Killed by Finn, "*Great Falls Tribune*, Nov. 30, 1917, 5.

41. William Preston Jr., *Aliens and Dissenters: Federal Suppression of Radicals, 1903–1933* (Cambridge, MA: Harvard University Press, 1963), 111.

42. Dubofsky, *We Shall Be All*, 401–3; Howd, "West Coast Lumber Industry," 73–74.

43. Clayton D. Laurie and Ronald D. Cole, *The Role of Federal Forces in Domestic Disorders, 1977–1945* (Washington, D.C.: Center of Military History), 223–53, 259–60; U.S. Army and Industrial Workers of the World, Background Material for Study on Federal Intervention in Domestic Issues, 101114-006-0438, DOJ-IWW; Department of Justice, Investigative Files, Part III: Use of Military Force by the Federal Government in Domestic Disturbances, 1900–1938 (DOJ-MF); Preston, *Aliens and Dissenters*, 103–7, 161–62.

44. "Wins Release of Seven I.W.W. Men," *Daily Missoulian*, July, 15, 1917, 3; "He Tore Down County's Flag," *Great Falls Tribune*, May 6, 1917, 3.

45. Letter from T.H. McDonald to the Attorney General, Aug. 21, 1917, IWW Cases and Activities–Montana, 002366-004-0784, DOJ-IWW.

46. Butte, Montana Copper Industry Strikes, 101114-010-0247, MIR.

47. Evans, "Montana's Role," 76.

48. Rebecca Lossin, "The Point of Destruction: Sabotage, Speech, and Progressive-Era Politics," PhD diss., Columbia University, 2020, pp. 90, 114–16; Howd, "West Coast Lumber Industry," 68, 75–76; U.S. House of Representatives, Subcommittee of the Select Committee on Expenditures, *Hearings on War Expenditures, Volume 2*, 66th Congress, 1st Session, 1919, pp. 957–58, 1182–92.

49. IWW Cases and Activities–Montana, 002366-004-0784, DOJ-IWW. See also Evans, "Montana's Role," 39–40.

50. Statements of U.S. Forest Service Supervisors Expressing Satisfaction with Industrial Workers of the World Labor Performance in Montana and Idaho Fire Control Programs, 002116-003-0668, Department of Labor, Records of the President's Mediation Commission; Evans, "Montana's Role," 39. On the employment of Wobblies in this work, see Mark Wyman, *Hoboes: Bindlestiffs, Fruit Tramps, and the Harvesting of the West* (New York: Hill and Wang, 2010), 107–9. On the death of two Wobblies, see Erik Loomis, *Empire of Timber: Labor Unions and the Pacific Northwest Forests* (New York: Cambridge University Press, 2015), 60. In one documented case, three union men, said to be working with Thomas Tracy, lead defendant in the Everett case, were convicted of conspiring to cause a strike among firefighters while a fire was burning in western Washington. Howd, "West Coast Lumber Industry," 76; IWW Cases and Activities–Western Washington, 002366-005-0968, DOJ-IWW.

51. "Annual Police Report," *Bemidji Daily Pioneer*, Feb. 6, 1917, 1.

52. Lara Vapnek, *Elizabeth Gurley Flynn: Modern American Revolutionary* (New York: Taylor and Francis, 2015), 66.

53. Elizabeth Gurley Flynn, *Sabotage* (Chicago: IWW, 1917); Émile Pouget, *Sabotage* (Chicago: Charles H. Kerr, 1913).

54. "Citizens Deport I.W.W.," *Bemidji Daily Pioneer*, July 25, 1917, 1.

55. Art Lee, "Hometown Hysteria: Bemidji at the Start of World War I," *Minnesota History* 49 (1984): 65, 74; "Petty Political Clacquers Fall in Attacks upon Truthfulness of 'Pioneer,'" *Bemidji Daily Pioneer*, Oct. 10, 1917, 1.

56. Gary Kaunonen, *Flames of Discontent: The 1916 Minnesota Iron Ore Strike* (Minneapolis: University of Minnesota Press, 1917), 207–9; Lee, "Hometown Hysteria," 70, 74; "Convicted as Criminal Syndicalist," *Industrial Worker*, Oct. 6, 1917, 3; "Bemidji I.W.W. to Prison," *Brainerd Daily Dispatch*, Oct. 3, 1917, 1.

57. Dowell, "Criminal Syndicalism," 185–86; "I.W.W. Is Outlaw, Declares Jurist," *Bemidji Daily Pioneer*, June 29, 1917, 1; "Dodge Registration, Aim to Tie Up Mines," *Brainerd Daily Dispatch*, June 8, 1917, 1; "Government's Drive on Slackers Starts with Arrests Today," *Minneapolis Morning Tribune*, June 13, 1917, 2; "Seven I.W.W. Men Refuse to Register," *Brainerd Daily Dispatch*, June 11, 1917, 1; "Harry Lisk Arrested," *Duluth News-Tribune*, Oct. 26, 1917, 5; "Hater of America Gets 60-Day Term," *Duluth News-Tribune*, July 12, 1917, 5; "Look Out, Agitators," *Duluth News-Tribune*, July 10, 1917, 5; "Lehtonen Acquitted," *Duluth News-Tribune*, Aug. 31, 1917, 5.

There were more cases like these in 1919 and 1920. Dowell, "Criminal Syndicalism," 1073; *Report of the Attorney General to the Governor of the State of*

Minnesota, 1919–1920 (Minneapolis, MN: Syndicate Printing Company, 1920), 21; *Report of the Attorney General to the Governor of the State of Minnesota, 1917–1918* (Minneapolis, MN: Syndicate Printing Company, 1918), 26.

58. Four Finnish Wobblies were arrested by police in Biwabik, Minnesota, three months before Dunning and charged with felony criminal syndicalism after being found posting IWW stickers around town. One of them, thirty-seven-year-old miner Elia Maki, was convicted in late September. But the trial judge put off sentencing and trial of the others and asked the state supreme court to resolve the defense lawyers' claim that the statute violated the U.S. Constitution because it inadequately defined sabotage, imposed cruel and unusual punishment, and was a discriminatory form of "class legislation" that violated the Equal Protection Clause. The following April, the court rejected these claims, as well as the assertion that the facts did not support Maki's conviction. This freed the trial court to sentence Maki to six months in jail or a $1,000 fine and to try the others, who were convicted and got three months or $500. State v. Moilen, 167 N.W. 345 (Minn. 1918); Dowell, "Criminal Syndicalism," 1072–73.

In January 1920, six men with the Workers Socialist Publishing Company were indicted, along with the company, for publishing the Finnish IWW paper *Industrialisti*. Four, as well as the company, were tried, convicted, and fined $1,000 each. Dowell, "Criminal Syndicalism," 1074; State v. Workers' Socialist Publishing Company, 185 N.W. 931 (Minn. 1921); "Gruesome Story Installment No. 4," *One Big Union Monthly*, June 1920, 37.

59. "Syndicalism Law Secures Its First Victim," *Boise Evening Capital News*, Oct. 24, 1917, 5; Description of Convict, Record of J. J. McMurphy, No. 2570, Inmate Records, Idaho State Archives and Idaho Historical Society (ISA); Affidavit, Nov. 26, 1920, ibid.

60. "Labor Agitator Is Guilty," *Portland Oregonian*, Oct. 27, 1917, 6.

61. Information Furnished Prison Board by the Judge, Record of John Otis Ellis, No. 2567, Inmate Records, ISA; Order of Commitment, ibid.; Robert C. Sims, "Idaho's Criminal Syndicalism Act: One State's Response to Radical Labor," *Labor History* 15, no. 4 (1974): 511, 519; Jail and Penitentiary Calendar, Box 135, Files 2–4, IWW Collection, WRML; "Criminal Syndicalism Cases," *Industrial Worker*, Jan. 12, 1919, 8; "Labor Agitator Is Received at the Penitentiary," *Boise Evening Capital News*, Nov. 15, 1917, 7.

62. Quoted in Sims, "Idaho's Criminal Syndicalism," 515.

63. Letter from E. M. Grant to Moses Alexander, July 1, 1917, in Moses Alexander Papers, Box 1, File 1, WRML; Letter from Moses Alexander to Emerson Frazier, May 18, 1918, in Moses Alexander Papers, Box 1, File 2, WRML.

64. Sims, "Idaho's Criminal Syndicalism Act," 515–16; IWW Cases and Activities–Idaho, 002366-004-0246, DOJ-IWW.

65. "Bonners Ferry Banishes I.W.W.," *Spokane Spokesman-Review*, July 13, 1917, 1.

66. "Mass Meeting in Moscow," *Kendrick Gazette*, July 20, 1917, 1.

67. Sims, "Idaho's Criminal Syndicalism Act," 516.

68. Letter from Latah County Protective Association to Moses Alexander, Aug. 10, 1917, in Moses Alexander Papers, Box 1, File 2, WRML; Letter from Senator J. F. Nugent to Attorney General A. Mitchell Palmer, June 25, 1920, in

CPUSA Casefiles, 002367-014-0927, 0941, Department of Justice Investigative Files: Communist Party.

69. See, for example, "Build Stockade for Idaho I.W.W.," *Spokane Spokesman-Review,* July 20, 1917, 5.

70. "Rock Pile for Klamath I.W.W.," *Klamath Falls Evening Herald,* July 16, 1917, 1; Evans, "Montana's Role," 42.

71. "Strike Trouble at Seattle May Be Settled," *Salem Daily Capital Journal,* July 24, 1917, 1; "Citizens of Klamath Have Taken Stand," *Klamath Falls Evening Herald,* July 16, 1917, 1.

72. "Drastic Measures May Be Taken," *Salem Statesman Journal,* July 31, 1917, 3; "Twenty-One Men Are Sentenced on Vagrancy Charge," *Klamath Falls Evening Herald,* July 31, 1917, 1; "Found Guilty of Vagrancy," *Klamath Falls Evening Herald,* July 26, 1917, 1.

73. Quoted in Dowell, "Criminal Syndicalism," 533–34.

74. Hall, *Harvest Wobblies,* 128–29; "Dempsey Mill at Tacoma Crippled," *Spokane Spokesman-Review,* July 25, 1917, 2; "I.W.W. Wenatchee Stockade," *Spokane Spokesman-Review,* July 26, 1917, 10; "I.W.W. Armies Are Lining Up," *Tacoma Times,* July 13, 1917, 1; "Yakima Jail Full," *Oregon Statesman,* July 17, 1917, 1.

75. "30 Taken in Net at Pasco," *Spokane Spokesman-Review,* July 14, 1917, 11.

76. IWW Cases and Activities–Centralia and Seattle, Washington, 002366-007-0000, DOJ-IWW; Hall, *Harvest Wobblies,* 131–32; "Hunger Strike in Ellensburg," *Spokane Spokesman-Review,* July 16, 1917, 10; "Arrest I.W.W. Leaders," *Spokane Spokesman-Review,* July 19, 1917, 10; "Let No One Talk to I.W.W. in Jail," *Spokane Spokesman-Review,* July 21, 1917, 1.

77. Memorandum for the Solicitor General, re James Rowan, IWW Cases and Activities–James H. Rowan Citizenship, 002366-010-0870, DOJ-IWW.

78. Evans, "Montana's Role," 79; "The Spokane Labor Council Acted under Excitement," *Everett Labor Journal,* Sept. 7, 1917, 1; Sims, "Idaho's Criminal Syndicalism Act," 518. See also "Mass Meeting at Moscow," *Kendrick Gazette,* July 20, 1917, 1; "Workers of Inland Empire Spurn I.W.W. Strike Call," *Spokane Spokesman-Review,* Aug. 24, 1917, 1.

79. "I.W.W. Prisoners Denied Writ of Habeas Corpus, *Spokane Spokesman-Review,* Aug. 28, 1917, 3.

80. Tyler, *Rebels of the Woods,* 23.

81. Evans, "Montana's Role," 71–72; Howd, "Industrial Relations," 6; Rader, "Montana Lumber Strike," 190.

82. "Local I.W.W. Names Are Made Public," *Klamath Falls Evening Herald,* July 16, 1917, 1.

83. "I.W.W. Escapes from the County Jail," *Klamath Falls Evening Herald,* Nov. 17, 1917, 1; "Klamath I.W.W. Are Convicted," *Ashland Tidings,* July 30, 1917, 1.

84. Dubofsky, *We Shall Be All,* 406; Philip Taft, "The Federal Trials of the IWW," *Labor History* 3, no. 1 (1962): 60; Property to be Returned, Box 11, File 15, Frederick Thompson Papers WRML; Order, United States v. Haywood, n.d., ibid.

85. Charles Ashleigh–Imprisonment and Deportation, 002371-002-0426, MIR; Raids and Plots, 1917–1919, Box 99, IWW Collection, WRML.

86. National Industrial Conference Board, *Strikes in American Industry in Wartime, April 6 to October 6, 1917* (Boston: National Industrial Conference Board, 1918), 19–20.

87. Dubofsky, *We Shall Be All*, 393–94; Evans, "Montana's Role," 70–72.

88. Chester, *The Wobblies*, 165; "Creation of State Fund to Is Advocated by Committee," *Bemidji Daily Pioneer*, Mar. 21, 1917 1. See also Murphy, *World War I*, 88–89.

89. IWW Cases and Activities–Simon Lubin, 002366-007-0072, DOJ-IWW; Chester, *The Wobblies*, 165–66, 194; Dubofsky, *We Shall Be All*, 393–97; Kathryn S. Olmsted, *Right Out of California: The 1930s and the Big Business Roots of Modern Conservatism* (New York: New Press, 2015), 122, 124.

90. Affidavit in Support of Indictment, IWW Cases and Activities–William D. Haywood, 002366-008-0465, DOJ-IWW; Statement Concerning the Present Legal Status of the I.W.W. Cases, in Pardon Attorney Case Files: William D. Haywood, 002366-012-0580, DOJ-IWW.

91. Chaplin, *Wobbly*, 234–37; DOJ Memo, Mar. 4, 1918, IWW Cases and Activities–William D. Haywood, 002366-008-0465, DOJ-IWW.

92. "Scotch the Snake," *Washington Post*, Sept. 30, 1917, S4.

93. "Putting down the I.W.W.," *St. Louis Post-Dispatch*, Sept. 7, 1917, 20. See also "Moving to Indict Socialist Leaders," *N.Y. Times*, Sept. 8, 2017, 1; "The I.W.W. Traitors," *Minneapolis Morning Tribune*, Oct. 3, 1917, 6.

94. Transcript of Record, United States v. Anderson, no. 763, in Pardon Attorney Case Files: C. W. Anderson Trial Transcript, 002366-015-0001, DOJ-IWW, p. 406; Dowell, "Criminal Syndicalism," 630–39; Nigel Anthony Sellars, *Oil, Wheat, and Wobblies: The Industrial Workers of the World in Oklahoma, 1905–1930* (Norman: University of Oklahoma Press, 1998), 74–76. See also United States v. C. W. Anderson, et al., Box 126, Files 1–9, IWW Collection, WRML.

95. D. D. Lescohier, "Harvest Labor Problems in the Wheat Belt," in *U.S. Department of Agriculture Bulletin No. 1020* (Washington, D.C.: GPO, 1922), 4–5; U.S. Bureau of the Census, *Statistical Abstract of 1918* (Washington, D.C.: GPO), 158.

96. With some thirty thousand wells, thousands of miles of pipeline, and an output of over 107 million barrels, Oklahoma was the country's largest producer in 1917. Production in Kansas was about one-third that level. But this represented an elevenfold increase over 1914. Sellars, *Oil, Wheat, and Wobblies*, 109–12; U.S. Bureau of the Census, *Statistical Abstract of 1917* (Washington, D.C.: GPO, 1918), 158–59; Tom G. Hall, "Wilson and the Food Crisis: Agricultural Price Control during World War I," *Agricultural History* 47, no. 1 (1973): 25.

97. Sellars, *Oil, Wheat, and Wobblies*, 57–67.

98. On OWIU organizing efforts in the state, see Sellars, *Oil, Wheat, and Wobblies*, 71–76; IWW Activities in the Kansas Oil Fields, 002371-002-0003, MIR; Earl Bruce White, "The Wichita Indictments and Trial of the Industrial Workers of the World, 1917–1919," PhD diss., University of Colorado, 1980, pp. 41–77.

99. Sellars, *Oil, Wheat, and Wobblies,* 77–78; Hall, *Harvest Wobblies,* 125; IWW Activities in Tulsa Oklahoma, 002371-006-0242, MIR; Earl White, "Wichita Indictments," 6–10.

100. Dowell, "Criminal Syndicalism," 292–93.

101. "Unearth I.W.W. Plot to Destroy Crops," *N.Y. Times,* July 7, 1917, 10.

102. Dowell, "Criminal Syndicalism," 293; "'Democracy' in Aberdeen," *Solidarity,* Aug. 11, 1917, n.p.

103. Hall, *Harvest Wobblies,* 137; "Headquarters Closed," *Sioux Falls Argus-Leader,* July 31, 1917, 3; "Aberdeen Curbs Activities of the I.W.W. Horde," *Sioux Falls Argus-Leader,* July 30, 1917, 1.

104. On League politics and wartime persecution of members, see Michael Lansing, *Insurgent Democracy: The Nonpartisan League in North Dakota Politics* (Chicago: University of Chicago Press, 2015), passim.

105. Dowell, "Criminal Syndicalism," 709–41, 1257–58. The state did enact a criminal sabotage statute, but it was enforceable only during wartime and was rarely, if ever, used. Ahmed A. White, "A Different Kind of Labor Law: Vagrancy Law and the Regulation of Harvest Labor, 1913–1924," *University of Colorado Law Review* 75, no. 3 (2004): 668, 733–34; Act of Jan. 30, 1918, ch. 12, § 1, North Dakota Special Session Laws 1918.

106. U.S. Bureau of the Census, *Statistical Abstract of 1918,* 158–59.

107. Hall, *Harvest Wobblies,* 134–35; Charles James Haug, "The Industrial Workers of the World in North Dakota, 1913–1917," *North Dakota Quarterly* 39, no. 1 (1971): 85, 101–2.

108. Thorstein Veblen, "Unpublished Paper on the I.W.W.," *Journal of Political Economy* 40, no. 6 (1932): 797.

109. See, for example, "Jamestown to Tolerate No I.W.W. Interference," *Fargo Forum and Daily Republican,* July 20, 1917, 2; "Want $4.50 Day at Jamestown," *Fargo Forum and Daily Republican,* Aug. 1, 1917, 10. See also Ahmed White, "Vagrancy Law," 707.

110. "Call for Help from Edmore: Get Men Here," *Fargo Forum and Daily Republican,* Sept. 1, 1917, 8.

111. Sellars, *Oil, Wheat, and Wobblies,* 105–7; "I.W.W. Plot Breaks Premature," *Morning Tulsa Daily World,* Oct. 30, 1917, 1.

112. Sellars, *Oil, Wheat, and Wobblies,* 106–7; *War-Time Prosecutions and Mob Violence* (New York: National Civil Liberties Bureau, 1919), 20–21; "'Go and Stay,' Commanded Black-Robed Leader," *Tulsa Democrat,* Nov. 10, 1917,1.

113. *War-Time Prosecutions,* 20–21; Earl White, "Wichita Indictments," 63–64.

114. "Several Arrests Are Made Today," *Augusta Daily Gazette,* Nov. 21, 1917, 1; "I.W.W. Roundup Is on in Kansas, Scores Arrested," *Topeka Capital Journal,* Nov. 21, 1917, 1; Earl White, "Wichita Indictments," 66–68.

115. *The Truth about the I.W.W. Prisoners* (New York: ACLU, 1918), 21–23.

116. Earl White, "Wichita Indictments," 198–99.

117. U.S. House of Representatives, Committee on the Judiciary, *Amnesty for Political Prisoners,* 67th Congress, 2nd Session (1922), Testimony of Caroline

Lowe and of Albert De Sliver, p. 32; Clayton R. Koppes, "The Kansas Trial of the IWW, 1917–1919," *Labor History* 16, no. 3 (1975): 338, 341–42; Earl White, "Wichita Indictments," 174–75; Lever Food and Fuel Control Act of 1917, Pub. L. 65–41, 40 Stat. 276.

118. Jeffrey J. Johnson, *The 1916 Preparedness Day Bombing: Anarchy and Terrorism in Progressive Era America* (New York: Routledge, 2017).

119. "Two I.W.W. Carrying Dynamite Are Captured in Sacramento," *San Francisco Examiner,* Dec. 23, 1927, 1.

120. Letter from Acting Attorney General to the President, in Pardon Attorney Sacramento Case Files–William Hood, 002366-013-0401, DOJ-IWW; "Dynamiter Suspect Admits He Stole Explosives," *San Francisco Examiner,* Sept. 25, 1917, 1; "U.S. Sleuths Follow Trail of Suspects," *San Francisco Examiner,* Dec. 23, 1917, 2.

121. Chester, *The Wobblies,* 188, 190–91.

122. Hyman Weintraub, "The I.W.W. in California: 1905–1931," MA thesis, University of California, Los Angeles, 1947, pp. 145–46.

123. See, for example, John H. Laslett, *Sunshine Was Never Enough: Los Angeles Workers, 1880–2010* (Berkeley: University of California Press, 2012), 62; Olmsted, *Right Out of California,* 35–36; U.S. Senate, Committee on Education and Labor, *Employers' Associations and Collective Bargaining in California,* Report No. 1150, Pt. 2, 77th Congress, 2nd Session (Washington, D.C.: GPO, 1942), 71–72.

124. Telegram to Attorney General, Aug. 23, 1917, IWW Cases and Activities–California, 002366-004-0080, DOJ-IWW.

125. Dowell, "Criminal Syndicalism," 355–56.

126. Weintraub, "I.W.W. in California," 138.

127. "Shall the Capital City Be Run by Disloyal I.W.W.," *Sacramento Bee,* Dec. 29, 1917, 12.

128. Weintraub, "I.W.W. in California," 141–47; Statement Concerning the Present Legal Status of the I.W.W. Cases, in Pardon Attorney Case Files: William D. Haywood, 002366-012-0580, DOJ-IWW; Anderson v. United States, 269 F. 65 (9th Cir. 1921). Five more were also made defendants in the Chicago case. Weintraub, "I.W.W. in California," 138–59; Ralph Shaffer, "Radicalism in California, 1869–1929," PhD diss., University of California, 1965, pp. 277–80; Correspondence Cases–IWW, ACLU Records, Volume 86, pp. 42–145.

129. "Idaho News Notes," *Kendrick Gazette,* Nov. 2, 1917, n.p.; "Eighteen I.W.W. Freed," *Kendrick Gazette,* Oct. 19, 1917, 1.

130. "Idaho I.W.W. Goes to Pen," *Idaho Falls Times,* Apr. 11, 1918, 4; "Hold I.W.W.s for Investigation," *Anaconda Standard,* Apr. 18, 1918, 2.

131. "Start Campaign for Clean-Up of All Idaho I.W.W.," *Daily Missoulian,* Mar. 19, 1919, 1; "I.W.W. Leader Found Guilty," *Boise Idaho Statesman,* Apr. 3, 1918, 1; Sims, "Idaho's Criminal Syndicalism Act," 521.

132. Description of Convict, Record of William Nelson, No. 2627, Inmate Records, ISA.

133. Telegram from J. T. Moran to Moses Alexander, Mar. 22, 1918, Box 1, File 2, Moses Alexander Papers, WRML.

134. Records of Dennis McCarthy, Joe Martin, Fred Morgan, John Shea, Bert Banker, Frank Fleury, J.L. O'Brien, George Kopp, Robert Wilson, Charles Carlson, Lyman Moore, and Frank Farmer in Inmate Records, ISA.

135. "Citizens of Ione Drive out IWW," *Spokane Spokesman-Review,* Jan. 1, 1918, 1.

136. "I.W.W.s Get 30 Days in Jail," *Spokane Spokesman-Review,* Apr. 6, 1918, 7; "To Curb I.WW. in Spokane," *Spokane Spokesman-Review,* Mar. 21, 1918, 6; "Not Swiss, He Says," *Spokane Spokesman-Review,* Feb. 8, 1918, 10.

137. "Rock Pile Asked for Local I.W.W.," *Spokane Daily Chronicle,* Apr. 11, 1918, 15. See also "Hands Off Spokane Police," *Spokane Spokesman-Review,* Apr. 7, 1918, 6; "Carried I.W.W. Songs to Court; City to Feed Him," *Spokane Daily Chronicle,* July 6, 1918, 1.

138. "Federal and Police Officers Make Raid on I.W.W. Quarters," *Portland Oregon Daily Journal,* Feb. 24, 1918, 4.

139. "150 I.W.W. Arrested in Raid Still Held," *Seattle Star,* May 13, 1918, 7; "I.W.W. Are Bound Over," *Seattle Star,* May 11, 1918, 3; "I.W.W. Held in Jail to Fight in Courts," *Seattle Star,* May 6, 1918, 7; "Chief Warren Raids I.W.W. Here; 213 Taken," *Seattle Star,* May 3, 1918, 1.

140. "Release Yearout and Wife, Taken in I.W.W. Raid," *Spokane Daily Chronicle,* May 4, 1918, 1.

141. City of Spokane v. Grady, 105 P. 1043 (Wash. 1921); "Superior Court Ruling Upholds City I.W.W. Law, "*Spokane Daily Chronicle,* June 28, 1918, 1.

142. "Fines Greek for Assault," *Spokane Spokesman-Review,* July 26, 1918, 7; "I.W.W. Leader Has Case Continued," *Spokane Daily Chronicle,* Aug. 21, 1918, 1; "Nab I.W.W. Agent Planning Strike," *Spokane Spokesman-Review,* Aug. 21, 1918, 1; "Get Evidence Against I.W.W.," *Spokane Spokesman-Review,* Aug. 30, 1918, 6.

143. Dean A. Strang, *Keep the Wretches in Order: America's Biggest Mass Trial, the Rise of the Justice Department, and the Fall of the IWW* (Madison: University of Wisconsin Press, 2019), 89–90; IWW Cases and Activities–William D. Haywood, Pending List of Defendants, 002366-009-0237, DOJ-IWW. See also Taft, "Federal Trials of the IWW," 63.

144. Bryant et al. v. United States, 257 F. 378 (5th Cir. 1919); Correspondence Cases–Amnesty, ACLU Records, Volume 196, p. 190. On other IWW prosecutions, see, for example, "Seven I.W.W. Found Guilty," *Tacoma Daily Ledger,* Jan. 31, 1918, 1.

145. Strang, *Keep the Wretches in Order,* 77–80. Count one alleged that the defendants, in violation of a general provision of the federal code, had conspired to "prevent, hinder and delay" the execution of ten federal statutes, including the Espionage Act, along with nine separate sections of the federal penal code and various presidential proclamations related to war production. Count two, which also rested on a general conspiracy provision, charged the defendants with conspiring to use sabotage and other such acts to deprive businesses engaged in war production of their constitutional right to fulfill their contractual obligations. Counts three and four both charged a conspiracy to undermine the implementation of the Selective Draft Act and cause desertion

from the military and insubordination in the ranks; count three rested on a general provision in the federal code, while count four, the most serious charge, invoked section four of the Espionage Act, the conspiracy provision. Count five charged a conspiracy to defraud employers of defense workers. Philip S. Foner, "United States of America vs. Wm. D. Haywood, et al.: The I.W.W. Indictment," *Labor History* 11, no. 4 (1970): 500, 506–30; Statement Concerning the Present Legal Status of the I.W.W. Cases, Pardon Attorney Case Files: William D. Haywood, 002366-012-0580, DOJ-IWW.

146. David Pietrusza, *Judge and Jury: The Life and Times of Judge Kennesaw Mountain Landis* (Providence, RI: Taylor Trade Publishing, 2001), 34–25, 67, 223.

147. Application for Executive Clemency, in Pardon Attorney Case Files: Charles Ashleigh, 002366-011-0001, DOJ-IWW; Chester, *The Wobblies*, 167, 179–80, 182–83; Strang, *Keep the Wretches in Order*, 104, 111–12.

148. "Soldiers Guard as 104 I.W.W. Are Arraigned Here," *Chicago Daily Tribune*, Dec. 16, 1917, 9.

149. On the tendency to evaluate the case without due regard for the nature of conspiracy law, see, for example, Taft, "Federal Trials of the IWW"; Richard Brazier, "The Mass I.W.W. Trial of 1918: A Retrospect," *Labor History* 7, no. 2 (1966): 178.

150. Dubofsky, *We Shall Be All*, 434–35; United States v. Haywood, et al., Boxes 104–105, IWW Collection, WRML; Report of Pardon Attorney, in Pardon Attorney Cases–Charles Lambert et al., 002366-011-0761, n.f., DOJ-IWW.

151. United States v. Haywood, et al., Boxes 105–108, IWW Collection, WRML.

152. Report on the Haywood Case, Haywood v. U.S., 001759-004-0192, Louis Brandeis Papers, Harvard Law Library. St. John had either declined or never received a request from the union's general executive board to replace Haywood in the event of the latter's arrest. For years, prosecutors insisted that St. John remained active in union affairs and that his mining work was for benefit of the IWW. Pardon Attorney Case Files: Charles Ashleigh, 002366-011-0001, passim, DOJ-IWW; IWW Cases and Activities–William D. Haywood, 002366-008-0873, passim, DOJ-IWW.

153. "Ex-Governor Loses Evidence in I.W.W. Case," *Chicago Daily Tribune*, May 20, 1918, 9; Chaplin, *Wobbly*, 245–46.

154. Chester, The Wobblies, 180–81.

155. Strang, *Keep the Wretches in Order*, 112–13, 144–50; Taft, "Federal Trials of the IWW," 70–74; Dubofsky, *We Shall Be All*, 435; United States v. Haywood, et al., Boxes 109–118, IWW Collection, WRML.

156. For reasons that remain unclear, Vanderveer gave no closing. As Chester suspects, it is possible that Vanderveer thought he had reached a secret deal with Landis and the Justice Department and that this is why he gave no closing. Or maybe, as Dubofsky contends, Vanderveer believed that a closing would serve no purpose. Chester, *The Wobblies*, 183–85; Dubofsky, *We Shall Be All*, 436.

157. Taft, "Federal Trials of the IWW," 74.

158. Strang, *Keep the Wretches in Order,* 161–63; Chester, *The Wobblies,* 182–85. The fifth count in the indictment, which charged conspiracy to interfere with the employment of defense workers, was withdrawn during the trial.

159. Lowell S. Hawley and Ralph Bushnell Potts, *Counsel for the Damned: A Biography of George Francis Vanderveer* (Philadelphia: J.B. Lippincott, 1953), 238–39; "Convict 100 I.W.W. Chiefs," *Chicago Daily Tribune,* Aug. 18, 1918, 1.

160. Strang, *Keep the Wretches in Order,* 166–67.

161. Benjamin Fletcher, 002371-003-0686, MIR; Strang, *Keep the Wretches in Order,* 165–69; "Haywood Given 20 Year Term," *Chicago Daily Tribune,* Aug. 31, 1918, 1. The fate of Fletcher's union, Marine Transport Workers Industrial Union No. 8, is a remarkable story unto itself. Largely disconnected from the IWW's experience in the West, it has been well told by others, most notably by Peter Cole in his *Wobblies on the Waterfront: Interracial Unionism in Progressive-Era Philadelphia* (Chicago: University of Illinois Press, 2013). At least one other black Wobbly, Oscar Black, arrested in Pacific County, Washington, in 1921 and convicted of criminal syndicalism 1921, was also imprisoned on felony charges.

162. "Haywood Given 20 Year Term," *Chicago Daily Tribune,* Aug. 31, 1918, 1; Taft, "Federal Trials of the IWW," 75; United States v. Haywood, et al., Box 118, File 6, IWW Collection, WRML.

163. Strang, *Keep the Wretches in Order,* 187–89; *The Autobiography of Big Bill Haywood* (New York: International Publishers, 1977), 324–26; Christina Heatherton, "University of Radicalism: Ricardo Flores Magón and Leavenworth Penitentiary," *American Quarterly* 66, no. 3 (2014): 557.

164. State v. Griffith, 184 P. 219 (Mont. 1918); Description List of the Convict, J.A. Griffith, Montana State Prison, Montana Historical Society Research Center; "Court Not Censor over Language is Ruling," *Great Falls Tribune,* Sept. 23, 1919, 4.

165. Evans, "Montana's Role," 86–95; Montana Sedition Project, http://www.seditionproject.net/index.html; Rader, "Montana Lumber Strike," 206–7.

166. "Convict Burans as Seditionist," *Missoulian,* May 24, 1918, 2; "I.W.W. Attorney in City on Business," *Billings Gazette,* Dec. 7, 1918, 2.

167. Gutfeld, "Years of Hysteria," 62–68; Letter to B.K. Wheeler, Nov. 16, 1917, IWW Cases and Activities–Montana, 002366-004-0784, DOJ-IWW; Butte, Montana, Copper Industry Disturbances and Use of Federal Military Force, 101114-003-0837, DOJ-MF; "Butte Officials Arrest 41 I.W.W.," *Missoulian,* Mar. 26, 1918, 1.

168. The sedition statute essentially declared it unlawful, during wartime, to disparage the government or the military, to display the flag of the enemy, and to say or publish anything that might undermine or be calculated to undermine the war effort. Act of Feb. 21, 1918, ch. 11, § 1, Montana Extraordinary Session Laws 1918. During the war nine states and two territories enacted sedition laws. Dowell, "Criminal Syndicalism," 10–11; Chafee, *Free Speech in the United States,* 575–97.

The state's criminal syndicalism law was first used in April 1918, when Missoula police arrested and charged the union's acting secretary and raided the

IWW hall, arresting fifteen who were also charged with criminal syndicalism. But the men were acquitted in that pro-union town. "Roundup Wobblies Securing Evidence," *Great Falls Tribune*, Apr. 8, 1918, 4. There was a scattering of other arrests on this charge later in 1918, in Flathead, Granite, and Lincoln counties. Dowell, "Criminal Syndicalism," 1078–81. On the enactment of this statute, which required two attempts, see Dowell, "Criminal Syndicalism," 273–86, 1257.

169. Letter from Burton Wheeler to the Attorney General, Oct. 4, 1918, in Butte, Montana Copper Industry Disturbances and the Use of Federal Troops, 101114-003-0837, n.f., DOJ-MF; Preston, *Aliens and Dissenters*, 113–14; Evans, "Montana's Role," 62, 78–79, 95–97; Gutfeld, "Years of Hysteria," 68–72, 106–15.

170. Preston, *Aliens and Dissenters*, 113–14; Butte, Montana, Copper Industry Disturbances and Use of Federal Military Force, 101114-003-0837, DOJ-MF.

171. IWW Cases and Activities–Butte, Montana, 002366-010-0642, DOJ-IWW; Chester, *The Wobblies*, 109–11; Letter from Baldwin Robertson to the Attorney General, Sept. 8, 1920, IWW Cases and Activities–Butte, 002366-101-642, DOJ-IWW; Letter from Governor S. V. Stewart to the Attorney General, IWW Cases and Activities–Butte, 002366-010-0499, DOJ-IWW.

CHAPTER 4. I'LL TAKE NEITHER MERCY NOR PITY

1. *The Silent Defense* (Chicago: IWW, n.d.), 5–6; Party Attorney Case Files–Chicago, 002366-012-0001, Department of Justice Investigative Files: Industrial Workers of the World (DOJ-IWW); Eleanor Dunbar and Frederick Esmond Activities, 002371-008-0126, DOJ-IWW; IWW Cases and Activities–Sacramento, California, 002366-006-0286, DOJ-IWW.

2. Eric Thomas Chester, *The Wobblies in Their Heyday* (Santa Barbara, CA: Praeger, 2014), 190–93; William Preston Jr., *Aliens and Dissenters: Federal Suppression of Radicals, 1903–1933* (Cambridge, MA: Harvard University Press, 1963), 135.

3. IWW Cases and Activities–Sacramento, 002366-005-1000, DOJ-IWW.

4. "Burden of War Is Now on United States," *Sacramento Bee*, Nov. 8, 1917, 6.

5. IWW Cases and Activities–Sacramento, 002366-006-0407, DOJ-IWW; IWW Cases and Activities–Sacramento, 002366-005-1000, DOJ-IWW.

6. Melvyn Dubofsky, *We Shall Be All: A History of the Industrial Workers of the World* (Urbana: University of Illinois Press, 1969), 439–41.

7. Leo Tulin, Summary of Criminal Syndicalism Cases, pp. 58–59, Box 1, Ralph Chaplin Papers, University of Michigan Special Collections.

8. "Raid on I.W.W. Room Bares New Evidence," *Chicago Daily Tribune*, Dec. 18, 1917, 5.

9. Dean A. Strang, *Keep the Wretches in Order: America's Biggest Mass Trial, the Rise of the Justice Department, and the Fall of the IWW* (Madison: University of Wisconsin Press, 2019), 146–48.

10. Chester, *The Wobblies,* 196–97. Pollok quarreled with the IWW about funding for the defense. Correspondence Cases–IWW, Records of the National Office of the American Civil Liberties Union (ACLU Records), Volume 86, pp. 103–22.

11. See, for example, Letter from John Murray to E.J. Costello, July 21, 1921, Correspondence Cases-Amnesty, ACLU Records, Volume 198, pp. 12–14; Eldridge Foster Dowell, "A History of the Enactment of Criminal Syndicalism Legislation in the United States," PhD diss., Johns Hopkins University, 1936, p. 345.

12. Chester, *The Wobblies,* 197–200; Ralph Shaffer, "Radicalism in California, 1869–1929," PhD diss., University of California, 1965, pp. 177–283. See also Correspondence Cases–IWW, ACLU Records, Volume 86, pp. 42–145; IWW Cases and Activities–Sacramento, 00266-006-0240, DOJ-IWW; IWW Cases and Activities–Fresno, 002366-009-0750, DOJ-IWW.

13. Hyman Weintraub, "The I.W.W. in California: 1905–1931," MA thesis, University of California, Los Angeles, 1947, pp. 153–57; Dowell, "Criminal Syndicalism," 344; IWW Cases and Activities, 002366-006-0000, DOJ-IWW; Earl Bruce White, "The Wichita Indictments and Trial of the Industrial Workers of the World, 1917–1919," PhD diss., University of Colorado, 1980, p. 35.

14. Weintraub, "I.W.W. in California," 157.

15. Weintraub, "I.W.W. in California," 153, 157.

16. Weintraub, "I.W.W. in California," 162–63; Dowell, "Criminal Syndicalism," 363.

17. Dowell, "Criminal Syndicalism," 326–30.

18. David M. Struthers, *The World in a City: Multiethnic Radicalism in Early Twentieth-Century Los Angeles* (Urbana: University of Illinois Press, 2019), 197–98. On newspaper coverage, see, for example, "Bolshevist Conspiracy Bared," *L.A. Times,* Jan. 31, 1919, 13; "Guilty I.W.W. Bailed Out," *L.A. Times,* Feb. 2, 1919, 7; "Protect Orange Pickers," *L.A. Times,* Feb. 5, 1919, 13.

19. Dowell, "Criminal Syndicalism," 359, 362–66, 368–70, 1217–18; Weintraub, "I.W.W. in California," 162–63.

20. Michael Kazin, "The Great Exception Revisited: Organized Labor and Politics in San Francisco and Los Angeles, 1870–1940," *Pacific Historical Review* 55 (1986): 381, 393–95; Dowell, "Criminal Syndicalism," 368; Act of Apr. 30, 1919, ch. 382, §§ 1–4, California Session Laws 1919.

21. Seattle Shipyard Labor Disturbances, 101114-005-0609, Department of Justice, Investigative Files, Part III: Use of Military Force by the Federal Government in Domestic Disturbances, 1900–1938, pp. 73–78; Dowell, "Criminal Syndicalism," 201–2.

22. Dowell, "Criminal Syndicalism," 202–11; "Syndicalism Bill Passed," *Seattle Star,* Jan. 14, 1919, 1.

23. Quoted in Joseph F. Tripp, "Reform and Repression in the Far West: The Washington Legislative Response to Labor Radicalism in 1919," *Rendezvous* 19 (1983): 43, 44. See also Joseph F. Tripp, "Law and Social Control: Historians' Views of Progressive-Era Labor Legislation," *Labor History* 28, no. 4 (1987): 447, 471–72.

24. Dowell, "Criminal Syndicalism," 218–20; Wash. Laws, 1919, ch. 3, p. 2, repealed by Wash. Laws, 1919, ch. 174, p. 518.

25. Victoria Johnson, *How Many Machine Guns Does It Take to Cook One Meal? The Seattle and San Francisco General Strikes* (Seattle: University of Washington Press, 2008), 31–68; Kathy Ferguson, "Creating a City to Resist the State: The Seattle General Strike of 1919," *Theory and Event* 22, no. 4 (2019): 911.

26. Terje I. Leiren, "Ole and the Reds: The 'Americanism' of Seattle Mayor Ole Hanson," *Norwegian-American Studies* 30 (1985): 75, 87.

27. Johnson, *How Many Machine Guns*, 45–46, 60–65; Clayton D. Laurie and Ronald D. Cole, *The Role of Federal Forces in Domestic Disorders, 1877–1945* (Washington, D.C.: Center of Military History), 262–65.

28. Dowell, "Criminal Syndicalism," 201–11; "Syndicalism Bill Passed," *Seattle Star,* Jan. 14, 1919, 1.

29. Clippings–IWW Cases, ACLU Records, Volume 85, pp. 39–41.

30. "Sentence I.W.W. to Month in Jail," *Spokane Daily Chronicle,* Jan. 30, 1919, 16; "New I.W.W. Office Raided," *Spokane Spokesman-Review,* Jan. 24, 1919, 3; "Spokane Oppression," *New Solidarity,* Feb. 8, 1919, 4.

31. See, for example, "I.W.W. Wants Judge to Testify," *Spokane Daily Chronicle,* July 9, 1919, 3; "Born on St. Patrick's Day Plea," *Spokane Spokesman-Review,* Mar. 18, 1919, 9; "Held on Syndicalism Charge," *Spokane Spokesman-Review,* Feb. 15, 1919, 6; "Grady Jury Disagrees," *Seattle Star,* Jan. 16, 1920, 12.

32. With Drops of Blood, IWW Cases and Activities–California, 002366-004-0080, DOJ-IWW; "Strangles Himself after Reading How," *Seattle Star,* Sept. 19, 1919, 10; "Buttons Undo Wobblies," *Spokesman-Review,* July 9, 1919, 6; "New Charges against 30 Reds," *Spokane Spokesman-Review,* Aug. 1, 1919, 6.

33. Erik Loomis, *Empire of Timber: Labor Unions and the Pacific Northwest Forests* (New York: Cambridge University Press, 2015), 54–55, 65–88; Robert L. Tyler, "The United States Government as Union Organizer: The Loyal Legion of Loggers and Lumbermen," *Mississippi Valley Historical Review* 47, no. 3 (1960): 434; Laurie and Cole, *Role of Federal Forces,* 237–40; Disque Report Regarding the Labor Situation in Washington and Oregon, in Brice P. Disque Papers, Accession No. 0316-001, Box 3/2, Pacific Northwest Historical Documents Collection, University of Washington Special Collections (UWSC); Cloice R. Howd, "Industrial Relations in the West Coast Lumber Industry," *U.S. Bureau of Labor Statistics Bulletin No. 349* (Washington, D.C.: GPO, 1923) 77–85.

34. Quoted in Adam Hodges, "Thinking Globally, Acting Locally: The Portland Soviet and the Emergence of American Communism, 1918–1920," *Pacific Northwest Quarterly* 98, no. 3 (2007): 115.

35. Adam Hodges, *World War I and Urban Order: The Local Class Politics of National Mobilization* (New York: Palgrave Macmillan, 2015) 127–48; Dowell, "Criminal Syndicalism," 552–53; Hodges, "Thinking Globally," 116.

36. Dowell, "Criminal Syndicalism," 532–57; Act of Feb. 3, 1919, ch. 12, §§ 1–4, 1919 Oregon Session Laws.

37. "City Authorities Put in Effect Oregon Criminal Syndicalism Law," *Portland Oregon Daily Journal,* Feb. 9, 1919, 1; "Court Releases Suspected Reds," *Portland Oregon Daily Journal,* Feb. 11, 1919, 1.

38. "22 I.W.W. Taken in Raid on Room of Local Order," *Portland Oregon Daily Journal,* Feb. 26, 1919, 18.

39. On Equi and her trial, see Heather Mayer, *Beyond the Rebel Girl: Women and the Industrial Workers of the World in the Pacific Northwest, 1905–1924* (Corvallis: Oregon State University Press, 2018), 141–56.

40. Hodges, "Thinking Globally," 116, 124–25.

41. "Radicals and Police Fight in Boston Riot," *N.Y. Times,* May 2, 1919, 3; "200 Arrests in Fatal Riots in Cleveland," *St. Louis Post-Dispatch,* May 2, 1919, 8; "May 1 Riots Deadly," *Chicago Daily Tribune,* May 2, 1919, 1.

42. Jeffrey P. Simon, "The Forgotten Terrorists: Lesson from the History of Terrorism," *Terrorism and Political Violence* 20, no. 2 (2008): 195; Robert K. Murray, *Red Scare: A Study in National Hysteria, 1919–1920* (New York: McGraw-Hill, 1955), 67–81.

43. Fred Thompson, *The I.W.W.: Its First Fifty Years* (Chicago: IWW, 1955), 18.

44. In spring 1918, the Neutrality Squad raided the IWW's San Francisco headquarters every week for four months and then, in May, moved to close the building and declared that all IWWs would be arrested "on sight." "Police Close Out I.W.W. Office," *San Francisco Examiner,* May 23, 1918, 13; "I.W.W. Bagged in Raid Convicted," *San Francisco Chronicle,* June 16, 1918, N1; "All I.W.W. to Be Jailed on Sight," *Salinas Californian,* May 11, 1918, 5. See also "8 Arrested in Raid on I.W.W.," *San Francisco Chronicle,* May 10, 1918, 3; "9 Taken in Raid on I.W.W.," *San Francisco Examiner,* Apr. 10, 1918, 5; "Arrests Reveal Spies' Activities," *Oakland Tribune,* Mar. 27, 1918, 5.

45. "Radical Is Held on New Charge, *San Francisco Chronicle,*" May 23, 1919, 5; "First Arrest Made Under Anti-Red Law," *San Francisco Examiner,* May 23, 1919, 2. See also Woodrow W. Whitten, "Criminal Syndicalism and the Law in California: 1919–1927," *Transactions of the American Philosophical Society* 59, no. 2 (1969): 3, 27.

46. "Police Arrest 18 I.W.W. in 2 Raids," *San Francisco Examiner,* Jan. 25, 1919, 11.

47. Whitten, "Criminal Syndicalism," 26–27; Criminal Syndicalism in California, Legal Defense Requests, ACLU Records, Volume 90, pp. 98–99; George W. Kirchwey, *A Survey of the Workings of the Criminal Syndicalism Law of California* (Los Angeles: ACLU, 1926), 13; "Syndicalism Cases in San Francisco," *Industrial Worker,* July 16, 1919, 2.

48. Letter from Emanuel Levin to Albert de Silver, Aug. 22, 1919, Legal Defense Requests, ACLU Records, Volume 90, pp. 103–4.

49. Levin likely was an IWW, although probably transferring his allegiance to the communist movement. Ralph E. Shaffer, "Communism in California: 1919–1924," *Science and Society* 34, no. 4 (1970): 412, 426.

50. Tulin, Summary of Criminal Syndicalism Cases, pp. 1–12; Whitten, "Criminal Syndicalism," 27, 29–30; Weintraub, "I.W.W. in California," 165–66; "Federal Officers Raid I.W.W.," *Stockton Daily Evening Record,* June 30, 1919, 14; "California Syndicalist Cases," *Industrial Worker,* Aug. 9, 1919, 4; "California Cases of Criminal Syndicalism," *New Solidarity,* Sept. 6, 1919, 3; "I.W.W. Editor Taken in Raid Is Released," *San Francisco Chronicle,*

Mar. 6, 1919, 11; "Local Publisher Nabbed in Raid," *Oakland Tribune,* Feb. 28, 1919, 1.

51. Whitten, "Criminal Syndicalism," 31; Tulin, Summary of Criminal Syndicalism Cases, 12–15; "Latest News," *L.A. Herald,* Nov. 11, 1919, 1.

52. "40 Are Quizzed in L.A. Probe of I.WW.," *L.A. Herald,* Oct. 6, 1919, 1. See also "Plot to Arm L.A. Reds is Revealed," *L.A. Herald,* Nov. 18, 1919, 1. The U.S. senator in question may have been John Works, a Progressive who had opposed America's entry into the war.

53. Murray, *Red Scare,* 123–34; Cameron McWhirter, *Red Summer: The Summer of 1919 and the Awakening of Black America* (New York: St. Martin's Press, 2012), passim.

54. Murray, *Red Scare,* 190–222; Matthew Guariglia, "Wrench in the Deportation Machine: Louis F. Post's Objection to Mechanized Red Scare Bureaucracy," *Journal of American Ethnic History* 38, no. 1 (2018): 62.

55. Robert Evans, "Montana's Role in the Enactment of Legislation Designed to Suppress the Industrial Workers of the World," MA thesis, Montana State University, 1964, pp. 98–121.

56. Sedition Act of 1918, Pub. L 65–160, 40 Stat. 553.

57. Dowell, "Criminal Syndicalism," 1209–11.

58. Only a few dozen Espionage Act cases of any kind were brought from July 1919 through June 1920, and only six cases were even commenced the following fiscal year. *Annual Report of the U.S. Attorney General, 1921* (Washington, D.C.: GPO, 1921), 98. Days before the armistice, the attorney general directed all U.S. attorneys to obtain his approval before initiating any more grand jury proceedings under sections three or four of Title I of the Espionage Act. *Annual Report of the U.S. Attorney General, 1919* (Washington, D.C.: GPO, 1919), 631.

59. On this deportation campaign, see Preston, *Aliens and Dissenters,* 181–237; Chester, *The Wobblies,* 135–43. On the deportation of IWWs, see also U.S. House of Representatives, Subcommittee of the Committee on Immigration and Naturalization, *Hearings on I.W.W. Deportation Cases,* 66th Congress, 2nd Session, 1920. These developments convinced the head of the Bureau of Investigation's "Radical Division," an ambitious young lawyer named John Edgar Hoover, that the federal government should begin arresting Wobblies in batches of five hundred until the organization ceased to exist. Preston, *Aliens and Dissenters,* 225–26. On federal resources in this period, see Michael Belknap, "Uncooperative Federalism: The Failure of the Bureau of Investigation's Intergovernmental Attack on Radicalism," *Publius* 12, no. 2 (1982): 25, 26.

60. Tom Copeland, *The Centralia Tragedy of 1919: Elmer Smith and the Wobblies* (Seattle: University of Washington Press, 1993), 37; Robert L. Tyler, "The I.W.W. in the Pacific N.W.: Rebels of the Woods," *Oregon Historical Quarterly* 55, no. 1 (1954): 3, 28.

61. Copeland, *Centralia Tragedy,* 42–43, 84; "Sentences Three Men as Syndicalists," *Seattle Star,* July 14, 1920, 2.

62. Copeland, *Centralia Tragedy,* 45–46; Tyler, "I.W.W. in the Pacific N.W.," 28–29.

63. Copeland, *Centralia Tragedy,* 50–54; Tyler, "I.W.W. in the Pacific N.W.," 29–30.

64. Copeland, *Centralia Tragedy* 50–54.

65. "I.W.W. Desperadoes Still Raging," *Tacoma Daily Ledger,* Nov. 18, 1919, 1; "I.W.W. Gunmen Surrounded," *Tacoma Daily Ledger,* Nov. 17, 1919, 1.

66. "Judge Bars Weapons from Court," *Seattle Star,* Jan. 29, 1920, 1; "Arrests Grimm Case Witnesses," *Spokane Weekly Spokesman,* Mar. 3, 1920, 1; Copeland, *Centralia Tragedy,* 57–70; Shawn Daley, "Centralia, Collective Memory, and the Tragedy of 1919," MA thesis, Portland State University, 1995, pp. 30–35; Dowell, "Criminal Syndicalism," 121. On the course of this litigation, see also Centralia, Box 124, IWW, Walter Reuther Memorial Library (WRML); IWW Cases and Activities–Centralia and Seattle, Washington, 002366-006-0705, DOJ-IWW.

67. Copeland, *Centralia Affair,* 65–87; IWW Cases and Activities–Centralia and Seattle, Washington, 002366-007-0000, DOJ-IWW.

68. The Tragedy of Centralia, IWW Cases and Activities–Seattle and Centralia, 002366-006-0705, DOJ-IWW. See also "Demand Prosecution of Every Wobbly Found," *Spokane Daily Chronicle,* Nov. 29, 1919, 3.

69. Decision upon Demur to Indictment, IWW Cases and Activities–Seattle and Centralia, 002366-006-0705, DOJ-IWW. See also IWW Cases and Activities–Seattle and Centralia, 002366-007-0000, DOJ-IWW.

70. See generally, Correspondence Cases–Washington, ACLU Records, Volume 140. See also Dowell, "Criminal Syndicalism," 1056–57.

71. "To Speed Trial of 500 Radicals," Clippings–IWW Cases, ACLU Records, Volume 85, pp. 39–41; Dowell, "Criminal Syndicalism," 1055.

72. Raids! Raids! Raids!, IWW Cases and Activities–William D. Haywood, 002366-008-1136, DOJ-IWW. See also Letter from Crowder Brown to A. Mitchell Palmer, Nov. 28, 1919, IWW Cases and Activities–Seattle and Tacoma, 002366-006-0679, DOJ-IWW.

73. Albert F. Gunns, *Civil Liberties in Crisis: The Pacific Northwest, 1917–1920* (New York: Garland Press, 1983), 42; Robert Tyler, *Rebels of the Woods: The IWW in the Pacific Northwest* (Eugene: University of Oregon Press, 1967), 150; "The Gruesome Story of American Terrorism," *One Big Union Monthly,* Apr. 20, 1920, 12, 14. On the extent of criminal syndicalism enforcement in Washington during this period, see also Correspondence Cases–Washington, ACLU Records, Volume 140; Appellant's Opening Brief, Hennessy v. Washington, Washington State Supreme Court, pp. 6–8, Box 126, File 20, IWW Collection, WRML (also available in UWSC–IWW Collection, Box 2); "Northwest Defense Bulletin," *Industrial Worker,* Feb. 14, 1920, 1; "Northwest Defense Bulletin," *Industrial Worker,* Feb. 7, 1920, 1; "Northwest Defence [*sic*] Bulletin," *Industrial Worker,* Dec. 20, 1920, 1.

74. "36 I.W.W. Are Found Guilty by Tacoma Jury," *Tacoma Daily Ledger,* Feb. 2, 1920, 1; "Tacoma I.W.W. Are Sentenced," *Seattle Star,* Mar. 2, 1920, 1; "Centralia Reds Called to Plead," *Seattle Star,* Dec. 27, 1919, 1.

75. "Seattle Men Will Go to I.W.W. Trial," *Seattle Star,* Jan. 26, 1920, 1; "Frank Hastings Released on Bonds Pending Appeals," *Washington Standard,* Oct. 5, 1920, 8; "Driven Insane," *Industrial Worker,* May 29, 1920, 1.

76. "Eight Are Guilty of Criminal Syndicalism," *L.A. Times*, Feb. 28, 1920, 114; "Northwest Defense Bulletin," *Industrial Worker*, May 8, 1920, 1; "Northwest Defense Bulletin," *Industrial Worker*, May 1, 1920, 1; "Northwest Defense Bulletin," *Industrial Worker*, Apr. 23, 1920, 1; "Northwest Defense Bulletin," *Industrial Worker*, Apr. 16, 1920, 1; "Northwest Defense Bulletin," *Industrial Worker*, Apr. 9, 1920, 1; "Northwest Defense Bulletin," *Industrial Worker*, Apr. 1, 1920, 1; "Northwest Defense Bulletin," *Industrial Worker*, Mar. 26, 1920, 1; "Northwest Defense Bulletin, *Industrial Worker*, Mar. 19, 1920, 1; "Northwest Defense Bulletin," *Industrial Worker*, Mar. 6, 1920, 1.

77. Michael Cohen, "'The Ku Klux Government': Vigilantism, Lynching, and the Repression of the IWW," *Journal for the Study of Radicalism* 1, no. 1 (2006): 32, 49.

78. Letter from Pay Boyd to ACLU, December 6, 1920, Correspondence Cases–Washington, ACLU Records, Volume 140, pp. 38–40.

79. Correspondence Cases–Washington, ACLU Records, Volume 140, pp. 47–65; "Will Let I.W.W. Gang Get Out," *Spokane Daily Chronicle*, Aug. 6, 1921, 1.

80. Letter from William Ferguson to Lucille Milner, June 22, 1920, Correspondence Cases–Washington, ACLU Records, Volume 140, pp. 47–48, 53–56.

81. "Olcott Calls upon State Official to Wage War upon Red Propaganda," *Salem Capital Journal*, Nov. 18, 1919, 1.

82. "22 Alleged I.W.W. Members Indicted," *Salem Capital Journal*, Nov. 21, 1919, 10.

83. "The Gruesome Story of American Terrorism," *One Big Union Monthly*, Apr. 1920, 12, 14. On other enforcement, see "I.W.W. and Reds are Rounded Up at Fossil," *Heppner Gazette-Times*, Nov. 27, 1919, 1; "Three I.W.W. Held Guilty," *Salem Capital Journal*, May 10, 1920, 4; "22 Alleged I.W.W. Members Indicted in Portland," *Salem Daily Capital Journal*, Nov. 21, 1919, 10; "Medford Man Indicted on Syndicalism Charge," *Salem Capital Journal*, Feb. 21, 1920, 12; "Faces Syndicalism Charge," *Pendleton East Oregonian*, Dec. 9, 1919, 4.

84. "Cantwell Convicted," *Everett Labor Journal*, Nov. 26, 1920, 2.

85. Hodges, "Thinking Globally," 126; "Fellow Worker J. Laundy Is Found Guilty in Portland," *Industrial Worker*, Apr. 9, 1920, 1; "Professional Witness Used in Portland Trial," *Industrial Worker*, Apr. 2, 1920, 1. See also State v. Laundy, 204 P. 958 (Ore. 1922); "Laundy Sentenced to 2 Years," *Salem Capital Journal*, Apr. 19, 1920, 2; "Laundy Criminal Case Nears End Today," *Salem Capital Journal*, Apr. 3, 1920, 4.

86. "I.W.W. Swarming to North Idaho Will Be Seized," *Boise Evening Capital News*, Nov. 16, 1917, 1.

87. "Present Plan to Handle 'Em Rather Rough," *Caldwell Tribune*, Nov. 21, 1919, n.p.; "Idaho Launches Move to Drive out the I.W.W.," *Boise Evening Capital News*, Nov. 18, 1919, 1.

88. "I.W.W. in North Tearing Up Cards," *Boise Evening Capital News*, Nov. 24, 1919, 5; "First Haul of I.W.W. Is Made in North Idaho," *Boise Evening Capital News*, Nov. 17, 1919, 1; "Idaho Law Enforcement Head Asks Federal Government to Deport Alien I.W.W. Members," *Boise Sunday Capital News*, Nov. 30, 1919, 1.

89. State v. Dingman, 219 P. 760 (Idaho 1923); Brief of Appellant, State v. Dingman, Idaho Supreme Court, p. 6., Box 127, File 5, IWW Collection, WRML; "Syndicalism Law Upheld by Court in Dingman Case," *Idaho Statesman*, Jun. 1, 1923, 7. The court found that the evidence used to demonstrate Dingman's membership in the IWW also constituted hearsay and ordered a new trial, which never took place.

90. "Tragical Ending of a Syndicalist Case," *Industrial Worker*, Jun. 5, 1920, 1; "Jovanovich Tries Suicide Twice," *Kendrick Gazette*, May 20, 1920, n.p.; "Shaving in Jail, Cuts His Throat," *Pendleton East Oregonian*, Mar. 5, 1920, 11.

91. "Legion Offers 1000 Men to Quell Reds," *Oakland Tribune*, Nov. 15, 1919, 2.

92. "All I.W.W. Told to Get Out of City," *San Francisco Examiner*, Nov. 15, 1919, 1.

93. "Service Men Wreck Headquarters of I.W.W. Hall Here," *L.A. Times*, Nov. 15, 1919, I1.

94. "Legion's Men Sworn In to War on Radicals," *L.A. Times*, Nov. 18, 1919, III1.

95. "Reds' Plot for U.S. Uprising Bared Here," *L.A. Herald*, Dec. 3, 1919, A7; "Reds Threaten Legion Leader," *L.A. Times*, Nov. 22, 1919, II1.

96. "Post Guards to Protect Heads of Drive on I.W.W.," *L.A. Herald*, Nov. 17, 1919, 1; "Foil I.W.W. Jail Break Attempt," *L.A. Herald*, Nov. 21, 1919, 1.

97. Claude Erwin, Record of California Criminal Syndicalism Convictions, p. 1, Box 135, File 1, IWW Collection, WRML; News Bulletin No. 1, Labor Defense League of California, Labor Defense Requests, ACLU Records, Volume 90, pp. 94–95; California Prison and Correctional Records, San Quentin, Book No. 10, Inmate No. 33280.

98. Letter from Harry McKee to Roger Baldwin, Correspondence Cases–California, ACLU Records, Volume 213, p. 155. See also Letter from George West [?] to Granville MacFarland, June 28, 1922, Correspondence Cases–California, ACLU Records, Volume 213, p. 158; Letter from Charlotte Whitney to Roger Baldwin, Mar. 13, 1922, Correspondence Cases–California, ACLU Records, Volume 213, p. 157; Eldridge Foster Dowell, *A History of Criminal Syndicalism in the United States* (Baltimore, MD: Johns Hopkins University Press, 1939), 51n18, 56–58.

99. John S. Gambs, *The Decline of the I.W.W.* (New York: Russell and Russell, 1966), 29; Kirchwey, *Criminal Syndicalism Law of California*, 16–17.

100. See, for example, CDDC Bulletin, March 1922, Box 4, IWW Seattle Joint Branches Collection, UWSC; Out of Their Own Mouths: Statements of the Three Men Who Sent One Hundred Men to Prison Under the Criminal Syndicalism Law, Box 169-O, IWW Collection, WRML; California the Beautiful and the Damned, pp. 16–29, Box 158-C, IWW Collection, WRML; "Woolvine Investigator Sticks to Ku Klux Klan," *Fresno Morning Republican*, May 23, 1922, 15. Dymond apparently deserted the U.S. Marine Corps thirteen times. "Sensation Sprung in I.W.W. Trial," *Sacramento Union*, Dec. 27, 1922, 1.

101. "Jury to Get I.W.W. Case in Oakland," *L.A. Herald*, Dec. 3, 1919, A10; Strang, *Keep the Wretches in Order*, 134, 287n1.

102. On McHugo's trial, see Correspondence Cases–California, ACLU Records, Volume 133, pp. 131–68; Whitten, "Criminal Syndicalism," 41–42; Erwin, Record of California Criminal Syndicalism Convictions, 1; "Legal Persecution Starts in the West," *One Big Union Monthly*, July 1919, 9; "Jury Convicts James McHugo," *San Francisco Chronicle*, Dec. 4, 1919, 1.

103. "I.W.W. Gets His Sentence," *Santa Cruz News*, Dec. 17, 1919, 1; "Second I.W.W. Convicted of Syndicalism," *San Francisco Examiner*, Dec. 11, 1919, 3. See also "Alleged Anarchists Arrested as Vagrants," *San Francisco Examiner*, Nov. 27, 1919, 11.

104. Erwin, Record of California Criminal Syndicalism Convictions, 1; Tulin, Summary of Criminal Syndicalism Cases, 4; California Prison and Correctional Records, San Quentin, Book No. 10, Inmate No. 33281.

105. "'Red' Terrorist to Testify at I.W.W. Trial," *L.A. Herald*, Mar. 19, 1920, B4; "Secrets of 'Sabotage Factory' Told," *L.A. Herald*, Mar. 18, 1920, 1; "Bombs and Poisons of I.W.W. Ravagers Shown," *L.A. Times*, Mar. 19, 1920, II12. See also Transcript, U.S. v. Elmer Anderson, IWW Cases and Activities–Fresno, 002366-009-0750, DOJ-IWW.

106. "Red Songs Recited in Court by Deputy," *L.A. Herald*, Mar. 19, 1920, A1.

107. Erwin, Record of California Criminal Syndicalism Convictions, 5–7; Tulin, Summary of Criminal Syndicalism Cases, 15; California Prison and Correctional Records, San Quentin, Book No. 10, Inmate Nos. 33735, 33744; "Secret Code of I.W.W. Read to Jury," *L.A. Herald*, Mar. 15, 1920, A12. See also "Boxes of I.W.W. Propaganda in Court," *L.A. Herald*, Mar. 16, 1920, A1; Clippings-California, ACLU Records, Volume 140, pp. 4–25.

108. R. W. Henderson, Constructive Conspiracy and Membership Clause of the California Criminal Syndicalist Act, n.d., pp. 8–17, Box 125, File 2, IWW Collection, WRML. See also Geoffrey Pommer, "The Political Use of the Conspiracy Charge in America," PhD diss., NYU, 1976, pp. 48–49; Leo Daly, "Freedom of Speech as Guaranteed by the Constitution of the State of California in Relation to the Criminal Syndicalism Law," LLM thesis, University of Southern California, 1926, pp. 21–22.

109. Appellant's Opening Brief, Hennessy v. Washington, Washington State Supreme Court, pp. 4–5, Box 126, File 20, IWW Collection, WRML; State v. Hennessy, 195 P. 211 (Wash. 1921); People v. Stewart, 230 P. 221, 224 (Cal. Dist. Ct. App. 1924); People v. Thompson, 229 P. 896, 898 (Cal. Dist. Ct. App. 1924); People v. Bailey, 225 P. 752, 757–59 (Cal. Dist. App. 1924); People v. Eaton, 213 P. 275 (Cal. Dist. Ct. App. 1923); People v. Wieler, 204 P. 410, 413 (Cal. Dist. Ct. App. 1922). In this respect, the nature of criminal syndicalism was understood by the Wobblies themselves. See, for example, Interview of Helen Gallagher, Meridel Le Sueur Papers, Audio Recordings, Box 37, Tape 37, Side 2, Minnesota Historical Society .

110. See, for example, State v. Laundy, 204 P. 958 (Or. 1922); People v. Bailey, 225 P. 752 (Dist. Ct. App. Cal. 1924); People v. Wagner, 225 P. 464 (Dist. Ct. App. Cal. 1924).

111. People v. Steelik [sic], 203 P. 78, 84 (Cal. 1921); People v. Wright, 226 P. 952, 954–55 (Cal. Dist. Ct. App. 1922). On the courts' endorsement of con-

spiracy doctrine in criminal syndicalism prosecutions, see People v. McClennegen, 234 P. 91 (Cal. 1925); People v. Thompson, 229 P. 896 (Cal. Dist. Ct. App. 1924); People v. Ware, 226 P. 956 (Cal. Dist. Ct. App. 1924).

112. See, for example, State v. McLennen, 200 P. 319 (Wash. 1921).

113. See, for example, "I.W.W. Wins in Spokane Trial," *Industrial Worker*, Jan. 20, 1923, 1; "Not Guilty," *New Solidarity*, Oct. 25, 1919, 8; "Walter Smith Is Acquitted at Everett," *Industrial Worker*, Dec. 11, 1920, 1; "Wobs Freed; Jury Acquits," *Industrial Worker*, Sept. 24, 1921, 1.

114. "Hold Propaganda as State Evidence," *Seattle Star*, Mar. 13, 1920, 9.

115. "Moudy Acquitted of Criminal Syndicalism," *Industrial Worker*, July 3, 1920, 1; "Moudy Acquitted of Syndicalism," *Seattle Star*, June 28, 1920, 8.

116. See, for example, "Northwest Defense Bulletin," *Industrial Worker*, June 5, 1920, 1; "Northwest Defense Bulletin," *Industrial Worker*, May 8, 1920, 1; "To Try I.W.W. Fourth Time," *L.A. Times*, Apr. 15, 1920, 14; "Northwest Defense Bulletin," *Industrial Worker*, June 12, 1920, 1.

117. Appellants' Opening Brief, State v. Pico, Washington State Supreme Court, pp. 12–17, Box 126, File 21, IWW Collection, WRML.

118. "Convict I.W.W. at Ellensburg," *Spokane Spokesman-Review*, Jan. 19, 1920, 8; "36 I.W.W. Are Found Guilty," *Seattle Star*, Feb. 2, 1920, 2.

119. Weintraub, "I.W.W. in California," 173.

120. Strang, *Keep the Wretches in Order*, 134–35.

121. Letter from Harry McKee to Roger Baldwin, Correspondence Cases–California, ACLU Records, Volume 213, p. 155.

122. Erwin, Record of California Criminal Syndicalism Convictions, 4.

123. "California Legion Mob Exiles Centralia Man," *Industrial Solidarity*, Apr. 3, 1922, 5; "Elmer Smith Will Defy Mob and Handle Eureka Defense," *Industrial Worker*, Apr. 22, 1922, 1.

124. "Sheriff Deports Red Lawyer with Warning not to Return Here," Clippings-Alabama, ACLU Records, Volume 208, pp. 90–91; Letter from James Kennedy to Roger Baldwin, Mar. 31, 1922, Correspondence Cases–California, ACLU Records, Volume 213; *American Civil Liberties Union Annual Report No. 3* (New York: ACLU, 1924), 16; "I.W.W. Attorney Given Ten Days," *Spokane Daily Chronicle*, Mar. 20, 1923, 3; "Elmer Smith Arrested in Centralia," *Industrial Worker*, Mar. 24, 1923, 1; "California Legion Mob Exiles Centralia Man," *Industrial Solidarity*, Apr. 3, 1922, 5. Smith gave 250 speeches between 1921 and 1924. Copeland, *Centralia Tragedy*, 104.

125. Correspondence Cases–Oregon, ACLU Records, Volume 139, pp. 26–27.

126. "Alleged 'Civil Liberties League' Agent Is Escorted from the City," *Shreveport Times*, Jan. 14, 1922, 1; "Flogged Lawyer May Quit Hospital Today," *Fort Worth Star-Telegram*, Jan. 16, 1922, 1; "Texas Kidnappers Beat I.W.W. Lawyer," *N.Y. Times*, Jan. 15, 1922, 1.

127. Clayton R. Koppes, "The Kansas Trial of the IWW, 1917–1919," *Labor History* 16, no. 3 (1975): 338, 342–44.

128. "I.W.W. Men Flock to Omaha Convention," *N.Y. Tribune*, Nov. 12, 1917, 14.

129. Raid I.W.W. Headquarters, in Socialist and IWW Matters in Chicago, 002371-004-0001, U.S. Military Intelligence Reports: Surveillance of Radicals,

1917–1941 (MIR); David Wagaman, "The Industrial Workers of the World in Nebraska, 1914–1920," *Nebraska History* 56 (1975): 295, 315.

130. "Scald Guard with Coffee," *Lincoln Star Journal,* June 29, 1918, 15.

131. IWW Activities in Omaha, Nebraska, 002371-003-0468, MIR.

132. Letter from T. S. Allen to Attorney General, June 29, 1918, IWW Cases and Activities–Nebraska, 002366-004-0931, DOJ-IWW.

133. Letter from T. S. Allen to Attorney General, Apr. 10, 1919, IWW Cases and Activities–Nebraska, 002366-004-0931, DOJ-IWW; Dubofsky, *We Shall Be All,* 442–43; Strang, *Keep the Wretches in Order,* 208–9.

134. Letter from T. S. Allen to Attorney General, Apr. 10, 1919, IWW Cases and Activities–Nebraska, 002366-004-0931, DOJ-IWW; Dubofsky, *We Shall Be All,* 442–43. This was not the only case in which officials in Washington, D.C., balked. On September 24, 1918, twenty-eight Wobblies were indicted on two counts of conspiring to violate the Espionage Act, among them A. S. Embree and men who had just served time for violating the city's criminal syndicalism ordinance. They never went to trial, and the U.S. attorney was admonished by his superiors that the statute was intended to punish utterances aimed at undermining the war effort, not those arising from labor disputes. Letter from John O'Brian to Francis Garrecht, Sept. 14, 1918, IWW Cases and Activities–Washington, 002366-005-0539, DOJ-IWW; Indictment, U.S. v. W. S. Hall, et al., IWW Cases and Activities–Washington, 002366-005-0539, DOJ-IWW.

135. Koppes, "Kansas Trial of the IWW," 348. See also Winthrop Lane, *Uncle Sam, Jailer: A Study of the Conditions of Federal Prisoners in Kansas Jails* (New York: National Civil Liberties Union, 1919); Correspondence Cases–IWW, ACLU Records, Volume 86, pp. 146–79; White, "Wichita Indictments" 123–32, 150, 214–16.

136. Letter from Frank McFarland to James Finch, Dec. 5, 1922, Pardon Attorney Wichita Case Files–Michael Sapper, 002366-014-0952, DOJ-IWW.

137. Koppes, "Kansas Trial of the IWW," 341; Memorandum In Re Anderson et al., Pardon Attorney Wichita Case Files, 002366-014-0612, DOJ-IWW; White, "Wichita Indictments," 60–64, 188–89.

138. IWW Cases and Activities, 002366-006-0000, DOJ-IWW. Among these witnesses was Elbert Coutts, who impressed Justice Department officials with his "star" performance in the Sacramento conspiracy case. However, Coutts could offer no relevant evidence.

139. Transcript of Record, United States v. Anderson, no. 763, Pardon Attorney Case Files: C. W. Anderson Trial Transcript, 002366-015-0001, DOJ-IWW, pp. 797–98; Koppes, "Kansas Trial of the IWW," 347–54; White, "Wichita Indictments," 221–27.

140. Transcript of Record, United States v. Anderson, no. 763, Pardon Attorney Case Files: C. W. Anderson Trial Transcript, 002366-015-0001, DOJ-IWW, pp. 1041–68. Moore and Lowe were aided for a time by a local lawyer named John Atwood, but he left the defense before trial.

141. Koppes, "Kansas Trial of the IWW," 353–54; White, "Wichita Indictments," 236, 259.

142. Sacramento I.W.W. Cases, Pardon Attorney Sacramento Case Files, 002366-014-0155, DOJ-IWW; IWW Cases and Activities–Sacramento, 002366-006-0407, DOJ-IWW; Philip Taft reports that twenty-seven defendants were convicted. "Guilty Wobblies in High Spirits on Entering Pen," *Leavenworth Times*, Dec. 20, 1919, 1.

143. Quoted in White, "Wichita Indictments," 263.

144. U.S. House of Representatives, Committee on the Judiciary, *Hearings on Amnesty for Political Prisoners*, 67th Congress, 2nd Session, 1922, Testimony of Caroline Lowe and of Albert De Sliver, p. 32.

145. Dowell, "Criminal Syndicalism," 657–62; Act of Jan. 31, 1920, ch. 37, Kansas Session Laws 1920.

146. Nigel Anthony Sellars, *Oil, Wheat and Wobblies: The Industrial Workers of the World in Oklahoma, 1905–1930* (Norman: University of Oklahoma Press, 1998), 122.

147. Sellars, *Oil, Wheat, and Wobblies*, 125, 239n; White, "Wichita Indictments," 196–98. ACLU records document an $800 donation from Lowe to the IWW in 1918. I.W.W. Collections, Correspondence Cases–Amnesty, ACLU Records, Volume 27, p. 87. See also U.S. House of Representatives, Committee on the Judiciary, *Hearings on Amnesty for Political Prisoners*, 67th Congress, 2nd Session, 1922, Testimony of Caroline Lowe, pp. 31–36.

148. Sellars, *Oil, Wheat, and Wobblies*, 122–33; White, "Wichita Indictments," 119–21.

149. Dowell, *History of Criminal Syndicalism*, 52, n. 20; Dowell, "Criminal Syndicalism," 521–26; Sellars, *Oil, Wheat, and Wobblies*, 134.

150. Sellars, *Oil, Wheat, and Wobblies*, 137–39. See also "Oklahoma 'Justice,'" *Solidarity*, Mar. 13, 1920, 4.

CHAPTER 5. DEALING THE DEATH BLOW

1. Trial Transcript, People v. Embree, pp. 4–8, 10, Record of A. S. Embree, No. 2994, Inmate Records, Idaho State Archives and Idaho Historical Society (ISA); IWW Cases and Activities–Bisbee Deportations, 002366-007-0380, Department of Justice Investigative Files: Industrial Workers of the World (DOJ-IWW); Hugh T. Lovin, "Idaho and the 'Reds,' 1919–1926," *Pacific Northwest Quarterly* 69, no. 3 (1978): 107, 111.

2. Weekly Report, General Conditions in Montana, Apr. 28, 1920, IWW Cases and Activities–Butte, Montana, 002366-010-0767, DOJ-IWW; "Murder of Manning Is Laid at Door," *Butte Daily Bulletin*, May 12, 1920, 1; "Jury Returns Open Verdict from Inquest," *Anaconda Standard*, May 14, 1920, 1.

3. Eric Thomas Chester, *The Wobblies in Their Heyday* (Santa Barbara, CA: Praeger, 2014), 113–14; Clayton D. Laurie and Ronald D. Cole, *The Role of Federal Forces in Domestic Disorders, 1977–1945* (Washington, D.C.: Center of Military History), 259–60.

4. Harrison George, "Jack Gaveel, I.W.W., Favors United Front," *Daily Worker*, Feb. 23, 1925, 6; California Prison and Correctional Records, San Quentin, Book No. 10, Inmate No. 34989; Leo Tulin, Summary of Criminal

Syndicalism Cases, p. 28, Box 1, Ralph Chaplin Papers, University of Michigan Special Collections.

5. "I.W.W. Given 1 to 14 Year Prison Term," *L.A. Herald,* May 24, 1921, A11. On Gaveel's sentence, see California Prison and Correctional Records, San Quentin, Book No. 10, Inmate No. 34989.

6. State of Facts, Record of Harry Breen, No. 6979, Kansas State Penitentiary at Lansing Records, Kansas State Archives and Kansas Historical Society (KSA).

7. Opening Brief and Argument of Appellant, State v. Breen, Kansas Supreme Court, No. 23954, Box 126, File 12, IWW Collection, Walter Reuther Memorial Library (WRML); Kansas State Penitentiary at Lansing Records, Id. No. 3776; State v. Breen, 205 P. 632 (Kan. 1922). Breen was freed almost two years later. "Kansas Forced to Free I.W.W.," *Industrial Worker,* Oct. 28, 1922, 2.

8. Brief of Appellants, State v. Dilgar and Thomas Paine, Kansas Supreme Court, Box 126, File 17, IWW Collection, WRML; State v. Dilgar, 208 P. 620 (Kan. 1922).

9. Prisoner Interview, Record of Thomas Paine, No. 7058, Kansas State Penitentiary at Lansing Records, KSA; Statement of Facts, Records of Thomas Paine, No. 7058, Kansas State Penitentiary at Lansing Records, KSA; Statement of Fact, Record of Robert Dilgar, No. 7059, Kansas State Penitentiary at Lansing, KSA.

10. "Defy Police to Put Them Out of Refuge," *Anaconda Standard,* Jan. 3, 1916, 7.

11. Statement of Fact, Record of William Murphy, No. 7057, Kansas State Penitentiary at Lansing Records, KSA. See also Abstract of Appellant, State v. Murphy et al., Supreme Court of Kansas, Box 126, File 18, IWW Collection, WRML; State v. Murphy, 212 P. 654 (Kan. 1923).

12. Inmate Note, William Murphy, No. 7057, Kansas State Penitentiary at Lansing, Records KSA.

13. "I.W.W. Gets Jail Sentence," *Bismarck Tribune,* Aug. 6, 1923, 2.

14. "I.W.W. Ordinance," *Wichita Daily Eagle,* July 31, 1920, 5.

15. "Judge Sargent Frees 18-Year-Old I.W.W.," *Wichita Beacon,* July 17, 1920, 11.

16. "Boy I.W.W. Sues County Officers; Charges Beating," *Wichita Daily Eagle,* July 25, 1920, 5; "Asks Habeas Corpus," *Wichita Daily Eagle,* July 16, 1920, 2. Six days after Barker was first arrested, organizer William Danton was arrested and charged with criminal syndicalism in Lyons. "Another I.W.W. in Toils," *Wichita Beacon,* July 10, 1920, 3; "Police Arrest 5 Men with I.W.W. Literature," *Wichita Beacon,* June 17, 1919, 8. Danton, also known as George Denton, languished in jail for ten weeks before Caroline Lowe and Harold Mulks got the Kansas Supreme Court to order him released on a $500 bond. "Man Ordered Released," *Hutchinson News,* Sept. 20, 1920, 9. See also In re Danton, 195 P. 981 (Kan. 1921); John Martin, "Defense News," *Industrial Pioneer,* Apr. 1923, 53.

17. "Lying in Ambush," *Topeka State Journal,* May 4, 1920, 1. See also "Reception for I.W.W.s is Planned by Kansans," *Topeka State Journal,* June 3, 1920, 1.

18. "I.W.W. Plead Not Guilty to Vagrancy," *Pratt Daily Tribune,* July 28, 1920, 3; "Get Another I.W.W.," *Caldwell Messenger,* June 29, 1920, 3; "Arrest

an I.W.W.," *Great Bend Tribune,* June 17, 1920, 1; "Bunch of IWWs Is Gathered In," *Wellington Monitor-Press,* June 23, 1920, n.p.

19. *Twenty-Fifth Biennial Report of the Attorney General of Kansas, 1921–1922* (Topeka: Kansas State Printing Plant, 1922), 18.

20. "Kansas Vigilance Check Mates Efforts of Wobblies in Harvest," *Hutchinson Gazette,* Aug. 8, 1920, 1.

21. State ex rel. Hopkins, 214 P. 617 (Kan. S. Ct. 1923); Appellants' Brief before Kansas Supreme Court, State ex rel. Hopkins, No. 24405 Box 126, File 10, IWW Collection, WRML. See also "A Hunt for I.W.W. Agents," *Hutchinson News,* June 24, 1920, 1.

22. "I.W.W. Tries His Own Case," *Hutchinson News,* Sept. 21, 1921, 11; "'Wob' Cuts Loose from Attorneys, Wins Own Case," *Hutchinson Gazette,* Sept. 22, 1921, 2. See also "I.W.W. Sending Counsel to Johnson," *Hutchinson News,* July 8, 1920, 1; "Tries and Wins His Own Case in Kansas," *Industrial Solidarity,* Oct. 1, 1921, 1.

23. "I.W.W. Pleads Guilty," *Hutchinson Gazette,* Dec. 14, 1921, 1.

24. "File Additional Charges against Alleged I.W.W.'s," *Wichita Daily Eagle,* June 30, 1922, 23.

25. "I.W.W. Released from County Jail," *Anthony Bulletin,* Sept. 7, 1922, 2.

26. "Convicted I.W.W. Sentenced to Pen," *Hutchinson News,* Oct. 7, 1922, 11; Records of Joe Neil, No. 7950, Kansas State Penitentiary at Lansing Records, KSA; Minutes of the 14th General Convention of the Industrial Workers of the World, 1922, 23 Box 3, File 2, IWW Collection, WRML; "Joe Neil Released, Rearrested," *Industrial Worker,* June 30, 1928, 1; "Paulen Paroles 38," *Emporia Gazette,* June 19, 1928, 6.

27. "I.W.W. Talked Too Much," *Abilene Daily Reflector,* Oct. 9, 1922, 1.

28. "Prisoners Resent Radical Talk of Convicted Wobbly," *Hutchinson News,* Oct. 9, 1922, 11; "Neal Charged with Assault," *Hutchinson News,* Oct. 11, 1922, 13.

29. Transcript of Record, Fiske v. Kansas, 274 U.S. 380 (1925) (no. 305), 20–21.

30. State v. Fiske, 230 P. 88, 89 (Kan. 1924).

31. Transcript of Record, Fiske v. Kansas, 2, 9, 19–21. See also Richard Cortner, "The Wobblies and Fiske v. Kansas: Victory and Disintegration," *Kansas History* 4 (1981): 30; State v. Fiske, 230 P. 88, 89 (Kan. 1924); Abstract of the Record, Fiske v. Kansas, 274 U.S. 380 (1925) (no. 305); Plaintiff's Brief, Fiske v. Kansas, 274 U.S. 380 (1925) (no. 305).

32. State v. Breen, 205 P. 632, 633 (Kan. 1922).

33. Ex parte Clancy, 210 P. 487, 489 (Kan. 1922); In re Danton, 195 P. 981 (Kan. 1921).

34. Act of Apr. 3, 1917, ch. 167, §§1–2, Kansas Session Laws 1917. *Clancy* was consistent with the weight of most precedent in the early twentieth century, when courts typically upheld vagrancy prosecutions against similar challenges and, regardless of whether the laws relied on were specific in this respect, validated this means of persecuting IWWs and other radicals. See, for example, Ex parte Strittmatter, 124 S.W. 906 (Tex. Cr. App. 1910); Ex parte Karnstrom, 249 S.W. 595 (Mo. 1923); Ex parte Branch, 137 S.W. 886 (Mo. 1911); State v.

McCormick, 77 So. 288 (La. 1918). Compare Ex parte Taft, 225 S.W. 457 (Mo. 1920).

35. "War Breaks Out among Harvesters in Oklahoma," *Wichita Daily Eagle*, June 17, 1922, 1; "One Killed in Battle among Harvest Hands," *Hutchinson Gazette*, June 17, 1922, 1. The shooter was exonerated on grounds of self-defense. See also "Alfalfa County Quiet Again as Troubles End," *Chickasha Daily Express*, June 17, 1922, 1; "Bold Move to Wreck Train," *Morning Tulsa Daily World*, Sept. 12, 1922, 7; "I.W.W. Camp Broken Up," *Morning Tulsa Daily News*, June 13, 1922, 2; "Alleged I.W.W. Agent Is Taken by Police," *Morning Tulsa Daily World*, Aug. 1, 1921, 1; "Officers Search for I.W.W. Thought to Be Boy's Killer," *Guthrie Daily Leader*, Aug. 2, 1921, 1.

36. Transcript of Record, State v. Berg, Pittsburg County District Court, No. 2146, pp. 168–69, Box 127, File10, IWW Collection, WRML.

37. Nigel Anthony Sellars, "Oil, Wheat, and Wobblies: The Industrial Workers of the World in Oklahoma, 1905–1930," PhD diss., Oklahoma State University, 1994, pp. 448–49.

38. Transcript of Record, State v. Berg, pp. 168–93.

39. Transcript of Record, State v. Berg, pp. 194–95.

40. Transcript of Record, State v. Berg, pp. 222–24.

41. "Lecture Goes with Fine and Sentence," *Blackwell Journal-Tribune*, Mar. 1, 1923, 1; Nigel Anthony Sellars, *Oil, Wheat, and Wobblies: The Industrial Workers of the World in Oklahoma, 1905–1930* (Norman: University of Oklahoma Press, 1998), 167–70. See also Berg v. State, 233 P. 497, 499 (Okla. Crim. App. 1925); Von Russell Creel, "The Case of the Wandering Wobblie [*sic*]: The State of Oklahoma v. Arthur Berg," *Chronicles of Oklahoma* 73 (1995): 404, 406, 415–16.

42. "Six Years in Prison for Convicted I.W.W. Agent," *Miami Record-Herald*, Sept. 28, 1923, 1; Sellars, *Oil, Wheat, and Wobblies*, 170–73. See also "C. S. Charge in Oklahoma," *Industrial Solidarity*, Sept. 1, 1923, 6.

43. "I.W.W. Organizer Gets Ten Days at Hard Labor," *Ward County Independent*, Aug. 5 1920, 1; "Judge Gives an I.W.W. Ten Days of Street Work," *Bismarck Tribune*, Aug. 4, 1920, 1. On similar arrests in 1920, see, for example, "In Police Court: Alleged I.W.W. Arrested," *Minot Daily News*, Sept. 13, 1920, 7; "I.W.W. Disbeliever in Government Taken," *Minot Daily News*, Sept. 11, 1920, 1; "Wobblie [*sic*] Wires Chicago for Aid When Arrested," *Minot Daily News*, Aug. 20, 1920, 1.

44. "'Yours for Revolution' Is Signature of Casey; Defended by Tom Arnold," *Aberdeen Daily News*, July 26, 1921, 1; "I.W.W. Members Are Escorted from Town by Sheriff[']s Posse," *Aberdeen Journal*, July 17, 1921, 1; "An Advocate of Syndicalism Is Lodged in Cell," *Aberdeen Journal*, July 15, 1921, p 1.

45. "Guilty, but to Manslaughter, Schmidt Plea," *Aberdeen Daily News*, Oct. 8, 1921, 1; "Syndicalism in Charge Brought in Court Today," *Aberdeen Journal*, July 25, 1925, 1.

46. "Two I.W.W. Are Arrested Here for Criminal Syndicalism," *Sioux Falls Argus-Leader*, July 26, 1921, 1.

47. "In Circuit Court," *Sioux Falls Argus-Leader*, Nov. 16, 1921, 5; "Bosinger's Jury Is Dismissed," *Sioux Falls Argus-Leader*, Nov. 7, 1921, 2.

48. "Complaint Made to Commission against I.W.W. Menace in City," *Fargo Forum and Daily Republican,* July 21, 1921, 5.

49. "I.W.W. Element Warned to Quit Plan to March on Langdon, N.D.," *Fargo Forum and Daily Republican,* Aug. 31, 1921, 1; "Wobblies at Larimore Quit," *Fargo Forum and Daily Republican,* Sept. 2, 1921, 1; "Three I.W.W. Leaders in Langdon Invasion Held," *Fargo Forum and Daily Republican,* Sept. 5, 1921, 1.

50. "Harvest Hands Attacked by Mob of Boozy Bankers," *Industrial Worker,* Aug. 18, 1921, 1.

51. "Work of Lake Officials Causes 200 I.W.W. to Quit," *Fargo Forum and Daily Republican,* Aug. 24, 1921, 5.

52. "Fargo Police Use Guns on Citizens," *Industrial Worker,* Oct. 1, 1921, n.p.; "I.W.W. Leaders Arrested after Mob Assault Is Made on Police," *Fargo Forum and Daily Republican,* Sept. 16, 1921, 1.

53. "Nestos Urges War on Loafers," *Grand Forks Herald,* Aug. 17, 1922, 2. In August, the director of the state employment bureau in Minot complained to police that "agitators" were driving up wages by convincing the hands to "hold out." The chief responded by declaring that organizers would be charged with vagrancy or run out of town. "Police to Act Today against Activities of I.W.W. Agitators," *Minot Daily News,* Aug. 2, 1922, 2. Some did leave, but several were arrested for defying a "go to work or leave town" order and persisting in "organizing I.W.W. farm hands and endeavoring to get them to quit their jobs at $4 a day, and demand $5 a day." "Transient Organizer for I.W.W. Draws Ten Days," *Minot Daily News,* Aug. 17, 1922, 8; "I.W.W. Organizer Arrested," *Ward County Independent,* Aug. 17, 1922, 9; "I.W.W. Organizer Is Again Under Arrest," *Minot Daily News,* Sept. 16, 1922, 2; "Wobbly Who Lectured to Street Crowd Now Soliloquizes in Cell," *Minot Daily News,* Sept. 7, 1922, 1.

54. "Organizer for I.W.W. Is Fined as Vagrant," *Minot Daily News,* Aug. 11, 1923, 1; "Organizers for I.W.W. Find Minot Decidedly Inhospitable," *Minot Daily News,* Aug. 21, 1923, 1; "I.W.W. Organizer Given Choice of Fine or Jail," *Minot Daily News,* Aug. 22, 1923, 2; "Two Arrested When I.W.W. Meeting Is Visited by Police," *Minot Daily News,* Aug. 30, 1923, 1; "Trials of I.W.W. Speaker and Secretary Scheduled in Police Court Today," *Minot Daily News,* Aug. 21, 1923, 1; "Trio of Alleged I.W.W. Delegates Are Arrested," *Minot Daily News,* Sept. 17, 1923, 5; "Third I.W.W. Taken to Jail," *Fargo Forum and Daily Republican,* June 18, 1923, 1; "I.W.W. Held to District Court," *Fargo Forum and Daily Republican,* June 18, 1923, 12; "Two Wobblies Jailed: One Resisted Officer," *Fargo Forum and Daily Republican,* July 26, 1923, 5; "Cass County Organized to Prevent Harvest Strike," *Fargo Forum and Daily Republican,* July 24, 1923, 1.

55. Record of Richard Quackenbush, No. 3005, Inmate Records, ISA.

56. Clippings-Alabama, Records of the National Office of the American Civil Liberties Union (ACLU Records), Volume 175, pp. 80–82.

57. "Quackenbush Returned to State Penitentiary," *Boise Idaho Statesman,* Apr. 26, 1923, 10.

58. Questionnaire of Prosecutor, June 1, 1921, Record of A.S. Embree, No. 2994, Inmate Records, ISA.

59. Record of Conviction, May 23, 1921, Record of A.S. Embree, No. 2994, Inmate Records, ISA.

60. Letter from John O'Brian to Francis Garrecht, Sept. 14, 1918, IWW Cases and Activities–Washington, 002366-005-0539, DOJ-IWW; Indictment, U.S. v. W.S. Hall, et al., IWW Cases and Activities–Washington, 002366-005-0539, DOJ-IWW.

61. Transcript, People v. Embree, pp. 4–123, Record of A.S. Embree, No. 2994, Inmate Records, ISA.

62. Transcript, People v. Embree, pp. 125–26; Description of Convict, Record of A.S. Embree, No. 2994, Inmate Records, ISA.

63. Record of Edwin Krier, No. 3338, Inmate Records, ISA.

64. Letter from ACLU, Aug. 24, 1923, Record of H.E. Herd, No. 2628, Inmate Records, ISA; "Governor Again Refuses to Free I.W.W. Convicts," *Boise Idaho Statesman*, Dec. 20, 1923, 2.

65. Letter from A.S. Embree to Ed Krier, Oct. 12, 1924, Record of A.S. Krier, No. 2994, Inmate Records, ISA; Leigh Campbell-Hale, "Remembering Ludlow but Forgetting the Columbine: The 1927–1928 Colorado Coal Strike," PhD diss., University of Colorado-Boulder, 2013, pp. 75–76; "Board Pardons Six Prisoners Now on Parole," *Boise Idaho Statesman*, Jan. 17, 1926, 7; "News that You May Have Overlooked," *Boise Idaho Statesman*, Apr. 7, 1924, 4.

66. "I.W.W. Are Busy Here," *Portland Oregonian*, Jan. 7, 1921, 12.

67. Eldridge Foster Dowell, "A History of the Enactment of Criminal Syndicalism Legislation in the United States," PhD diss., Johns Hopkins University, 1936, pp. 558–63. During the Great Lumber Strike, Benewah County, Idaho, prosecutor Allen Holsclaw proposed, unsuccessfully, that this problem be dealt with by dispensing with trials altogether. Letter from Allen Holsclaw to Clement Wilkins, Sept. 18, 1917, Box 1, File 2, Moses Alexander Papers, WRML. It is not clear how much of an impediment the wording of the law actually was, and other prosecutors were not concerned with the statute's wording. "Idaho Law Being Violated by Reds, Attorneys Decide," *Boise Evening Capital News*, Dec. 15, 1919, 7. The bigger problem prosecutors faced, especially in remote counties where many trials took place, was jurors' hostility to the lumber companies and penchant for sympathizing with defendants. Nevertheless, the legislature changed the statute to criminalize "being or continuing to be" a member. Robert C. Sims, "Idaho's Criminal Syndicalism Act: One State's Response to Radical Labor," *Labor History* 15, no. 4 (1975): 511, 522.

68. "Portland Reds Under Arrest," *Salem Capital Journal*, Jan. 24, 1921, 1.

69. "Radical Is Bound Over," *Portland Oregon Daily Journal*, Oct. 8, 1921, 5; "I.W.W. Suspects Are Arrested," *Portland Oregonian*, Mar. 25, 1921, 6; "Alleged Syndicalist Held," *Portland Oregonian*, Feb. 27, 1921, 6; "Alleged Syndicalist Held," *Portland Oregonian*, Feb. 25, 1921, 11.

70. In May 1922, three Wobblies were convicted of criminal syndicalism and one sentenced to prison in Montesano. "Syndicalists Sentenced at Montesano," *Athena Press*, May 26, 1922, 1. On arrests in the first half of the year, see also "Criminal Syndicalism Charged to Man Here," *Salem Capital Journal*, June 17, 1922, 1; "I.W.W. Members Are Indicted by Grand Jury," *Klamath Falls Evening Herald*, June 14, 1922, 1; "Syndicalism Charged to Man Here," *Salem Capital*

Journal, June 17, 1922, 1; "Wobblies Held for Grand Jury," *Salem Capital Journal,* May 30, 1922, 1; "Arraign I.W.W. 19th," *Klamath Falls Evening Herald,* June 16, 1922, 1; "Wobbly Bound Over," *Klamath Falls Evening Herald,* May 24, 1922, 1; "I.W.W. Suspects Captured in Raid," *Portland Oregon Daily Journal,* May 24, 1922, 6. On increasing enforcement in the fall, see "I.W.W. Hold Meeting," *Portland Oregonian,* Oct. 18, 1922, 5; "Three I.W.W. Sentenced," *Portland Oregonian,* Oct. 25, 1922, 6.

71. "Court to 'Kick' Out Wobblies," *Portland Oregon Daily Journal,* Oct. 19, 1922, 1; "Offer by Portland Wobblies Rejected," *Salem Capital Journal,* Oct. 25, 1922, 1; "I.W.W.'s Declare War on Portland," *Medford Mail Tribune,* Oct. 19, 1922, 1. In December, two more organizers were charged with criminal syndicalism for passing out literature in Astoria. "I.W.W. Suspects Jailed," *Portland Oregonian,* Dec. 3, 1922, 6.

72. "Two IWW Delegates Arrested in North Bend, Oregon" *Industrial Worker,* Feb. 21, 1923, 1; "Sam Holcomb Indicted," *Portland Oregonian,* Feb. 23, 1923, 16.

73. "I.W.W. Trial in Tillamook Is Held Again," *Albany Evening Herald,* Mar. 12, 1923, 1; "Police to Curb I.W.W. Activity," *Portland Oregonian,* Apr. 25, 1923, 1.

74. "Two I.W.W.s Bound Over," *Portland Oregonian,* May 9, 1923, 7; "Alleged Red Arrested," *Portland Oregonian,* Sept. 14, 1923, 15.

75. "Seven I.W.W.s to State Prison," *Spokane Spokesman-Review,* June 24, 1921, 7; State v. Smith et al., 197 P. 770 (Wash. 1921).

76. "Iron Heel in Northwest; Status of Cases to Date," *Industrial Worker,* Jan. 15, 1921, 1; Dowell, "Criminal Syndicalism," 1063. See also "A. S. Embree Sentenced in Anti-Labor Court," *Solidarity,* June 4, 1921, 3; "Four I.W.W. Held on Syndicalism Charge," *Industrial Solidarity,* Oct. 15, 1921, 4; "Police Stop Amnesty Meeting in Spokane," *Solidarity,* Apr. 13, 1921, 1. Nearly two years later, the secretary of the general defense committee, Harry Feinberg, could not really say how many were still behind bars in the state. Minutes of the 14th General Convention of the Industrial Workers of the World, 1922, 24, Box 3, File 2, IWW Collection, WRML.

77. Weekly Situation Report, Sept. 22–29, 1921, Military Intelligence Report, 9th Corps District, in CPUSA Casefile, 002367-015-0889, Department of Justice Investigative Files: Communist Party; "Acquit Wenatchee I.W.W.," *Spokane Spokesman-Review,* Jan. 12, 1922, 1; "Spindler Says He Is IWW Chief," *Spokane Daily Chronicle,* Nov. 10, 1921, 1; "Arrest Carroll on I.W.W. Count," *Spokane Daily Chronicle,* Sept. 7, 1921, 1; "Fulton Denies I.W.W. Charge," *Spokane Spokesman-Review,* June 25, 1921, 10; "Faces Syndicalism Charge," *Spokane Spokesman-Review,* May 4, 1921, 9.

78. "Jail Sentences for Eight Men," *Spokane Daily Chronicle,* Feb. 19, 1921, 1; "Won't Agree to Quit Sale of Wob Paper," *Spokane Daily Chronicle,* Feb. 11, 1921, 28. On vagrancy and misdemeanor criminal syndicalism, see also "Natural-Born Wobblies Let Off," *Spokane Daily Chronicle,* Sept. 10, 1923, 6; "Wobbly Given 30-Day Term," *Spokane Daily Chronicle,* Mar. 17, 1923, 7; "Four Arrested as I.W.W.," *Spokane Spokesman-Review,* Dec. 22, 1922, 6; "Send Malden Men to Jail for Month," *Spokane Daily Chronicle,* Oct. 31,1922,

1; "Says He's I.W.W., Gets a Month," *Spokane Spokesman-Review,* Mar. 19, 1921, 1; "Police Hear of Five Burglaries," *Spokane Spokesman-Review,* Feb. 7, 1921, 6.

79. "Get Vanderveer to Defend Wobs," *Spokane Daily Chronicle,* Feb. 12, 1921, 1; "Eight I.W.W. Sent to Jail," *Spokane Spokesman-Review,* Feb. 20, 1921, 7.

80. On misdemeanor arrests, see, for example, "I.W.W. Charge Brings Sentence," *Spokane Daily Chronicle,* Feb. 9, 1922, 6; "Gets Thirty Days for Syndicalism," *Spokane Daily Chronicle,* June 10, 1922, 3. On felony arrests, see, for example, "I.W.W. Records Seized in Police Raid Here," *Spokane Daily Chronicle,* Dec. 21, 1922, 6; "Grab Alleged I.W.W. Organizer," *Spokane Spokesman-Review,* Aug. 6, 1922, 7; "Raid I.W.W. at Aberdeen," *Spokane Spokesman-Review,* May 31, 1922, 1.

81. "Not Guilty of Syndicalism," *Spokane Spokesman-Review,* Oct. 25, 1922, 7.

82. Tom Copeland, *The Centralia Tragedy of 1919: Elmer Smith and the Wobblies* (Seattle: University of Washington, 1993), 136–59.

83. Complaint, In the Matter of the Proceeding for the Disbarment of Elmer S. Smith, Box 126, File 26, IWW Collection, WRML; Notice of Hearing in the Matter of the Proceedings for the Disbarment of Elmer Smith, Box 126, File 25, IWW Collection, WRML. See also Disbarment Proceeding against Workers Attorney Checked, Box 16, File 1, IWW Collection, WRML.

84. In re Smith, 233 P. 288 (Wash. 1925). See also Brief on Behalf of Defendant Elmer Smith, State Bar Association of the State of Washington v. Elmer Smith, Washington State Supreme Court, Box 126, File 27, IWW Collection, WRML.

85. "Lumber Lords Disbar Elmer Smith," *Industrial Solidarity,* Mar. 4, 1925, 1. See also "Class Interests of Supreme Court," *Industrial Worker,* Mar. 18, 1925, 1.

86. Copeland, *The Centralia Tragedy,* 176–77.

87. Speeches by Elmer Smith, et al., pp. 1, 8, in Washington State Historical Society ; "Elmer Smith Reinstated After Abandoning His Radical Beliefs," *Portland Oregonian,* Mar. 20, 1930, 1.

88. CDDC Bulletin, December 1921, Box 4, IWW Seattle Joint Branches Collection, University of Washington Special Collections (UWSC).

89. Stephen M. Kohn, *American Political Prisoners: Prosecutions under the Espionage and Sedition Acts* (Westport, CT: Praeger, 1994), 166; California Prison and Correctional Records, San Quentin, Book No. 10, Inmate No. 35785; Clippings-Alabama, ACLU Records, Volume 208, 19; Clippings-Alabama, ACLU Records, Volume 175, pp. 19–31; Report on IWW Matters, Sept. 24, 1921, IWW Cases and Activities–San Francisco, 002366-007-0287, DOJ-IWW; "I.W.W. Counsel Withdraws," *Sacramento Union,* Dec. 13, 1921, 2. Although Kohn describes Roe as over seventy, his prison record gives an age of about sixty-six upon conviction.

90. People v. Malley, 194 P. 48 (Ca. Dist. Ct. App. 1920).

91. Report on IWW Matters, July 2, 1921, IWW Cases and Activities–San Francisco, 002366-007-0287, DOJ-IWW.

92. Clippings-Alabama, ACLU Records, Volume 175, pp. 13–17; Immediate Attention, Documents, Correspondence Cases–California, ACLU Records, Volume 213, 51.

93. CDDC Bulletin, April 1923, Box 4, IWW Seattle Joint Branches Collection, UWSC.

94. Hyman Weintraub, "The I.W.W. in California: 1905–1931," MA thesis, University of California, Los Angeles, 1947, pp. 128–32; Woodrow C. Whitten, "Criminal Syndicalism and the Law in California: 1919–1927," *Transactions of the American Philosophical Society* 59, no. 2 (1969): 3, 58. See also "Trials of I.W.W. Are Set by Judge," *Sacramento Union*, Dec. 3, 1922, 5; "Five Alleged I.W.W. Members Indicted," *Sacramento Union*, Nov. 16, 1922, 9; "I.W.W. Pickets Plan to Block Strike-Breakers," *Oakland Tribune*, Nov. 17, 1922, 20; "I.W.W. Raided in Sacramento," *Reno Gazette-Journal*, Oct. 25, 1922, 5; "Officers Raid Fresno I.W.W. Headquarters," *San Francisco Chronicle*, Nov. 1, 1922, 15.

95. Weintraub, "I.W.W. in California," 126–28, 133–35.

96. Weintraub, "I.W.W. in California," 190–210; Archie Sinclair, "Hypocritical California," *Industrial Pioneer*, Dec. 1923, 7; "General Strike Call," *Industrial Pioneer*, May 1923, 8.

97. "I.W.W. Striker Is Shot by Watchman," *Eugene Guard*, May 3, 1923, 1; "Aged Mill Guard Held for Murder," *Spokane Daily Chronicle*, May 8, 1923, 6. "Mill Watchman Freed of Murder," *Tacoma Daily Ledger*, Nov. 22, 1923, 10. On arrests in 1923, see "Arrest Wobblies," *Spokane Daily Chronicle*, Feb. 24, 1923, 1; "Wobbly Organizers Held at Walla Walla," *Spokane Daily Chronicle*, Aug. 20, 1923, 1; "I.W.W. Are Released," *Spokane Spokesman-Review*, Aug. 21, 1923, 9. See also Albert F. Gunns, *Civil Liberties in Crisis: The Pacific Northwest, 1917–1920* (New York: Garland Press, 1983), 55; "I.W.W. Wins in Spokane Trial," *Industrial Worker*, Jan. 20, 1923, 1.

98. John S. Gambs, *The Decline of the I.W.W.* (New York: Russell and Russell, 1966), 70–73; Robert L. Tyler, "The I.W.W. in the Pacific N.W.: Rebels of the Woods," *Oregon Historical Quarterly* 55, no. 1 (1954): 3, 37–39. See also Clippings-Alabama, ACLU Records, Volume 208; "I.W.W. General Strike Hits Lumber and Shipping," *San Francisco Chronicle*, Apr. 26, 1923, 1; "Wob Strike Spreads," *Spokane Daily Chronicle*, Apr. 28, 1923, 1; "General Strike Called by Wobs," *Spokane Daily Chronicle*, Apr. 25, 1923, 1; "I.W.W. Try to Hold Up Coast Ships," *Oakland Tribune*, Apr. 26, 1923, 1; "I.W.W. Threaten Coast Firms," *Great Falls Tribune*, Apr. 28, 1923, 1.

99. "'Wobblies' No Longer Feared by Employers," *Oakland Tribune*, Apr. 29, 1923, 1. See also "Ship Strike Move Fails in Bay District," *San Francisco Examiner*, Apr. 27, 1923, 1; "I.W.W. Issue Threat When Strike Wanes," *San Francisco Chronicle*, Apr. 28, 1923, 3; "Backbone of I.W.W. Strike Broken," *San Francisco Chronicle*, Apr. 29, 1923, 1.

100. Louis B. Perry and Richard S. Perry, *A History of the Los Angeles Labor Movement, 1911–1941* (Berkeley: University of California Press, 1963), 176–82.

101. Boris Stern, "Cargo Handling and Longshore Labor Conditions," *U.S. Bureau of Labor Statistics, Bulletin No. 550* (Washington, D.C.: GPO, 1932), 71–74, 98–100; Betty Schneider and Abraham Seigel, *Industrial Relations in the*

Pacific Coast Longshore Industry (Berkeley, CA: Institute of Industrial Relations, 1956), 7–10; Howard Kimeldorf, *Reds or Rackets: The Making of Radical and Conservative Unions on the Waterfront* (Berkeley: University of California Press, 1988), 32–35; John Laslett, *Sunshine Was Never Enough: Los Angeles Workers, 1880–2010* (Oakland: University of California Press, 2014), 70–73.

102. "Shipowners to Fight I.W.W.," *L.A. Times,* Aug. 3, 1922, 1. See also "Asserted Wobbly Held," *L.A. Times,* Feb. 19, 1923, II7; "L. A. Arrests Wob Pickets," *Industrial Worker,* Dec. 23, 1922, 1; "200 Arrests in Cal.[;] Jury Trials Clog Courts," *Industrial Worker,* Jan. 6, 1923, 1; "Unjust Criminal Syndicalism Law Issue in San Pedro Fight," *Industrial Solidarity,* Dec. 30, 1922, 1; "Thirty-Six Reds Seized in Police Harbor Raids," *L.A. Times,* Nov. 9, 1922, II1; "Record Haul of Reds Caught in Harbor Net," *L.A. Times,* Dec. 19, 1922, II1.

103. Memorandum from Kate Crane Gartz, Feb. 16, 1923, Box 6, File 23, Leo Gallagher Papers, University of Kansas Special Collections; "Launch War against I.W.W.," *Santa Ana Register,* Feb. 28, 1923, 1.

104. Perry and Perry, *Los Angeles Labor Movement,* 183–86; "Ships Not Hampered," *L.A. Times,* Apr. 25, 1923, 1; "Wobbly Plans Failing," *L.A. Times,* Apr. 26, 1923, 1; "Raids on Wobbly Nest at Harbor Net 300 Reds," *L.A. Times,* May 15, 1923, II1; Clippings-Alabama, ACLU Records, Volume 208, pp. 40–46.

105. George P. West, "After Liberalism Had Failed," *Nation,* May 30, 1923, 629.

106. Richard Fisher, quoted in Martin Zanger, "Politics of Confrontation: Upton Sinclair and the Launching of the ACLU in Southern California," *Pacific Historical Review* 38, no. 4 (1969): 383, 386.

107. Anthony Arthur, *Radical Innocent: Upton Sinclair* (New York: Random House, 2007), 193–94; Weintraub, "I.W.W. in California," 228–32.

108. Zanger, "Politics of Confrontation," 394–95; "Sinclair Held for Trial," *L.A. Times,* May 17, 1923, II. See also Clippings-Alabama, ACLU Records, Volume 236, pp. 16–38.

109. Tulin, Summary of Criminal Syndicalism Cases, 40, 45–46; Weintraub, "I.W.W. in California," 233–24; Whitten, "Criminal Syndicalism," 58; "300 Alleged Wobblies in L.A. Freed," *Santa Ana Register,* June 2, 1923, 1.

110. Laslett, *Sunshine Was Never Enough,* 82. Another waterfront strike, a five-day walkout called July 12 to protest the criminal syndicalism convictions that followed the first strike, accomplished little more than to get a few more men arrested on vagrancy charges.

111. Address of E.S. Smith, Apr. 10, 1922, People v. Casdorf and Firey, Superior Court, County of Sacramento, Box 125, File 6, IWW Collection, WRML, pp. 22–23, 36, 45. See also "I.W.W. Found Guilty in 20 Minutes," *Sacramento Union,* Apr. 11, 1922, 1.

112. "Call Sent for More Witnesses," *Sacramento Union,* Apr. 2, 1922, 1.

113. California the Beautiful and the Damned, p. 5, Box 158-C, IWW Collection, WRML; "Ten Witnesses Start Sentences," *Industrial Solidarity,* Aug. 25, 1923, 6; Clippings-Alabama, ACLU Records, Volume 208, pp. 50–57; "Witnesses on Trial Again at Sacramento," *Industrial Solidarity,* Oct. 28, 1922, 1; "Witnesses' Trial Again Postponed," *Industrial Solidarity,* Dec. 23, 1922, 8.

114. Tulin, Summary of Criminal Syndicalism Cases, 32, 35–36, 59.

115. See, for example, "Witness in I.W.W. Trial Nabbed as He Leaves Court," *L.A. Herald,* Nov. 30, 1921, A3.

116. Claude Erwin, Record of California Criminal Syndicalism Convictions, p.11, Box 135, File 1, IWW Records, WRML; California Prison and Correctional Records, San Quentin, Book No. 10, Inmate No. 36502; California Prison and Correctional Records, Folsom, Inmate No. 12540. On the prosecution of the witnesses, see also Clippings-Alabama, ACLU Records, Volume 208; "I.W.W. Members Get Stiff Sentence," *Sacramento Union,* Apr. 13, 1923, 2; "Thirteen Indictments Are Returned," *Sacramento Union,* Apr. 8, 1922, 1.

117. Tulin, Summary of Criminal Syndicalism Cases, 27–42; "Radicals Are Sent to Prison," *L.A. Times,* Mar. 22, 1923, II1. In July 1919, a number of "spectators" at the criminal syndicalism trial of Wobbly John Rittenhaus in Spokane police court were arrested under Washington State's "red flag" law for wearing red neckties and carnations. "Wear I.W.W. Label, Nabbed by Police," *Anaconda Standard,* July 9, 1919, 1. In the summer of 1922, a judge in Eureka, California, committed C.A. Ward, a minor and the secretary of the union's Lumber Workers Industrial Union local, to reform school after arresting him for watching the trial of another Wobbly. "California Has First Minor in Syndicalist Case," Clippings-Alabama, ACLU Records, Volume 208, 34.

118. Tulin, Summary of Criminal Syndicalism Cases, 51.

119. Tulin, Summary of Criminal Syndicalism Cases, 41; "Sentences Given Two of I.W.W.; Attorney Jailed," *Sacramento Bee,* May 19, 1923, 1.

120. Whitten, "Criminal Syndicalism," 58–59, n75; "Fresno Sets I.W.W. Trial," *L.A. Times,* Sept. 15, 1923, I9; "Wobblies Can Sell Wares in Fresno Freely," *L.A. Times,* Aug. 26, 1923, II1. See also, for example, "Jurist Offers Cure for Reds," *L.A. Times,* May 27, 1923, II12.

121. State ex rel. Lindsley v. Wallace, 195 P. 1049, 1050 (Wash. 1921). See also Appellant's Opening Brief, State v. Grady et al., Box 2, IWW Seattle Joint Branches Collection.

122. "Threats Made by IWW upon Spokane Judge," *Salem Capital Journal,* Feb. 4, 1920, 1. On other instances of enforcement, see Ex parte Parent, 192 P. 947 (Wash. 1920); State ex rel. Lindsley v. Wallace, 195 P. 1049, 1050 (Wash. 1921); State ex rel. Lindsley v. Grady, 199 P. 980 (Wash. 1921); William Haywood, "General Defense," *One Big Union Monthly,* Sept. 1920, 58. Authorities sought injunctions of this kind in an undetermined number of other cases. Correspondence Regarding Bellingham, Washington, Correspondence Cases–Washington, ACLU Records, Volume 140, pp. 27–30. However, they were not always granted, as a case from Bellingham, Washington reveals. Dowell, "Criminal Syndicalism," 1059–60.

123. People v. IWW et al., Superior Court, County of Sacramento, No. 31125 (1923), Box 125, File 5, IWW Collection, WRML. See also Whitten, "Criminal Syndicalism," app. E. 66; Ex parte Wood, 227 P. 908 (Cal. 1924).

124. Whitten, "Criminal Syndicalism," 59.

125. Memo from Ed Delaney to General Defense Committee, Oct. 1, 1924, Box 1, File 4, IWW Seattle Joint Branches Records, UWSC; Minutes of the 16th General Convention of the IWW, pp. 17–18, Box 1, File 13, IWW Seattle Joint Branches Collection, UWSC.

126. Weintraub, "I.W.W. in California," 186–88; Tulin, Summary of Criminal Syndicalism Cases, 52; "Fifteen Wobs Released," *Industrial Solidarity*, Oct. 29, 1924, 1. A lack of funds prevented the union properly contesting the Busick injunction in court.

127. "Frame-Up Charged by Convicted I.W.W.," *Sacramento Union*, Oct. 28, 1921, 6.

128. "Man Jailed for Court Contempt," *L.A. Herald*, Nov. 24, 1921, A12.

129. "I.W.W. Trial is Guarded after Near Riot," *L.A. Herald*, Nov. 18, 1921, A11; "9 I.W.W.'s Yell and Cheer at Sentence," *L.A. Herald*, Dec. 9, 1921, 3; Weintraub, "I.W.W. in California," 171.

130. "Four Wobblies Guilty," *L.A. Times*, May 12, 1923, 15.

131. On the Sacramento prosecutor's record and his questionable ethics, see "William Cowan Breaks a Home," *Industrial Solidarity*, Mar. 29, 1924, 1; "Prosecutor of Wobs Rewarded?," *Industrial Solidarity*, Jan. 12, 1924, 6; "I.W.W. Faces New California Battle," *Industrial Worker*, Aug. 27, 1924, 2. On other occasions involving the use of special prosecutors, see, for example, "District Attorney Names New Deputy," *L.A. Herald*, Jan. 23, 1920, 1; "Eureka Court Fails to Convict 9 Wobs," *Industrial Solidarity*, Mar. 1, 1924, 1; "Powell Case Lost in Courts," *Industrial Solidarity*, Mar. 18, 1925, 6; "Sacramento I.W.W. Released from Jail," *L.A. Times*, Jan. 21, 1923, IV12.

132. Clippings-Alabama, ACLU Records, Volume 236, pp. 62–64; Tulin, Summary of Criminal Syndicalism Cases, 52. See also "Intimidation Tactics of I.W.W. Brought Out in Trial," *Feather River Bulletin*, Oct. 25, 1923, 1.

133. "Wobs Hold Own in Los Angles," *Industrial Solidarity*, May 3, 1924, 6.

134. "Sacramento Fight Reopened," *Industrial Solidarity*, Mar. 8, 1924, 1.

135. Weintraub, "I.W.W. in California," 236.

136. Directive from Commanding Captain, Mar. 22, 1924, Correspondence Cases–California, ACLU Records, Volume 257, p. 25. On the continued enforcement efforts in Southern California during this period, see Minutes of the 16th General Convention of the IWW, pp. 74–75, Box 1, File 13, IWW Seattle Joint Branches Collection, UWSC; "More Arrests in Southern Cal.," *Industrial Solidarity*, Apr. 19, 1924, 1; "Last Round Near in Calif. Fight for Right to Exist," *Industrial Solidarity*, Apr. 19, 1924, 6.

137. Weintraub, "I.W.W. in California," 238–39; Correspondence Cases–California, ACLU Records, Volume 257, pp. 38–45.

138. Weintraub, "I.W.W. in California," 242–45.

139. "21 Arrested in Radical Raid," *San Francisco Examiner*, Dec. 4, 1924, 5. See also, for example, "Merced Roundup of Hoboes Drives Fifty from Town," *San Francisco Examiner*, Dec. 15, 1924, 5; "12 'Wobblies' Jailed in Three Police Raids," *San Francisco Examiner*, June 17, 1924, 8; "13 I.W.W. Nabbed in S.F. Arson Quiz," *Oakland Tribune*, June 16, 1924, 1; "180 Days in Jail," *Bakersfield Californian*, Apr. 16, 1924, 7.

140. Tulin, Summary of Criminal Syndicalism Cases, 52–56.

141. See, for example, "Wobblies Told Spirit of Law," *L.A. Times*, May 27, 1924, II10; "Five Wob Cases Dismissed," *Industrial Solidarity*, Sept. 10, 1924, 1; "Eureka Court Fails to Convict 9 Wobs," *Industrial Solidarity*, Mar. 1, 1924, 1.

142. Archie Sinclair, "Now That the Storm Is Receding," *Industrial Pioneer,* March 1924, 11.

143. Tulin, Summary of Criminal Syndicalism Cases, 56; California Prison and Correctional Records, San Quentin, Book No. 10, Inmate No. 40054; "John Bruns Is Out of Quentin," *Industrial Solidarity,* Nov. 23, 1927, 1. Bruns's prison record is inconsistent with respect to both his name and his age.

CHAPTER 6. BETWEEN THE DROWNING AND THE BROKEN

1. Clippings–Amnesty Cases, Records of the National Office of the American Civil Liberties Union (ACLU Records), Volume 233, p. 182.

2. Ralph Chaplin, *Wobbly: The Rough-and-Tumble Story of an American Radical* (Chicago: University of Chicago Press, 1948), 251–52, 254–55; Box 2, Files 13, 26, Ralph Chaplin Papers, Washington State Historical Society (WSHS).

3. Clippings–Amnesty Cases, ACLU Records, Volume 233, p. 182.

4. Correspondence Cases–Amnesty, ACLU Records, Volume 196, pp. 153–54, 190; *Annual Report of the U.S. Attorney General, 1923* (Washington, D.C.: GPO, 1923), p. 373; U.S. Senate, *Government Prosecutions under the Espionage Act,* 67th Congress, 2nd Session, 1922, pp. 5, 16.

5. Kumpula v. United States, 261 F. 49, 50 (9th Cir. 1920); "Kumpula Committed to Jail," *Eugene Morning Register,* Jan. 3, 1920, 3.

6. Harry N. Schreiber, *The Wilson Administration and Civil Liberties* (Ithaca, NY: Cornell University Press, 1960), 58, 78; U.S. Senate, Subcommittee of the Committee on the Judiciary, *Hearings on Amnesty and Pardon for Political Prisoners,* 66th Congress, 3rd Session, 1921, Testimony of A. Mitchell Palmer, pp. 69–75; U.S. House of Representatives, Committee on the Judiciary, *Hearings on Amnesty and Pardon for Political Prisoners,* 67th Congress, 2nd Session, 1922, Testimony of Albert De Sliver, pp. 1–2.

7. Between 1919 and 1925, 128 people, all of them IWWs, were imprisoned on criminal syndicalism charges in California, out of 164 who were convicted of the crime. See Leo Tulin, Summary of Criminal Syndicalism Cases, p. 72, Box 1, Ralph Chaplin Papers, University of Michigan Special Collections; Woodrow C. Whitten, "Criminal Syndicalism and the Law in California: 1919–1927," *Transactions of the American Philosophical Society* 59, no. 2 (1969): 52–53, 65–66 (app. c); Eldridge Foster Dowell, "A History of the Enactment of Criminal Syndicalism Legislation in the United States," PhD diss., Johns Hopkins University, 1936, p. 935; Claude Erwin, Record of California Criminal Syndicalism Convictions, Box 135, File 1, IWW Collection, Walter Reuther Memorial Library (WRML). Thirty—29 Wobblies and one supporter—were imprisoned in Idaho. See *Inmates of the Idaho State Penitentiary, 1864–1947* (Boise, ID: Idaho Historical Society, 2008), vii; Fifty-nine, nearly all Wobblies, were imprisoned in Washington. Washington State Archive, Washington State Penitentiary, Commitment Registers, https://www.digitalarchives.wa.gov/. According to one commonly cited, though unreliable, estimate, by April 1920, 86 people had been convicted of felony criminal syndicalism in Oregon. Mildred Cline, "A Study of Criminal Syndicalism in Oregon," BA thesis, Reed College, 1933,

p. 6; "Exile of All Alien I.W.W. Requested," *Portland Oregonian*, Apr. 4, 1920, 10. In fact, about two dozen met this fate. See Albert F. Gunns, *Civil Liberties in Crisis: The Pacific Northwest, 1917–1920* (New York: Garland Press, 1983), 42; "Iron Heel in Northwest," *Industrial Worker*, Jan. 15, 1921, 1; "Four I.W.W. Held on Syndicalism Charge," *Industrial Solidarity*, Oct. 15, 1921, 4; "Police Stop Amnesty Meeting in Spokane," *Solidarity*, Apr. 13, 1921, 1.

About 531 people were formally charged with felony criminal syndicalism in California. Tulin, Summary of Criminal Syndicalism Cases, 72; Whitten, "Criminal Syndicalism," 65–66 (app. c). Likewise, according to a report published in 1936 by an antiradical group that supported these laws, between the time that California's law went into effect in 1919 and the end of the 1927–28 fiscal year, 873 people were arrested *and fingerprinted* on criminal syndicalism charges, of whom a great majority were Wobblies. *The California Criminal Syndicalism Law: A Factual Analysis* (San Francisco: The California Crusaders, 1936), 10. According to a defense organization associated with the Communist Party, as many as 1,100 Wobblies were, in some fashion or another, charged with criminal syndicalism in California from 1919 through 1921, with another 105 in 1924. Civil Rights Survey, 1940, Correspondence-Labor, ACLU Records, Volume 2295, p. 16. For a partial accounting of serious criminal cases involving IWWs, see also Jail and Penitentiary Calendar, Box 135, File 2, IWW Collection, WRML.

8. See, e.g., Henry G. Weise, "Nailing Christ to the Cross Again," *Industrial Pioneer*, Dec. 1923, 6.

9. Brief of Appellant, State v. Payne, Washington State Supreme Court, pp. 2–8, Box 126, File 22, IWW Collection, WRML; Washington State Archive, Washington State Penitentiary, Commitment Registers, https://www.digital archives.wa.gov/. Besides his prominence in the union, Payne's criminality consisted in permitting his place to be used by strikers during a sawmill strike in nearby Newport.

10. C.E. Payne, "At Walla Walla," *Seattle Star*, Sept. 21, 1922, 1; C.E. Payne, "At Walla Walla," *Seattle Star*, Sept. 22, 1922, 7. On Payne's situation, including his role in the tumultuous period of the mid 1920s, see, generally, C.E. Payne Papers, Oregon Historical Society.

11. *The Autobiography of Big Bill Haywood* (New York: International Publishers, 1977), 333–35, 338.

12. Jack London, *The Star Rover* (Orinda, CA: SeaWolf Press, 2018), 21–31; *Big Bill Haywood*, 337.

13. Criminal Syndicalism Law in California, Correspondence Cases–California, ACLU Records, Volume 284C, pp. 32, 33; California Prison and Correctional Records, San Quentin, Book No. 10, Inmate No. 33739. See also CDDC Bulletin, Aug. 11, 1923, Box 4, IWW Seattle Joint Branches Collection, University of Washington Special Collections (UWSC); Archie Sinclair, "A Visit to San Quentin," *Industrial Pioneer*, Oct. 1923, 27.

14. How Justice Is Meted Out, Correspondence Cases-California, ACLU Records, Volume 213, pp. 69–71; "C. S. Deportees are Sick in New York," *Industrial Worker*, Aug. 30, 1924, 2.

15. CDDC Bulletin, June 7, 1924, Box 4, IWW Seattle Joint Branches Collection, UWSC; "Solitary Cells Break Wobbly Strike," *L.A. Times*, June 20,

1924, 5; "San Quentin 'Reds' Again on Strike," *Santa Rosa Press Democrat,* June 21, 1924, 1. See also Clippings-Alabama, ACLU Records, Volume 208, pp. 35–36; Hyman Weintraub, "The I.W.W. in California: 1905–1931," MA thesis, University of California, Los Angeles, 1947, pp. 194–195; "Prisoners at San Quentin Go on Strike," *San Francisco Chronicle,* Aug. 2, 1925, 2; "No Work Strike Is Conducted by Quentin Inmates," *Sacramento Union,* Aug. 2, 1922, 1; "Wobblies in Solitary," *L.A. Times,* Jun. 23, 1923, 1.

16. "'Bum Chuck,' Say I.W.W. Kickers, So They Strike," *Boise Idaho Statesman,* Apr. 25, 1919, 6.

17. Ralph Chaplin, *Wobbly,* 257; Eric Thomas Chester, *The Wobblies in Their Heyday* (Santa Barbara, CA: Praeger, 2014), 210–11; "I.W.W. Mutiny in Prison," *Wichita Daily Stockman,* Dec. 12, 1918, 2. The protests occurred in the shadow of a mass strike at the prison in January 1919, which involved hundreds of inmates.

18. End San Quentin Strike, Clippings-Alabama, ACLU Records, Volume 236, p. 97; Syndicalism Prisoners on Another Strike, Is Rumor, Clippings–Amnesty Cases, ACLU Records, Volume 233, p. 353; Class War Prisoners Strike in San Quentin, ibid., p. 354; CDDC Bulletin, Oct. 6, 1923, Box 4, IWW Seattle Joint Branches Collection, UWSC.

19. CDDC Bulletin, Nov. 24, 1923, Box 4, IWW Seattle Joint Branches Collection, UWSC.

20. CDDC Bulletin, Sept. 29, 1924, Box 4, IWW Seattle Joint Branches Collection, UWSC; California Prison and Correctional Records, San Quentin, Prison Register, 1918–1922 (Allen was transferred to Folsom in 1922.).

21. Biennial Report of the State Board of Prison Directors of the State of California, Fiscal Years 1921–1922 (San Quentin, CA: San Quentin Press, 1922), 15.

22. Conditions in San Quentin, Correspondence Cases-California, ACLU Records, Volume 213, p. 39; Weintraub, "I.W.W. in California," 192–93.

23. Christina Heatherton, "University of Radicalism: Ricardo Flores Magón and Leavenworth Penitentiary," *American Quarterly* 66, no. 3 (2014): 557.

24. Pardon Attorney Chicago Case Files–Richard Brazier, 002366-012-0323, Department of Justice Investigative Files: Industrial Workers of the World (DOJ-IWW).

25. Disciplinary Note, May 29, 1924, Joe Neil, No. 7950, Kansas State Penitentiary at Lansing Records, Kansas State Archives and Kansas Historical Society (KSA).

26. Letter from H. F. Brown to Warden, Kansas State Penitentiary, Jan. 17, 1923, in Joe Neil, No. 7950, Kansas State Penitentiary at Lansing Records, KSA; Marcet Haldeman-Julius, "Joe Neil, Victim of a Great State's Bigotry," Clippings-Georgia, ACLU Records, Volume 352, pp. 54–70; "Little Known of Hill at Kankakee," *Janesville Daily Gazette,* July 18, 1910, 8.

27. Description of Convict, Record of William Nelson, No. 2627, in Inmate Records, Idaho State Archives and Idaho Historical Society (ISA); "Bloodhounds Placed on Convicts' Trial," *Portland Oregon Daily Journal,* Jul. 20, 1929, 1.

28. Tulin, Summary of Criminal Syndicalism Cases, 19; Claude Erwin, Record of California Criminal Syndicalism Convictions, p. 15, in Box 135, File 1, IWW

Collection, WRML; California Prison and Correctional Records, Folsom, Inmate No. 14388.

29. Washington State Archive, Department of Health, Death Certificates, https://www.digitalarchives.wa.gov/Record/View/0D252977D7C7A6256300B 91240DC22FC; Washington State Archive, Washington State Penitentiary, Commitment Registers, https://www.digitalarchives.wa.gov/Record/View /A16501011CBE6D55857027348E5CD075F. Over a dozen political prisoners and religious and conscientious objectors died at Leavenworth in this period. One of them was Ricardo Flores Magón, the architect of the Magónista Rebellion. Flores Magón's volatile but often close relationship to the IWW was manifested when Wobblies jammed the courtroom to support him during his 1912 trial in San Diego for violating the Neutrality Act. Flores Magón died at Leavenworth on November 21, 1922, three years into a twenty-year sentence for violating the Espionage Act. Although it is generally thought that he succumbed to diabetes, aggravated by poor medical care, it is possible that Flores Magón was murdered by guards. David M. Struthers, *The World in a City: Multiethnic Radicalism in Early Twentieth-Century Los Angeles* (Urbana: University of Illinois Press, 2019), 110, 178–82, 202–3; Heatherton, "University of Radicalism," passim. On other deaths at Leavenworth, see Stephen M. Kohn, *American Political Prisoners: Prosecutions under the Espionage and Sedition Acts* (Westport, CT: Praeger, 1994), 183–89.

30. Kohn, *American Political Prisoners,* 119, 139; "Prison Tuberculosis Takes the Life of Another Wobbly," *Daily Worker,* May 12, 1924, 4.

31. Claude Erwin, Record of California Criminal Syndicalism Convictions, p. 6, Box 135, File 1, IWW Collection, WRML; Tulin, Summary of Criminal Syndicalism Cases, 20.

32. Tulin, Summary of Criminal Syndicalism Cases, 54.

33. Kohn, *American Political Prisoners,* 84–85.

34. IWW Cases and Activities–Sacramento, California, 002366-006-0286, DOJ-IWW; Circumstances Surrounding the Sacramento Trial, in Pardon Attorney Case Files–Carl Ahlteen, Ragner Johanson, and Sigfried Stenberg, 002366-011-0001, DOJ-IWW; Kohn, *American Political Prisoners,* 98.

35. "Sacramento I.W.W. Insane in Prison," *San Francisco Examiner,* June 26, 1921, 2.

36. Kohn, *American Political Prisoners,* 122.

37. Transcript of Record, United States v. Anderson, no. 763, in Pardon Attorney Case Files: C. W. Anderson Trial Transcript, 002366-015-0001, DOJ-IWW, pp. 1095, 1107–8.

38. Letter from H. E. Held to State Pardon Board, Apr. 4, 1921, Record of H. E. Held, Inmate Records, ISA.

39. Letters from Steelink to Fannia Steelink, Apr. 4, 1920, Apr. 9, 1920, Box 1, File 1, Nicolaas Steelink Papers, WRML. Fannia's name is sometimes spelled "Fania."

40. People v. Steelik [sic], 203 P. 78, 84 (Cal. 1921). See Correspondence Cases–California, ACLU Records, Volume 213, pp. 91–94.

41. See, for example People v. Sullivan, 211 P. 467, 468–69 (Cal. Dist. Ct. App. 1922); People v. Wismer, 209 P. 259, 261 (Cal. Dist. Ct. App. 1922). In

1921 and 1922, the Washington State Supreme Court considered eleven criminal syndicalism cases and reversed convictions in five of those cases—three because of the admission of impermissible hearsay and two because of faulty jury instructions. Dowell, "Criminal Syndicalism," 1060–61.

42. See, for example, People v. Thornton, 219 P. 1020 (Cal. Dist. Ct. App. 1923).

43. Ex parte Moore, 224 P. 662 (Idaho 1924). The decision, which came when the state was done with prosecuting Wobblies for this crime, was swiftly overturned by the legislature, which amended the law to criminalize "slack work" and "work done in an improper manner." Act of Feb. 21, 1925, ch. 51, Idaho Laws. See also Correspondence Cases–Colorado et al., ACLU Records, Volume 258, pp. 76–95.

44. State v. Moilen, 167 N.W. 345, 346 (Minn. 1918). See also, for example State v. Dingman, 219 P. 760, 762–64 (Idaho 1923); Brief of Appellant, State v. Dingman, Idaho Supreme Court, p. 6., Box 127, File 5, IWW Collection, WRML. When defendants got their convictions overturned because of the indefinite way that terms like *sabotage* or *terrorism* were defined, this was usually because trial courts had erred by expanding the meaning of these terms in their jury instructions. See, for example, State v. Tonn, 191 N.W. 530, 538 (Iowa 1923); State v. Aspelin, 203 P. 964, 965 (Wash. 1922).

45. State v. Hennessy, 195 P. 211, 216 (Wash. 1921). See also Appellants Opening Brief, Hennessy v. Washington, Washington State Supreme Court, pp. 3–4, Box 126, File 20, IWW Collection, WRML.

46. See, for example, People v. Eaton, 213 P. 275, 276–77 (Cal. Dist. Ct. App. 1923).

47. See, for example People v. Powell, 236 P. 311, 314 (Cal. Dist. Ct. App. 1925); People v. Stewart, 230 P. 221, 224 (Cal. Dist. Ct. App. 1924); People v. Roe, 209 P. 381, 383–84 (Cal. Dist. Ct. App. 1922). For an example of how such arguments were framed, see Appellant's Brief, State v. Sorllie, pp. 21–24, Washington State Supreme Court, Box 2, IWW Seattle Joint Branches Collection, UWSC. The claim that prosecutions premised on actions of the IWW before these laws were enacted comprised an unconstitutional form of ex post facto punishment was rejected on similar grounds. People v. Steelik [sic], 203 P. 78, 84 (Cal. 1921). Some courts were concerned that guilt should require proof that defendants knew at least something about the nature of the IWW if they were to be convicted based only on their membership in the union, but they were usually satisfied that this could be inferred from membership. See, for example, People v. Cox, 226 P. 14, 16 (Cal. Dist. Ct. App. 1924).

48. See, for example People v. Taylor, 203 P. 85, 87–89 (Cal. 1921); People v. Lesse, 199 P. 46, 47 (Cal. Dist. Ct. App. 1921); State v. Moilen, 167 N.W. 345, 348–49 (Minn. 1918). Some courts did take exception to this practice. See, for example People v. Erickson, 226 P. 637 (Cal. Dist. Ct. App. 1924); People v. Leonard, 225 P. 461, 462 (Cal. Dist. Ct. App. 1924).

49. See People v. Steelik [sic], 203 P. 78, 84–85; State v. Tonn, 191 N.W. 530, 537–38 (Iowa 1923); People v. Casdorf, 212 P. 237, 238 (Cal. Dist. Ct. App. 1922). For an example of how such claims were framed, see Appellants'

Opening Brief, People v. La Rue, et al., California District Court of Appeal, No. 684, pp. 5–12, Box 2, IWW Seattle Joint Branches Collection, UWSC.

50. Most courts simply held that this provision of the Constitution governed only the type of punishment that could be imposed on defendants, not its severity, and otherwise limited the extent of punishment only where a legislature might have exceeded its own discretion. State v. Moilen, 167 N.W. 345, 347 (Minn. 1918). Cf. State v. Hennessy, 151 P. 211, 215 (Wash. 1921).

51. See, for example, People v. Wieler, 204 P. 410, 411 (Cal. Dist. Ct. App. 1921); State v. Dingman, 219 P. 760, 764 (Idaho 1923); State v. Hennessy, 195 P. 211, 215 (Wash. 1921).

52. State v. Moilen, 140 Minn. 112, 116 (Minn. 1919). A handful of state court decisions invalidated antiradical prosecutions for sedition because they violated defendants' free speech rights. See, for example, State v. Diamond, 202 P. 988 (N.M. 1921); State v. Gabriel, 112 A. 611 (N.J. 1919); State v. Tachin, 106 A. 145 (N.J. 1919); State v. Smith, 109 P. 107 (Mont. 1920); State v. Dunn, 57 Mont. 591 (Mont. 1920); State v. Griffith, 184 P. 219 (Mont. 1918).

53. State v. Berg, 233 P. 497, 501 (Okla. Ct. Crim. App. 1925).

54. People v. Taylor, 203 P. 85, 88 (Cal. 1921). The court also rejected Taylor's claim that the trial court erred in refusing to instruct the jury as to the "general right of the masses to strike" and the right to sympathize with "the soviet government of Russia." It rejected, too, the claim that the state had not drafted the indictment clearly enough. Ibid., 90–91. See also People v. Cox, 226 P. 14, 15–16 (Cal. Dist. Ct. App. 1924); People v. Wagner, 225 P. 464, 466–67 (Cal. Dist. Ct. App. 1924); State v. Hennessy, 195 P. 211, 216 (Wash. 1921). On Taylor's case, see also Clippings-California, ACLU Records, Volume 140, pp. 44–55.

55. Schenck v. United States, 249 U.S. 47, 48 (1919).

56. David M. Rabban, "The Emergence of Modern First Amendment Doctrine," *University of Chicago Law Review* 50 (1983): 1205, 1210–14, 1265–83; Richard L. Sklar, "The Fiction of the First Freedom," *Western Political Quarterly* 6, no. 3 (1953): 302, 305–6. On the bad tendency test, see Edward J. Bloustein, "The First Amendment 'Bad Tendency' of Speech Doctrine," *Rutgers Law Review* 43 (1990–91): 507.

57. Abrams v. United States, 215 U.S. 616, 628–29 (1919). On *Abrams* and the transformation of Holmes's and Brandeis's views, see Richard Polenberg, *Fighting Faiths: The Abrams Case, The Supreme Court, and Free Speech* (Ithaca, NY: Cornell University Press, 1999). On the limits of this transformation, see Jacob Kramer, *The New Freedom and the Radicals: Woodrow Wilson, Progressive Views of Radicals, and the Origins of Repressive Tolerance* (Philadelphia: Temple University Press, 2015), 105–8.

58. Dean A. Strang, *Keep the Wretches in Order: America's Biggest Mass Trial, the Rise of the Justice Department, and the Fall of the IWW* (Madison: University of Wisconsin Press, 2019), 224.

59. Haywood v. United States, 268 F. 795 (7th Cir. 1920). The court ruled that Judge Landis was wrong to admit the defendants' statements and conduct before the enactment of the Espionage Act to show their criminal intent, but he also ruled that such evidence was properly admitted to show the defendants'

"possession and knowledge" of criminal "means." Ibid., 807. On the litigation of the defendants' appeal, see United States v. Haywood, et al., Boxes 122–123, IWW Collection, WRML.

60. Anderson v. United States, 269 F. 65 (9th Cir. 1921).

61. Anderson v. United States 273 F. 20 (8th Cir. 1921); Clayton R. Koppes, "The Kansas Trial of the IWW, 1917–1919," *Labor History* 16, no. 3 (1975): 338, 356. In at least one other case, Wobblies convicted of violating the Espionage Act benefited from a technical ruling by an appellate court. In January 1918, federal prosecutors in Tacoma convicted seven IWW construction workers of violating the Espionage Act by speaking against the war in the camp bunkhouse while draft-eligible workers were present. In February, the men received sentences that ran from one year to five years, but their convictions were thrown out because of a defect in the indictment. Indictment, U.S. v. Foster, et al., IWW Cases and Activities–Washington, 002366-005-0539, DOJ-IWW; Foster v. United States, 253 F. 481 (9th Cir. 1918); *War-Time Prosecutions and Mob Violence* (New York: National Civil Liberties Bureau, 1919), 14.

62. Heatherton, "University of Radicalism," 557.

63. William Preston Jr., *Aliens and Dissenters: Federal Suppression of Radicals, 1903–1933* (Cambridge, MA: Harvard University Press, 1963), 258.

64. Chaplin, *Wobbly*, 332.

65. For an overview of this campaign, see *American Civil Liberties Union Annual Report No. 2* (New York: ACLU, 1923), 9–16; Preston, *Aliens and Dissenters*, 259–67; Ben Fletcher, "I.W.W. Organizer," *Pennsylvania History: A Journal of Mid-Atlantic Studies* 46, no. 3 (1979): 212, 224.

66. Robert C. Cottrell, *Roger Nash Baldwin and the American Civil Liberties Union* (New York: Columbia University Press, 2001), 80–102, 108–9.

67. Among the archived collections of ACLU records that document these efforts, see, Correspondence Cases–Amnesty, ACLU Records, Volumes 195–198; Clippings–Amnesty Cases, ACLU Records, Volumes 199, 233. On the origins of these organizations, see Laura Weinrib, *The Taming of Free Speech: America's Civil Liberties Compromise* (Cambridge, MA: Harvard University Press, 2016), 52–57, 67–70, 108–10.

68. For a review of such opposition, see Clippings–Amnesty Cases, ACLU Records, Volume 199. See also Clippings–Amnesty Cases, ACLU Records, Volume 233.

69. On the revelations about prisoners and their families, see U.S. House, Committee on the Judiciary, *Hearings on Amnesty*, pp. 175–93. On the support of newspapermen, see, for example, "Mercy or 50 Prisoners," *Washington Post*, May 9, 1919, 6; "The Superfluous Espionage Act," *Boston Daily Globe*, Feb. 10, 1919, 6.

70. U.S. Senate, *Amnesty and Pardon for Political Prisoners*, 75–76.

71. Debs v. United States, 249 U.S. 211 (1919).

72. Letter from John Murphy to Dora Haines, May 19, 1921, in Correspondence Cases–Alabama, ACLU Records, Volume 165, pp. 24–26; Chester, *The Wobblies*, 216–19. See also Report of the General Defense Committee, in Minutes of the 14th General Convention of the Industrial Workers of the World, 1922, 25–26, Box 3, File 2, IWW Collection, WRML; Clippings–Amnesty

Cases, ACLU Records, Volume 199; Correspondence Cases–Amnesty, ACLU Records, Volume 198.

73. London, *Star Rover,* 16.

74. *An Open Letter to President Harding from 52 Members of the I.W.W. at Leavenworth* (Chicago: IWW General Defense Committee, 1922), 3–5, 10–11, 18, 20–22.

75. See, for example, Executive Pardon, in Pardon Attorney Case Files–Ralph Chaplin, 002366-012-370, DOJ-IWW.

76. Kohn, *American Political Prisoners,* 91; Chester, *The Wobblies,* 219–21; U.S. House, Committee on the Judiciary, *Hearings on Amnesty,* Testimony of Albert De Silver 1–4.

77. Chester, *The Wobblies,* 220–21; Philip Taft, "The Federal Trials of the IWW," *Labor History* 3, no. 1 (1962): 60, 80–91. See also Commutation Controversy, Box 17, Files 35–37, IWW Collection, WRM; Kohn, *American Political Prisoners,* 20; Correspondence Cases–Alabama, ACLU Records, Volume 165, pp. 101, 106; *Annual Report of the Attorney General,* 1924 (Washington, D.C.: GPO, 1924), 404.

78. Warden's Office, in Pardon Attorney Case Files–James Rowan, 002366-012-0491, DOJ-IWW; Strang, *Keep the Wretches in Order,* 229.

79. Lois Phillips Hudson, *The Bones of Plenty* (Minneapolis: Minnesota Historical Society, 1984), 338–39.

80. See Pardon Attorney Case Files–Chicago, 002366-012-0001, DOJ-IWW; U.S. Senate, *Government Prosecutions under the Espionage Act,* U.S. Senate, 66th Congress, 2nd Session, 1922; Preston, *Aliens and Dissenters,* 252–65; Kohn, *American Political Prisoners,* 86, 110, 115–17; Richard Brazier, "The Amazing Deportation Mania," *Industrial Pioneer,* Feb. 1924, 43.

81. IWW Cases and Activities–James H. Rowan Citizenship, 002366-010-0870, DOJ-IWW.

82. John Dos Passos, *U.S.A.* (New York: Library of America, 1996), 750.

83. Robert L. Tyler, "The I.W.W. in the Pacific N.W.: Rebels of the Woods," *Oregon Historical Quarterly* 55, no. 1 (1954): 3, 32; Tom Copeland, *The Centralia Tragedy of 1919: Elmer Smith and the Wobblies* (Seattle: University of Washington, 1993), 171–85.

84. *American Civil Liberties Union Annual Report No. 5* (New York: ACLU, 1926), 15; *American Civil Liberties Union Annual Report No. 4* (New York: ACLU, 1925), 16; "Criminal Syndicalism Prisoners Refuse to Leave Centralia Boys," *Industrial Solidarity,* Apr. 29, 1925, 3. The criminal syndicalism defendants were not released until 1926. *American Civil Liberties Union Annual Report No. 6* (New York: ACLU, 1927), 12.

85. San Quentin Bunch on Record against Parole, Clippings-Amnesty Cases, ACLU Records, Volume 233, p. 384.

86. Letter from John Shea to State Board of Pardons, July 1, 1919, Record of John Shea, No. 2638, Inmate Records, ISA.

87. Letter from Charles Anderson to State Board of Pardons, n.d., Record of Charles Anderson, No. 2648, Inmate Records, ISA.

88. Letter from W. Marks to Warden, Idaho State Prison, July 7, 1921, Record of Joe Martin, No. 2636, Inmate Records, ISA.

89. Letter from Mrs. A. C. Banker to Governor D.W. Davis, Dec. 14, 1920, Record of Bert Banker, No. 2639, Inmate Records, ISA. Banker was paroled to his mother a year later.

90. Letter from Howard Clifford to D. W. Davis, Dec. 4, 1920, Record of Charles Clifford, No. 2629, Inmate Records, ISA.

91. Letter from Ada Howard to Governor D.W. Davis, Nov. 20, 1920, Record of Charles Clifford, No. 2629, Inmate Records, ISA.

92. Letter from W. H. Eller to Pardon Board, Dec. 6, 1920, Record of Gust Haraldson, No. 2828, Inmate Records, ISA.

93. Letter from Robert Terrell to Governor D. W. Davis, May 10, 1922, Record of Thomas O'Hara, No. 3039, Inmate Records, ISA. See also Telegram from General Defense Committee to Governor D. W. Davis, May 10, 1922, ibid.

94. Letter from L. E. Clapp to Thomas O'Hara, May 16, 1956, Record of Thomas O'Hara, No. 3039, Inmate Records, ISA.

95. "Released I.W.W. Holds to Economic Views," Clippings–Amnesty Cases, ACLU Records, Volume 199, p. 9; IWW Cases and Activities–William Haywood, 002366-009-0237, DOJ-IWW; Kohn, *American Political Prisoners*, 103.

96. *Solidarity Forever: An Oral History of the IWW* (Chicago: Lake View Press, 1985), 201.

97. Cletus E. Daniel, "In Defense of the Wheatland Wobblies: A Critical Analysis of the IWW in California," *Labor History* 19, no. 4 (1978): 485, 506. The three miners who pleaded guilty to manslaughter in the last days of the 1916 Mesabi strike had their sentences commuted a few months later. Neil Betten, "Riot, Revolution, Repression in the Iron Range Strike of 1916," *Minnesota History* 41 (1968): 82, 90.

98. Erwin, Record of California Criminal Syndicalism Convictions, 26; Pardon Attorney Case Files-James Price, 002366-013-0892, DOJ-IWW.

99. Tulin, Summary of Criminal Syndicalism Cases, pp. 45–46; Earl Bruce White, "The Wichita Indictments and Trial of the Industrial Workers of the World, 1917–1919," PhD diss., University of Colorado, 1980, p. 289.

100. On the difficulties that inhere in determining membership levels, see, for example, Eric Chester, "The Rise and Fall of the IWW: As Viewed through Membership Figures," *Anarcho-Syndicalist Review* 55 (2011): 13; Letter from Fred Thompson to Martin McLaughlin, Feb. 3, 1973, Box 11, File 14, Frederick Thompson Papers, WRML; Paul Brissenden, *The I.W.W.: A Study of American Syndicalism* (New York: Columbia University Press, 1919), 352; Fred Thompson, "They Didn't Suppress the IWW," *Radical America* 1, no. 2 (1967): 1, 2–5.

101. According to Thompson, IWW membership rebounded strongly after the Red Scare, reaching nearly 60,000 in 1923. Fred Thompson, *The I.W.W.: Its First Fifty Years* (Chicago: IWW, 1955), 111, 129–31; Thompson, "They Didn't Suppress the IWW," 2–5. This figure is questionable, as Chester has shown. He estimates a membership of somewhere between 15,000 and 20,000 from the end of the war into the early 1920s. Chester, "Rise and Fall of the IWW," 15–17. But Chester's figures may also be on the low side, given their reliance on members' payment of dues. Moreover, as he makes clear, membership figures offer "only a very limited glimpse into the life of any organization." Ibid., 16. On the union's viability in the early 1920s, see also Greg Hall, *Harvest Wobblies: The Industrial*

Workers of the World and Agricultural Workers in the American West, 1905–1930 (Corvallis: Oregon State University Press, 2001), 206–8; Frank Tobias Higbie, "Indispensable Outcasts: Seasonal Laborers and Community in the Upper Midwest, 1880–1930," PhD diss., University of Illinois, Urbana-Champaign, 2000, p. 295; Patrick Renshaw, "The IWW and the Red Scare, 1917–1924," *Journal of Comparative History* 3, no. 4 (1968): 63.

102. "Throws Scare into Wobblies," *L.A. Times,* Apr. 19, 1920, I19.

103. Kohn, *American Political Prisoners,* 84–85.

104. Chester, *The Wobblies,* 222.

105. White, "Wichita Indictments," 287.

106. "Vincent St. John, I.W.W. Aide, Dies," *San Francisco Examiner,* June 23, 1929, 16.

107. Dubofsky, *We Shall Be All,* 262–63.

108. *The Wobblies* (film), 1:23:23–33. See also Chester, *The Wobblies,* 222.

109. Dubofsky, *We Shall Be All,* 443; John S. Gambs, *The Decline of the I.W.W.* (New York: Russell and Russell, 1966), 53. On the post office's interference, see Chester, *The Wobblies,* 173–75. Some researchers have focused too little on repression at the state and local levels, which also tends to distract from what the union endured after federal prosecutions ended. See, for example, Dubofsky, *We Shall Be All,* 349–468; Preston, *Aliens and Dissenters;* Chester, *The Wobblies,* 203–10; Michael Johnson, "The I.W.W. and Wilsonian Democracy," *Science & Society* 28, no. 3 (1964): 257.

110. Preston, *Aliens and Dissenters,* 141; Dubofsky, *We Shall Be All,* 443–44; Letter from Roger Baldwin, Jan. 3, 1918, Correspondence Cases–Amnesty, ACLU Records, Volume 27, p. 45. See also *Solidarity Forever,* 114.

111. Financial Statement, Box 28, Files 1–4, IWW Collection, WRML; General Office Bulletins, Box 31, Files 1–5, IWW Collection, WRML; *Big Bill Haywood,* 344–45. Actual litigation costs during this one period, which account for very few vagrancy cases and probably only some criminal syndicalism cases, exceeded $200,000. Weinrib, *Taming of Free Speech,* 101.

112. On the union's defense-related expenditures in 1920, see Financial Statements of the IWW, Recruiting Union Reports for January, 1920 through January 1, 1921, Box 28, File 2, IWW Collection, WRML. The $100,000 figure is based on reports from nine months of that year (statements from May, June, and October are missing) which document $75,699 in total defense-related expenses, of which $25,250 went toward legal expenses, $6,113 to relief, and $15,469 for bail. The balance went toward printing and postage, publicity, and speakers' fees. In the fiscal year ending April 1, 1921, union expenses totaled $192,000 and general defense committee disbursement about $83,000. Minutes of the 13th General Convention of the IWW, pp. 31–32, Box 1, File 13, IWW Seattle Joint Branches Collection, UWSC.

113. This figure includes $18,848 for legal defense, $5,220 for relief for prisoners and their families, and $4,115 in a special account involving defense work in California. Industrial Workers of the World, Financial Statement for the Fiscal Year October 1, 1923–October 1, 1924, Box 28, File 7, IWW Collection, WRML. The following fiscal year, the union still spent $21,406 on defense work, including $6,909 on legal expenses. Industrial Workers of the World,

Financial Statement for the Fiscal Year October 1, 1924–October 1, 1925, Box 28, File 8, IWW Collection, WRML.

114. In 1925, with the felony prosecutions over but funds still needed for defense work and inmates' relief, the union also began to receive help from International Labor Defense, an organization created that year by the Communist Party to enlist the IWW in a common effort to counter legal persecution. Minutes of the 15th General Convention of the IWW, pp. 31–33, Box 1, File 13, IWW Seattle Joint Branches Collection, UWSC; Jacob A. Zumoff, *The Communist International and US Communism, 1919–1929* (Chicago: Haymarket Books, 2014), 196–204.

115. See, for example, the financial reports of the California Branch of the General Defense Committee, Box 4, IWW Seattle Joint Branches Collection, UWSC.

116. CDDC Bulletin, April 22, 1923, Box 4, IWW Seattle Joint Branches Collection, UWSC.

117. "Necktie Performs Patriotic Service," *Roseburg News-Review,* Apr. 8, 1918, 1; "Dr. Equi Claims Body of Suicide," *Portland Oregon Daily Journal,* Apr. 10, 1918, 4. On the harassment of people doing defense work, see also "Connors is 40950," *Industrial Solidarity,* June 24, 1925, 5; "California Frame-Up Artists Try Again to Get Connors," *Industrial Solidarity,* May 27, 1925, 1; "Tom Connors, Defense Secretary, in Jail in Sacramento," *Industrial Solidarity,* Apr. 21, 1923, 5; John Martin, "General Defense News," *Industrial Pioneer,* May 1921, 55.

118. Chaplin, *Wobbly,* 290–95.

119. Correspondence Cases–IWW, ACLU Records, Volume 86, p. 164.

120. Marcet Haldeman Julius, "Joe Neil, Victim of a Great State's Bigotry," Clippings-Georgia, ACLU Records, Volume 352, pp. 54–70.

121. For instance, in the spring of 1921, the IWW had to muster $37,000 in bail for ten members facing criminal syndicalism charges in Los Angeles. Roster of Cases Now Pending, Correspondence Cases–Alabama, ACLU Records, Volume 165, pp. 122–24. "Defense News," *Industrial Pioneer,* July 1921, 52. That same summer, the IWW raised $23,000 to bail out four of the Kansas conspiracy case defendants.

122. See, for example, Report on IWW Matters, July 2, 1921, IWW Cases and Activities–San Francisco, 002366-007-0287, DOJ-IWW; White, "Wichita Indictments," 142–44.

123. IWW Cases and Activities–San Francisco, 002366-007-0287, DOJ-IWW. See also IWW Instability, 002371-009-0809, DOJ-IWW.

124. Hall, *Harvest Wobblies,* 225–29.

125. James P. Cannon, "The I.W.W.," *Fourth International* 16 (1955): 75; Elizabeth Gurley Flynn, *Memories of the Industrial Workers of the World* (New York: Institute for Marxist Studies, 1977), 24–25.

126. Gambs, *Decline of the I.W.W.,* 77.

127. William Chamberlin, "Russian Recollections," *The Russian Review* 21, no. 4 (1962): 333, 337–38; Kohn, *American Political Prisoners,* 85.

128. Chester, *The Wobblies,* 204–6; Dubofsky, *We Shall Be All,* 462–65; Gambs, *Decline of the I.W.W.,* 182–83; Roy Brown, "'High Spots' of the 13th

I.W.W. Convention," *Industrial Pioneer,* July 21, pp. 36, 39–40; Chaplin, *Wobbly,* 302–3. For a summary of the IWW's official basis for rejecting the Comintern's invitation, see The I.W.W. Reply to the Red Trade Union International, in IWW Collection, WSHS.

129. This conflict formed the basis of a destructive rift between the IWW's national leadership and Local 8 of the Marine Transport Workers Industrial Union, which had successfully organized black and white workers on the Philadelphia waterfront. The dispute, which grew out of the local's decision to load munitions destined for a White army fighting the Bolsheviks as well as questions concerning the local's business practices, mapped onto larger struggle over centralization that led first to Local 8's temporary expulsion and then, in 1923, to its effective reformation as an AFL union. Peter Cole, *Wobblies on the Waterfront: Interracial Unionism in Progressive-Era Philadelphia* (Chicago: University of Illinois Press, 2013), 128–47; Lisa Mcgirr, "Black and White Longshoremen in the IWW: A History of the Philadelphia Marine Transport Workers Industrial Union Local 8," *Labor History* 36, no. 3 (1995): 377, 395–400.

130. Chester, *The Wobblies,* 221–24; Gambs, *Decline of the I.W.W.,* 100–108, 164–67; Weintraub, "I.W.W. in California," 250. Cf. Dubofsky, *We Shall Be All,* 457–68.

131. Many of these conflicts revolved around the fate of the Centralia defendants and criminal syndicalism inmates in Washington State. See Correspondence, Box 1, File 4, IWW Seattle Joint Branches Collection, UWSC; Minutes of the 16th General Convention of the IWW, pp. 88–89, Box 1, File 13, IWW Seattle Joint Branches Collection, UWSC.

132. Gambs, *Decline of the I.W.W.,* 100–125, 164–67.

133. Nigel Anthony Sellars, *Oil, Wheat and Wobblies: The Industrial Workers of the World in Oklahoma, 1905–1930* (Norman: University of Oklahoma Press, 1998), 149–54, 175–76.

134. Hall, *Harvest Wobblies,* 214; *American Labor Yearbook, 1923–1924* (New York: Rand, 1924), 93; Weintraub, "I.W.W. in California," 215–16; "Harvest Drive Gets into Dakota," *Industrial Solidarity,* July 29, 1925, 1; "I.W.W. Ready for Harvest Drive, *Industrial Solidarity,* May 20, 1925, 1; "Wobblies Fill Jail in Fargo for Right to Ride Freights," *Industrial Solidarity,* Aug. 26, 1925, 1.

135. Sellars, *Oil, Wheat, and Wobblies,* 178–79; Weintraub, "I.W.W. in California," 253–54; Hall, *Harvest Wobblies,* 220–22; Sellars, *Oil, Wheat, and Wobblies,* 179–82; Higbie, "Indispensable Outcasts," 285, 295–96.

136. Fiske v. Kansas, 274 U.S. 380, 383–87 (1927).

137. Burns v. United States, 274 U.S. 328 (1927); CDDC Bulletins, May 6, 1923, July 11, 1923, Nov. 24, 1923, Oct. 18, 1924, Box 4, IWW Seattle Joint Branches Collection, UWSC; Tulin, Summary of Criminal Syndicalism Cases, 51–54. See also Conviction of Bill Burns Upheld by U.S. Supreme Court" *Industrial Worker,* May 28, 1927, 3; "Strange Case of Wm. Burns," *Industrial Solidarity,* Nov. 19, 1924, 1.

138. Charges against one defendant were dropped when he renounced the IWW. It is not clear what happened to the other. Tulin, Summary of Criminal Syndicalism Cases, 53; Letter from Roger Baldwin to Harlan Stone, Dec. 9,

1924, Correspondence Cases–California, ACLU Records, Volume 257, p. 108; California Cases, Industrial Worker, Mar. 25, 1924, 1. On the offer tendered to Burns, see CDDC Bulletin, May 6, 1923, Box 4, IWW Seattle Joint Branches Collection, UWSC.

139. Burns v. United States, 274 U.S. 328, 331–37 (1927); Tulin, Summary of Criminal Syndicalism Cases, 49.

140. Lisa Rubens, "The Patrician Radical: Charlotte Anita Whitney," *California History* 65, no. 3 (1986): 158, 160–61; Beth Slutsky, "Parlor Pink Turned Soapbox Red: The Trial of Charlotte Anita Whitney," *American Communist History* 9, no. 1 (2010): 35, 38–41.

141. Slutsky, "Parlor Pink," 41–42; Ralph E. Shaffer, "Formation of the California Communist Labor Party," *Pacific Historical Review* 36, no. 1 (1967): 59, 73–78.

142. Although not an appendage of the IWW, the CLP was closely connected to the union. The dissident left-wing delegates to the Socialist Party's national convention in Chicago who founded the CLP in early September 1919 had a fair number of Westerners and IWWs in their ranks. They also devised a program that focused on labor organizing, industrial unionism, and "direct action." Shaffer, "Communist Labor Party," 59, 71. See also Theodore Draper, *The Roots of American Communism* (New York: Viking, 1957), 178–79; IWW Cases and Activities–San Francisco, 002366-007-0287, DOJ-IWW; Letter from A.M. Kidd to Mrs. Elmo Robinson, Jan. 8, 1927, Box 19, File 389, ACLU Records.

143. Whitten, "Criminal Syndicalism," 47; Slutsky, "Parlor Pink," 46–49; Vincent Blasi, "The First Amendment and the Ideal of Civic Courage," *William and Mary Law Review* 29, no. 4 (1987–88): 658–59. Whitney faced four other counts of criminal syndicalism by aiding and abetting, publication, advocacy, and justification, but the jury could not reach unanimity. Whitten, "Criminal Syndicalism," 47. On Whitney's case, see also Clippings-California, ACLU Records, Volume 140, pp. 57–108.

144. Whitney v. California, 274 U.S. 357, 371 (1927). Cf. Gitlow v. New York, 268 U.S. 652 (1925).

145. Whitney v. California, 274 U.S. 357, 368–70 (1927).

146. David M. Rabban, "The Emergence of Modern First Amendment Doctrine," *University of Chicago Law Review* 50, no. 4 (1983): 1205, 1323–25.

147. Whitney v. California, 274 U.S. 357, 373 (1927).

148. Whitney v. California, 274 U.S. 357, 379 (1927).

149. Whitney v. California, 274 U.S. 357, 379 (1927). On the tension between Brandeis's position in Whitney's case and his stance in Ruthenberg's, see Ronald K.L. Collins and David M. Skover, "Curious Concurrence: Justice Brandeis's Vote in Whitney v California," *Supreme Court Review* (2005): 333.

150. Leigh Campbell-Hale, "Remembering Ludlow but Forgetting the Columbine: The 1927–1928 Colorado Coal Strike," PhD diss., University of Colorado-Boulder, 2013, pp. 132–35, 216–19; Ronal L. McMahan, "'Rang-U-Tang': The I.W.W. and the 1927 Colorado Coal Strike," in Joseph R. Conlin, ed., *At the Point of Production: The Local History of the IWW* (Westport, CT:

Greenwood Press, 1981), 191. The strikers killed or mortally wounded at the Columbine were Jerry Davis, John Eastenes, Rene Jacques, Frafnk Kovich, Nick Spanudakhis, and Mike Vidovich.

CONCLUSION

1. Eyrna Jones Heisler, "The Thin Red Line Between Truth and Lies," *James Jones Literary Society Newsletter* 18, no. 2 (2012): 4, 11.

2. James Jones, *From Here to Eternity* (New York: Dial Press, 2012), 628–33.

3. Jones, *From Here to Eternity*, 629–33.

4. Jones, *From Here to Eternity*, 582, 633.

5. Jones, *From Here to Eternity*, 341–44.

6. Jones, *From Here to Eternity*, 15.

7. Correspondence Cases–Kentucky, Records of the National Office of the American Civil Liberties Union (ACLU Records), Volume 484, pp. 3–12, 36; California Prison and Correctional Records, San Quentin, Book No. 11, Inmate No. 38990; CDDC Bulletins, Feb. 2, 1924, Feb. 9, 1924, in Box 4, IWW Seattle Joint Branches Collection, University of Washington Special Collections; Box 6, Folder 8, Leo Gallagher Papers, University of Kansas Special Collections.

8. Laura Weinrib, *The Taming of Free Speech: America's Civil Liberties Compromise* (Cambridge, MA: Harvard University Press, 2016), 184; Stromberg v. California, 283 U.S. 359 (1931); Appellant's Brief, pp. 10–11, Stromberg v. California, 283 U.S. 359 (1931) (no. 584); People v. Mintz, 290 P. 93 (Ca. Dist. Ct. App. 1930).

9. De Jonge v. Oregon, 299 U.S. 353, 365 (1937).

10. See for example Mark Tushnet, "The Hughes Court and Radical Political Dissent: The Cases of Dirk De Jonge and Angelo Herndon," *Georgia State Law Review* 29, no. 2 (2011–12): 333. On the transformation of the concept of civil liberties and its main champion, the ACLU, see Weinrib, *Taming of Free Speech*.

11. Herndon v. Lowry, 301 U.S. 242, 262 (1937); De Jonge v. Oregon, 299 U.S. 353, 363–64 (1937).

12. The main purpose of the Smith Act was to destroy the Communist Party. But the party was not the first target of prosecution. That honor fell to Trotskyist unionists in Minnesota, chief among them a group who had led the remarkably militant teamsters strike in Minneapolis in 1934. But these radicals—"more communistic than the Communist Party"—had since became an intolerable inconvenience to International Brotherhood of Teamsters' increasingly conservative and corrupt national leadership, who followed up on a number of other stratagems to purge these people by imploring the Roosevelt Administration to aid them in this effort. The government's answer, it seems, came in June 1941, when the Justice Department indicted twenty-nine members of the Trotskyist Socialist Workers Party in the Twin Cities on charges of violating the Smith Act. Eighteen, including one-time Wobbly and Communist James P. Cannon, were convicted and sentenced to prison. Dunne v. United States, 138 F.2d 137 (8th Cir. 1943); Ralph C. James and Estelle James, "The Purge of the Trotskyites

from the Teamsters," *Western Political Quarterly* 19, no. 1 (1966): 5, 7; Michal R. Belknap, *Cold War Political Justice: The Smith Act, the Communist Party, and American Civil Liberties* (Westport, CT: Greenwood Press, 1977), 19, 37–41; Thomas L. Pahl, "G-String Conspiracy, Political Repression or Armed Revolt?: The Minneapolis Trotskyite Trial," *Labor History* 8 (1967): 30.

13. U.S. House of Representatives, *Report of the Special Committee on Un-American Activities,* 76th Congress, 1st Session (Washington, D.C.: GPO, 1939); U.S. House of Representatives, Special Committee on Un-American Activities, *Investigation of Un-American Propaganda Activities,* 75th Congress, 3rd Session, Volumes 1–3, 1938. The surviving legislative history does not reference this fact, but parallels between the Smith Act's provisions on subversion (especially by membership in radical organizations) and the criminal syndicalism laws leave little doubt as to their kinship. The Supreme Court would note this in its most important case on the statute. Dennis v. United States, 341 U.S. 494, 536, 562 n. 2 (1951). And lawyers on both sides in this and other Smith Act cases would take as given that the statute was based on these earlier anti-radical laws. See Brief for United States, pp. 246–47, United States v. Dennis, 341 U.S. 494 (1951) (no. 336); Brief for Petitioners, pp. 17–19, n. 24, Scales v. United States, 367 U.S. 203 (1958) (no. 665); Brief for United States, p. 26, Scales v. United States, 367 U.S. 203 (1958) (no. 665). See also Mark A. Sheft, "The End of the Smith Act: A Legal and Historical Analysis of Scales v. United States," *American Journal of Legal History* 36, no. 2 (1992): 164, 167, 181; Belknap, *Cold War Political Justice,* 136.

14. See Dennis v. United States, 341 U.S. 494, 509–10 (1951); Dennis v. United States, 183 F.2d 201 (2d Cir. 1950); Elizabeth Gurley Flynn, *The Rebel Girl: An Autobiography* (New York: International, 1955), 163–64, 205–6. See also Belknap, *Cold War Political Justice,* 129–30; Rebecca Lossin, "The Point of Destruction: Sabotage, Speech, and Progressive-Era Politics," PhD diss., Columbia University, 2020, p. 15, n3.

15. Newspaper reports and IWW's records do nothing to suggest that Warren's role in assisting the other prosecutor, A. A. Rogers, was in any way unconventional. Leo Tulin, Summary of Criminal Syndicalism Cases, p. 24, Box 1, Ralph Chaplin Papers, University of Michigan Special Collections; "James C. Taylor Is Found Guilty," *San Francisco Examiner,* May 19, 1919, 1.

16. *The Memoirs of Earl Warren* (New York: Doubleday, 1977), 62; Ronald K. L. Collins and David M. Skover, "Curious Concurrence: Justice Brandeis's Vote in Whitney v California," *Supreme Court Review* (2005): 333, 377.

17. Brandenburg v. Ohio, 395 U.S. 444, 448–49 (1969).

18. "F.B.I. Kept Close Watch on Douglas," *N.Y. Times,* July 22, 1984, 42.

19. Aldan Whitman, "Vigorous Defender of Rights," *N.Y. Times,* Jan. 20, 1980, 28.

20. William O. Douglas, *Go East, Young Man: The Early Years* (New York: Vintage, 1974), 80–83.

21. Brandenburg v. Ohio, 395 U.S. 444, 454 (1969).

22. Papachristou v. City of Jacksonville, 405 U.S. 156, 163, 170 (1972). On the constitutional campaign against vagrancy laws, its resonance with New Left

politics, and Douglas's role pushing this position on the Supreme Court, see Risa Golubuff, *Vagrant Nation: Police Power, Constitutional Change, and the Making of the 1960s* (New York: Oxford University Press, 2016).

23. Brandenburg v. Ohio, 395 U.S. 444, 454 (1969).

24. On Winston's case, see Smith Act Cases–Winston and Green, ACLU Records, Volume B899.

25. Jack London, "The Question of the Maximum," in *The War of the Classes* (Orinda, CA: SeaWolf Press, 2018), 93, 116.

26. On the ACLU's divestment from the politics of labor radicalism, see Weinrib, *Taming of Free Speech*.

27. Jack London, *The Iron Heel* (Orinda, CA: SeaWolf Press, 1908), 223–24.

28. On IWW activism in recent decades, see, for example, John Silvano, ed., *Nothing in Common: An Oral History of IWW Strikes, 1971–1992* (Cedar Rapids, IA: Cedar Publishing, 1999); Chronology of IWW History, https://archive.iww.org/history/chronology/.

29. Ralph Chaplin, *Wobbly: The Rough-and-Tumble Story of an American Radical* (Chicago: University of Chicago Press, 1948), 351, 367–68; Kevin J. Christiano, "Labor Poet Ralph Chaplin: Resister to the 'Great War,' Prisoner of the 'Class War,'" *Journal for the Study of Radicalism* 14, no. 2 (2020): 157; Ralph Chaplin, *American Labor's Case against Communism: How the Operations of Stalin's Red Quislings Look from Inside the Labor Movement* (Seattle, WA: Educator Publishing, 1947).

30. Ralph Chaplin, "Why I Wrote 'Solidarity Forever,'" *American West* 5, no.1 (1968): 18, 20, 25.

31. Record of John O'Shea, No. 2638, Inmate Records, Idaho State Archives and Idaho Historical Society.

32. Earl Bruce White, "The Wichita Indictments and Trial of the Industrial Workers of the World, 1917–1919," PhD diss., University of Colorado, 1980, pp. 285–91.

33. Alex Kershaw, *Jack London: A Life* (New York: St. Martin's Press, 1999), 15, 28–29, 40–41.

34. U.S. Bureau of the Census, *King County, Washington, Population Schedule*, Seattle, ED 40–325, Sheet 6-B, House No. 6015; "Hagbard M. Edwards (Obituary)," *Seattle Daily Times*, May 14, 1977, 49.

35. Earle Labor et al., eds., *The Letters of Jack London, Volume Three: 1913–1916* (Stanford, CA: Stanford University Press, 1988), 1122, 1537–38.

36. "'Helping Hand' or 'Iron Heel'?," *Solidarity*, Dec. 2, 1916, 2; Minutes of the 10th General Convention of the Industrial Workers of the World, 1916,71, Box 2, File 2, IWW Collection, Walter Reuther Memorial Library.

37. Alfred Kazin, *On Native Grounds: An Interpretation of Modern American Prose Literature* (New York: Reynal and Hitchcock, 1942), 111.

38. George Sterling, "Testimony of the Suns," in *Selected Poems* (New York: Henry Holt 1923), 192, 229.

39. Marcet Haldeman-Julius, "Joe Neil, Victim of a Great State's Bigotry," ACLU Records, Volume 352, pp. 54–70.

40. Letter from Caroline Lowe to Lucille Milner, Nov. 9, 1925, Correspondence Cases–Kansas, ACLU Records, Volume 286, p. 63.

41. "Joe Neil Thanks Fellow Workers," *Industrial Worker,* July 14, 1928, 1. On efforts to deport Neil, see Clippings-Georgia, ACLU Records, Volume 352, pp. 54–70. "Arrested as He Leaves Penitentiary, Man Now Faces Federal Charges," *Emporia Gazette,* June 23, 1928, 8.

Bibliography

ARCHIVAL COLLECTIONS

American Civil Liberties Union of Northern California Records, California Historical Society, San Francisco, California.

California Prison and Correctional Records. California State Archives, Sacramento, California.

C. E. Payne Papers. Oregon Historical Society, Portland, Oregon.

Communist Party of the United States. Records. Tamiment Library and Robert Wagner Labor Archives, New York University, New York.

Description Lists of Convicts. Montana State Prison. Montana Historical Society Research Center, Helena, Montana.

Fargo, North Dakota. Justice of the Peace Records, 1893–1947. Institute for Regional Studies Archive Collection. North Dakota State University, Fargo, North Dakota.

Fred Thompson Collection. Walter Reuther Memorial Library, Detroit, Michigan.

Hagbard Edwards Papers. Walter Reuther Memorial Library, Wayne State University, Detroit, Michigan.

Industrial Workers of the World Collection. Walter Reuther Memorial Library, Wayne State University, Detroit, Michigan.

Industrial Workers of the World Collection. Washington State Historical Society, Tacoma Washington.

Industrial Workers of the World Seattle Joint Branches Collection. University of Washington Special Collections, Seattle, Washington.

Inmate Records. Idaho State Archives and Idaho Historical Society, Boise, Idaho.

Inmate Records. Kansas State Archives and Kansas Historical Society, Topeka, Kansas.

International Labor Defense Records. New York Public Library Archives and Manuscripts. Schomburg Center for Research in Black Culture, Manuscripts, Archives and Rare Books Division, New York, New York.

Leo Gallagher Papers. University of Kansas Special Collections. Kenneth Spencer Research Library, Lawrence, Kansas.

Louis Dembitz Brandeis Papers. Harvard Law School Library, Cambridge, Massachusetts.

Meridel Le Sueur Papers. Minnesota Historical Society, Saint Paul, Minnesota.

Moses Alexander Papers. Walter Reuther Memorial Library, Wayne State University, Detroit, Michigan.

Nicholaas Steelink Papers. Walter Reuther Memorial Library, Wayne State University, Detroit, Michigan.

Ralph Chaplin Papers. Special Collections Research Center, University of Michigan, Ann Arbor, Michigan.

Ralph Chaplin Papers. Washington State Historical Society, Tacoma, Washington.

Records of the National Office of the American Civil Liberties Union. Princeton University, Princeton, New Jersey, accessed via microfilm and Proquest History Vault.

U.S. Department of Justice. Investigative Files, Part I: Industrial Workers of the World. Accessed via Proquest History Vault.

U.S. Department of Justice. Investigative Files, Part II: Communist Party. Accessed via ProQuest History Vault.

U.S. Department of Justice. Investigative Files, Part III: The Use of Military Force by the Federal Government in Domestic Disturbances, 1900-1938. Accessed via Proquest History Vault.

U.S. Department of Labor. Records of the President's Mediation Commission. Accessed via Proquest History Vault.

U.S. Military Intelligence Reports: Surveillance of Radicals, 1917–1941. Accessed via ProQuest History Vault.

Washington State Penitentiary. Commitment Registers. Washington State Archives. Olympia, Washington.

STATUTES, BILLS, AND ORDINANCE
Federal Statutes

Espionage Act of 1917. Public Law 65-24, *U.S. Statutes at Large* 40 (1917): 217–31.

Espionage Act. S.2, 55th Congress (1917).

Espionage Act. H.R. 291, 55th Congress (1917).

Lever Food and Fuel Control Act of 1917. Public Law 65-41, *U.S. Statutes at Large* 40 (1917): 276–87.

Sedition Act of 1918. Public Law 65-160, *U.S. Statutes at Large* 40 (1918): 553–54.

State Statutes

California: Act of Apr. 30, 1919, ch. 382, §§ 1–4. California Session Laws, Criminal Syndicalism.

Kansas: Act of Apr. 3, 1917, ch. 167, §§ 1–3. Kansas Session Laws 1917, Vagrancy.

Kansas: Act of Jan. 31, 1920, ch. 37. Kansas Session Laws 1920, Criminal Syndicalism.

Idaho: Act of Mar. 14, 1917, ch. 145, §§ 1–4. Idaho Session Laws 1917, Criminal Syndicalism.

Idaho: Act of Feb. 21, 1925, ch. 51, §§ 1–4. Idaho Session Laws 1925, Criminal Syndicalism.

Minnesota: Act of Apr. 13, 1917, ch. 215, §§ 1–4. Minnesota Session Laws 1917, Criminal Syndicalism.

Montana: Act of Feb. 21, 1918, ch. 11, § 1. Montana Extraordinary Session Laws 1918, Sedition.

Oregon: Act of Feb. 3, 1919, ch. 12, §§ 1–4. Oregon Session Laws 1919 Criminal Syndicalism.

North Dakota: Act of Jan. 30, 1918, ch. 12, § 1. North Dakota Special Session Laws 1918, Sabotage.

Washington: Act of Mar. 19, 1919, ch. 174, § 1. Washington Session Laws 1919, Criminal Syndicalism.

Local Ordinance
Title I, § 23. Fargo, ND, Charter and Ordinances, 1908, Vagrancy.

PUBLISHED JUDICIAL OPINIONS
U.S. Court Cases
Abrams v. United States, 215 U.S. 616 (1919).
Anderson v. United States, 269 F. 65 (9th Cir. 1921).
Anderson v. United States 273 F. 20 (8th Cir. 1921).
Brandenburg v. Ohio, 395 U.S. 444 (1969).
Bryant et al. v. United States, 257 F. 378 (5th Cir. 1919).
Burns v. United States, 274 U.S. 328 (1927).
De Jonge v. Oregon, 299 U.S. 353 (1937).
Debs v. United States, 249 U.S. 211 (1919).
Dennis v. United States, 183 F.2d 201 (2d Cir. 1950).
Dennis v. United States, 341 U.S. 494 (1951).
Dunne v. United States, 138 F.2d 137 (8th Cir. 1943).
Fiske v. Kansas, 274 U.S. 380 (1927).
Gitlow v. New York, 258 U.S. 652 (1925).
Haywood v. United States, 268 F. 795 (7th Cir. 1920).
Herndon v. Lowry, 301 U.S. 242 (1937).
Kumpula v United States, 261 F. 49 (9th Cir. 1920).
Papachristou v. City of Jacksonville, 405 U.S. 156 (1972).
Schenck v. United States, 249 U.S. 47 (1919).
Stromberg v. California, 283 U.S. 359 (1931).
United States v. Wheeler, 245 U.S. 281 (1920).
Whitney v. California, 274 U.S. 357 (1927).

State Court Cases

State v. Starr, 113 P.2d 356 (Ariz. 1941).

Ex parte Wood, 227 P. 908 (Cal. 1924).

People v. Bailey, 225 P. 752 (Cal. Dist. App. 1924).

People v. Casdorf, 212 P. 237 (Cal. Dist. Ct. App. 1922).

People v. Cox, 226 P. 14 (Cal. Dist. Ct. App. 1924).

People v. Eaton, 213 P. 275 (Cal. Dist. Ct. App. 1923).

People v. Erickson, 226 P. 637 (Cal. Dist. Ct. App. 1924).

People v. Leonard, 225 P. 461 (Cal. Dist. Ct. App. 1924).

People v. Lesse, 199 P. 46, 47 (Cal. Dist. Ct. App. 1921).

People v. Malley, 194 P.48 (Ca. Dist. Ct. App. 1920).

People v. McClennegen, 234 P. 91 (Cal. 1925).

People v. Mintz, 290 P. 93 (Cal. Dist. Ct. App. 1930).

People v. Powell, 236 P. 311(Cal. Dist. Ct. App. 1925).

People v. Roe, 209 P. 381 (Cal. Dist. Ct. App. 1922).

People v. Schoon, 171 P. 680 (Cal. 1918).

People v. Steelik [*sic*], 203 P. 78 (Cal. 1921).

People v. Stewart, 230 P. 221 (Cal. Dist. Ct. App. 1924).

People v. Sullivan, 211 P. 467 (Cal. Dist. Ct. App. 1922).

People v. Taylor, 203 P. 85 (Cal. 1921).

People v. Thompson, 229 P. 896 (Cal. Dist. Ct. App. 1924).

People v. Thornton, 219 P. 1020 (Cal. Dist. Ct. App. 1923).

People v. Wagner, 225 P. 464 (Cal. Dist. Ct. App. 1924).

People v. Wieler, 204 P. 410 (Cal. Dist. Ct. App. 1921).

People v. Wismer, 209 P. 259 (Cal. Dist. Ct. App. 1922).

Ex parte Moore, 224 P. 662 (Idaho 1924).

In re Hostede, 173 P. 1087 (Idaho 1918).

State v. Dingman, 219 P. 760 (Idaho 1923).

State v. Tonn, 191 N.W. 530 (Iowa 1923).

Ex Parte Clancy, 210 P. 487 (Kan. 1922).

In re Danton, 195 P. 981 (Kan. 1921).

State v. Breen, 205 P. 632 (Kan. 1922).

State v. Dilgar, 208 P. 620 (Kan. 1922).

State v. Fiske, 230 P. 88 (Kan. 1924).

State v. Murphy, 212 P. 654 (Kan. 1923).

State v. McCormick, 77 So. 288 (La. 1918).

State v. Moilen, 167 N.W. 345 (Minn. 1918).

State v. Workers' Socialist Publishing Company, 185 N.W. 931 (Minn. 1921).

Ex Parte Branch, 137 S.W. 886 (Mo. 1911).

Ex Parte Karnstrom, 249 S.W. 595 (Mo. 1923).

Ex Parte Taft, 225 S.W. 457 (Mont. 920).

State v. Dunn, 57 Mont. 591 (Mont. 1920).

State v. Griffith, 184 P. 219 (Mont. 1918).

State v. Smith, 109 P. 107 (Mont. 1920).

State v. Boyd, 91 A. 586 (N.J. 1914).

State v. Gabriel, 112 A. 611 (N.J. 1919).

State v. Tachin, 106 A. 145 (N.J. 1919).

State v. Tachin, 108 A. 318 (N.J. Ct. of Err. & App. 1919).
State v. Diamond, 202 P. 988 (N.M. 1921).
State v. Berg, 233 P. 497 (Okla. Ct. Crim. App. 1925).
Ex parte Strittmatter, 124 S.W. 906 (Tex. Cr. App. 1910).
City of Spokane v. Grady, 105 P. 1043 (Wash. 1921).
Ex parte Parent, 192 P. 947 (Wash. 1920).
In re Smith, 233 P. 288 (Wash. 1925).
Lindsley v. Grady, 199 P. 980 (Wash. 1921).
Lindsley v. Wallace, 195 P. 1049 (Wash. 1921).
State v. Aspelin, 203 P. 964 (Wash. 1922).
State v. Hennessy, 195 P. 211 (Wash. 1921).
State v. McLennen, 200 P. 319 (Wash. 1921).
State v. Smith et al., 197 P.770 (Wash. 1921).

TRANSCRIPTS AND COURT CASE MATERIALS
NOT ASSOCIATED WITH SPECIFIC ARCHIVAL
COLLECTIONS

Abstract of the Record. Fiske v. Kansas, 274 U.S. 380 (1925) (no. 305).
Appellant's Brief. Stromberg v. California, 283 U.S. 359 (1931) (no. 584).
Brief for Petitioners. Scales v. United States, 367 U.S. 203 (1958) (no. 665).
Brief for United States. Scales v. United States, 367 U.S. 203 (1958) (no. 665).
Plaintiff's Brief. Fiske v. Kansas. 274 U.S. 380 (1925) (no. 305).
Transcript of Record. Fiske v. Kansas, 274 U.S. 380 (1925) (no. 305).

PUBLISHED GOVERNMENT HEARINGS AND ADMINISTRATIVE
AND LEGISLATIVE DOCUMENTS

U.S. Government Documents
Annual Report of the U.S. Attorney General, 1919. Washington, D.C.: GPO, 1919.
Annual Report of the U.S. Attorney General, 1921. Washington, D.C.: GPO, 1921.
Annual Report of the U.S. Attorney General, 1923. Washington, D.C.: GPO, 1923.
Report of the President's Mediation Commission to the President of the United States. Washington, D.C.: GPO, 1918.
U.S. Bureau of the Census. *Historical Statistics of the United States, Colonial Times to 1957.* Washington, D.C.: GPO, 1960.
———. *Historical Statistics of the United States, Colonial Times to 1970.* Washington, D.C.: GPO, 1975.
———. *King County, Washington, Population Schedule, Seattle, ED 40-325, Sheet 6-B.* Washington, D.C.: GPO, 1940.
———. *Statistical Abstract of 1917.* Washington DC: GPO 1918.
———. *Statistical Abstract of 1918.* Washington DC: GPO, 1919.
U.S. Bureau of Corporations. *The Lumber Industry: Part 1, Standing Timber.* Washington, D.C.: GPO, 1913.

U.S. Commission on Industrial Relations. *Final Report.* 64th Congress, 1st Session. S. Doc. 415. Washington, D.C.: GPO, 1916.

U.S. Commission on Public Information. *Report of President Wilson's Mediation Commission on the Bisbee, Ariz., Deportation.* Bisbee, Ariz., November 5, 1917.

U.S. House of Representatives. Committee on Labor. *Hearings on Peonage in Western Pennsylvania.* 62nd Cong., 1st Session, 1911.

———. Committee on the Judiciary, *Hearings on Amnesty and Pardon for Political Prisoners.* 67th Congress, 2nd Session, 1922.

———. *55th Congressional Record,* 1917.

———. Special Committee on Un-American Activities. *Hearings on Un-American Propaganda Activities.* Vol. 1–3. 75st Congress, 3rd Session, 1938.

———. Special Committee on Un-American Activities. *Report of the Special Committee on Un-American Activities.* 76th Congress, 1st Session, 1939.

———. Subcommittee of the Committee on Immigration and Naturalization. *Hearings on I.W.W. Deportation Cases.* 66th Congress, 2nd Session, 1920.

———. Subcommittee of the Select Committee on Expenditures. *Hearings on War Expenditures, Volume 2,* 66th Congress, 1st Session, 1919.

U.S. Senate. Committee on Education and Labor. *Employers' Associations and Collective Bargaining in California.* Report No. 1150, Pt. 2. 77th Congress, 2nd Session, 1942.

———. *55th Congressional Record,* 1917.

———. *Government Prosecutions under the Espionage Act.* 67th Congress, 2nd Session, 1922.

———. *Report on Strike of Textile Workers in Lawrence, Massachusetts in 1912.* 62nd Congress, 2nd Session, 1912.

———. Subcommittee of the Committee on the Judiciary. *Hearings on Amnesty and Pardon for Political Prisoners.* 66th Congress, 3rd Session, 1921.

———. *Violations of Free Speech and the Rights of Labor: Private Police Systems.* Report No. 6, pt. 2. 76th Congress, 1st Session, 1939.

State Documents

Biennial Report of the State Board of Prison Directors of the State of California, Fiscal Years 1921–1922. San Quentin, CA: San Quentin Press, 1922.

Report of the Attorney General to the Governor of the State of Minnesota, 1917–1918. Minneapolis, MN: Syndicate Printing Company, 1918.

Report of the Attorney General to the Governor of the State of Minnesota, 1919–1920. Minneapolis, MN: Syndicate Printing Company, 1920.

Twenty-Fifth Biennial Report of the Attorney General of Kansas, 1921–1922. Topeka: Kansas State Printing Plant, 1922.

NEWSPAPERS

Labor and Related Publications

Daily Worker

Industrial Pioneer

Industrial Solidarity
Industrial Worker
New Solidarity
Northwest Worker
One Big Union Monthly
Solidarity

Other Newspapers
Aberdeen (South Dakota) *Daily News*
Aberdeen (South Dakota) *Journal*
Abilene (Kansas) *Daily Reflector*
Albany (Oregon) *Evening Herald*
Athena (Oregon) *Daily Press*
Alton (Kansas) *Empire*
Anaconda (Montana) *Standard*
Anthony (Kansas) *Bulletin*
Ashland (Oregon) *Tidings*
Atwater (California) *Signal*
Augusta (Kansas) *Daily Gazette*
Bakersfield Californian
Bemidji (Minnesota) *Daily Pioneer*
Bisbee (Arizona) *Review*
Bismarck (North Dakota) *Tribune*
Blackwell (Oklahoma) *Journal-Tribune*
Boise Evening Capital News
Boise Idaho Statesman
Bonners Ferry (Idaho) *Herald*
Brainerd (Minnesota) *Daily Dispatch*
Butte (Montana) *Daily Bulletin*
Butte (Montana) *Miner*
Caldwell (Idaho) *Tribune*
Chicago Daily Tribune
Chickasha (Oklahoma) *Daily Express*
Daily (Missoula, MT) *Missoulian*
Duluth (Minnesota) *Labor World*
Duluth (Minnesota) *News-Tribune*
Emporia (Kansas) *Gazette*
Eugene (Oregon) *Morning Register*
Everett (Washington) *Labor Journal*
Fargo (North Dakota) *Forum and Daily Republican*
Feather River (California) *Bulletin*
Fort Worth Star-Telegram
Grand Forks (North Dakota) *Herald*
Great Falls (Montana) *Tribune*
Guthrie (Oklahoma) *Daily Leader*
Hays (Kansas) *Free Press*

Helena (Montana) *Independent Record*
Heppner (Oregon) *Gazette-Times*
Hutchinson (Kansas) *Gazette*
Hutchinson (Kansas) *News*
Janesville (Wisconsin) *Daily Gazette*
Kendrick (Idaho) *Gazette*
Klamath Falls (Oregon) *Evening Herald*
Leavenworth (Kansas) *Times*
Lincoln (Nebraska) *Star Journal*
Los Angeles Herald
Los Angeles Times
Medford (Oregon) *Mail Tribune*
Minneapolis Morning Tribune
Minot (North Dakota) *Daily News*
Modesto (California) *Bee*
Morning Tulsa Daily World
New York Times
New York Tribune
Oakland Tribune
Pendleton East Oregonian
Portland Oregon Daily Journal
Portland Oregonian
Pratt (Kansas) *Daily Tribune*
Reno (Nevada) *Gazette-Journal*
Roseburg (Oregon) *News-Review*
Sacramento Bee
Sacramento Union
Salinas Californian
Santa Ana (California) *Register*
Shreveport (Louisiana) *Times*
St. John (Kansas) *Daily News*
St. Louis Post-Dispatch
Salem (Oregon) *Daily Capital Journal*
Salem (Oregon) *Statesman Journal*
Salina (Kansas) *Evening Journal*
San Francisco Examiner
Santa Rosa (California) *Press Democrat*
Seattle Daily Times
Seattle Star
Sioux Falls (South Dakota) *Argus-Leader*
Spearfish (South Dakota) *Queen City Mail*
Spokane (Washington) *Daily Chronicle*
Spokane (Washington) *Spokesman-Review*
Spokane (Washington) *Weekly Spokesman*
Sterling (Kansas) *Bulletin*
Tacoma (Washington) *Daily Ledger*
Topeka (Kansas) *Capital Journal*

Trego County (Kansas) *Reporter*
Tulsa Democrat
Ward County (North Dakota) *Independent*
Washburn (North Dakota) *Leader*
Olympia (Washington) Standard
Washington Post
Wellington (Kansas) *Monitor-Press*
Westphalia (Kansas) *Times*
Wichita Beacon
Wichita Daily Eagle
Wichita Daily Stockman

INTERNET SITES

Industrial Workers of the World. "Chronology of IWW History." https:// archive.iww.org/history/chronology/.

University of Washington. "IWW History Project: Industrial Workers of the World 1905–1935." https://depts.washington.edu/iww/.

University of Montana, "Montana Sedition Project." http://www.seditionproject .net/.

Washington Secretary of State. "Washington State Archive: Digital Archives." https://www.digitalarchives.wa.gov.

DISSERTATIONS AND THESES

Campbell-Hale, Leigh. "Remembering Ludlow but Forgetting the Columbine: The 1927–1928 Colorado Coal Strike." PhD diss., University of Colorado–Boulder, 2013.

Cline, Mildred. "A Study of Criminal Syndicalism in Oregon." BA thesis, Reed College, 1933.

Cohen, Michael Mark. "'The Conspiracy of Capital': American Popular Radicalism and the Politics of Conspiracy." PhD diss., Yale University, 2004.

Daley, Shawn. "Centralia, Collective Memory, and the Tragedy of 1919." MA thesis, Portland State University, 1995.

Daly, Leo. "Freedom of Speech as Guaranteed by the Constitution of the State of California in Relation to the Criminal Syndicalism Law." LLM thesis, University of Southern California, 1926.

Dowell, Eldridge Foster. "A History of the Enactment of Criminal Syndicalism Legislation in the United States." PhD diss., Johns Hopkins University, Baltimore, 1936.

Dreyfus, Philip Jacques. "Toward Industrial Organization: Timber Workers, Unionism and Syndicalism in the Pacific Northwest, 1900–1917." PhD diss., CUNY, 1993.

England, Shawn L. "Anarchy, Anarcho-Magonismo, and the Mexican Peasant: The Evolution of Ricardo Flores Magon's Revolutionary Philosophy." MA thesis, University of Calgary, 1995.

Evans, Robert. "Montana's Role in the Enactment of Legislation Designed to Suppress the Industrial Workers of the World." MA thesis, Montana State University, 1964.

Goings, Aaron. "Red Harbor: Class, Violence, and Community in Grays Harbor, Washington." PhD diss., Simon Fraser University, 2011.

Gutfeld, Aaron. "Years of Hysteria, Montana, 1917–1921: A Study in Local Intolerance." PhD diss., University of California, Los Angeles, 1971.

Higbie, Frank Tobias. "Indispensable Outcasts: Seasonal Laborers and Community in the Upper Midwest, 1880–1930." PhD diss., University of Illinois, Urbana-Champaign, 2000.

Lossin, Rebecca. "The Point of Destruction: Sabotage, Speech, and Progressive-Era Politics." PhD diss., Columbia University, 2020.

Peterson, Nicholas. "A Rip in the Social Fabric: Revolution, Industrial Workers of the World, and the Paterson Silk Strike of 1913 in American Literature, 1908–1927." PhD diss., Temple University, 2011.

Pommer, Geoffrey. "The Political Use of the Conspiracy Charge in America," PhD diss., NYU, 1976.

Sellars, Nigel Anthony. "Oil, wheat, and Wobblies: The Industrial Workers of the World in Oklahoma, 1905–1930." PhD diss., Oklahoma State University, 1994.

Shaffer, Ralph. "Radicalism in California, 1869–1929." PhD diss., University of California, 1965.

Weintraub, Hyman. "The I.W.W. in California: 1905–1931" MA thesis, University of California, Los Angeles, 1947.

White, Earl Bruce. "The Wichita Indictments and Trial of the Industrial Workers of the World, 1917–1919." PhD diss., University of Colorado, 1980.

BOOKS

Adler, William M. *The Man Who Never Died: The Life, Times, and Legacy of Joe Hill, American Labor Icon*. New York: Bloomsbury Press, 2011.

Allen, Ruth A. *East Texas Lumber Workers: An Economic and Social Picture, 1870–1950*. Austin: University of Texas Press, 1961.

American Civil Liberties Union Annual Report No. 2. New York: ACLU, 1923.

American Civil Liberties Union Annual Report No. 3. New York: ACLU, 1924.

American Civil Liberties Union Annual Report No. 4. New York: ACLU, 1925.

American Civil Liberties Union Annual Report No. 5. New York: ACLU, 1926.

American Civil Liberties Union Annual Report No. 6. New York: ACLU, 1927.

American Labor Yearbook, 1919–1920. New York: Rand, 1920.

American Labor Yearbook, 1923–1924. New York: Rand, 1924.

An Open Letter to President Harding from 52 Members of the I.W.W. at Leavenworth. Chicago: General Defense Committee, 1922.

Anderson, Nels. *The Hobo: The Sociology of the Homeless Man*. Chicago: University of Chicago Press, 1922.

Ashleigh, Charles. *The Rambling Kid: A Novel about the IWW*. New York: Charles H. Kerr, 2004.

The Autobiography of Big Bill Haywood. New York: International Publishers, 1977.

Barrett, James R. *William Z. Foster and the Tragedy of American Radicalism.* Urbana: University of Illinois Press, 1999.

Belknap, Michal R. *Cold War Political Justice: The Smith Act, the Communist Party, and American Civil Liberties.* Westport, CT: Greenwood Press, 1977.

Bird, Stewart, et al., eds. *Solidarity Forever: An Oral History of the IWW.* Chicago: Lake View Press, 1985.

Blum, Howard. *Dark Invasion: 1915: Germany's Secret War and the Hunt for the First Terrorist Cell in America.* New York: Harper, 2014.

Botkin, Jane Little. *Frank Little and the IWW: The Blood That Stained a Family.* Norman: University of Oklahoma Press, 2017.

———. *The Girl Who Dared to Defy: Jane Street and the Rebel Maids of Denver.* Norman: University of Oklahoma Press, 2021.

Brissenden, Paul F. *The I.W.W.: A Study of American Syndicalism.* New York: Columbia University Press, 1919.

———. *The Launching of the Industrial Workers of the World.* New York: Johnson Reprint Group, 1966.

Brody, David. *Labor in Crisis: The Steel Strike of 1919.* Urbana: University of Illinois Press, 1965.

———. *Workers in Industrial America: Essays on the Twentieth Century Struggle.* New York: Oxford, 1980.

Byrkit, James W. *Forging the Copper Collar: Arizona's Labor-Management War of 1901–1921.* Tucson: University of Arizona Press, 1982.

The California Criminal Syndicalism Law: A Factual Analysis. San Francisco: The California Crusaders, 1936.

Carlson, Peter. *Roughneck: The Life and Times of Big Bill Haywood.* New York: W.W. Norton, 1983.

Chafee, Zechariah, Jr. *Free Speech in the United States.* Cambridge, MA: Harvard University Press, 1954.

Chaplin, Ralph. *American Labor's Case against Communism: How the Operations of Stalin's Red Quislings Look from Inside the Labor Movement.* Seattle: Educator Publishing, 1947.

———. *The Prison Poems.* New York: Leonard Press, 1922.

———. *Wobbly: The Rough-and-Tumble Story of an American Radical.* Chicago: University of Chicago Press, 1948.

Chester, Eric Thomas. *The Wobblies in Their Heyday.* Santa Barbara, CA: Praeger, 2014.

Clymer, Jeffory A. *America's Culture of Terrorism: Violence, Capitalism, and the Written Word.* Chapel Hill: University of North Carolina Press, 2003.

Cohen, Michael. *The Conspiracy of Capital: Law, Violence, and American Popular Radicalism in the Age of Monopoly.* Amherst: University of Massachusetts Press, 2019.

Cole, Peter, et al. *Wobblies of the World: A Global History of the IWW.* London: Pluto, 2017.

———. *Wobblies on the Waterfront: Interracial Unionism in Progressive-Era Philadelphia.* Chicago: University of Illinois Press, 2013.

Conlin, Joseph R., ed. *At the Point of Production: The Local History of the I.W.W.* Westport, CT: Greenwood, 1981.

The Cook County Jail Survey. Chicago: Chicago Community Trust, 1922.

Copeland, Tom. *The Centralia Tragedy of 1919: Elmer Smith and the Wobblies.* Seattle: University of Washington Press, 1993.

Cottrell, Robert C. *Roger Nash Baldwin and the American Civil Liberties Union.* New York: Columbia University Press, 2001.

De Caux, Len, *Labor Radical: From the Wobblies to the CIO.* New York: Beacon, 1970.

Depastino, Todd. *Citizen Hobo: How a Century of Homelessness Shaped America.* Chicago: University of Chicago Press, 2003.

Douglas, William O. *Go East, Young Man: The Early Years.* New York: Vintage, 1974.

Dowell, Eldridge Foster. *A History of Criminal Syndicalism Legislation in the United States.* Baltimore, MD: Johns Hopkins University Press, 1939.

Draper, Theodore. *The Roots of American Communism.* New York: Viking, 1957.

Dreiser, Theodore. *Sister Carrie.* New York: B. W. Dodge & Company, 1907.

Dubofsky, Melvyn. *Industrialism and the American Worker, 1865–1920.* Arlington Heights, IL: H. Davidson, 1985.

———. *We Shall Be All: A History of the Industrial Workers of the World.* Urbana: University of Illinois Press, 1969.

Engstrom, Emil. *The Vanishing Logger.* New York: Vantage, 1956.

Fishman, Joseph F. *Crucibles of Crime: The Shocking Story of the American Jail.* New York: Cosmopolis, 1923.

Flynn, Elizabeth Gurley. *Memories of the Industrial Workers of the World.* New York: Institute for Marxist Studies, 1977.

———. *The Rebel Girl: An Autobiography.* New York: International, 1955.

———. *Sabotage.* Chicago: IWW, 1917.

Flynt, Josiah. *Tramping with Tramps.* New York: Century, 1899.

Foner, Philip S. *Fellow Workers and Friends: IWW Free Speech Fights as Told by Participants.* Westport, CT: Greenwood Press, 1981.

———. *The Industrial Workers of the World.* New York: International, 1965.

Forrant, Robert, and Jurg Siegenthaler, eds., *The Great Lawrence Textile Strike of 1912: New Scholarship on the Bread and Roses Strike.* New York: Routledge, 2016.

Foster, James C., ed. *American Labor in the Southwest.* Tucson: University of Arizona Press.

Founding Convention of the IWW: Proceedings. New York: Merit Publishers, 1969.

Gambs, John S. *The Decline of the I.W.W.* New York: Russell and Russell, 1966.

Goings, Aaron. *The Port of Missing Men: Billy Gohl, Labor, and Brutal Times in the Pacific Northwest.* Seattle: University of Washington Press, 2020.

Golin, Steve. *The Fragile Bridge: The Paterson Silk Strike, 1913.* Philadelphia: Temple University Press, 1992.

Golubuff, Risa. *Vagrant Nation: Police Power, Constitutional Change, and the Making of the 1960s.* New York: Oxford University Press, 2016.

Greene, Julie. *Pure and Simple Politics: The American Federation of Labor and Political Activism, 1881–1917.* New York: Cambridge University Press, 1998.

Gunns, Albert F. *Civil Liberties in Crisis: The Pacific Northwest, 1917–1920.* New York: Garland Press, 1983.

Gutman, Herbert G. *Work, Culture, and Society in Industrializing America.* New York: Vintage, 1977.

Hall, Greg. *Harvest Wobblies: The Industrial Workers of the World and Agricultural Workers in the American West, 1905–1930.* Corvallis: Oregon State University Press, 2001.

Hammett, Dashiell. *Red Harvest.* New York: Vintage, 1989.

Hawley, Lowell S., and Ralph Bushnell Potts. *Counsel for the Damned: A Biography of George Francis Vanderveer.* Philadelphia: J.B. Lippincott, 1953.

Higbie, Frank Tobias. *Indispensable Outcasts: Hobo Workers and Community in the American Midwest, 1880–1930.* Urbana: University of Illinois Press, 2003.

Hodges, Adam. *World War I and Urban Order: The Local Class Politics of National Mobilization.* New York: Palgrave Macmillan, 2015.

Industrial Workers of the World, *The Lumber Industry and Its Workers.* 3d ed. Chicago: IWW, 1921.

Inmates of the Idaho State Penitentiary, 1864–1947. Boise: Idaho Historical Society, 2008.

Isern, Thomas D. *Bull Threshers and Bindlestiffs: Harvesting and Threshing on the North American Plains.* Lawrence: University of Kansas Press, 1990.

Johnson, Jeffrey J. *The 1916 Preparedness Day Bombing: Anarchy and Terrorism in Progressive Era America.* New York: Routledge, 2017.

Johnson, Victoria. *How Many Machine Guns Does It Take to Cook One Meal? The Seattle and San Francisco General Strikes.* Seattle: University of Washington Press, 2008.

Johnson, Diane. *Dashiell Hammett: A Life .* New York: Random House, 1983.

Jones, James. *From Here to Eternity.* New York: Dial Press, 2012.

Kaunonen, Gary. *Flames of Discontent: The 1916 Minnesota Iron Ore Strike.* Minneapolis: University of Minnesota, 1917.

Kazin, Alfred. *On Native Grounds: An Interpretation of Modern American Prose Literature.* New York: Reynal and Hitchcock, 1942.

Kelly, Desmond. *The Elimination of the Tramp.* New York: Putnam and Sons, 1908.

Kershaw, Alex. *Jack London: A Life.* New York: St. Martin's Press, 1999.

Kimeldorf, Howard. *Reds or Rackets: The Making of Radical and Conservative Unions on the Waterfront.* Berkeley: University of California Press, 1988.

Otto Kirchheimer, *Political Justice: The Use of Legal Procedure for Political Ends*: Princeton, NJ: Princeton University Press, 1961.

Kirchwey, George W. *A Survey of the Workings of the Criminal Syndicalism Law of California.* Los Angeles: ACLU, 1926.

Kramer, Jacob. *The New Freedom and the Radicals: Woodrow Wilson, Progressive Views of Radicals, and the Origins of Repressive Tolerance.* Philadelphia: Temple University Press, 2015.

Kohn, Stephen M. *American Political Prisoners: Prosecutions under the Espionage and Sedition Acts*. Westport, CT: Praeger, 1994.

Labor, Earle, et al., eds., *The Letters of Jack London, Volume Three: 1913–1916*. Stanford, CA: Stanford University Press, 1988.

Laidler, Harry W. *History of Socialism*. New York: Crowell, 1968.

Lane, Winthrop. *Uncle Sam, Jailer: A Study of the Conditions of Federal Prisoners in Kansas Jails*. New York: National Civil Liberties Union, 1919.

Lansing, Michael. *The Nonpartisan League in North Dakota Politics*. Chicago: University of Chicago Press, 2015.

Laslett, John H. *Sunshine Was Never Enough: Los Angeles Workers, 1880–2010*. Berkeley: University of California Press, 2012.

Laubach, Frank C. *Why There Are Vagrants*. New York: Columbia University Press, 1916.

Laurie, Clayton D., and Cole, Ronald D. *The Role of Federal Forces in Domestic Disorders, 1877–1945*. Washington, D.C.: Center of Military History, 1997.

Leiter, Robert. *The Teamsters Union: A Study of its Economic Impact*. New York: Bookman Associates, 1957.

Lescohier, D.D. *The Labor Market*. New York: Macmillan, 1919.

London, Jack. *The Iron Heel*. Orinda, CA: SeaWolf Press, 2017.

———. *The Road*. New Brunswick, NJ: Rutgers University Press, 2006.

———. *War of the Classes*. Orinda, CA: SeaWolf Press, 2018.

———. *What Life Means to Me, in Revolution*. Orinda, CA: SeaWolf Press, 2018.

London, Joan. *Jack London and His Times*. New York: Doubleday, 1939.

Loomis, Erik. *Empire of Timber: Labor Unions and the Pacific Northwest Forests*. New York: Cambridge University Press, 2015.

Lukas, Anthony. Big Trouble: *A Murder in a Small Town Sets Off a Struggle for the Soul of America*. New York: Simon and Schuster, 1997.

May, Mathew. *Soapbox Rebellion: The Hobo Orator Union and the Free Speech Fights of the Industrial Workers of the World, 1909–1916*. Tuscaloosa: University of Alabama Press, 2013.

Mayer, Heather. *Beyond the Rebel Girl: Women and the Industrial Workers of the World in the Pacific Northwest, 1905–1924*. Corvallis: Oregon State University Press, 2018.

McGerr, Michael. *A Fierce Discontent: The Rise and Fall of the Progressive Movement in America*. New York: Oxford University Press, 2003.

The Memoirs of Earl Warren. New York: Doubleday, 1977.

Murphy, Paul L. *World War I and the Origin of Civil Liberties in the United States*. New York: W.W. Norton and Company, 1978.

Murray, Robert K. *Red Scare: A Study in National Hysteria, 1919–1920*. New York: McGraw-Hill, 1955.

National Industrial Conference Board. *Strikes in American Industry in Wartime, April 6 to October 6, 1917*. Boston: National Industrial Conference Board, 1918.

Neumann, Franz L. *Behemoth: The Structure and Practice of National Socialism, 1933-1944*: Chicago: Ivan R. Dee, 2009.

Olmsted, Kathryn S. *Right Out of California: The 1930s the Big Business Roots of Modern Conservatism*. New York: New Press, 2015.

Palmer, Bryan D. *James P. Cannon and the Origins of the American Revolutionary Left, 1890–1928.* Urbana: University of Illinois Press, 2010.

Parker, Carlton. *The California Casual.* New York: Harcourt, Brace and Howe, 1920.

———. *The Casual Laborer and Other Essays.* New York: Harcourt, Brace and Howe, 1920.

Pearson, Chad. *Reform or Repression: Organizing America's Anti-Union Movement.* Philadelphia: University of Pennsylvania Press, 2016.

Perlman, Selig. *A Theory of the Labor Movement.* New York: Macmillan, 1923.

Perry, Louis B., and Richard S. Perry, *A History of the Los Angeles Labor Movement, 1911–1941.* Berkeley: University of California Press, 1963.

Pietrusza, David. *Judge and Jury: The Life and Times of Judge Kennesaw Mountain Landis.* Providence, RI: Taylor Trade Publishing, 2001.

Polenberg, Richard. *Fighting Faiths: The Abrams Case, The Supreme Court, and Free Speech.* Ithaca, NY: Cornell University Press, 1999.

Pouget, Émile. *Sabotage.* Chicago: Charles H. Kerr, 1913.

Preston, William, Jr. *Aliens and Dissenters: Federal Suppression of Radicals, 1903–1933.* Cambridge, MA: Harvard University Press, 1963.

Proceedings of the National Convention of the Socialist Party, 1912. Chicago: Socialist Party, 1912.

Queen, Stuart Alfred. *The Passing of the County Jail.* Menasha, WI: Banta, 1920.

Ross, Jack. *The Socialist Party of America: A Complete History.* Lincoln, NE: Potomac Books, 2015.

Salerno, Salvatore. *Red November, Black November: Culture and Community in the Industrial Workers of the World.* Albany: SUNY Press, 1989.

Salgado, Sebastião. *An Uncertain Grace.* New York: Aperture, 2005.

Scheuerman, William E., ed. *The Rule of Law under Siege: Selected Essays of Franz L. Neumann and Otto Kirchheimer.* Berkeley, CA: University of California Press, 1996.

Schmidt, James D. *Industrial Violence and the Legal Origins of Child Labor.* New York: Cambridge University Press, 2010.

Schneider, Betty and Seigel, Abraham. *Industrial Relations in the Pacific Coast Longshore Industry.* Berkeley, CA: Institute of Industrial Relations, 1956.

Sellars, Nigel Anthony. *Oil, Wheat and Wobblies: The Industrial Workers of the World in Oklahoma, 1905–1930.* Norman: University of Oklahoma Press, 1998.

The Silent Defense. Chicago: IWW, n.d.

Silvano, John, ed. *Nothing in Common: An Oral History of IWW Strikes, 1971–1992.* Cedar Rapids, IA: Cedar Publishing, 1999.

Smith, Walker, C. *The Everett Massacre: A History of the Class Struggle in the Lumber Industry.* Chicago: IWW, 1917.

———. *Sabotage: Its History, Philosophy, and Function.* Chicago: Solidarity Bookshop, 1913.

Sterling, George. *Selected Poems.* New York: Henry Holt and Company, 1923.

Stevenson, Archibald E., ed. *Revolutionary Radicalism: Its History, Purpose and Tactics with an Exposition and Discussion of the Steps Being Taken and Required to Curb It.* Albany, NY: Lyon, 1920.

Stormquist, Shelton. *Re-inventing "The People": The Progressive Movement, the Class Problem, and the Origins of Modern Liberalism.* Urbana: University of Illinois Press, 2006.

Strang, Dean A. *Keep the Wretches in Order: America's Biggest Mass Trial, the Rise of the Justice Department, and the Fall of the IWW.* Madison: University of Wisconsin Press, 2019.

Struthers, David M. *The World in a City: Multiethnic Radicalism in Early Twentieth-Century Los Angeles.* Urbana: University of Illinois Press, 2019.

Thompson, Fred. *The I.W.W.: Its First Fifty Years.* Chicago: IWW, 1955.

Traven, B. *The Cotton-Pickers.* Chicago: Ivan R. Dee, 1995.

Tripp, Anne Huber. *The I.W.W. and the Paterson Silk Strike of 1913.* Urbana: University of Illinois Press, 1987.

Trotsky, Leon. *My Life.* London: Scribner, 1930.

The Truth about the I.W.W. Prisoners. New York: ACLU, 1918.

Tyler, Robert L. *Rebels of the Woods: The IWW in the Pacific Northwest.* Eugene: University of Oregon Press, 1967.

Vapnek, Lara. *Elizabeth Gurley Flynn, Modern American Revolutionary.* New York: Taylor and Francis, 2015.

Voss, Kim. *The Making of American Exceptionalism: The Knights of Labor and Class Formation in the Nineteenth Century.* Ithaca, NY: Cornell, 1994.

War-Time Prosecutions and Mob Violence. New York: National Civil Liberties Bureau, 1919.

Weinstein, James. *The Decline of Socialism in America, 1912–1925.* New York: Vintage, 1967.

Witcover, Jules. *Sabotage at Black Tom: Imperial Germany's Secret War in America, 1914–1917.* Chapel Hill, NC: Algonquin Books, 1989.

Work, Clemens. *Darkest before Dawn: Sedition and Free Speech in the American West.* Albuquerque: University of New Mexico Press, 2005.

Wyman, Mark. *Hoboes: Bindlestiffs, Fruit Tramps, and the Harvesting of the West.* New York: Hill and Wang, 2010.

Zanjani, Sally, and Guy Louis Rocha. *The Ignoble Conspiracy: Radicalism on Trial in Nevada.* Reno: University of Nevada Press, 1986.

Zumoff, Jacob A. *The Communist International and US Communism, 1919–1929.* Chicago, IL: Haymarket Books, 2014.

PERIODICALS AND BOOK CHAPTERS

"Accidents in the Logging Industry of Oregon." *Monthly Labor Review* 15 (1922): 148–49.

Adamic, Louis. "Sabotage." *Harper's Monthly Magazine,* Jan. 1931.

Appleman, Roy. "Timber Empire from the Public Domain." *Mississippi Valley Historical Review* 26, no. 2 (1939): 193–208.

"Arouse, Ye Slaves." In *Debs: His Life, Writings and Speeches,* 309–11. Chicago: Charles H. Kerr, 1908.

Atack, Jeremy, et al. "Skill Intensity and Rising Wage Dispersion in Nineteenth-Century American Manufacturing." *Journal of Economic History* 64, no. 1 (2004): 172–92.

Belknap, Michael. "Uncooperative Federalism: The Failure of the Bureau of Investigation's Intergovernmental Attack on Radicalism." *Publius* 12, no. 2 (Spring 1982): 25–47.

Berliner, Jonathan. "Jack London's Socialistic Social Darwinism." *American Literary Realism* 41, no. 1 (Fall 2008): 52–78.

Betten, Neil. "Riot Revolution, Repression in the Iron Range Strike of 1916." *Minnesota History* 41 (Summer 1968): 82.

———. "Strike on the Mesabi—1907." *Minnesota History* 40 (Fall 1967): 340-47.

Biggs, Michael. "Strikes as Sequences of Interaction: The American Strike Wave of 1886." *Social Science History* 26, no. 3 (Fall 2002): 583–617.

Blasi, Vincent. "The First Amendment and the Ideal of Civic Courage." *William and Mary Law Review* 29, no. 4 (1988): 653–97.

Bloustein, Edward J. "The First Amendment 'Bad Tendency' of Speech Doctrine." *Rutgers Law Review* 43, no. 3 (Spring 1991): 507–38.

Brazier, Richard. "The Mass I.W.W. Trial of 1918: A Retrospect." *Labor History* 7, no. 2 (1966): 178–92.

Byrkit, James. "The Bisbee Deportation." In *American Labor in the Southwest,* edited by James C. Foster, 86–102. Tucson: University of Arizona Press.

Cannon, James P. "The I.W.W." *Fourth International* 16 (Summer 1955): 75

Chamberlain, William. "Russian Recollections." *Russian Review* 21, no. 4 (1962): 333–47.

Chaplin, Ralph. "Why I Wrote 'Solidarity Forever,' *American West* 5, no.1 (January 1968): 18.

Chester, Eric. "The Rise and Fall of the IWW: As Viewed through Membership Figures." *Anarcho-Syndicalist Review* 55 (Winter 2011): 13–18.

Christiano, Kevin J. "Labor Poet Ralph Chaplin: Resister to the 'Great War,' Prisoner of the 'Class War.'" *Journal for the Study of Radicalism* 14, no. 2 (2020): 157–82.

Cobble, Dorothy Sue. "Pure and Simple Radicalism: Putting the Progressive AFL in Its Time." *Labor* 10, no. 4 (2013): 61–87.

Cohen, Michael. "'The Ku Klux Government': Vigilantism, Lynching, and the Repression of the IWW." *Journal for the Study of Radicalism,* 1, no. 1 (Spring 2007): 31–56.

Collins, Ronald K.L., and David M. Skover. "Curious Concurrence: Justice Brandeis's Vote in *Whitney v California.*" *Supreme Court Review* (2005): 333–97.

Conlin, Joseph R. "The I.W.W. and the Socialist Party." *Science and Society* 31, no. 1 (Winter 1967): 22–36.

Cortner, Richard. "The Wobblies and *Fiske v. Kansas:* Victory and Disintegration." *Kansas History* 4 (Spring 1981): 30–38.

Creel, Von Russell. "The Case of the Wandering Wobblie [*sic*]: *The State of Oklahoma v. Arthur Berg.*" *Chronicles of Oklahoma* 73 (1995): 404–23.

Daniel, Cletus E. "In Defense of the Wheatland Wobblies: A Critical Analysis of the IWW in California." *Labor History* 19, no. 4 (1978): 485–509.

Davis, Mike. "The Stopwatch and the Wooden Shoe: Scientific Management and the Industrial Workers of the World." *Radical America* 9, no. 1 (1975): 69–113.

Debs, Eugene. "Arouse, Ye Slaves." In *Debs: His Life, Writings and Speeches.* Chicago: Charles H. Kerr, 1908.

Doree, E. F. "Gathering in the Grain." *International Socialist Review* 15, no. 12 (1915): 740–43.

"Dust Explosions and Fires in Grain Separators in the Pacific Northwest." In *U.S. Department of Agriculture, Bulletin No. 379.* Washington, D.C.: GPO, 1916.

Eleff, Robert M. "The 1916 Minnesota Miners' Strike Against U.S. Steel." *Minnesota History* 51 (Summer 1988): 63–74.

Elliott, Russell R. "Labor Troubles in the Mining Camps at Goldfield, Nevada, 1906–1908." *Pacific Historical Review* 19, no. 4 (1950): 369–84.

Fahey, John. "Big Lumber in the Inland Empire: The Early Years, 1900–1930." *Pacific Northwest Quarterly* 76, no. 3 (1985): 95–103.

Ferguson, Kathy. "Creating a City to Resist the State: The Seattle General Strike of 1919." *Theory & Event* 22, no. 4 (2019): 911–50.

Fickle, James F. "Race, Class, and Radicalism: The Wobblies in the Southern Lumber Industry, 1900–1916." In *At the Point of Production: The Local History of the IWW,* edited by Joseph R. Conlin, 97–113. Westport, CT: Greenwood Press, 1981.

Fishbein, Meyer H. "The President's Mediation Commission and the Arizona Copper Strike, 1917." *Southwest Social Science Quarterly* 30, no. 3 (1949): 175–82.

Foner, Philip S. "*United States of America vs. Wm. D. Haywood, et al.:* The I.W.W. Indictment." *Labor History* 11, no. 4 (1970): 500–530.

Goldstein, Robert J. "The Anarchist Scare of 1908: A Sign of Tensions in the Progressive Era." *American Studies* 15, no. 2 (Fall 1974): 55–78.

Green, James R. "The Brotherhood of Timber Workers, 1910–1913: A Radical Response to Industrial Capitalism in the Southern U.S.A." *Past and Present,* no. 60 (1973): 161–200.

Greene, Julie. "Not So Simple: Reassessing the Politics of the Progressive Era AFL." *Labor* 10, no. 4 (2013): 105–10.

Guariglia, Matthew. "Wrench in the Deportation Machine: Louis F. Post's Objection to Mechanized Red Scare Bureaucracy." *Journal of American Ethnic History* 38, no. 1 (2018): 62–77.

Gutfeld, Aron. "The Murder of Frank Little: Radical Labor Agitation in Butte, Montana, 1917." *Labor History* 10, no. 2 (1969): 177–92.

Hall, Tom G. "Wilson and the Food Crisis, Agricultural Price Control During World War I." *Agricultural History* 47, no. 1 (1973): 25–46.

Harring, Sidney L. "Class Conflict and the Suppression of Tramps in Buffalo, 1892–1894." *Law and Society Review* 11, no. 5 (1977): 873–911.

Haug, Charles James Haug. "The Industrial Workers of the World in North Dakota, 1913–1917." *North Dakota Quarterly* 39, no. 1 (1971): 85–102.

Haynes, John E. "Revolt of the 'Timber Beasts': IWW Lumber Strike in Minnesota." *Minnesota History* 42 (Spring 1971): 162–74.

Heatherton, Christina. "University of Radicalism: Ricardo Flores Magón and Leavenworth Penitentiary." *American Quarterly* 66, no. 3 (2014): 557–81.

Heisler, Eyrna Jones. "The Thin Red Line between Truth and Lies." *James Jones Literary Society Newsletter* 18, no. 2 (2012): 4.

Hodges, Adam J. "Thinking Globally, Acting Locally: The Portland Soviet and the Emergence of American Communism, 1918–1920." *Pacific Northwest Quarterly* 98, no. 3 (2007): 115–29.

Hoffman, Dennis E., and Vincent J. Webb. "Police Response to Labor Radicalism in Portland and Seattle, 1913–19." *Oregon Historical Quarterly* 87, no. 4 (Winter 1986): 341–66.

Howd, Cloice, R. "Industrial Relations in the West Coast Lumber Industry." In *U.S. Bureau of Labor, Bulletin No. 349*. Washington, D.C.: GPO, 1923.

Hoxie, R. F. "The Truth about the IWW." *Journal of Political Economy* 21, no. 9 (1913): 785–97.

"Improvements in Workplace Safety—United States, 1900–1999." *Morbidity and Mortality Weekly Report* 48, no. 22 (1999): 461-69.

Ingham, John N. "A Strike in the Progressive Era: McKees Rocks, 1909." *Pennsylvania Magazine of History and Biography* 90, no. 3 (1966): 353–77.

Interstate Commerce Commission. "Accident Bulletins, Railway Age." Mar. 7, 1919, 10.

"Jack London, in Memoriam." *International Socialist Review* 17, no. 10 (1917): 578–638.

James, John A. and Mark Thomas. "A Golden Age? Unemployment and the American Labor Market." *Journal of Economic History* 63, no. 4 (2003): 959–94.

James, Ralph C. and Estelle James. "The Purge of the Trotskyites from the Teamsters." *Western Political Quarterly* 19, no. 1 (1966): 5–15.

Johnson, Michael R. "The I.W.W. and Wilsonian Democracy." *Science & Society* 28, no. 3 (1964): 257–74.

Kazin, Michael. "The Great Exception Revisited: Organized Labor and Politics in San Francisco and Los Angeles, 1870–1940." *Pacific Historical Review* 55, no. 3 (1986): 371–402.

Koppes, Clayton R. "The Kansas Trial of the IWW, 1917–1919." *Labor History* 16, no. 3 (1975): 338–58.

Leier, Mark. "Kipling Gets a Red Card." *Labour/Le Travail* 30 (1992): 163–68.

Leiren, Terje I. "Ole and the Reds: The 'Americanism' of Seattle Mayor Ole Hanson." *Norwegian-American Studies* 30 (1985): 75–95.

Lescohier, Don D. "Conditions Affecting the Demand for Harvest Labor in the Wheat Belt." In *U.S. Department of Agriculture, Bulletin No. 1230*. Washington, D.C.: GPO, 1924.

———. "Harvest Labor Problems in the Wheat Belt," In *U.S. Department of Agriculture, Bulletin No. 1020*. Washington, D.C.: GPO, 1922.

———. "Sources of Supply and Conditions of Employment of Harvest Labor in the Wheat Belt." *U.S. Department of Agriculture, Bulletin No. 1211*. Washington, D.C.: GPO, 1924.

Lescohier, Donald D. "With the I.W.W. in the Wheat Lands," *Harper's Monthly Magazine*, Aug. 1923.

London, Jack. "The Dream of Debs." *International Socialist Review* 9, no. 7 (1909): 481–89.

———. "The Dream of Debs." *International Socialist Review* 9, no. 8 (1909): 561–70

———. "How I Became a Socialist." In *War of the Classes,* 165. Orinda, CA: SeaWolf Press, 2018.

———. "A New Law of Development." In *War of the Classes,* 135. Orinda, CA: SeaWolf Press, 2018.

———. "Preface." In *War of the Classes,* vii. Orinda, CA: SeaWolf Press, 2018.

Lovin, Hugh T. "Idaho and the 'Reds,' 1919–1926." *The Pacific Northwest Quarterly* 69, no. 3 (1978): 107–15.

Marcy, Leslie. "The Iron Heel on the Mesaba [*sic*] Range." *International Socialist Review* 17, no. 2 (1917): 474-80.

Marsh, Benjamin C. "Causes of Vagrancy and Methods of Eradication." *Annals of the American Academy of Political and Social Science* 23, no. 3 (1904): 37–48.

Mcgirr, Lisa. "Black and White Longshoremen in the IWW: A History of the Philadelphia Marine Transport Workers Industrial Union Local 8." *Labor History* 36, no. 3 (1995): 377–402.

McMahan, Ronal L. "'Rang-U-Tang:' The I.W.W. and the 1927 Colorado Coal Strike." In *At the Point of Production: The Local History of the IWW,* edited by Joseph R. Conlin, 191. Westport, CT: Greenwood Press, 1981.

Mittelman, Edward B. "The Loyal Legion of Loggers and Lumbermen: An Experiment in Industrial Relations." *Journal of Political Economy* 31, no. 3 (1923): 313–41.

Myers, Gustavas. "A Study of the Causes of Industrial Accidents." *Publication of the American Statistical Association* 14, no. 111 (1915): 672–94.

Orenic, Liesl Miller. "The Base of the Empire: Teamsters Local 743 and Montgomery Ward." *Labor* 15, no. 2 (2018): 49–75.

"Organization or Anarchy." *New Republic,* July 21, 1917.

Pahl, Thomas L. "G-String Conspiracy, Political Repression or Armed Revolt?: The Minneapolis Trotskyite Trial." *Labor History* 8 (Winter 1967): 30–51.

Parker, Carlton. "The I.W.W." *Atlantic Monthly,* Nov. 1917.

Peterson, Florence. "Review of Strikes in the United States." *Monthly Labor Review,* 46, no. 5 (1938): 1047–67.

———. "Strikes in the United States, 1880–1936," In *U.S. Bureau of Labor Statistics, Bulletin No. 651.* Washington, D.C.: GOP, 1938.

Peterson, Larry. "The Intellectual World of the IWW: An American Worker's Library in the First Half of the 20th Century." *History Workshop Journal* 22, no. 1 (Autumn 1986): 153–72.

Pinsolle, Dominque. "Sabotage, the IWW, and Repression." In *Wobblies of the World: A Global History of the IWW,* edited by Peter Cole, et al., 44–58. London: Pluto, 2017.

Portelli, Alessandro. "Jack London's Missing Revolution: Notes on 'The Iron Heel.'" *Science Fiction Studies* 9, no. 2 (1982): 1801–94.

Rabban, David M. "The Emergence of Modern First Amendment Doctrine." *University of Chicago Law Review* 50, no. 4 (1983): 1205–1355.

Rader, Benjamin G. "The Montana Lumber Strike of 1917." *Pacific Historical Review* 36, no. 2 (1967): 189–207.

Raskin, Jonah. "Jack London, Burning Man: Portrait of an American Socialist." *Socialism and Democracy* 19, no. 2 (2005): 57–68.

Reed, Merl E. "Lumberjacks and Longshoremen: The I.W.W. in Louisiana." *Labor History* 13, no. 1 (1972): 41–59.

Renshaw, Patrick. "The IWW and the Red Scare, 1917–1924." *Journal of Comparative History* 3, no. 4 (1968): 63–72.

Rubens, Lisa. "The Patrician Radical: Charlotte Anita Whitney." *California History* 65, no. 3 (1986): 158–71.

Seraile, William. "Ben Fletcher, I.W.W. Organizer." *Pennsylvania History: A Journal of Mid-Atlantic Studies* 46, no. 3 (1979): 213–232.

Shaffer, Ralph E. "Communism in California: 1919–1924." *Science & Society* 34, no. 4 (1970): 412–29.

———. "Formation of the California Communist Labor Party." *Pacific Historical Review* 36, no. 1 (1967): 59–78.

Sheft, Mark A. "The End of the Smith Act: A Legal and Historical Analysis of *Scales v. United States*." *American Journal of Legal History* 36, no. 2 (1992): 164–202.

Shor, Francis. "The Iron Heel's Marginal(ized) Utopia." *Extrapolation* 35, no. 3 (1994): 211–29.

———. "The IWW and Oppositional Politics in World War I: Pushing the System Beyond Its Limits." *Radical History Review* 64 (1996): 74–94.

Simon, Jeffrey P. "The Forgotten Terrorists: Lesson from the History of Terrorism." *Terrorism and Political Violence* 20, no. 2 (2008): 195–214.

Sims, Robert C. "Idaho's Criminal Syndicalism Act: One State's Response to Radical Labor." *Labor History* 15, no. 4 (1975): 511–27.

Sklar, Richard L. "The Fiction of the First Freedom." *Western Political Quarterly* 6, no. 2 (June 1953): 302–19.

Slutsky, Beth. "Parlor Pink Turned Soapbox Red: The Trial of Charlotte Anita Whitney." *American Communist History* 9, no. 1 (2010): 35–39.

Stanley, Amy Dru. "Beggars Can't Be Choosers: Compulsion and Contract in Postbellum America." *Journal of American History* 78, no. 4 (1992): 1265–93.

Steckel, Richard. "Stature and the Standard of Living." *Journal of Economic History* 33, no. 4 (1995): 1903–40.

Stern, Boris. "Cargo Handling and Longshore Labor Conditions." *U.S. Bureau of Labor Statistics, Bulletin No. 550* (1932).

Taft, Philip. "The Federal Trials of the IWW." *Labor History* 3, no. 1 (1962): 57–91.

———. "The I.W.W. in the Grain Belt." *Labor History* 1, no. 1 (1960): 53–67.

Thompson, E.P. "Time, Work-Discipline, and Industrial Capitalism." *Past & Present* no. 38 (1967): 56–97.

Thompson, Fred. "They Didn't Suppress the IWW." *Radical America* 1, no. 2 (September–October 1967): 1–5.

Tomlins, Christopher. "Necessities of State. Police, Sovereignty, and the Constitution." *Journal of Police History* 20, no. 1 (2008): 47–63.

Tripp, Joseph F. "Law and Social Control: Historians' Views of Progressive-Era Labor Legislation." *Labor History* 28, no. 4 (1987): 447–83.

———. "Reform and Repression in the Far West: The Washington Legislative Response to Labor Radicalism in 1919." *Rendezvous* 19 (1983): 43–54.

Tushnet, Mark. "The Hughes Court and Radical Political Dissent: The Cases of Dirk De Jonge and Angelo Herndon." *Georgia State University Law Review* 28, no. 2 (Winter 2012): 333–78.

Tyler, Robert L. "The I.W.W. in the Pacific N.W.: Rebels of the Woods." *Oregon Historical Quarterly* 55, no. 1 (1954): 3–44.

———. "The United States Government as Union Organizer: The Loyal Legion of Loggers and Lumbermen." *Mississippi Valley Historical Review* 47, no. 3 (1960): 434–51.

Veblen, Thorstein. "Unpublished Paper on the I.W.W." *Journal of Political Economy*, 40, no. 6 (1932): 797–807.

Voss, Kim. "Disposition Is Not Action: The Rise and Demise of the Knights of Labor." *Studies in American Political Development* 6, no. 2 (1992): 272–321.

Wagaman, David. "The Industrial Workers of the World in Nebraska, 1914–1920." *Nebraska History* 56 (1975): 295–338.

"Wages in the United States and Europe, 1870–1898." *U.S. Bureau of Corporations, Bulletin No. 18*. Washington, D.C.: GPO, 1898.

Wakstein, Allen M. "The Origins of the Open-Shop Movement, 1919–1920." *Journal of American History* 51, no. 3 (1964): 460–75.

West, George P. "After Liberalism Had Failed." *Nation*, May 30, 1923.

White, Ahmed A. "The Crime of Economic Radicalism: Criminal Syndicalism Laws and the Industrial Workers of the World, 1917–1927." *Oregon Law Review* 85 (2006): 649–769.

———. "A Different Kind of Labor Law: Vagrancy Law and the Regulation of Harvest Labor, 1913–1924." *University of Colorado Law Review* 75, no. 3 (2004): 668–743.

Whitten, Woodrow W. "Criminal Syndicalism and the Law in California: 1919–1927" *Transactions of the American Philosophical Society* 59, no. 2 (1969): 3–73.

Zanger, Martin. "Politics of Confrontation: Upton Sinclair and the Launching of the ACLU in Southern California." *Pacific Historical Review* 38, no. 4 (1969): 383–406.

DOCUMENTARY FILM

The Wobblies. Directed by Stewart Bird and Deborah Shaffer. 1979.

Index

Founded in 1893,
UNIVERSITY OF CALIFORNIA PRESS
publishes bold, progressive books and journals
on topics in the arts, humanities, social sciences,
and natural sciences—with a focus on social
justice issues—that inspire thought and action
among readers worldwide.

The UC PRESS FOUNDATION
raises funds to uphold the press's vital role
as an independent, nonprofit publisher, and
receives philanthropic support from a wide
range of individuals and institutions—and from
committed readers like you. To learn more, visit
ucpress.edu/supportus.